Trends and Challenges in International Law

Maurizio Arcari • Irini Papanicolopulu •
Laura Pineschi
Editors

Trends and Challenges in International Law

Selected Issues in Human Rights, Cultural Heritage, Environment and Sea

Springer

Editors
Maurizio Arcari
School of Law
University of Milano-Bicocca
Milan, Italy

Irini Papanicolopulu
School of Law
University of Milano-Bicocca
Milan, Italy

Laura Pineschi
Department of Law, Politics and International Studies, Center for Studies in European and International Affairs (CSEIA)
University of Parma
Parma, Italy

ISBN 978-3-030-94386-8   ISBN 978-3-030-94387-5 (eBook)
https://doi.org/10.1007/978-3-030-94387-5

This Springer imprint is published by the registered company Springer Nature Switzerland AG
The registered company address is: Gewerbestrasse 11, 6330 Cham, Switzerland

Contents

Contributors

Maurizio Arcari School of Law, University of Milano-Bicocca, Milan, Italy

Elena Carpanelli Department of Law, Political and International Studies, University of Parma, Parma, Italy
Center for Studies in European and International Affairs, University of Parma, Parma, Italy

Gabriella Citroni University of Milano-Bicocca, Milan, Italy

Matteo Fornari University of Milano-Bicocca, Milan, Italy

Maria Clara Maffei University of Parma, Parma, Italy

Angelo Merialdi Genoa, Italy

Irini Papanicolopulu School of Law, University of Milano-Bicocca, Milan, Italy

Laura Pineschi Department of Law, Politics and International Studies, Center for Studies in European and International Affairs (CSEIA), University of Parma, Parma, Italy

Luigi Santosuosso Division for Ocean Affairs and the Law of the Sea, Office of Legal Affairs, United Nations, New York, NY, USA

Tullio Treves University of Milano, Milan, Italy

Sabrina Urbinati University of Milano-Bicocca, Milan, Italy

Introduction

Maurizio Arcari, Irini Papanicolopulu, and Laura Pineschi

Abstract This Introduction explains the facts at the genesis of this volume, the wider context within which contributions are set and some of the fundamental questions raised by them.

1 An Ever Evolving Discipline

International law is a fascinating field of study, not least because of its continuous evolution. Changes within the international community and new developments in legal thinking lead to a continuous tension between the certainty of existing regulation and the expectations generated by emerging rules. The past, present and future appear to be interlinked, with past concerns and theories having an impact on present day regulation, which in turn will inevitably affect the future of this discipline.

The proliferation of legal instruments and institutions over the last few decades[1] has added interest, enlarging the horizons of international lawyers, who today deal with topics that would have been unheard of even a few decades ago. Human rights and environmental protection are bright examples of how relatively recent concepts and principles have revolutionised the nature and structure of international law. Given the primary role of human rights in today's international legal and political

[1] On this phenomenon suffice it to mention the work by the International Law Commission (ILC) on the topic of "Fragmentation of international law: difficulties arising from the diversification and expansion of international law", the results of which have been published in the website of the ILC https://legal.un.org/ilc/summaries/1_9.shtml.

M. Arcari · I. Papanicolopulu (✉)
School of Law, University of Milano-Bicocca, Milan, Italy
e-mail: maurizio.arcari@unimib.it; irini.papanicolopulu@unimib.it

L. Pineschi
Department of Law, Politics and International Studies, Center for Studies in European and International Affairs (CSEIA), University of Parma, Parma, Italy
e-mail: laura.pineschi@unipr.it

M. Arcari et al. (eds.), *Trends and Challenges in International Law*,
https://doi.org/10.1007/978-3-030-94387-5_1

discourse,[2] one may wonder at the fact that the Universal Declaration of Human Rights[3] is, after all, less than a hundred years old. Similarly, the current focus of States, civil society and individuals on climate change[4] may make us wonder at the fact that less than fifty years have elapsed since the adoption of the Stockholm Declaration on the Human Environment.[5]

At the same time, change has not left unaltered old and solid branches of international law, such as the law of the sea, which is rightly considered as one of the pillars of the traditional, Westphalian, conception of international law. The adoption of the United Nations Convention on the Law of the Sea (UNCLOS) in 1982[6] was seen by many as the final point of a long process of development, that had interested most of the twentieth century. The 'Constitution for the Oceans', introducing the 'new' law of the sea,[7] was expected to settle issues relating to marine spaces. Yet even before the entry into force of the UNCLOS, new concerns started emerging, from maritime security[8] and the application of human rights in the maritime context[9] to exploitation of biodiversity of areas beyond national jurisdiction[10] and the persistent problem of ensuring sustainable fisheries.[11] Today, the ongoing 'Intergovernmental Conference on an international legally binding instrument under the United Nations Convention on the Law of the Sea on the conservation and sustainable use of marine biological diversity of areas beyond national

---

[2]For example, the 2030 Agenda for Sustainable Development (Transforming our world: the 2030 Agenda for Sustainable Development, U.N. Doc. A/RES/70/1 of 25 December 2015) "is grounded in the Universal Declaration of Human Rights [and] international human rights treaties" (para. 10) and its 17 Sustainable Development Goals (SDGs) "seek to realize the human rights of all and to achieve gender equality and the empowerment of all women and girls" (Preamble).

[3]U.N. Doc. A/RES/217 (III) of 10 December 1948.

[4]Suffice it to recall that SDG 13 is devoted to "Climate Action" and that States constantly refer to climate change and its effect upon the planet and its inhabitants in their high-level statements, for example in front of the UN General Assembly.

[5]Declaration of the United Nations Conference on the Human Environment (Stockholm, 5–12 June 1972), U.N. Doc. A/CONF.48/14/Rev.1, p. 3.

[6]United Nations Convention on the Law of the Sea (Montego Bay, 10 December 1982), entered into force on 16 November 1994, in 1833 UNTS 397.

[7]As recalled by Bardonnet and Virally (1983) in the very title of the book edited by them.

[8]Leading to the adoption, in 1988, of the Convention for the Suppression of Unlawful Acts Against the Safety of Maritime Navigation (10 March 1988), entered into force on 1 March 1992, in 1678 UNTS 201. The Convention was subsequently amended in 2005.

[9]Sohn (1988).

[10]Glowka (1996).

[11]Leading to the adoption of the Agreement for the Implementation of the Provisions of the United Nations Convention on the Law of the Sea of 10 December 1982 relating to the Conservation and Management of Straddling Fish Stocks and Highly Migratory Fish Stocks (New York, 4 August 1995), entered into force on 11 December 2001, 2167 UNTS 3.

jurisdiction'[12] is one of the very few global diplomatic conferences currently convened by the United Nations with a view to adopting a new multilateral treaty.

The enduring quest of lawyers for a better understanding of old and new issues and developments is at the heart of this volume. Its title may indeed appear rather ambitious. There is no single field of international law which is not witnessing "trends and challenges"; and should every major trend and challenge be addressed, this would have been a book series, instead of a single volume. However, the aim of this book is more modest, and commensurate to its size. It proposes to consider some of the key trends and challenges that currently characterise international law, looking in particular at four subfields—human rights law, cultural heritage law, environmental law, and law of the sea. With this introduction, we would like to present the content of the book and briefly explain its origin and characteristics.

2 A Common Background

As mentioned before, the book is divided into four sections: human rights law, cultural heritage law, environmental law, and law of the sea. The authors are all Italian scholars or international lawyers. However, the choice of topics and of authors is not by chance, but rather is motivated by the events taking place at the genesis of this volume. The book was in fact conceived of and written by a group of scholars and practitioners that share the same mentor: Professor Tullio Scovazzi. Around the time that Professor Scovazzi's service at the University of Milano-Bicocca was drawing to a close, we started to think about how best to pay tribute to him. Well aware of the natural reserve that has always characterised him, we realised that the usual *festschrift*, in which his numerous friends and colleagues could have contributed a chapter, would be at odds with his minimalist style.

We have therefore preferred a more intimate tribute, in the form of a collective volume, in which his closest pupils and collaborators have taken part, and which addresses four fields where Tullio Scovazzi has excelled, not only in his more than 600 pieces of scholarly writing, but also in his practice. As to contributors, all of them grew up or collaborated with him at the Universities of Parma, Genoa, Milan, or Milano-Bicocca, where he taught from 1980 to 1991, 1991 to 1994, 1994 to1998 and 1998 to 2021, respectively. With regard to the topics, the law of the sea was the first field to which he turned his attention with his first monographs[13] and in which he has subsequently always been active.[14] Human rights law has prompted some of

[12] International legally binding instrument under the United Nations Convention on the Law of the Sea on the conservation and sustainable use of marine biological diversity of areas beyond national jurisdiction, U.N. Doc. A/RES/72/249 of 19 January 2018.

[13] Scovazzi (1977, 1979, 1984).

[14] Suffice it to recall his 1999 Hague course, reprinted in Scovazzi (2001b, 2005b, 2014d, 2015, 2016a); and the atlases edited with Giampiero Francalanci: Francalanci et al. (1986); Scovazzi et al. (1989); Francalanci and Scovazzi (1994).

his most cogent pieces[15] and has seen him work on the adoption of the International Convention for the Protection of All Persons from Enforced Disappearance.[16] In the field of environmental law, his multiple publications[17] have been matched by concrete action, in particular with the UNEP-MAP and ACCOBAMS Secretariats. Last but not least, is cultural heritage law, where he has not only published key contributions,[18] but has played a crucial role in both the adoption of the UNESCO Convention on the Protection of Underwater Cultural Heritage[19] and the restitution of cultural objects which had been illegally exported.

Furthermore, the different contributions in this volume share a certain approach to legal research and a certain method, that pay tribute to the authors' common mentor. Professor Tullio Scovazzi certainly belongs to the Italian positivist school, characterised by 'logical rigor and correctness of method'.[20] At the same time, he has developed a peculiar method in addressing international law, that privileges an inductive approach to legal analysis and shuns *ex ante* systems in favour of a realist description and analysis of international law as it emerges from the complex and often contradictory practice of States. He has himself sketched that method in the Introduction to his manual of international law:

> È un metodo descrittivo, e non ricostruttivo, basato sulla ricerca, analisi ed esposizione di dati della pratica internazionale dai quali è possibile desumere il convincimento di coloro che agiscono per conto degli Stati circa l'esistenza di una data norma e sul suo contenuto. Si tratta di cogliere tendenze, a volte solide, a volte molto instabili. [. . .] Le conclusioni alle quali sono pervenuto sono il risultato di un lavoro di reperimento, descrizione e sintesi di dati della pratica internazionale e di un costante tentativo di ricercare la banalità e di fuggire da qualsiasi ambizione di originalità.[21]

[15] Among many others Scovazzi (2005a); Citroni and Scovazzi (2006); Scovazzi (2006b); Scovazzi (2009); Scovazzi et al. (2009); Citroni and Scovazzi (2013); Scovazzi (2014a); Scovazzi (2014b); Westra et al. (2015); Scovazzi (2016b); Antonucci et al. (2016); Scovazzi (2017).

[16] New York, 20 December 2006, entered into force on 23 December 2010, 2716 UNTS 3. On the Convention see Scovazzi and Citroni (2007).

[17] Among many others Francioni and Scovazzi (eds) (1991); Maffei et al. (1996); Scovazzi and Arcari (1999); Scovazzi (1999b); Scovazzi (2001a); Scovazzi (ed) (2001c); Juste Ruiz and Scovazzi (eds) (2005); Scovazzi (2014d).

[18] Among many others Camarda and Scovazzi (2002); Garabello and Scovazzi (2003); Scovazzi (2004); Nafziger and Scovazzi (eds) (2008); Scovazzi (2011); Scovazzi (2012); Scovazzi et al. (2012); Scovazzi (2014c); Scovazzi (2019).

[19] Paris, 2 November 2001, entered into force on 2 January 2009, 2562 UNTS I-45694.

[20] Cassese (1990), p. 146. More extensively on the Italian school of international law, see Bartolini (2020).

[21] "It is a descriptive method, and not a reconstructive one, based on the research, analysis and presentation of data from international practice, from which it is possible to deduce the belief of those who act on the behalf of States concerning the existence of a certain norm and its content. It is a matter of catching trends, sometimes solid, other times very instable. [. . .] The conclusions which I have reached are the result of a work of discovery, description and synthesis of data from international practice and a constant effort to look for banality and avoid any ambition of originality" Scovazzi (2018), pp. v–vi (translation by the authors). See also Scovazzi (1999a).

This method is considered better suited to discuss international law, which is still, to a significant extent, composed of customary rules that evolve on the basis of informal schemes.[22] It is often accompanied by a taste for the unusual[23] and a preference for contradiction, rather than consistency. In his scholarly writings, Tullio Scovazzi has often highlighted, in clear language, the gaps and inconsistencies of modern international law and its many regimes.[24] At the same time, however, he has played a significant role, as a negotiator, in filling these gaps and addressing these inconsistencies. This activity testifies to the fact that his critique is not a sterile, self-centred, monologue, but is part of the global dialogue aiming at progressing international law. This method, which clearly departs from those that are most popular at the moment, is certainly worth highlighting.[25] At a time when the scholarly community is very much troubled by the—at least apparent—homogenisation of legal scholarship and its lack of diversity,[26] we have seized the opportunity, in paying tribute to our common background, to present alternatives to the dominant method, which often monopolises the global international law discourse and silences alternative approaches.

3 The Function of International Law

The occasion which triggers this book is therefore linked to a specific event and would by itself justify the choice of authors and topics. Yet there are some further linkages, that connect the topics addressed in the chapters of this book, and which are worth briefly mentioning. All fields, with the exception of the law of the sea, are new ones, which came into being during the twentieth century. As such, they share some common concerns relating to sources, actors and principles, as well as the fact that their emergence has changed the face of current international law—and this is certainly true for human rights law and environmental law. Furthermore, all fields are rapidly developing ones, with new legal instruments that have been adopted in the last few decades and with a growing case law that testifies to their vitality, as the chapters of this volume show.

Human rights law, environmental law, cultural heritage law, and, to a certain extent, also the law of the sea, tend to address interests that go beyond single States and aim at the protection of common concerns: human dignity, the natural

[22] Scovazzi (1999a), p. 618.

[23] As sometimes reflected in the titles of his writings: Scovazzi (2002a, 2006a, 2007, 2008, 2021).

[24] Scovazzi (2002b); his chapter on "A Contradictory and Counterproductive Regime" in Garabello and Scovazzi (2003), pp. 3–17; his chapter on "Bioprospecting on the deep seabed: a legal gap requiring to be filled" in Francioni and Scovazzi (2006), p. 81.

[25] It is up to the reader to find out how much of this method has trickled down into his pupils' and collaborators' writings.

[26] Roberts (2017).

environment, cultural heritage, spaces beyond national jurisdiction and the common heritage of (hu)mankind. As such, they all pose significant challenges to the traditional, Westphalian, conception of international law, causing a tension between the old concepts of State security and sovereignty, on the one hand, and the new concepts, incorporated in the concept of human dignity and the United Nations Sustainable Development Goals (SDGs)[27] that put the human person and the natural environment at the centre of the picture. Are "old" rules and institutions of international law prepared to address new challenges for (or the concerns of) the international community as a whole? Have the above-mentioned new fields succeeded in their aim, to shift the perspective from a State-centred to a human- and environment-centred one? Is it possible to strike the right balance between environment, development, human rights, national and international security? Even more provocatively, and specifically, is there room for new subjects of international law, like nature and animals, for the benefit of the environment, as discussed by Maria Clara Maffei?

These are fundamental questions at the background of most chapters in this book, which are devoted to particular instances that well exemplify some of the fundamental choices with which international lawyers are faced today. Elena Carpanelli discusses the extent to which human rights law and the adjudicative bodies established by it may contribute to the protection of the environment through the adoption of measures to prevent and combat transboundary pollution. Gabriella Citroni critically examines the extent to which human rights law has impacted on the concept of security. Matteo Fornari considers whether international humanitarian law can effectively counteract modern methods of warfare which still disregard fundamental humanitarian principles. Maurizio Arcari addresses the extent to which secondary rules of international law can be used to further compliance with, and eventually the effectiveness, of primary rules concerning the protection of the natural environment. Laura Pineschi analyses whether the principal global multilateral security actor, the UN Security Council, is adequately equipped to address the emerging threats stemming out of climate change. Irini Papanicolopulu follows the historical evolution of the notion of "law of the sea" in light of the changing composition and primary interests of the international community.

Another aspect that brings together different contributions in this book concerns the interconnectedness of specialised fields of international law and their relationship. 'International law is a legal system' as the International Law Commission (ILC) has forcefully asserted.[28] Its different subfields, therefore, are not isolated islands but parts of the continent, and present points of contact and interchange that should be maximised, in order to get the most out of the system. In this light, many chapters of this book address issues at the intersection of different regimes, through

[27] As presented in Transforming our world: the 2030 Agenda for Sustainable Development, U.N. Doc. A/RES/70/1 of 25 December 2015.

[28] ILC, *Conclusions of the Work of the Study Group on the Fragmentation of International Law: Difficulties A rising from the Diversification and Expansion of International Law* (hereafter ILC Conclusions), https://legal.un.org/ilc/texts/instruments/english/draft_articles/1_9_2006.pdf, para. 1. See also Higgins (1991), p. 23: "[i]nternational law is not rules. It is a normative system".

an intra-systemic or an inter-systemic perspective. Elena Carpanelli discusses human rights and environmental law; Angelo Merialdi brings together the law of the sea and cultural heritage law; Laura Pineschi joins environmental law and the law of collective security; Sabrina Urbinati examines cultural heritage law and European Union law.

A final common thread that characterises several chapters in this book relates to the expectations raised in the twentieth century with the institutionalisation of the international community and their critical assessment in light of the present state of affairs in international law. Thanks to crucial developments, first and foremost the creation of the United Nations, international law has acquired an institutional dimension that was unthinkable before the twentieth century. Stemming from the ashes of World War II, the expectation of States, scholars and the global community was that the institutionalisation of law-making, law-applying and law-adjudicating would bring peace to the world and would promote the law of cooperation (as opposed to the previous law of co-existence). Have international institutions lived up to their expectations? Have they truly contributed to the advancement of the "civilising mission" of international law? Or do they represent a missed opportunity? This is an issue that troubles much current international law scholarship and that is addressed in different chapters of this book. Laura Pineschi questions whether the UN system of collective security is prepared to address new global challenges, such as climate change and their impact on local conflicts. Maurizio Arcari examines the work of the International Law Commission (ILC) in light of the modern concern of environmental degradation, questioning whether the traditional rules on international responsibility developed by the ILC are fit to cope with the challenge of the prevention of environmental damage. Irini Papanicolopulu considers whether UNCLOS has truly said the last word in this field, or whether normative processes have continued beyond this, undeniably monumental, UN treaty. Luigi Santosuosso examines the Commission for the Limits of the Continental Shelf, a technical body in a political world, as it has been aptly termed, and asks questions that go beyond this specific body. Can technical bodies work in a still highly politicised world? Can they, through technical means, settle issues that involve the very foundations of States, that is, the powers stemming from sovereignty over their maritime zones? In the regional context, Elena Carpanelli looks at the jurisprudence of the Inter-American Court of Human Rights, in an effort to evaluate whether regional courts may be more proactive in their role, not only of custodians of human rights law, but also of normative actors that may prompt developments where States dare not.

These are some common threads that run through multiple chapters in this book. Certainly, they are just some among the many trends that characterise modern international law and the many challenges that the international community is facing. Yet we believe that highlighting them and illustrating how States and other international actors are dealing with them may contribute towards proving that 'the typical function of any legal system is to demonstrate by facts that it is not true that the stronger is always right'.[29]

Acknowledgments We would like to close this brief introduction with some words of gratitude. Like all collective works, this volume could not have taken shape without the enthusiasm and dedication of many people. The editors are first indebted to Dr. Mariana Clara De Andrade for having assisted them in the setting up of this volume for publication. Special thanks are also due to the Department of Law, Legal and International Studies of the University of Parma, which financed the linguistic revision of all contributions by a native English speaker, Mr. Chris Callan. Above all, our gratitude goes to the authors of the individual chapters for their patient collaboration in the completion of this collective effort.

References

Antonucci A, Papanicolopulu I, Scovazzi T (eds) (2016) L'immigrazione irregolare via mare nella giurisprudenza italiana e nell'esperienza europea. Giappichelli, Torino
Bardonnet D, Virally M (1983) Le nouveau droit international de la mer. Pedone, Paris
Bartolini G (ed) (2020) A history of international law in Italy. Oxford University Press, Oxford
Camarda G, Scovazzi T (eds) (2002) The protection of the underwater cultural heritage - legal aspects. Giuffrè, Milano
Cassese A (1990) Diritto internazionale. In: Bonanate L (ed) Studi internazionali. Edizioni della Fondazione Agnelli, Torino, p 113
Citroni G, Scovazzi T (2006) Vos vas a aparecer muerto como aparecieron tus amigos, los demás. In: Pineschi (ed) La tutela internazionale dei diritti umani. Giuffrè, Milano, pp 616–635
Citroni G, Scovazzi T (2013) Corso di diritto internazionale, Parte III: La tutela internazionale dei diritti umani. Giuffrè, Milano
Francalanci G, Scovazzi T (eds) (1994) Lines in the sea. Martinus Nijhoff, Dordrecht
Francalanci G, Romanò D, Scovazzi T (eds) (1986) Atlas of the straight baselines. Giuffrè, Milano
Francioni F, Scovazzi T (eds) (1991) International responsibility for environmental harm. Graham and Trotman, London
Francioni F, Scovazzi T (eds) (2006) Biotechnology and international law. Hart, Oxford
Garabello R, Scovazzi T (eds) (2003) The protection of the underwater cultural heritage - before and after the 2001 UNESCO Convention. Brill, Leiden
Glowka L (1996) The deepest of ironies: genetic resources, marine scientific research, and the area. Ocean Yearb 12:154–178
Higgins R (1991) International law and the avoidance, containment and resolution of disputes: general course on public international law. Recueil des Cours 230:9
Juste Ruiz J, Scovazzi T (eds) (2005) La práctica internacional en materia de responsabilidad por accidentes industriales catastróficos. Tirant lo Blanch, Valencia
Maffei MC, Pineschi L, Scovazzi T, Treves T (eds) (1996) Participation in world treaties on the protection of the environment - a collection of data. Kluwer Law International, London
Nafziger JAR, Scovazzi T (eds) (2008) Le patrimoine culturel de l'humanité – the cultural heritage of mankind. Martinus Nijhoff, Leiden
Roberts A (2017) Is international law international? Oxford University Press, Oxford
Scovazzi T (1977) Gli accordi bilaterali sulla pesca. Giuffrè, Milano
Scovazzi T (1979) La pesca nell'evoluzione del diritto del mare, vol I. Giuffrè, Milano

[29]"Il filo conduttore dell'esposizione è che la funzione tipica di qualsiasi sistema giuridico è di dimostrare nei fatti che non è vero che il più forte ha sempre ragione", Scovazzi (2018), p. viii.

Scovazzi T (1984) La pesca nell'evoluzione del diritto del mare, vol II. Giuffrè, Milano
Scovazzi T (1999a) Casi, esempi e divagazioni: riflessioni sul metodo descrittivo dei fenomeni giuridici. La Comunità Internazionale 54:595–618
Scovazzi T (ed) (1999b) Marine specially protected areas - the general aspects and the Mediterranean regional system. Kluwer Law International, The Hague
Scovazzi T (2001a) State responsibility for environmental harm. Yearb Int Environ Law 12:43–67
Scovazzi T (2001b) The evolution of international law of the sea: new issues, new challenges. Recueil des Cours 286:39–243
Scovazzi T (ed) (2001c) The protection of the environment in a context of regional economic integration - the case of the European Community, the MERCOSUR and the NAFTA. Giuffrè, Milano
Scovazzi T (2002a) Un'effimera isola e un ipotetico quesito. Rivista di Diritto Internazionale 85: 946–953
Scovazzi T (2002b) Una fase di crisi nel sistema di mantenimento della pace delle Nazioni Unite. Affari Esteri 34:372–402
Scovazzi (ed) (2004) La protezione del patrimonio culturale sottomarino nel Mare Mediterraneo. Giuffrè, Milano
Scovazzi T (2005a) Il terrorismo di Stato nell'opera di Giulio Douhet. Rivista di Diritto Internazionale 88:703–720
Scovazzi T (2005b) Maritime delimitations in the Mediterranean Sea. In Cursos Euromediterraneos Bancaja de Derecho Internacional. pp 349–501
Scovazzi T (2006a) L'osso duro del proselitismo. In: Pineschi L (ed) La tutela internazionale dei diritti umani. Giuffrè, Milano, pp 433–441
Scovazzi T (2006b) Tortura e formalismi giuridici di basso profilo. Rivista di Diritto Internazionale 89:905–947
Scovazzi T (2007) Saint-Pierre riproposto da Rousseau. Rivista di Diritto Internazionale 90:1067–1078
Scovazzi T (2008) L'attaccamento del gregario scelto Mohamed Salem alla bandiera italiana. In Studi in onore di Umberto Leanza, vol III. Editoriale Scientifica, Napoli, pp 1781–1788
Scovazzi T (2009) La Repubblica riconosce e garantisce i diritti inviolabili della segretezza delle relazioni tra servizi informativi italiani e stranieri? Rivista di Diritto Internazionale 92:959–992
Scovazzi T (2011) Diviser c'est Détruire: ethical principles and legal rules in the field of return of cultural property. Rivista di Diritto Internazionale 94:341–395
Scovazzi T (2012) The definition of intangible cultural heritage. In: Borelli S, Lenzerini F (eds) Cultural heritage, cultural rights, cultural diversity. Martinus Nijhoff, Leiden, pp 179–200
Scovazzi T (2014a) Human rights and immigration at sea. In: Rubio-Marín R (ed) Human rights and immigration. Oxford University Press, Oxford, pp 212–260
Scovazzi T (2014b) Il lato oscuro dei diritti umani: aspetti di diritto internazionale. In: Meccarelli M, Palchetti P, Sotis C (eds) Il lato oscuro dei diritti umani. Dykinson, Madrid, pp 115–134
Scovazzi T (ed) (2014c) La restituzione dei beni culturali rimossi con particolare riguardo alla pratica italiana. Giuffrè, Milano
Scovazzi T (2014d) Negotiating conservation and sustainable use of marine biological diversity in areas beyond national jurisdiction: prospects and challenges. Ital Yearb Int Law 24:61–93
Scovazzi T (2015) The origin of the theory of sovereignty of the sea. In: Del Castillo L (ed) Law of the sea, from Grotius to the international tribunal for the law of the sea – Liber Amicorum Judge Hugo Caminos. Brill/Nijhoff, Leiden, pp 48–63
Scovazzi T (2016a) Harlequin and the Mediterranean. In: Wolfrum R, Seršić M, Šošić T (eds) Contemporary developments in international law – essays in honour of Budislav Vukas. Brill/Nijhoff, Leiden, pp 291–230
Scovazzi T (2016b) Segreto di Stato e diritti umani: il sipario nero sul caso Abu Omar. Diritti Umani e Diritto Internazionale, pp 157–184

Scovazzi T (2017) Il diritto umano all'acqua e all'igiene personale. In: Pineschi L (ed) La tutela della salute nel diritto internazionale ed europeo tra interessi globali e interessi particolari. Editoriale Scientifica, Napoli, pp 213–254
Scovazzi T (2018) Corso di diritto internazionale Parte I, 3rd edn. Giuffrè, Milano
Scovazzi T (2019) Sunken Spanish ships before American courts. Int J Mar Coast Law 34:245–290
Scovazzi T (2021) Come se non esistesse. Rivista di Diritto Internazionale 104:167–181
Scovazzi T, Arcari M (1999) Diritto internazionale e ambiente. In: Nespor S, De Cesaris AL (eds) Codice dell'ambiente. Giuffrè, Milano, pp 3–35
Scovazzi T, Citroni G (2007) The struggle against enforced disappearance and the 2007 United Nations Convention. Martinus Nijhoff, Leiden
Scovazzi T et al (eds) (1989) Atlas of the straight baselines, 2nd edn. Giuffrè, Milano
Scovazzi T, Papanicolopulu I, Urbinati S (eds) (2009) I diritti umani di fronte al giudice internazionale – Atti della giornata di studio in memoria di Carlo Russo. Giuffrè, Milano
Scovazzi T, Ubertazzi B, Zagato L (eds) (2012) Il patrimonio culturale intangibile nelle sue diverse dimensioni. Giuffrè, Milano
Sohn LB (1988) International law of the sea and human rights issues. In: Clingan TA Jr (ed) The law of the sea: what lies ahead? The Law of the Sea Institute, Honolulu, pp 51–71
Westra L, Juss S, Scovazzi T (eds) (2015) Towards a refugee oriented right of asylum. Routledge, Farnham

Part I
Human Rights Law

International Human Rights Law and Transboundary Environmental Harm: Trends and Challenges

Elena Carpanelli

Abstract In its landmark Advisory Opinion on the Environment and Human Rights, issued on 15 November 2017, the Inter-American Court of Human Rights recognized that the American Convention on Human Rights, under certain circumstances, involves extraterritorial obligations with respect to environmental matters. The Court further specified the content of the State obligations to protect individuals from transboundary environmental harm under the Convention. By doing so, the Court dealt with two core aspects of the relationship between human rights and the environment that, despite having been neglected so far, have the potential to increasingly come up before international bodies (and possibly, domestic courts) in the near future: the extraterritorial scope of human rights treaties in cases of cross-border environmental harm and the content of the State's obligations to protect human rights in the face of such harm. The central argument defended in this chapter is that the Inter-American Court of Human Rights' main findings shed new light on the role of international human rights law in addressing transboundary environmental harm and, contextually, provide an opportunity to critically examine not only some of the most significant current trends, but also future challenges, with respect to the relationship between human rights and the environment.

1 Introduction

A degraded or polluted environment adversely affects the enjoyment of human rights in several ways. A healthy environment is in fact instrumental to the full exercise of a multitude of rights, including the rights to life and to health. At the same time, the exercise of certain rights, such as the right to participation in environmental decision-making, is conducive to, and might strengthen, environmental protection.

E. Carpanelli (✉)
Department of Law, Political and International Studies, University of Parma, Parma, Italy

Center for Studies in European and International Affairs, University of Parma, Parma, Italy
e-mail: elena.carpanelli@unipr.it

M. Arcari et al. (eds.), *Trends and Challenges in International Law*,
https://doi.org/10.1007/978-3-030-94387-5_2

Recently, increasing attention has been given to the mutual relationship between human rights and the environment. This has led lawmakers, institutions and courts—at the universal, regional and domestic level—to acknowledge this close nexus.[1]

Whilst the contours of the relationship between human rights and the environment in the dynamics of international law have become progressively clearer, mostly thanks to human rights treaty bodies' decisions, some aspects are still contentious. An issue long overlooked is, for instance, whether existing international human rights instruments, including their monitoring mechanisms, have a part to play with respect to transboundary environmental harm.

Yet, pollution often overcomes physical boundaries, affecting the rights of individuals abroad. One example among many is haze pollution in Southeast Asia: forest fires in Indonesia linked to the uncontrolled expansion of palm oil plantations lead to a deterioration in air quality and adversely affect people in neighbouring countries, such as Malaysia, Singapore and Thailand.[2] Similarly, transboundary pollution might stem from offshore oil and gas extraction activities, as made evident by the 2009 Montara oil spill in the Australian Exclusive Economic Zone, which led to local populations in neighbouring States suffering from serious environmental damage.[3]

As early as 2012, Alan Boyle, in a seminal work on the environment and human rights, questioned whether "human rights law has any role in tackling transboundary pollution or global climate change", contextually underlining the absence of judicial precedents and the paucity of literature on the subject matter.[4] While literature remains scarce[5] and no decision on individual claims has addressed this issue so far,[6] some important clarifications on this aspect have come from the Inter-American Court of Human Rights' Advisory Opinion on the Environment and Human Rights (hereinafter also 'Advisory Opinion' or 'Opinion OC-23/17').[7] The Court recognized in fact that, under certain circumstances, the American Convention on Human Rights[8] might apply extraterritorially in the context of cross-border environmental issues and contextually elaborated on the extent of the related State obligations under the Convention.

This chapter purports to examine the Inter-American Court's main findings and to rely on them as a starting point for outlining some broader reflections about current

---

[1] See infra, Sect. 2.

[2] See Metha (2020).

[3] On this case see, among others, Lyons (2015).

[4] Boyle (2012), pp. 633 ff.

[5] Scc, however, the recent study by Banda (2019).

[6] There are, however, pending cases. See infra, Sect. 5.

[7] Environment and Human Rights (State Obligations in Relation to the Environment in the Context of the Protection and Guarantee of the Rights to Life and to Personal Integrity—Interpretation and Scope of the Articles 4(1) and 5(1) of the American Convention on Human Rights), Advisory Opinion OC-23/17. For an overview on this case see, among others, Banda (2018), Papantoniou (2018), Vega-Barbosa and Aboagye (2018) and Lima (2020).

[8] San José, 22 November 1969, entered into force on 18 July 1978, 1144 UNTS 23.

trends and future challenges in the relationship between human rights and the environment generally and about the role of international human rights law with respect to cross-border environmental harm more specifically. Accordingly, the following questions will be discussed: did the Inter-American Court of Human Rights definitively admit "diagonal claims", that is claims brought by individuals or groups against States different from their own from which transboundary harm originates?[9] Is the Inter-American Court's approach in this respect fully convincing? Did the Court's decision influence or could it influence future practice and, in the affirmative, what might its implications be? What are, the main challenges (if any) ahead with respect to the role of international human rights law in transboundary environmental harm disputes?

The chapter is structured as follows. After a brief overview of the progressive recognition of the interdependence between human rights and environmental protection (Sect. 2) and of the issue of diagonal environmental rights under international human rights law (Sect. 3), the content of the Inter-American Court of Human Rights' Advisory Opinion on the environment and human rights will be examined, focusing on the main novelties it has brought about with respect to the role of international human rights law for cross-border environmental disputes (Sect. 4). Section 5 will address the limits of the said Opinion, as well as the key challenges that diagonal environmental claims under international human rights law might continue to encounter.

2 Setting the Scene: Human Rights and Environmental Protection

Principle 1 of the 1972 Stockholm Declaration on the Human Environment[10] is commonly regarded as the first provision acknowledging the close relationship between human rights and environmental protection at the international level.[11] It provides that:

> Man has the fundamental right to freedom, equality and adequate conditions of life, in an environment of a quality that permits a life of dignity and well-being, and he bears the

[9] This expression is commonly used in literature to indicate those claims that are brought by an individual against a State different from his own from which the environmental harm originates. See, for instance, Knox (2010) and by Feria-Tinta and Milnes (2018). The concept of diagonal claims will be explained more in depth infra, in Sect. 3.

[10] Stockholm Declaration on the Human Environment, in Report of the United Nations Conference on the Human Environment, 5–16 June 1972, UN Doc. A/CONF.48/14.

[11] Much has been written about the relationship between human rights and the environment. In this section, the main developments in the recognition of this nexus from an international legal standpoint will be retraced briefly, without any ambition to be exhaustive. For a collection of contributions by the most prominent scholars on the subject matter see, among many, Shelton (2011).

> solemn responsibility to protect and improve the environment for present and future generations.[12]

The interdependence between human rights and the environment has been subsequently upheld in several other non-binding instruments,[13] including the 2018 Framework Principles on Human Rights and the Environment.[14] According to those Principles, which have been outlined in the context of the United Nations special procedure on human rights and the environment,[15] States "should ensure a safe, clean, healthy and sustainable environment in order to respect, protect and fulfil human rights"[16] and, *vice versa*, "should respect, protect and fulfil human rights in order to ensure a safe, clean, healthy and sustainable environment".[17]

The progressive recognition of the nexus between human rights and the environment has been sealed by the inclusion of human rights references in legally binding international environmental instruments. The Paris Agreement has in fact been welcomed as the first international environmental agreement to refer specifically to human rights.[18] The Draft Global Pact for the Environment, which could eventually set the basis for an international legally binding treaty of general reach,[19] also incorporates a human rights dimension.[20]

---

[12] Notably, this statement has not been replicated in more recent instruments, such as the 1992 Rio Declaration on Environment and Development (in Report of the United Nations Conference on Environment and Development, 3–14 June 1992, UN Doc. A/CONF.151/26/Rev.1) and the 2012 Rio+20 outcome document "The Future we Want" (Resolution I, "The Future We Want", 22 June 2012, in Report of the United Nations Conference on Sustainable Development, Rio De Janeiro, 20–22 June 2012, UN Doc. A/CONF.216/16). Principle 1 of the Rio Declaration only states: "human rights are at the center of concerns for sustainable development. They are entitled to a healthy and productive life in harmony with nature".

[13] See, for instance, UN Commission on Human Rights, Sub-Commission on Prevention of Discrimination and Protection of Minorities, Special Rapporteur Fatma Zohra Ksentini, "Human Rights and the Environment", UN Doc. E/CN.4/Sub.2/1994/9, 6 July 1994, para. 22. The Draft Principles proposed by the Special Rapporteur were however not adopted by the Commission.

[14] Report of the Special Rapporteur on the issue of human rights obligations relating to the enjoyment of a safe, clean, healthy and sustainable development, UN Doc. A/HRC/37/59, 24 January 2018, Annex.

[15] See Knox (2019a), pp. 44 ff.

[16] Ibidem, Principle 1.

[17] Ibidem, Principle 2.

[18] See Paris Agreement (Paris, 12 December 2015, entered into force on 4 November 2016), Preamble ("Parties should, when taking action to address climate change, respect, promote and consider their respective obligations on human rights (. . .)"). For a more cautious approach on the significance of this human rights reference in the Paris Agreement see Boyle (2018).

[19] The Pact was promoted at the United Nations level by the French Government in 2017. In 2018, the UN General Assembly adopted a resolution, whereby it de facto opened inter-State discussion on it. See Towards a Global Pact for the Environment, UN Doc. A/RES/72/277 of 10 May 2018.

[20] In particular, it makes express reference to the right to a sound environment (Article 1). This has led John Knox to consider it as a potential "milestone" in the relationship between the environment and human rights. See Knox (2019b), p. 40.

In parallel, over the last few decades the progressive recognition of the close relationship between the environment and human rights has also resulted in—and has occurred through—an

> expansion of human rights provisions to account for some measures of environmental protection, bringing human rights (provided in treaties but also in domestic constitutions) and their institutional arsenal (. . .) to bear on questions of environmental regulation.[21]

Notably, this process has followed different directives:[22] the recognition of a right to a healthy environment in regional treaties; the progressive upholding of an environmental dimension of existing human rights, such as the right to life or to the enjoyment of private life or property (so-called "greening" of existing human rights law);[23] and the provision of certain procedural rights applicable to environmental issues, such as the right to access environmental information, to take part in environmental decision-making processes and to obtain redress for environmental harm (so-called "proceduralisation of environmental rights").[24]

2.1 *The Right to a Healthy Environment*

The protection of the environment was not perceived as a concern until the early 1970s, when, as anticipated, the relationship between human rights and the environment was first acknowledged in the Stockholm Declaration. It is thus not surprising that the first development highlighted above, namely the *assertion of a substantive right to a healthy environment,* has focused on—at least at its outset—human rights treaty regimes established in the "post-Stockholm era". The right to a healthy environment features, in fact, in Article 24 of the 1981 African Charter on Human and Peoples Rights,[25] in Article 11(1) of the 1988 Additional Protocol to the American Convention on Human Rights in the Area of Social, Cultural and

---

[21] Dupuy and Viñuales (2018), p. 357.

[22] The existence of different approaches has been acknowledged, among others, by Chuffart and Viñuales (2014), especially at p. 288.

[23] See, among others, Boyle (2012), p. 614.

[24] See, among many, Francioni (2010), p. 42.

[25] Nairobi, 27 June 1981, entered into force on 21 October 1986, 1520 UNTS 217. This provision states: "All people shall have the right to a general satisfactory environment favorable to their development". The scope and content of this right has been better defined by the case law of the African Commission on Human and Peoples' Rights and the African Court of Human and Peoples' Rights. See, for instance, African Commission, *The Social and Economic Rights Action Center and the Center for Economic and Social Rights v. Nigeria,* 27 October 2001 and African Court, *African Commission on Human and Peoples' Rights v. Republic of Kenya,* 26 May 2017, para. 199. See also the ECOWAS Court of Justice which has dealt with Article 24 of the African Charter. See *SERAP v. Federal Republic of Nigeria,* judgment No. ECW/CCJ/JUD/18/12, 14 December 2012. For an overview and critical analysis of this judgment, see Pineschi (2014). More generally, see Lumina (2020).

Economic Rights (so-called "Protocol of San Salvador"),[26] and in Article 38 of the 2004 Arab Charter of Human Rights.[27] Moreover, the right to a healthy environment is enshrined in regional agreements establishing procedural rights in environmental matters adopted after the seventies, such as the 1998 Regional Agreement on Access to Information, Public Participation in Decision-Making and Access to Justice in Environmental Matters (so-called "Aarhus Convention")[28] and the 2018 Regional Agreement on Access to Information, Public Participation and Justice in Environmental Matters in Latin America and the Caribbean (so-called "Escazú Agreement").[29]

The recognition of the right to a healthy environment as being "implicitly" incorporated in other pre-Stockholm human rights treaties is instead a recent contentious development, which—as will been explained *infra*—has concerned, for the time being, only one specific regional system of human rights protection—namely the Inter-American one.[30]

The same right has not been recognized—either *expressly* or *implicitly*—in legally binding instruments at the universal level.[31] That notwithstanding, the UN Special Rapporteur on human rights and the environment has called for such a development, highlighting the crucial role that this progress might have, especially as a way to ensure a more coherent normative framework.[32] To date, the content and

[26]This provision states: "Everyone should have the right to live in a healthy and sustainable environment". The Protocol was adopted in San Salvador on 17 November 1988 and entered into force on 16 November 1999, OAS Treaty Series no. 69.

[27]Tunis, 22 May 2004, entered into force on 15 March 2008. This article provides that: "Every person has (. . .) the right to a healthy environment (. . .)".

[28]See Preamble and Article 1. The agreement was adopted on 25 June 1998 and entered into force on 30 October 2001 (2161 UNTS 447).

[29]Article 4. The Agreement was adopted on 14 March 2018 and has not entered into force yet.

[30]The Inter-American Court of Human Rights, first in its Advisory Opinion OC-23/17 and then in its judgment in the case of *Indigenous Communities of the Lhaka Honaht (Our Land) v. Argentina* of 6 February 2020, found that the right to a healthy environment is also "implicitly" incorporated in Article 26 of the American Convention on Human Rights. See Advisory Opinion, para. 57 ff. and *Indigenous Communities of the Lhaka Honhat Association (Our Land) v. Argentina,* judgment of 6 February 2020, Series C 400, paras. 202 ff. This will be analyzed more in depth in Sect. 4. This approach has not met full consensus. See separate opinions attached to the Inter-American Court of Human Rights' Advisory Opinion and to the judgment in the *Lhaka Honhat v. Argentina* case. The lack of direct justiciability of Article 11(1) of the Protocol of San Salvador has instead prevented the Inter-American Commission and Court from elaborating on its content and scope. Yet, this provision was referred to in the judgment, rendered by the Inter-American Court of Human Rights, in the case of *Kawas Fernández v. Honduras*, of 3 April 2009 (Series C No. 196), para. 148.

[31]There are, however, global human rights agreements concluded after the 1970s that, even if do not uphold the right to a healthy environment, make explicit reference to the environment. See Article 24(2)(c) of the United Nations Convention on the Rights of the Child (New York, 20 November 1989, entered into force on 2 September 1990, 1577 UNTS 3).

[32]See Report of the Special Rapporteur on the issue of human rights obligations relating to the enjoyment of a safe, clean, healthy and sustainable environment, UN Doc. A/73/188, 19 July 2018. See also Knox and Pejan (2018), p. 15.

scope of the right to a healthy environment varies in fact depending on the instrument taken into account (and, at times, even on the interpretation offered by different bodies within the same system of human rights protection): thus, for instance, the African Charter on Human and Peoples' Rights attaches to the right enshrined in Article 24 a collective dimension (as made evident by the use of the expression "*all people* have the right to. . ."), which does not find equivalents in other conventions.[33] By way of additional example, the Aarhus Convention includes *future generations* among the right-holders; a recognition that differentiates it from other international instruments. On top of that, the use of inconsistent terminology ("healthy", "sustainable", "adequate" are all adjectives used next to the word "environment") not only leads to a definitional indeterminacy, but also opens the way to questions about the impact of the use of different words on the content of corresponding State obligations. This lack of convergence also features in domestic practice, where the right to a healthy environment has progressively been encapsulated in constitutional texts.[34]

Arguably, in light of these divergences both at the global and domestic level, there has also so far been a certain reluctance to infer from the recognitions highlighted above the emergence—whether accomplished or still in progress—of a right to a healthy environment in general international law.[35]

2.2 The Integration of Environmental Considerations Within the Realm of Existing Human Rights

The second development related to human rights and the environment—that is the *integration of environmental considerations within the realm of existing human rights*—has instead primarily concerned those human rights treaty regimes that do not provide for a freestanding right to a healthy environment enshrined in positive law.[36] Absent any express provisions in the texts, human rights treaty monitoring

[33] Yet, as will be noted in Sect. 4, the Inter-American Court of Human Rights has also acknowledged the collective dimension of the right to a healthy environment.

[34] Boyd (2012) and Daly and May (2018), especially pp. 50 ff.

[35] See, among others, Lewis (2012), p. 36 and Post (2019). It is also worth underlying that some scholars have contended that the recognition of the right to a healthy environment at the global level is neither necessary nor useful. See, for instance, Francioni (2010), p. 54.

[36] The main human rights treaties adopted before the 1970s—such as the International Covenant on Civil and Political Rights (New York, 16 December 1966, entered into force on 23 March 1976, 999 UNTS 171), the International Covenant on Economic, Social and Cultural Rights (New York, 16 December 1966, entered into force on 3 January 1976, 993 UNTS 3), the Convention for the Protection of Human Rights and Fundamental Freedoms (hereinafter also 'European Convention on Human Rights') (Rome, 4 November 1950, entered into force on 3 September 1953, ETS No. 005) and the European Social Charter (Turin, 18 October 1961, revised in Strasbourg on 6 May 1996)—do not contain any reference to the protection of the environment.

bodies have in fact interpreted extensively the existing provisions to include substantive obligations relating to environmental protection.

The Human Rights Committee, for instance, has recognized that the right to life in Article 6 of the International Covenant on Civil and Political Rights implies a corresponding obligation for States parties to take appropriate measures to address environmental degradation and to protect the environment against harm, pollution and climate change.[37] Accordingly, in its views in the *Portillo Cáceres* v. *Paraguay* case, the Committee found that the State concerned had breached, inter alia, the claimants' rights to life and to respect for one's private and family life, protected under the Covenant, by failing to enforce environmental regulation and properly address environmental harm caused by the mass use of agrotoxins.[38]

Likewise, both the European and the Inter-American Court of Human Rights have found that environmental harm may result in the violation of several rights protected under the European and American Conventions on Human Rights, including the right to life,[39] the right to property[40] and the right to respect for one's private and family life.[41]

Notably, the greening process has concerned not only civil and political rights, but also economic, social and cultural rights. The European Committee of Social Rights and the Committee on Economic, Social and Cultural Rights have interpreted the provisions on the right to health contained in the Charter[42] and in the Covenant[43] so as to encompass environmental considerations.[44]

In light of the above, one can argue that the conceptual assumption behind the greening process of human rights is well synthesized in Judge Weeramantry's

---

[37] General Comment No. 36, UN Doc. CCPR/C/GC/26, 3 September 2019, paras. 26 and 62.

[38] Communication No. 2751/2016, Views adopted on 25 July 2019, UN Doc. CCPR/C/126/D/2751/2016, 20 September 2019. For a comment on the recent "case-law" of the Human Rights Committee see, inter alia, Citroni (2020).

[39] See, e.g., ECtHR [GC], *Öneryildiz v. Turkey*, App. No. 48939/99, judgment of 30 November 2004, para. 118. See also the Inter-American Court of Human Rights' Advisory Opinion OC-23/17, para. 63. For an overview of the implementation status of the European Court of Human Rights' judgments in environmental matters see Council of Europe, Department for the Execution of Judgments of the European Court of Human Rights, Thematic Factsheet, October 2020.

[40] See, e.g., IACtHR, *Saramaka Peoples v. Suriname*, Series C No. 172, judgment of 28 November 2007, para. 158; *Indigenous Community of Yakye Axa v. Paraguay*, Series C No. 125, judgment of 17 June 2005, para. 143.

[41] See, e.g., ECtHR, *Fadayeva v. Russia*, App. No. 55723/00, judgment of 9 June 2005, para. 134; *Taşkin and others v. Turkey*, App. No. 46117/99, judgment of 10 November 2004, para. 126; *López Ostra v. Spain*, App. No. 16798/90, judgment of 9 December 1994, para. 58; *Cordella and others v. Italy*, App. Nos. 54414/13 and 54264/15, judgment of 24 January 2019, para. 174.

[42] Article 14.

[43] Article 12.

[44] See European Committee of Social Rights, *Marangopolous Foundation for Human Rights v. Greece*, decision of 6 December 2006, para. 195 ff. See also Committee on Economic, Social and Cultural Rights, General Comment No. 14, The Right to the Highest Attainable Standard of Health (Article 12), UN Doc. E/C.12/2000/4 of 11 August 2000, para. 15.

separate opinion on the *Gabcíkovo-Nagymaros Project* case, whereby he affirmed that "environmental protection is (...) a vital part of contemporary human rights doctrine, for it is a *sine qua non* for numerous human rights such as the right to health and the right to life itself".[45]

Yet, divergences also exist in the way in which judicial and quasi-judicial human rights treaty bodies have incorporated environmental considerations in human rights provisions. Thus, for instance, whereas certain human rights bodies have seemingly inferred a right to a healthy environment from existing human rights,[46] others have not gone so far or have clearly distinguished between the recognition of a self-standing right to a healthy environment "implicit" in treaty law and the environmental implications of other human rights.[47] By way of further example, certain treaty monitoring bodies have shown a more progressive attitude in upholding the collective dimension of environmental rights stemming from existing provisions, compared to others.[48] On top of that, human rights treaty monitoring bodies have examined comparable cases under different "heads" (e.g. the right to respect one's private and family life, rather than the right to life).[49] Similar inconsistencies have not only concerned different systems of human rights protection; even within the same treaty regime, environmental considerations have been upheld with respect to different human rights.

Despite this "fragmentation", there are however signs of an ongoing cross-fertilisation between international judicial and quasi-judicial human rights treaty bodies[50] that, in the long run, could increase convergence.

2.3 Procedural Environmental Rights

As stated earlier, a third critical development in the field of human rights and the environment has been the *proceduralisation of environmental rights*. This expression refers to two parallel phenomena: on the one hand, the progressive inclusion of procedural rights—such as the rights to access to information, to participate in

[45] ICJ, *Gabcíkovo-Nagymaros Project (Hungary v. Slovakia)*, 25 September 1997, separate opinion, p. 88.

[46] See again *Marangopolous Foundation for Human Rights v. Greece*, para. 195.

[47] Here the reference is once again to the Inter-American Court of Human Rights' Advisory Opinion OC-23/17, whose content will be better analysed infra, in Sect. 4.

[48] See again Francioni (2010), p. 51, who refers to the Inter-American system of protection of human rights. For a comparative study between the European and Inter-American system of human rights protection with respect to environmental rights see, among others, Pavoni (2015).

[49] See, e.g., European Court of Human Rights, *Cordella and others v. Italy* cit. (decided under Article 8 of the European Convention on Human Rights) and Human Rights Committee, *Portillo Cáceres v. Paraguay* cit. (decided on the basis of Articles 6 and 17 of the International Covenant on Civil and Political Rights).

[50] See, for instance, Human Rights Committee, *Portillo Cáceres v. Paraguay* cit., para. 7.4.

decision-making and to an effective remedy—in binding and non-binding international environmental law instruments;[51] on the other hand, the interpretation of procedural rights embodied in international human rights law instruments—such as the right to an effective remedy—so as to apply them to environmental matters.[52]

Despite an overall convergence, the case law of judicial and quasi-judicial human rights treaty bodies displays—also in this last respect—a number of inconsistencies, both between[53] and within different systems of human rights protection,[54] in a way that resembles the "greening" process of substantive human rights.

Yet, as a result of their recognition in international environmental instruments, procedural environmental rights have attained a higher level of maturity compared to substantive ones.[55]

3 A Neglected Aspect: Diagonal Environmental Rights Under International Human Rights Law

The above developments concerning the nexus between human rights and the environment have nourished scholarly debate, concerning, for instance, the status of an autonomous right to a healthy environment in international law[56] or the very opportunity to treat environmental protection as a human rights issue.[57] As stated above, in the absence of relevant practice, scant attention has until recently been devoted to a further aspect, namely the role that international human rights law might have with respect to transboundary environmental harm.[58]

The no-harm principle, which requires States to prevent those activities within their territories which may cause significant cross-border harm, is contained in many environmental law instruments[59] and is considered to be part of general international

---

[51] See, for instance, among many, Principle 10 of the Rio Declaration and the content of the Aarhus Convention.

[52] For a recollection of cases see, among others, Cournil (2016).

[53] For an in-depth analysis of the issue with respect to the case law of the European Court of Human Rights and the Inter-American Court of Human Rights see again Pavoni (2015).

[54] See, for instance, the different approach adopted by the European Court of Human Rights in the cases *Hatton and others v. United Kingdom* (GC, App. No. 36022/97, judgment of 8 July 2003) and *Taşkin v. Turkey* (App. No. 46117/99, judgment of 10 November 2004).

[55] Ong (2010), p. 165.

[56] See Knox and Pejan (2018), p. 1.

[57] On this debate, see also Adinolfi (2018), p. 211.

[58] But, see again Knox (2010), Boyle (2012) and Banda (2019). "Transboundary environmental harm" is understood here as the harm resulting from acts taken on a State's territory but producing effects outside it. It does not refer to the harm caused by State authorities acting outside of their territory.

[59] As far as non-binding instruments are concerned, see, for instance, Principle 21 of the Stockholm Declaration on the Human Environment and Principle 21 of the Rio Declaration on Environment

law.[60] However, it rests on State-to-State relations, meaning that generally only the State of nationality can act at the international level to seek reparation for the damage individuals have suffered as a result of another State's wrongful conduct.[61] Affected individuals could in any case seek remedies from private parties or States before domestic courts in the home State or in the foreign State from which the harm originated (indeed, the exhaustion of local remedies available in the foreign State is a pre-condition for the State of nationality to take up the claim on behalf of its national), provided that this is not precluded by national provisions.[62] Whereas this often leads to a multitude of contextual procedures, also known as "cluster-litigation",[63] it could also result in there being no effective remedy if domestic legislation does not allow such claims to be made.

The issue becomes more complex if transboundary harm is considered from an international human rights perspective. There is little doubt that, in the event that they have exhausted all domestic avenues without obtaining an effective remedy, individuals could bring a claim against their own State due to its failure to protect them from transboundary environmental harm. But can they also do so with respect to *other States* from whose territory the harmful effects originated? And, what would be the extent of State obligations in this respect?

---

and Development. With respect to binding instruments, see, among others, United Nations Framework Convention on Climate Change (New York, 9 May 1992, entered into force on 21 March 1994, 1771 UNTS 107), Preamble; and Convention on Biological Diversity (Rio De Janeiro, 5 June 1992, entered into force on 29 December 1993, 1760 UNTS 79), Article 3. For an overview of other instruments, see Lefeber (2018), pp. 92–93.

[60] See, for instance, Court of Arbitration, *Trial Smelter case (United States v. Canada)*, 16 April 1938, and 11 March 1941, p. 1965; International Court of Justice, *Corfu Channel case (The United Kingdom v. Albania)*, 9 April 1949, p. 22 and *Pulp Mills on the River Uruguay (Argentina v. Uruguay)*, 20 April 2010, para. 101. See also International Law Commission, Draft Articles on the Prevention of Transboundary Harm from Hazardous Activities, 12 December 2001, UN Doc. A/RES/56/82. The customary nature of this rule has also been upheld by Scovazzi (1986), p. 277. See also, *ex multis*, Dupuy and Viñuales (2018), pp. 63 ff., pursuant to whom the no-harm principle has crystallised into a more comprehensive principle of prevention. Bodansky considers instead the duty to prevent transboundary pollution as a general principle of international law or declarative law. See Bodansky (2010), p. 201. On the content of the no-harm rule, see again, among others, Scovazzi (2001). On the general reach of the no-harm rule beyond environmental protection, see Stephens (2009), p. 162.

[61] For existing exceptions, linked to environmental complaint mechanisms allowing "vertical" individual claims on the international plane, see Knox (2010).

[62] At times, national law remedies are provided for, in specific treaties. See, for instance, the Nordic Environmental Protection Convention (Stockholm, 19 February 1974, entered into force on 5 October 1976, 1092 UNTS 279), Article 3. For a practical example of claims brought in the courts of the State from which the harm originates see Prihandono and Dewanty (2015).

[63] Nollkaemper (2008).

3.1 The "Transboundary Application" of Human Rights Treaties and the "Jurisdiction" Conundrum

The "transboundary application" of human rights treaties in environmental matters, which could translate—provided that domestic remedies have been exhausted—to quasi-judicial or judicial proceedings at the international level against the State from which the harm originates,[64] is inherently linked to the debate about the interpretation of State jurisdictional clauses contained therein.[65] In this sense, the role that international human rights law might play with respect to transboundary environmental harm is emblematic of a matter of more general reach, namely the applicability of human rights treaties to the direct extraterritorial effects of domestic acts,[66] of which foreign surveillance and domestic economic policies (with extraterritorial effects on the enjoyment of human rights by individuals abroad) represent additional examples.[67]

Human rights treaties generally require States parties to respect and secure the rights and freedoms of the individuals *in their territories or within their jurisdiction.*[68] This has been traditionally interpreted by human rights treaty bodies—albeit with some climb-downs[69] and differences[70]—as meaning that human rights treaties would apply extraterritorially if the State exercises effective control or authority over a territory or individuals abroad (so-called "spatial and personal models of jurisdiction").[71]

---

[64] Treves (2019), p. 102.

[65] See, for instance, Article 2 of the International Covenant on Civil and Political Rights, Article 1 of the European Convention on Human Rights and Article 1 of the American Convention on Human Rights. On the notion of jurisdiction in human rights treaties and their extraterritorial application see, among many, De Sena (2002), Gondek (2009), Milanovic (2011), Besson (2012), Da Costa (2012), Den Hejer and Lawson (2013), and Raible (2020).

[66] See Altwicker (2018), p. 586.

[67] Ibid. There may however also be cases of indirect extraterritorial effects of domestic acts. Altwicker refers, by way of example, to the case of extradition (ibid., p. 585). Another example could be the licensing or exporting of arms, which are then used to commit human rights violations abroad.

[68] See again Article 2 of the International Covenant on Civil and Political Rights or Article 1 of the European Convention on Human Rights.

[69] See European Court of Human Rights, *Bankovic and others v. Belgium and others*, App. No. 52207/99, decision of 19 December 2001. On the interpretation of the notion of "jurisdiction" in Article 1 of the European Convention on Human Rights see, among many, Papanicolopulu (2009).

[70] The Human Rights Committee's "case-law" generally refers, for instance, to the "power" exercised over an individual; conversely, the European Court of Human Rights has generally used the expression "authority and control".

[71] These expressions have been used by Milanovic (2011). Among the relevant case-law, see, *ex multis*, International Court of Justice, *Legal Consequences of the Construction of a Wall in the Occupied Palestinian Territory*, Advisory Opinion, 9 July 2004, para. 109 ff.; Human Rights Committee, General Comment No. 31, UN Doc. CCPR/C/21/Rev.1/Add.1326, May 2004, para.

Human rights treaty bodies have however lately shown a progressively expansive approach towards extraterritoriality. Thus, for instance, in its General Comment No. 36, the Human Rights Committee upheld an "impact-approach", when it found that States also exercise *jurisdiction* over persons located outside a territory under their effective control, if the rights of those individuals are "*impacted*" by their activities in a direct and reasonably foreseeable manner.[72] While fitting with the personal model of jurisdiction, this approach arguably broadened its scope in a way that seemingly conceals a more universalistic attitude.[73]

The case law of the European Court of Human Rights concerning both the spatial and the personal models of jurisdiction also features expansive trends.[74] The Court has upheld, for instance, the extraterritorial application of certain positive obligations under the European Convention on Human Rights.[75] This latest drift has been based on the idea of a "*procedural* control" of individuals abroad, by means, inter alia, of the issuance of arrest warrants or of ongoing proceedings.[76]

In the case of transboundary environmental harm, States do not exercise authority or control over a territory or individuals abroad, but on activities that occur within their territory, whose harmful effects impact on rights-holders on foreign soil. It follows that, at least *prima facie*, human rights treaties would not apply to such scenario.

That notwithstanding, it has been argued that even if human rights treaty bodies have been reluctant to expressly acknowledge an additional model of jurisdiction which also encompass *extraterritorial effects of domestic measures*, there would be an *emerging*—and minoritarian—*trend* pointing in this direction, often concealed by means of references to the traditional models of jurisdiction. The expression "direct

10; European Court of Human Rights, *Al-Skeini v. United Kingdom*, GC, App. No. 55721/07, judgment of 7 July 2011, paras. 130–142. Scholars have conceptualized "more universalistic" approaches to jurisdiction. These include a so-called third model of jurisdiction, grounded on the distinction between positive and negative obligations: according to this view, States should be responsible for breaches of their negative obligations even where they do not exercise control or authority over a territory or individuals abroad; the same would not occur, instead, with respect to States' positive obligations. See again Milanovic (2011), pp. 209 ff. On the relevance of this approach to cases of domestic acts with extraterritorial effects (like foreign surveillance), see Milanovic (2015), p. 129. Other scholars have proposed a more "universalistic" conceptualization, pursuant to which also positive obligations would have an "extraterritorial application". See Altwicker (2018), p. 591. Finally, other scholars have stressed the general need for a dynamic interpretation of the concept of jurisdiction in international human rights treaties so to make States parties responsible also for "transboundary acts" (a category which includes domestic acts with extraterritorial effects) violating the rights of individuals abroad, without however specifying the grounds for such an extensive interpretation. See Vennemann (2006), p. 307.

[72] See General Comment No. 36, UN Doc. CCPR/C/GC/36, 30 October 2018, paras. 22 and 63. The expression "impact-approach" has been used by Møgster (2018).

[73] Ibid.

[74] For an overview of the relevant case law, see Milanovic (2018a), especially pp. 99–103.

[75] See, e.g., European Court of Human Rights, *Romeo Castaño v. Belgium*, App. No. 8351/17, judgment of 9 July 2019.

[76] This "procedural dimension" has been underlined by Besson (2020).

effects test" has been coined to refer to this approach, pursuant to which individuals would fall within a State's jurisdiction if they felt the effects of its domestic actions, even if they are on foreign soil.[77] In that sense, recent practice would have built on the dicta of the Inter-American Commission on Human Rights and of the European Court of Human Rights, which had in 1999 and 2004 already found, respectively, that

> a party to the American Convention may be responsible under certain circumstances for the acts and omissions of its agents which produce effects or are undertaken outside that State's own territory[78]

and that

> in exceptional circumstances the acts of Contracting States performed outside their territory, or which produce effects there, may amount to exercise by them of their jurisdiction within the meaning of Article 1 of the [European] Convention [on Human Rights].[79]

Until recently, however, human rights treaty monitoring bodies have not clarified on what grounds the rights-holders located abroad would fall within the jurisdiction of the State whose domestic actions had affected them. Moreover, even when they had the chance to do so in contentious cases, they have proved reluctant to clearly uphold that acts taking place in a State's territory, but impinging on the rights of individuals abroad, fall within the scope of application of the relevant treaties.[80]

Remarkably, not all human rights treaties which have been subjected to the so-called "greening" process contain jurisdictional clauses. Those which do not include them have generally been interpreted more extensively in the area of extraterritoriality.[81]

In lieu of a jurisdictional clause in the text of the International Covenant on Economic, Social and Cultural Rights, the Committee on Economic, Social and Cultural Rights has concluded, for instance, that the "obligations of States parties [stemming from the Covenant] do not stop at their territorial borders".[82] More specifically, the Committee upheld that

---

[77] See Banda (2019), pp. 1927 ff.

[78] See Inter-American Commission on Human Rights, *Saldaño v. Argentina*, 11 March 1999, para. 17.

[79] See European Court of Human Rights, *Ilascu and others v. Moldavia*, App. No. 48787/99, 8 July 2004, para. 314.

[80] See European Court of Human Rights, *Big Brothers Watch v. United Kingdom*, App. Nos. 58170/13, 62322/14 and 24960/14, judgment of 13 September 2018 (the case has been referred to the Grand Chamber), para. 271. On the Court's approach on this aspect see Milanovic (2018b).

[81] Treaties that expressly refer to the environment, such as the Convention on the Rights of the Child, have also been interpreted extensively. See, e.g., Committee on the Rights of the Child, General Comment No. 16 on State obligations regarding the impact of business on children's rights, UN Doc. CRC/C/GC/16, 17 April 2013, para. 43.

[82] General Comment No. 24 on State obligations under the International Covenant on Economic, Social and Cultural Rights in the context of business activities, UN Doc. E/C.12/GC/24, 10 August 2017, para. 26. On the alleged lack of clarity of the Committee's findings in the area of extraterritoriality see, among others, Raible (2020), pp. 26 ff. See also Langford (2013), p. 52.

> the extraterritorial obligation to respect requires States parties to refrain from interfering directly or indirectly with the enjoyment of the Covenant rights by persons outside their territories[83]

and that the

> extraterritorial obligation to prevent requires States parties to take steps to prevent and redress infringements of Covenant rights that occur outside their territories due to the activities of business entities over which they can exercise control, especially in cases where the remedies available to victims before the domestic courts of the State where the harm occurs are unavailable or ineffective.[84]

The significance of these divergences in approach towards extraterritoriality in general and towards diagonal claims specifically is, however, limited in practice. Despite the lack of "limits" in the convention text, in fact, jurisdictional clauses are often provided for in the instruments that establish monitoring mechanisms, with the result that the admissibility of individual communications would still depend on the existence of a jurisdictional link between the State and the individual whose rights have been violated. Article 2 of the Optional Protocol to the International Covenant on Economic, Social and Cultural Rights[85] provides, for instance, that

> communications may be submitted by or on behalf of individuals or groups of individuals, under the jurisdiction of a State Party, claiming to be victims of a violation of any of the economic, social and cultural rights set forth in the Covenant by that State Party.

3.2 State Human Rights Obligations in a Transboundary Environmental Context

Apart from the question of applicability, the extent of a State's duty under human rights treaties in a transboundary environmental harm context has been long unclear. What would be the States' obligations under human rights treaties if they were found to apply in the first place?

An indication in this respect, albeit of a non-legally binding character, might have come from Article 13 of the 2018 Framework Principles on Human Rights and the Environment, which provides for a duty to cooperate. It establishes in fact that:

---

[83] Ibid., para. 29.

[84] Ibid., para. 30. See also Principle 13 of the Maastricht Principles on the Extraterritorial Obligations of States in the Area of Economic, Social and Cultural Rights, adopted by human rights experts in 2011: "States must desist from acts and omissions that create a real risk of nullifying or impairing the enjoyment of economic, social and cultural rights extraterritorially. The responsibility of States is engaged where such nullification or impairment is a foreseeable result of their conduct. Uncertainty about potential impacts does not constitute justification for such conduct". The text of the Principles is reported in De Schutter et al. (2012).

[85] New York, 16 December 1966, entered into force on 3 January 1976, 993 UNTS 3. For other similar jurisdictional clauses, see again Langford (2013), p. 59.

> States should cooperate with each other to establish, maintain and enforce effective international legal frameworks in order to prevent, reduce and remedy transboundary and global environmental harm that interferes with the full enjoyment of human rights.

The uncertainty over the extent of States' obligations can be ascribed again to the paucity of relevant practice. Thus, for instance, of the two diagonal "claims" which have been filed before the Inter-American Commission on Human Rights so far, one has been rejected and the other is still pending.

The Inter-American Commission in fact did not pronounce on the petition filed in 2005 by the Inuit against the United States of America. The indigenous group claimed that this State had violated their human rights, as protected under the American Declaration of the Rights and Duties of Man, by not limiting its contribution to carbon emissions and thus to climate change.[86] The claim possessed a "diagonal dimension" as it was filed on behalf of the Inuit residing in the Artic regions not only of the United States of America, but also of Canada,[87] and could therefore provide an opportunity for clarifying States' obligations with respect to transboundary and global environmental harm. The Commission was however unable to establish, on the basis of the information received, whether the allegations constituted breaches of the rights protected under the Declaration.[88]

A further petition was filed before the American Commission on Human Rights in 2013 on behalf of the Arctic Athabaskan peoples of United States of America and Canada against the latter State.[89] Like in the Inuit petition, the indigenous group complained that Canada, by not regulating black carbon emissions, had caused human rights violations. Moreover, insofar as the petition refers also to the violations of rights concerning members of the group residing in the United States, it presents a "diagonal dimension". As stated, however, the case is still pending.

Notably, the petitioners argued in both claims that the American Declaration on the Rights and Duties of Man should also be interpreted in light of international environmental norms, thus arguing that States should be obliged to avoid transboundary environmental harm.[90]

---

[86] Petition to the Inter-American Commission on Human Rights Seeking Relief from Violations Resulting from Global Warming Caused by Acts and Omissions of the United States, filed on 12 August 2005.

[87] See again Knox (2010).

[88] The decision was issued on 16 November 2006.

[89] Petition to the Inter-American Commission on Human Rights Seeking Relief from Violations of the Rights of Arctic Athabaskan Peoples Resulting from Rapid Arctic Warming and Melting Caused by Emissions of Black Carbon by Canada, filed on 23 April 2013. On this petition see, among others, Szpak (2020).

[90] Apart from the petitions lodged before human rights treaties monitoring mechanisms, it is unfortunate that the International Court of Justice was prevented—due to the discontinuation of the Aerial Herbicide Spraying (Ecuador v. Colombia). In its memorial, Ecuador had alleged, inter alia, that Colombia's aerial herbicide spraying of coca leaf plantations, which were also having trans-boundary effects in Ecuador, had given rise to a violation of the Ecuadorians' right to a healthy and decent environment enshrined in Article 11(1) of the Protocol of San Salvador, to which both Colombia and Ecuador are parties. In spite of the fact that this application did not amount to a

4 The Inter-American Court of Human Rights' Advisory Opinion OC-23/17

The role that human rights treaties and their monitoring mechanisms might have with respect to transboundary environmental harm has gained momentum after the Inter-American Court of Human Rights arguably opened the path, with its Advisory Opinion OC-23/17, to future cross-border diagonal claims for the alleged violation of human rights caused by transboundary environmental harm.[91]

The Advisory Opinion was rendered in 2017 in response to a request filed on 14 March 2016 by the Republic of Colombia, as a result of its concerns over the severe degradation that the construction and operations of large-scale infrastructure projects by States that border the Caribbean Sea could cause to the marine environment, and thus to the human habitat, in the Wider Caribbean Region. In particular, Colombia submitted to the Court three questions on the interpretation of the American Convention on Human Rights, specifically: (1) whether a person on foreign soil could be anyhow considered subject to the jurisdiction of a State party to the American Convention as per its Article 1, provided that his or her rights had been violated as a result of the environmental damage or the risk of such damage coming from that State; (2) whether the conduct of a State party to that Convention that caused transboundary environmental harm was compatible with the State obligations stemming from Articles 4 (right to life) and 5 (right to personal integrity) of the American Convention, read in conjunction with Article 1 of the same instrument; (3) whether the Convention required States parties to abide by those norms of international environmental law that aim at preventing environmental damage and whether cooperation among the States concerned and environmental impact assessments could ensure compliance with the relevant obligations.[92]

In providing an answer to these questions, the Court "systematically addressed"[93] several issues concerning the relationship between the environment and human rights. The Court stressed, in fact, that it was not bound, in the exercise of its advisory function, by the literal terms of the requests received.[94]

"diagonal claim" in the traditional sense, it could have nonetheless led the International Court of Justice to deal with the extraterritorial application of the recalled provision and, in the event that this was confirmed, with the content of the corresponding State obligations. The removal of the case from the Court's docket has, however, definitively ruled out the possibility of any clarificatory indications deriving from the judgment. The Application was filed by Ecuador on 31 March 2008 and the agreement of the parties that resolved the dispute was concluded on 9 September 2013 and communicated to the Court on 12 September 2013.

[91] See again Feria-Tinta and Milnes (2018), pp. 74 ff.

[92] Advisory Opinion OC-23/17, para. 3.

[93] This expression has been used by Professor Scovazzi with respect to the right to a healthy environment. See Scovazzi (2019b).

[94] See Advisory Opinion OC-23/17, para. 27.

For the purpose of this contribution, three main 'findings' in the Court's Advisory Opinion[95] are of paramount importance and will therefore be taken into account. Two of them relate specifically to the role of the American Convention on Human Rights, and of its monitoring mechanism, with respect to transboundary environmental harm. The third one, which will be analysed first (albeit briefly), while being broader in scope, might also exert influence on future diagonal environmental claims.

4.1 On the Existence of an Autonomous Right to a Healthy Environment

One of the most significant findings of the Court is that the American Convention on Human Rights would also protect the right to a healthy environment.

Whereas Colombia's request only concerned the scope and meaning of the rights to life and personal integrity, protected under Articles 4 and 5 of the American Convention on Human Rights, the Court decided, in fact, to directly examine, at first, the relationship between human rights and environment and, more importantly, the existence of other human rights affected by environmental degradation.[96] In this context, after having acknowledged the well-established link between the protection of the environment and the enjoyment of human rights, as upheld also in universal non legally binding instruments,[97] the Court found that this nexus translated, under most systems of human rights protection, into the "greening of pre-existing human rights" and, in certain cases, into the recognition of an autonomous right to a healthy environment as in the case of the Inter-American system.[98] In this respect, the Court referred not only to Article 11 of the San Salvador Protocol, which, as discussed above, expressly recognizes a right to a healthy environment, but, what is new, also to Article 26 of the American Convention on Human Rights, pursuant to which:

> the States Parties undertake to adopt measures, both internally and through international cooperation, especially those of an economic and technical nature, with a view to achieving progressively, by legislation or other appropriate means, the full realization of the rights implicit in the economic, social, educational, scientific, and cultural standards set forth in the Charter of the Organization of American States as amended by the Protocol of Buenos Aires.[99]

---

[95] The Advisory Opinion is also significant in relation to other perspectives. Some commentators, for instance, have stressed its relevance for the recognition of the interdependency and indivisibility of human rights and for the resort to soft-law instruments. See again Feria-Tinta and Milnes (2018), pp. 69 ff.

[96] Advisory Opinion OC-23/17, paras. 47 ff.

[97] The Court mentioned, for instance, the Stockholm Declaration and the Agenda 2030 for Sustainable Development (see paras. 52–53).

[98] Advisory Opinion OC-23/17, para. 55.

[99] Ibid., paras. 56–57.

The Court reached this conclusion on the basis of the notion of "integral development" enshrined in the Organization of American States (OAS) Charter.[100] It found indeed that this concept should have been interpreted in light of other relevant international instruments so as to encompass environmental protection (as one of its pillars). By doing so, the Court's majority *de facto* found that the right to a healthy environment is "implicitly" protected under the American Convention on Human Rights and upheld its direct enforceability. In fact, whereas the Protocol of San Salvador limits the submission of individual petitions under the Inter-American system of human rights protection to the rights to education and to organize trade unions,[101] the economic, social and cultural rights "implicitly" protected under Article 26 of the American Convention do not *arguably* encounter any such restriction.

Clearly, this finding calls into the picture—and poses itself within the framework of—the Court's progressive recognition of economic, social and cultural rights as justiciable rights under the American Convention on Human Rights, and the debate stemming thereof.[102] Some members of the Court indeed openly shared their dissent with respect to the majority's conclusion concerning the direct justiciability of the right to a healthy environment, both because it exceeded the purpose of the Advisory Opinion and due to their view that economic, social and cultural rights would not have been directly enforceable, as standalone rights, under Article 26 of the American Convention.[103]

Ultimately, the direct justiciability of the right to a healthy environment was confirmed, albeit not unanimously, by the Inter-American Court of Human Rights in February 2020, when it adjudicated upon a contentious case concerning, inter alia, the alleged violation of this right.[104]

Notably, whilst this case concerned facts of an "intra-State" dimension,[105] nothing prevents, in principle (that is, provided that no other limits exist), that a similar

[100] Bogotá, 30 April 1948, entered into force on 13 December 1951, OAS Treaty Series Nos. 1-C and 61, Article 48.

[101] See Article 19, para. 6, of the Protocol.

[102] See, for instance, Inter-American Court of Human Rights, *Lagos del Campo v. Peru*, judgment of 31 August 2017, Series C No. 340. The Court found that the right to work is directly justiciable under Article 26 of the American Convention on Human Rights.

[103] See Concurring Opinions of judges Vio Grossi and Sierra Porto.

[104] Inter-American Court of Human Rights, *Indigenous Communities of the Lhaka Honat (Our Land) Association v. Argentina* cit., para. 201 ff. As already underlined, however, some judges dissented with the majority's stance. See the partially dissenting opinions of judges Vio Grossi, Sierra Porto and Pérez Manrique. On this case see again Lima (2020), pp. 514–519.

[105] The case concerned the alleged violation by Argentina of the rights of indigenous communities located in the Salta province, due to that State's inaction with respect to activities undertaken by private parties in the area which caused environmental degradation. The findings of the Court under Article 26 also concern the rights to cultural identity, to water and to adequate food.

finding would apply also to diagonal claims related to the right to a healthy environment.[106]

4.2 *On the Outer Limits of the American Convention on Human Rights*

Another significant aspect of the Court's Advisory Opinion, and the one that has attracted the greatest attention so far, is the finding that States parties to the American Convention might exercise, under certain circumstances, jurisdiction over individuals on foreign soil as a result of them being affected by activities undertaken within their territories.[107]

The Court began its analysis on this point by stressing that Article 1 of the American Convention on Human Rights, by means of which a State party to the American Convention "undertake to respect the rights and freedoms recognized herein and to ensure to all persons subject *to their jurisdiction* the free and full exercise of those rights and freedoms" (emphasis added), implies that those States are under an obligation to respect and ensure the rights not only of those persons that are within their territory, but also those that are under their authority, control or responsibility.[108] More precisely, the Court found that the term "jurisdiction" in Article 1 should be interpreted, in light of hermeneutical rules, to include "certain ways of exercising jurisdiction beyond the territory of the State in question".[109]

The Court then moved to examine in detail other human rights treaty monitoring bodies' case law, focusing on the situations in which they had found that the exercise of States' jurisdiction also concerned extraterritorial conduct.[110] Having excluded that a link between these scenarios and that at stake in the Colombian State's request existed, the Court found that, in the specific case, concerning the possibility of an extraterritorial exercise of jurisdiction with respect to compliance with environmental obligations, the "obligations derived from the American Convention must be analyzed in light of the State obligations in that regard".[111] The Court stressed in this respect that

---

106 Enforceability apart, in its Opinion OC-23/17 the Court also addressed the scope and content of the right to a healthy environment by upholding its collective and individual dimensions, by identifying the corresponding States' obligations, including promoting environmental protection and ensuring that every individual lives in a healthy environment, and by stressing the object of the protection, namely nature in itself. See Advisory Opinion OC-23/17, para. 59 ff.

107 Ibid., para. 71 ff.

108 Ibid., para. 73.

109 Ibid., para. 74.

110 Ibid., para. 79.

111 Ibid., para. 82.

> States have an obligation to avoid transboundary environmental damage that can affect the human rights of individuals outside their territory

and that, accordingly,

> for the purposes of the American Convention, when transboundary damage occurs that affects treaty-based rights, (...) the persons whose rights have been violated are under the jurisdiction of the State of origin, if there is a causal link between the act that originated in its territory and the infringement of the human rights of persons outside its territory.[112]

In upholding the above-mentioned conclusion on the meaning of the term "jurisdiction" in Article 1 of the American Convention, the Court stressed that the State of origin of the transboundary harm would exercise *effective control over the individuals abroad*,[113] thus "formally" relying on the traditional model of personal jurisdiction. That notwithstanding, the Court coined, in practice, a new model of jurisdiction, based on the exercise of *effective control over activities* (rather than persons) carried out in the States' territories and which cause damage abroad. As stressed by Maria Banda,

> rather than treating the direct effects as a separate basis of extraterritorial jurisdiction, the Court chose to subsume this approach under the effective control test. The Court thus essentially redefined the effective control test in the Advisory Opinion: in the Inter-American context, effective control now apparently also refers to the State's control over the *domestic* activities involved (as understood in international environmental law) and not merely control over a person or territory (as usually understood in human rights law).[114]

Through its findings, the Court therefore confirmed and elaborated further, albeit on the grounds of an apparently extensive interpretation of traditional models of jurisdiction, the emerging trend towards the recognition of a new direct effects model, pursuant to which, as discussed above, individuals would fall within a State's jurisdiction if they felt the effects of its domestic actions, even when on foreign soil. Rather, one could argue that the Opinion represents—to date—the most advanced and elaborated expression of the said trend, as the Court detailed the grounds upon which the rights-holders located abroad would fall within the jurisdiction of the State whose domestic actions affected them.

In principle, the Court's interpretation of the jurisdictional clause in Article 1 of the American Convention paves the way to diagonal claims for transboundary environmental damage. It is thus not surprising that, in the aftermath of the issuance of Opinion OC-23/17, scholars have already underlined this perspective[115] and, subsequently, announcements have been made that cross-border individual claims

[112] Ibid., para. 101.

[113] Ibid., para. 102.

[114] See again Banda (2019), p. 1931.

[115] See again Feria-Tinta and Milnes (2018).

would have been filed before human rights treaty bodies with respect to transboundary environmental harm.[116]

As will be seen *infra* (Sect. 5), the Court's reasoning on the new jurisdictional link gives rise, however, to some theoretical perplexities and operational shortcomings, which could reduce, in practice, its material influence on future diagonal claims in environmental matters. Moreover, the Court itself seemingly limited the possibility of presenting cross-border claims insofar as it stressed that "extraterritorial obligations are exceptional and should be restrictively construed".[117]

4.3 *On the Content of States' Human Rights Obligations with Respect to Transboundary Environmental Harm*

In the final part of its Advisory Opinion, the Court focused on the substantial and procedural obligations, under Articles 4 and 5 of the American Convention on Human Rights, relating to environmental protection. In doing so, the Court took into particular account the "transboundary dimension" inherent in Colombia's request. The Court, in fact, found that

> to comply with the obligations to respect and ensure the rights to life and personal integrity, in the context of environmental protection, States must fulfill a series of obligations with regard to both damage that has occurred within their territory and *transboundary damage*.[118]

In the attempt to identify the extent of these obligations, the Court relied on international environmental law and, more precisely, on the obligation to prevent, the precautionary principle, the obligation of cooperation and the procedural obligations relating to environmental protection.[119] The Court therefore engaged into a detailed examination of the aforesaid rules, which led it to conclude that States parties to the American Convention on Human Rights, in order to respect and ensure the rights to life and to personal integrity protected thereunder, should: (a) prevent significant environmental damage within or outside its territory; (b) regulate, supervise and monitor the activities within their jurisdiction that could produce significant environmental damage, conduct environmental impact assessments when there is a risk of such damage, and prepare a contingent plan to minimize and mitigate it; (c) act in accordance with the precautionary principle; (d) cooperate, in good faith, with the States potentially affected by transboundary environmental harm; (e) notify the latter States of the risk of damage and consult and negotiate with them in good faith; (f) ensure the right to access to information concerning potential environmental

---

[116] See the announcement related to the filing, in 2019, by West Timorese communities of a claim for transboundary harm against Australia in relation to the Montara oil spill. This information is available at: https://twentyessex.com/monica-feria-tinta-instructed-in-montara-oil-spill-case/.

[117] Advisory Opinion OC-23/17, paras. 81 and 104.

[118] Ibid., para. 125. Emphasis added.

[119] Ibid., paras. 125–241.

damage, the right to public participation in environmental policies and decision-making and the right to access to justice in environmental matters.[120]

Three aspects are of particular significance and should therefore be stressed. First, through these findings, the Court clarified for the first time the very extent of States human rights duties in a transboundary environmental harm context, albeit with reference to a specific system of human rights protection (i.e. the American Convention on Human Rights). In this respect, the Opinion represents relevant practice that, as discussed above, helps to fill the existing lacuna.

Second, the Court relied extensively on systemic interpretation in order to establish States' obligations under the Convention in the event of transboundary environment harm. While the resort to systemic interpretation is not novel for international human rights treaty monitoring bodies, especially as far as the relationship between the environment and human rights is concerned,[121] the extent of such "reliance" on other relevant rules of international law distinguishes the Inter-American Court's Advisory Opinion from previous human rights treaty bodies' practice. Moreover, if read together with the expansive approach concerning the notion of "jurisdiction", this element makes the Opinion at stake a "forerunner". It has been underlined, in fact, how

> recognizing regimes' congruence in theory and practice is important for both redress of the victim and unity of international law. Tribunals have already acknowledged this in one line of cases, where the harm originates and ends in the same State. The next line of cases will call on judges to give meaning to the regime nexus in case involving extraterritorial harm.[122]

It is hence not surprising that several commentators have welcomed Advisory Opinion OC-23/17 as a step forward in the direction of a progressive convergence between international environmental law and international human rights law[123] and, more generally, towards the "de-fragmentation" of international law.[124]

From this perspective, it is significative that the Court, despite limiting its analysis to some international environmental law provisions in accordance with the Colombia State's request, underlined the potential broader reach of its reasoning, which could extend to include other relevant rules of international environmental law applicable in the relations between the parties.

Lastly, the Court arguably hinted to the wider "scope" of the obligations listed above. Throughout its Opinion, the Court stressed, in fact, that, whilst its focus was on the rights to life and to personal integrity, the same obligations stemmed from other rights protected under the American Convention, especially the right to a healthy environment.[125]

---

[120] Ibid., para. 242.

[121] See, among others, with reference to the case law of the European Court of Human Rights, Rachovitsa (2017), p. 570.

[122] Banda (2019), p. 1957.

[123] Ibid.

[124] Feria-Tinta and Milnes (2019).

[125] Ibid., para. 69.

5 Diagonal Environmental Rights After Advisory Opinion OC-23/17: All Set?

Despite the "advancements" highlighted above, the significance of the Inter-American Court's Advisory Opinion for future diagonal environmental claims remains contentious.

What follows is an attempt to identify the most critical aspects, which contextually account for certain shortcomings in the Court's reasoning and, more generally, for the main challenges ahead as far as the role of human rights treaties with respect to transboundary environmental harm is concerned.[126]

5.1 A "Vague" Jurisdictional Link

From a theoretical perspective, the Inter-American Court of Human Right's stance on the extraterritorial applicability of the American Convention on Human Rights is not fully convincing. The Court, in upholding a newly construed jurisdictional model of "effective control over activities", allegedly conflated, in fact, the obligation to prevent transboundary harm—and the concept of control inherent to the due diligence standard of conduct required thereof—and the extraterritorial application of human rights treaties—which also implies a form, albeit different, of control.[127]

One could additionally question the effective impact of the Opinion, and in particular of its findings on jurisdiction, beyond environmental transboundary harm. More precisely, it might be contentious whether the Court's reliance on the criterion of systemic interpretation and, specifically, on the obligation to avoid transboundary environmental harm would prevent the application of the new reading of the notion of jurisdiction to cases in which the activities under the effective control of the State cause another kind of harm (such as, for instance, as a result of intelligence surveillance on individuals abroad).[128]

This uncertainty over the "extension" of the Court's findings to other kinds of scenarios arguably finds support in the statement of the same Court, recalled above, that "extraterritorial obligations are exceptional and should be restrictively construed", which precedes in the Opinion the reference to environmental norms.

---

[126] Whilst scholars have underlined the significance of the Court's Advisory Opinion in opening the path to cross-border human rights claims, little attention has indeed been paid so far to its potential shortcomings and the challenges that similar claims may continue facing. See Feria-Tinta and Milnes (2018) and Banda (2019).

[127] On this aspect see again Besson (2020), who underlines (and criticizes) a more general trend, in human rights treaties monitoring bodies' case law, towards conflation between due diligence and jurisdiction.

[128] For a critical stance with respect to the Court's approach see, e.g., Verga-Barbosa and Aboagye (2018), pp. 295–296.

Whereas these doubts could be easily overcome in view of the general scope of the no-harm principle in international law, the Court's reasoning on this aspect did not help in clarifying the point. To the contrary, the very meaning of the expression "should be restrictively construed" remains uncertain.[129]

Apart from the above considerations concerning the theoretical foundations of the Inter-American Court's approach and its overall significance also beyond a transboundary environmental harm context, a further critical aspect—and the one that could limit the practical "effectiveness" of the Advisory Opinion with respect to diagonal environmental claims—is the Court's failure to provide clear guidelines concerning the criteria that it posed as the basis of the operation of the new model of jurisdiction.[130]

As highlighted above, the Inter-American Court's approach requires, for the American Convention to apply extraterritorially, that a causal nexus is established between the conduct undertaken within the State's territory and the human rights violations occurring abroad. No further indication was provided by the Court, however, as far as the nature of this causal link is concerned.

In this respect, the Court did not seem to uphold other human rights treaty bodies' findings, which, despite the absence of a unambiguous formula by which to assess causation at the international level, have relied, inter alia, on foreseeability and directness (of the consequences of certain conducts) as viable tests.[131]

As a result, it has been noted that "the unlimited formulation by the Inter-American Court does not explain how causality can be interpreted as an exceptional situation of extraterritorial jurisdiction", thus feeding legal uncertainty.[132]

Clearly, one could question, in the first instance, the very adequacy of causation—whose reliance on can in itself be further evidence of the conflation between due diligence and jurisdiction and, therefore, between the assessment of State

[129] One interesting element that emerges from the Opinion, and that could signal an alternative "way forward" to overcome these issues, is the regional consensus towards an extensive reading of the term jurisdiction so as to admit diagonal environmental claims. A number of States parties to the American Convention on Human Rights submitted, in fact, observations whereby they supported its extraterritorial application in transboundary environmental harm cases and, as a result, the admissibility of diagonal environmental claims. These States are Guatemala, Honduras and Bolivia. Only one State, Panama, supported a more restrictive reading of the term "jurisdiction". As has been noted, the Inter-American Court of Human Rights has generally relied on a Latin-American consensus as a ground for upholding a progressive interpretation of the provisions of the American Convention (Lixinski 2017, pp. 65 ff). There is nothing to prevent, should a contentious case ever to be brought before the Inter-American Court of Human Rights entailing "diagonal environmental rights", that consensus could be used as a method of interpretation alternative to the systemic one, which, as stressed above, leaves room for concern.

[130] Berkes (2018).

[131] See, e.g., Human Rights Committee, General Comment No. 36 cit., para. 22 and European Court of Human Rights, *Andreou v. Turkey*, App. No. 45653/99, decision on admissibility of 3 June 2008, point A(c). On the concept of causation with respect to extraterritorial human rights obligations see Skogly (2013), p. 236.

[132] See again Berkes (2018).

responsibility and the application of a human rights treaty—for the purposes of the latter.[133] But, even leaving this argument aside, in the absence of more precise indications, the operation and actual "success" of diagonal environmental claims might be all but straightforward and downsized in practice.

Remarkably, this lack of clarity has not only concerned the "causal link", but also other elements, such as, for instance, the "significance" of the harm that should be caused to individuals abroad.[134]

5.2 *The Long Arm of the Court's Opinion: An (Un)Exportable Model?*

It is a widely known fact that interpretative pronouncements rendered by a human rights treaty monitoring body can, in principle, only exert influence within the relevant system of human rights protection. That notwithstanding, cross-fertilisation among human rights bodies has been on the rise and could, in the long run, "strengthen arguments of customary international law standards emergent from the terms of the conventions and contribute to the development of general principles of law".[135]

Against this backdrop, has Advisory Opinion OC-23/17 provided an "exportable model", that other human rights treaty monitoring bodies could replicate, thus paving the way themselves to diagonal environmental claims?[136]

While any definitive answer is strictly dependant on other human rights treaty monitoring bodies' future practice, and any assessment over the opportunity of such "exportability" is beyond the purpose of this contribution, a few considerations may already be made.

Hence, the reference to the Committee on Economic, Social and Cultural Rights' General Comments in the part of the Opinion dealing with the "new model of jurisdiction"[137] feeds the perception that the Court implicitly grounded its interpretation on the less restrictive approach to extraterritoriality that, as discussed above, has been developed with respect to economic, social and cultural rights. In this respect, the fact that the Court upheld, in the same Opinion, a stand-alone right to a healthy environment, protected under Article 26 of the American Convention on Human Rights, could have arguably played a role, albeit indirectly, and make it

[133] But see, instead, Scheinin (2013), p. 229.

[134] Ibid.

[135] See Boyle and Chinkin (2007), p. 278.

[136] It has been noted, at the same time, that the Inter-American Court's stance would find its origin in the practice of other human rights monitoring bodies. See, e.g., Ollino (2020), who, however, also raises some concerns as to the new jurisdictional link envisaged by the Court.

[137] See Advisory Opinion OC-23/17, footnote 194.

unlikely that a similar approach would be followed in other systems focused on the protection of civil and political rights.

To the opposite, the Inter-American Court's "subsumption" of the new model of jurisdiction (based on the control over activities) into a traditional one (the personal model) might be seen as a factor that could allegedly facilitate a convergence in human rights treaty bodies' practice, with a positive impact on diagonal environmental claims under other systems of human rights protection.

Yet, a pre-requisite for human rights treaty monitoring bodies to adopt a certain approach on jurisdiction and on the merits is the lack of further procedural hurdles that would make it possible for them to hear transboundary environmental harm cases. It follows that the "exportability" of the Inter-American model could be in practice halted by further procedural grounds, such as the previous exhaustion of domestic remedies, in the same way that such hurdles could halt the admissibility of a complaint in case of contentious jurisdiction within the Inter-American human rights protection system.

Proceedings are pending before human rights treaty monitoring bodies, which could well represent a test bed for the above considerations. For instance, on 3 September 2020, six Portuguese individuals (children and young adults) filed an application asking the European Court of Human Rights to hold 33 States parties to the European Convention on Human Rights responsible for the violations of their human rights caused by their failure to reduce greenhouse gas emissions.[138] As is evident, the application features a "diagonal environmental dimension", given that Portugal, being the State of nationality and residence, is only one out of the 33 States against whom the claim has been presented.

Remarkably, the applicants, when asserting that States parties to the European Convention on Human Rights would exercise jurisdiction, as per Article 1 of the same instrument, over the individuals located outside their territories, quoted, inter alia, the American Court of Human Rights' Advisory Opinion OC-23/17.[139]

In this case, a first issue is represented by the need for the applicants to overcome certain procedural requirements, such as proving their victim status, the exhaustion of domestic remedies and the significant disadvantage they suffered from.

Should the application not be rejected on these procedural grounds, the Court's stance on jurisdiction will likely clarify if and—to what extent—it will follow in its Inter-American counterpart's footsteps.

In a similar vein, the Committee on the Rights of the Child could also confirm or reject the Inter-American Court of Human Rights' approach with respect to the

[138]The text of the application is available at: https://youth4climatejustice.org/assets/images/Application_form+annex_(with_redactions)_for_website.pdf. For an early comment see Clark et al. (2020).

[139]Ibid., para. 24.

communication pending before it and filed by sixteen youths against Argentina, Brazil, France, Germany and Turkey.[140] The petitioners claimed that, by failing to curb emissions and to promote the use of fossil fuels, the respondents violated their rights protected under the Convention on the Rights of the Child. Like in the previous case, the communication has a "diagonal dimension", given that only some of the petitioners are nationals (and are located within the territory of) the respondent States. Furthermore, even in this case, references have been made to the Inter-American Court of Human Rights' Advisory Opinion OC-23/17 when asserting that each petitioner would be within the jurisdiction of each respondent State.[141] Also this communication can encounter procedural hurdles, such as, for instance, exhaustion of domestic remedies. Given that the Committee has already upheld a more expansive approach in interpreting the notion of jurisdiction compared, for instance, to the European Court of Human Rights,[142] it is however plausible that, if the communication is not "discharged" on other procedural grounds, it will, at least in principle, back the Inter-American Court's stance.

For the time being, it is noteworthy that the Advisory Opinion has been recalled in diagonal environmental claims as a ground to support their admissibility.

From another perspective, one could question whether, even in the event that the same approach to jurisdiction was eventually upheld by other monitoring bodies, some divergences on the merits in future "diagonal environmental practice" could emanate from the different approaches by which, as noted earlier, these same bodies have acknowledged the existing relationship between the environment and human rights. In its Advisory Opinion OC-23/17, the American Court of Human Rights repeatedly stressed, in fact, that States' obligations of the kind identified therein, as deriving from Articles 4 and 5 of the American Convention on Human Rights, should also stem from the right to a healthy environment, which the Court contextually upheld as a stand-alone and directly justiciable right protected under Article 26 of the same treaty.

It has been explained above, however, that this right has not been recognized as an autonomous right in all systems of human rights protection. As a result, diagonal environmental claims could be filed and argued on different grounds depending on the specific system of protection at stake.

Clearly, one might well argue that this "fragmentation" already characterizes the current practice of human rights treaty monitoring bodies with respect to the environment and human rights more generally. Yet, it might still be questioned whether similar "asymmetries" could hinder future cross-fertilisation as far as the

---

[140] Sacchi et al. v. Argentina, Brazil, France, Germany and Turkey. The application was lodged on 23 September 2019. The text is available at the website: https://earthjustice.org/sites/default/files/files/CRC-communication-Sacchi-et-al-v.-Argentina-et-al.pdf. For an early comment see La Manna (2020).

[141] Ibid., para. 247.

[142] See again General Comment No. 16, cit., para. 39 ff.

content of human rights obligations with respect to transboundary environmental harm is concerned.

5.3 *From Transboundary to Global Environmental Harm?*

The pending cases mentioned in the above section call into question a further critical aspect. In the face of global environmental threats, like climate change, an additional issue is, in fact, whether States could be held responsible for failing to respect and ensure the rights of those individuals that are located outside their territories, but that are nonetheless affected by the harmful impacts of their activities, such as greenhouse gas emissions.

Compared to a traditional-kind of "bilateral transboundary pollution" scenario, a "global-scale" one is characterized by the potentially remote location of the individual affected with respect to the State of origin of the environmental harm and by the difficulties in establishing with a certain degree of certainty the "responsible" State, given the number of countries contributing to the damage.[143]

The above considerations imply questioning if the Inter-American Court of Human Rights' findings in Advisory Opinion OC-23/17 has something to say also with respect to global environmental threats.

Again, while one should wait for human rights treaty bodies' future practice, there are already some elements that cast doubt on the significance of the Advisory Opinion with respect to global environmental issues, at least as far as the new jurisdictional link is concerned.

As stated, the Inter-American Court grounded the extraterritorial applicability of the American Convention on Human Rights on the existence of a causal nexus between the conduct undertaken within the State's territory and the human rights violations suffered by individuals located abroad. However, in "global settings", determining *if* and *which* State activities have *caused* a specific human rights violation may prove particularly hard. In the context of climate change, for instance, one of the most contentious issues is the establishment of a link between the high emissions recorded in a State, global warming and the interference with the enjoyment of human rights of individuals located elsewhere.[144] While States have control over the emissions they produce, their consequences are, in fact, the "products of incredibly complex and lengthy scientific processes".[145] Providing evidence that a particular interference with the enjoyment of human rights is due to climate change can therefore prove particularly arduous.

Moreover, the same challenges that have been underlined with respect to the establishment of causation under the law of State responsibility when multiple

---

[143] See again Boyle (2018), p. 772.

[144] See Adinolfi (2018), p. 220.

[145] Lewis (2018), p. 182.

factors (such as *multiple wrongdoers*) contribute towards a harmful outcome[146] could also be put forth as a result of the "use" of that same criterion as a ground to determine jurisdiction. As stated above, many States contribute to climate change and several other factors contribute to it. Accordingly, climate change can be seen as the cumulative output of multiple factors and actions. Therefore, even assuming that a specific human rights violation may be ascribed to climate change, the existence of a "nexus" between the activities conducted in a certain State and the interference with the enjoyment of human rights located abroad can be all but clear-cut.

Importantly, the issue of causation does not concern only the exercise of State's jurisdiction over individuals located outside its territory, even if this is the most relevant aspect with respect to the impact of Advisory Opinion OC-23/17 on future environmental diagonal claims. Even if jurisdiction were established, any individual claim would in fact meet with considerable challenges in proving State responsibility under international human rights treaties. Moreover, the lack of *locus standi* could also represent a bar to future diagonal environmental claims as regards climate change.

Apart from the above, one could also wonder whether the Inter-American Court's findings with respect to State obligations stemming from the rights to life and personal integrity might apply also in a climate change context. As discussed earlier, the Inter-American Court relied on systemic interpretation and, to this end, took into account several relevant international environmental norms applicable to the relations between the parties. Yet, it may be argued that, if the Court had considered more specifically international provisions on climate change in such a hermeneutical exercise, the conclusions, in terms of applicable standards of compliance, could have been slightly different. It has been noted, in fact, that

> (. . .) even if we accept that human rights law potentially has transboundary application as indicated by the Inter-American Court, it will still be hard to show that parties to the United Nations Framework Convention on Climate Change regime, including the major greenhouse gas emitters, have failed to strike the right balance between their own State's economic development and respect for human rights in other States when they have complied with or are exempted from greenhouse gas emissions reduction targets (. . .).[147]

Against this background, it is not surprising that scholars have underlined so far that the "prospect of bringing a successful claim under international human rights law for a violation based on climate change are somewhat limited"[148] and even challenged the opportunity to envisage diagonal environmental claims with respect to global environmental threats.[149]

[146] See, e.g., Plakokefalos (2015).

[147] Boyle (2018), p. 773.

[148] Lewis (2018), p. 188.

[149] Boyle (2018), p. 773. Boyle joined former UN Special Rapporteur John Knox in supporting the view that, in the face of global threats, such as climate change, the best approach is that human rights obligations inform the content of the duty to cooperate (id., p. 774).

The applications currently pending before human rights treaty monitoring bodies, which have been discussed in the previous section,[150] could eventually shed light on this specific aspect and reveal whether diagonal environmental claims might prove a successful avenue for holding States accountable in a climate change context.

6 Conclusive Remarks

As noted by Professor Scovazzi, the Inter-American Court of Human Rights' Advisory Opinion OC-23/17 represents an indispensable reference point for any future stance on human rights and the environment.[151] By building on this premise, this contribution has focused on Opinion OC-23/17 as a ground to examine, more generally, the role that international human rights law can play as regards transboundary environmental harm (and beyond).

In this respect, the Court's Opinion is noteworthy at least from two perspectives. First, it gave substance to certain obligations that States owe to individuals under the American Convention on Human Rights in relation to transboundary environmental harm, thus representing a step forward towards more clarity as far as the role that international human rights law may have with respect to cross-border environmental harm. Second, by relying on systemic interpretation, it confirmed a (desirable) trend towards a greater (and virtuous) interplay between international human rights law and international environmental law.

The definition of the content of human rights obligations in light of environmental rules might exert great influence domestically.[152] This occurs when—and to the extent that—human rights treaties have direct effects on a State party and national courts are required to take into account the treaty monitoring bodies' case law.[153] As a result, the Court's findings with respect to human rights obligations in a transboundary environmental harm context could "facilitate" reliance on human rights instruments in diagonal environmental claims before domestic courts.

---

[150] On the rise of human rights-based climate change cases see Savaresi (2021), pp. 1–3.

[151] Scovazzi (2019b), p. 713.

[152] One example in this respect (albeit relating to the obligations stemming from Articles 2 and 8 of the European Convention on Human Rights) is the *Urgenda* case before Dutch courts. On 24 June 2015, the Hague District Court issued an important decision, in which human rights considerations were taken into account in order to establish the State's failure to take sufficient actions to prevent climate change. This decision was upheld by the Hague Court of Appeals on 9 October 2018 and by the Dutch Supreme Court on 20 December 2019. See *Urgenda Foundation v. Kingdom of the Netherlands (Ministry of Infrastructure and the Environment)*, case no. C/09/456689/HA ZA 13-1396. For a comment see, ex multis, Scovazzi (2019a), pp. 619 ff.

[153] This consideration is particularly relevant in the Inter-American context, where the Court has upheld a "monistic" approach as far as the relationship between international and national law is concerned and where national courts exercise a decentralized control of conventionality. See, among others, Binder (2011), p. 1204.

Yet, the full significance of the above findings also depends on the possibility of "enforcing" the aforesaid obligations by means of individual claims brought before human rights treaty monitoring mechanisms.

In this respect, there is no doubt that, by upholding an extensive reading of the notion of "jurisdiction" in Article 1 of the American Convention on Human Rights, the Inter-American Court provided a "way out" to prevent victims of transboundary environmental damage being denied a remedy in the event that their State of nationality does not pursue their claims on the international stage and no further avenues are available before domestic courts (either of the home State or the State of origin of the environmental harm). By doing that, the Court provided a possible solution to an increasingly pressing need.

However, the analysis undertaken has shown that, despite the apparent leap forward brought about by the abovementioned Opinion, the Court's reasoning raises several perplexities and numerous hurdles still exist that may undermine the prospect of success of diagonal environmental claims either within or outside the Inter-American system of human rights protection.

The doubts concerning the theoretical soundness of the Court's finding concerning jurisdiction and the unpredictability of other human rights treaty monitoring bodies' practice in this respect are representative of the inconsistent way in which monitoring bodies have tackled the issue of the extra-territorial application of the main human rights treaties so far, and of the conceptual difficulties behind it. As stated, if and to what extent other human rights treaty monitoring bodies will follow the Inter-American Court's footsteps remains dubious. They might well in fact adopt a more restrictive approach in interpreting and applying jurisdictional clauses contained in human rights treaties and, accordingly, bar from the outset foreign individuals from bringing claims based on them against the States from which the transboundary environmental harm originates.

The uncertainties related to the practical operation of the "new jurisdictional link" envisaged by the Inter-American Court of Human Rights and its contentious use in a climate change context are, moreover, emblematic of the difficulties inherent in any attempt to connect certain activities to remote harmful effects that may affect the individuals.

Diagonal environmental claims can thus encounter different kinds of limits, related either to admissibility or to causation and evidence. Moreover, even if these obstacles were overcome, further issues could arise, which have so far been neglected in the absence of contentious proceedings, first and foremost that of appropriate remedies.

As a result, State obligations identified by the Inter-American Court of Human Rights in relation to transboundary environmental harm risk having limited application in practice or, worse, that they cannot be enforced (at least as far as international human rights monitoring mechanisms are at stake).

In 1999, Professor Scovazzi noted that environmental protection could be seen as a game with three players: those private operators responsible for damage, the State and the *individual* (or associations).[154] It is argued here that, for the third player to fully take part in the game, victims of transboundary environmental harm should be able to resort to the international systems of human rights protection in order to hold the polluting States accountable. Yet, whereas the Inter-American Court's Advisory Opinion OC-23/17 has signaled an important step in this respect, it has also implicitly reminded us of the current challenges that still hamper cross-border human rights claims in environmental matters.

If some of them could certainly be "overcome" by way of interpretation (even if ideally on the ground of hermeneutical criteria different from those relied on by the Inter-American Court of Human Rights) or clarifications stemming from future monitoring bodies' practice, others, such as the difficulties in addressing global environmental harm from a human rights perspective, might unsatisfactorily prove more difficult to "be solved" in practice.[155] As stated, however, some clarifications also in this respect could soon come from human rights treaty bodies, before whom contentious proceedings are currently pending.

Postscript After the submission of this Chapter (8 February 2021), an important development has occurred. On 11 October 2021, the Committee on the Rights of the Child published its five decisions, one for each respondent State, in the case Sacchi et al. v. Argentina et al. These decisions represent a "milestone" for diagonal environmental claims despite finding the petition inadmissible due to the non-exhaustion of domestic remedies. The Committee's decisions, in fact, confirmed the exportability of the Inter-American Court of Human Rights' approach to extra-territorial jurisdiction, emerging from Advisory Opinion OC-23/17, and shed new light on the role that international human rights law may play with respect not only to transboundary but also to global environmental harm.

References

Adinolfi G (2018) The right to a healthy environment: delineating the content (and contours) of a slippery notion. In: Bartolini G et al (eds) Routledge handbook of human rights and disaster. Routledge, London, pp 211–227

Altwicker T (2018) Transnationalizing rights: international human rights law in cross-border contexts. Eur J Int Law 29:581–606

Banda ML (2018) Inter-American Court of Human Rights Advisory Opinion on the environment and human rights. ASIL Insight

Banda ML (2019) Regime congruence: rethinking the scope of state responsibility for transboundary environmental harm. Minn Law Rev 103:1879–1959

Berkes A (2018) A new extraterritorial jurisdictional link recognized by the IACtHR. EJIL:Talk!

Besson S (2012) The extraterritoriality of the European Convention on Human Rights: why human rights depend on jurisdiction and what jurisdiction amounts to? Leiden J Int Law 25:857–884

[154] Scovazzi (1999), p. 508.

[155] See Boyle (2012), p. 641, pursuant to whom "existing human rights law is not the right medium for addressing the shared problem of climate change".

Besson S (2020) Due diligence and extraterritorial human rights obligations – mind the gap! ESIL Reflections
Binder C (2011) The prohibition of amnesties by the Inter-American Court of Human Rights. German Law J 12:1203–1229
Bodansky D (2010) The art and craft of international environmental law. Harvard University Press, Cambridge
Boyd D (2012) The environmental rights revolution: a global study of constitutions, human rights and the environment. UBC Press, Vancouver
Boyle A (2012) Human rights and the environment: where next? Eur J Hum Rights Law 23:613–642
Boyle A (2018) Climate change, the Paris Agreement and human rights. Int Comp Law Q 67:759–777
Boyle A, Chinkin C (2007) The making of international law. OUP, Oxford
Chuffart S, Viñuales JE (2014) From the other stone. Economic, social and cultural rights from an international environmental law perspective. In: Eibe R, Giacca G, Golay C (eds) Economic, social and cultural rights in international law: contemporary issues and challenges. OUP, Oxford, pp 286–307
Citroni G (2020) La "stagione dell'ambiente" del Comitato delle Nazioni Unite dei diritti umani. Rivista giuridica dell'ambiente 1:1–29
Clark P et al (2020) Climate change and the European Court of Human Rights: the Portuguese Youth Case. EJIL:Talk!
Cournil C (2016) "Verdissement" des systems régionaux de protection des droits de l'homme: circulation et standardisation des normes. Journal européen des droits de l'homme 1:3–31
Da Costa K (2012) The extraterritorial application of selected human rights treaties. Brill/Martinus Nijhoff, Leiden
Daly E, May J (2018) Learning from constitutional environmental rights. In: Knox HJ, Ramin P (eds) The human rights to a healthy environment. CUP, Cambridge, pp 42–58
De Schutter O et al (2012) Commentary to the Maastricht principles on extraterritorial obligations of states in the area of economic, social and cultural rights. Hum Rights Q 34:1084–1169
De Sena P (2002) La nozione di giurisdizione statale nei trattati sui diritti dell'uomo. Giappichelli, Torino
Den Hejer M, Lawson R (2013) Extraterritorial human rights and the concept of 'Jurisdiction'. In: Langford M et al (eds) Global justice, states duties. The extraterritorial scope of economic, social and cultural rights in international law. CUP, Cambridge, pp 153–191
Dupuy PM, Viñuales JE (2018) International environmental law, 2nd edn. CUP, Cambridge
Feria-Tinta M, Milnes S (2018) The rise of environmental law in international dispute resolution: Inter-American Court of Human Rights issues landmark advisory opinion on environment and human rights. Yearb Int Environ Law 27:64–81
Feria-Tinta M, Milnes S (2019) International environmental law in the 21st century: the constitutionalization of the right to a healthy environment in the Inter-American Court of Human Rights' Advisory Opinion No. 23. Anuario colombiano de derecho internacional 12
Francioni F (2010) International human rights in an environmental horizon. Eur J Int Law 21:41–55
Gondek M (2009) The reach of human rights in a globalising world: extraterritorial application of human rights treaties. Antwerp, Oxford: Intersentia
Knox HJ (2010) Diagonal environmental rights. In: Gibney M, Skogly S (eds) Universal human rights and extraterritorial obligations. University of Pennsylvania Press, Philadelphia, pp 82–103
Knox HJ (2019a) The United Nations mandate on human rights and the environment. In: May J, Daly E (eds) Human rights and the environment. Legality, indivisibility, dignity and geography. Edward Elgar, Cheltenham, pp 34–48
Knox HJ (2019b) The global pact for the environment: at the crossroads of human rights and the environment. Rev Eur Comp Int Environ Law 28:40–47
Knox HJ, Pejan R (eds) (2018) The human rights to a healthy environment. CUP, Cambridge

La Manna M (2020) Cambiamenti climatici e diritti umani delle generazioni presente e future: Greta Thumberg (e altri) dinnanzi al Comitato sui diritti del fanciullo. Diritti umani e diritto internazionale 14:217–224

Langford M (2013) Extraterritorial duties in international law. In: Langford M, Vandenhole W, Martin S, van Genugten W (eds) Global justice, states duties. The extraterritorial scope of economic, social and cultural rights in international law. CUP, Cambridge, pp 51–113

Lefeber R (2018) Responsibility not to cause transboundary environmental harm. In: Kramer L, Orlando E (eds) General principles of environmental law. Edward Elgar, Northampton, pp 92–102

Lewis B (2012) Environmental rights or a right to the environment? Exploring the nexus between human rights and environmental protection. Macquarie J Int Comp Law J 8:36–47

Lewis B (2018) Environmental human rights and climate change. Current status and future prospects. Springer, Singapore

Lima L (2020) The protection of the environment before the Inter-American Court of Human Rights: recent developments. Rivista giuridica dell'ambiente 3:495–521

Lixinski L (2017) The consensus method of interpretation by the Inter-American Court of Human Rights. Can J Comp Contemp Law 3:65–95

Lumina M (2020) The right to a clean, safe and healthy environment under the African Human Rights System. In: Addaney M, Oluborode Jegede A (eds) Human rights and the environment under African Union Law. Palgrave Macmillan, Cham, pp 25–54

Lyons Y (2015) Transboundary pollution from offshore activities: a study of the Montara offshore oil spill. In: Jayakumar S et al (eds) Transboundary pollution. Evolving issues of international law and policy. Edward Elgar, Cheltenham, pp 162–189

Metha T (2020) Accountability for environmental destruction – ecocide in national and international law, Part I. Opinio Juris

Milanovic M (2011) Extraterritorial application of human rights treaties: law, principles and policy. OUP, Oxford

Milanovic M (2015) Human rights treaties and foreign surveillance. Harv Int Law J 56:81–146

Milanovic M (2018a) Jurisdiction and responsibility: trends in the jurisprudence of the Strasbourg Court. In: van Aaken A, Motoc I (eds) The European Convention on Human Rights and general international law. OUP, Oxford, pp 97–111

Milanovic M (2018b) ECtHR Judgment in Big Brother Watch v. UK. EJIL:Talk!

Møgster D (2018) Towards universality: activities impacting the enjoyment of the right to life and the extraterritorial application of the ICCPR. EJIL:Talk!

Nollkaemper A (2008) Cluster-litigation in cases of transboundary environmental harm. In: Faure M, Ying S (eds) China and international environmental liability: legal remedies for transboundary pollution. Edward Elgar, Cheltenham, pp 11–37

Ollino A (2020) Reflections on the advisory opinion on human rights and the environment and the notion of extraterritorial jurisdiction. Die Friedens-Warte 93:56–69

Ong D (2010) Procedural environmental global justice? The evolution of procedural means for environmental protection: from inter-state obligations to individual-state rights. In: French D (ed) Global justice and sustainable development. Martinus Nijhoff Publishers, Leiden, pp 137–166

Papanicolopulu I (2009) La nozione di giurisdizione ai sensi dell'Articolo 1 della Convenzione europea dei diritti umani nella recente giurisprudenza della Corte europea dei diritti umani. In: Scovazzi T, Papanicolopulu I, Urbinati S (eds) I diritti umani di fronte al giudice internazionale. Atti della giornata di studio in memoria di Carlo Russo. Milano, Giuffrè, pp 83–130

Papantoniou A (2018) Advisory opinion on the environment and human rights (state obligations in relation to the environment in the context of protection and guarantee of the right to life and to personal integrity – interpretation and scope of Articles 4(1) and 5(1) of the American Convention on Human Rights). Am J Int Law 112:463–466

Pavoni R (2015) Environmental jurisprudence of the European and Inter-American Court of Human Rights: comparative insights. In: Boer B (ed) Environmental law dimensions of human rights. OUP, Oxford, pp 69–106
Pineschi L (2014) Un'evoluzione imperfetta nella tutela del diritto a un ambiente soddisfacente: la sentenza della Corte di giustizia dell'ECOWAS sul caso *SERAP* c. *Nigeria*. Diritti umani e diritto internazionale 8:103–132
Plakokefalos I (2015) Causation in the law of state responsibility and the problem of overdetermination: in search of clarity. Eur J Int Law 26:471–492
Post H (2019) The state of a human right to a healthy environment. Israel Yearb Int Law 49: 171–205
Prihandono I, Dewanty EH (2015) Litigating cross-border environmental dispute in Indonesian Civil Court. Indonesia Law Rev 1:14–32
Rachovitsa A (2017) The principle of systemic integration in human rights law. Int Comp Law Q 66:557–588
Raible L (2020) Human rights unbound. A theory of extraterritoriality. OUP, Oxford
Savaresi A (2021) Plugging the enforcement gap. The rise and rise of human rights in climate change litigation. Quest Int Law 77:1–3
Scheinin M (2013) Just another word? Jurisdiction in the roadmaps of state responsibility. In: Langford M et al (eds) Global justice, state duties. The extraterritorial scope of economic, social and cultural rights in international law. CUP, Cambridge, pp 212–229
Scovazzi T (1986) La responsabilità internazionale in caso di inquinamento transfrontaliero. Rivista giuridica dell'ambiente 1:272–283
Scovazzi T (1999) Il diritto dell'individuo ad agire per la tutela dell'ambiente: descrizioni e impressioni. Jus – Rivista di Scienze giuridiche 1:495–508
Scovazzi T (2001) State responsibility for environmental harm. Yearb Int Environ Law 12:43–67
Scovazzi T (2019a) L'interpretazione e l'applicazione "ambientalista" della Convenzione europea dei diritti umani, con particolare riguardo al caso "Urgenda". Rivista giuridica dell'ambiente 3: 619–632
Scovazzi T (2019b) La Corte interamericana dei diritti umani svolge una trattazione sistematica del diritto umano a un ambiente sano. Rivista giuridica dell'ambiente 4:713–716
Shelton D (ed) (2011) Human rights and the environment (vols I and II). Edward Elgar, Cheltenham
Skogly S (2013) Causality and extraterritorial human rights obligations. In: Langford M et al (eds) Global justice, state duties. The extraterritorial scope of economic, social and cultural rights in international law. CUP, Cambridge, pp 233–258
Stephens T (2009) International courts and environmental protection. CUP, Cambridge
Szpak A (2020) Arctic Athabaskan Council's petition to the Inter-American Commission on human rights and climate change—business as usual or a breakthrough? Clim Change 162:1575–1593
Treves T (2019) The expansion of international law. In: Recueil des cours de l'Académie de droit international 398. Brill, Leiden
Vega-Barbosa GL, Aboagye L (2018) Human rights and the protection of the environment: the advisory opinion of the Inter-American Court of Human Rights. EJIL:Talk!
Vennemann N (2006) Application of International Human Rights Conventions to transboundary acts. In: Bratispie R, Miller R (eds) Transboundary harm in international law. Lessons from the Trail Smelter Arbitration. CUP, New York, pp 295–307
Verga-Barbosa G, Aboagye L (2018) A commentary on the advisory opinion of the Inter-American Court of Human Rights on the environment and human rights. Diritto pubblico comparato ed europeo online 34:291–298

What Does a State Secure Make? Interpreting National Security in the Light of International Human Rights Law

Gabriella Citroni

Abstract This chapter aims at outlining trends and challenges relating to the somewhat elusive notion of national security and its troubled relationship with human rights, arguing that, instead of being necessarily seen as "inherently opposed" in the interests they pursue, the two should be looked at from a different perspective and reconciled. The chapter first illustrates the reasons behind the need to revisit the very notion of national security itself and to reinterpret the State's role and the corresponding limitations to its powers. The subsequent section makes the case for the necessity to depart from a merely State-centred interpretation of security, flagging—through the analysis of specific cases—that the assumption that the State is always a benign entity, whose interests are worth protection no matter what, may be tragically wrong. The State can actually be the "villain of the piece", often in the very (abused) name of national security and thus it should not be given *carte blanche*. Along these lines, the chapter then recounts instances where the "national security card" has been played by governments, unravelling the dangers entrenched therein and reaffirming the need to remain vigilant in order to avoid creating loopholes in the protection of human rights, which would ultimately endanger security, rather than protecting it. Section 5 of the chapter emphasises the importance of detecting and firmly rejecting recurrent attempts at relativizing—often in the name of national security—the absolute prohibition of torture. Finally, some conclusions are offered to answer the question underlying the entire chapter, which remains both a recurrent trend and a challenge in international law: "what does a State truly secure make"?

G. Citroni (✉)
University of Milano-Bicocca, Milan, Italy
e-mail: gabriella.citroni@unimib.it

M. Arcari et al. (eds.), *Trends and Challenges in International Law*,
https://doi.org/10.1007/978-3-030-94387-5_3

1 Introduction

Perhaps, at least compared to the law of the sea or environmental law, international human rights law could not be described as Professor Scovazzi's first love, however, as so often happens with more mature passions, the relationship that he has developed with it seems to be a close and long lasting one. Several fine writings and the number of students—including myself—who have benefitted from his thought-provoking lectures are a testimony to this.

Professor Scovazzi's approach to international human rights law can be regarded as an unprecedented mixture of Humanism, Pop-Culture and, at times, Surrealism: notions and theories, usually expressed with a razor-sharp irony, revolving around human beings and their real stories and experiences, conveyed in vivid detail and in simple, even raw, words, without falling into the trap of offering a deluge of footnotes and doctrinal references and carefully steering clear of the abhorred legal technicalities. This way of looking at, studying and teaching the subject, naïve as it may seem, is actually highly sophisticated in that it goes straight to the core of the issues, yet builds on the foundations of a deep knowledge of international law and adapts the latter to the peculiarities of human rights. The outcome are interpretations—perhaps at times unorthodox—that truly capture the purpose of international human rights law and are the most conducive to the protection of the human beings concerned.

The relationship between the State and the individuals (especially the most humble and forgotten ones) subject to its jurisdiction and the notion of national security and its use—and abuse—are at the core of Professor Scovazzi's work on international human rights law, which is inspired by the idea that there can be no security whatsoever in a State where human rights are grossly violated. In line with this understanding, while the notion of national security has frequently been invoked to restrict—or blatantly disregard—human rights, and the two have been seen as somehow "inherently opposed" in the interests they pursue, it is here argued that they should instead be looked at from a different perspective and reconciled.

In an attempt to pay a humble and heartfelt tribute to Professor Scovazzi's teachings, this chapter aims at collecting the fruits of his studies and reflections on the notion of national security, outlining trends and challenges in respect of such a concept and its troubled relationship with human rights. The chapter first illustrates the reasons behind the need to revisit the very notion of national security and to reinterpret the State's role, as well as the corresponding limitations to its powers. The subsequent section invokes a few characters that have deeply marked Professor Scovazzi's work, evidencing with their stories and words how the State can be regarded as the "villain of the piece", often in the very (abused) name of national security. Along these lines, the chapter then recounts instances where the "national security card" has been played rather slyly by governments, unravelling the dangers entrenched therein and reaffirming the need to remain vigilant in order to avoid creating loopholes in the protection of human rights, which would ultimately endanger security, rather than protecting it. Section 5 of the chapter makes the case for detecting and firmly rejecting recurrent attempts at relativizing—often in the name of national security—the absolute prohibition of torture. Finally, some conclusions are offered to answer the question underlying the entire chapter, which remains both a recurrent trend and a challenge in international law: "what does a State truly secure make"?

2 Revisiting the Notion of National Security

National security is a crucial concept in both domestic and international law and several restrictions—some significant—to certain human rights are permitted in its name.[1] In its name, violations—including those which are gross– of fundamental human rights have been committed.[2] Such a powerful term begs the question of what the notion of national security actually means.[3]

[1]For instance, under certain circumstances, Article 6.1, of the European Convention on Human Rights (ECHR), allows the exclusion of the press and public from all or part of trials in the interests of national security in a democratic society; Article 8.2 of the ECHR allows interferences by public authorities in the right to respect for private and family life; Article 10.2 of the ECHR allows restrictions to the freedom of expression in the interests of national security; Article 11.2 of ECHR allows restrictions to be placed on the exercise of the freedom of assembly and association in the interests of national security. Similarly, under certain circumstances, Article 2.3 of the Protocol No. 4 to the ECHR allows restrictions to the freedom of movement in the interests of national security; and Article 1.2 of Protocol No. 7 to the ECHR allows the expulsion of aliens if it is grounded on reasons of national security. In the same sense, Article 13.2 of the American Convention on Human Rights (ACHR) allows restrictions to the freedom of thought and expression to the extent necessary to ensure the protection of national security; and the same applies to the right to assembly (Article 15 of the ACHR), the freedom of association (Article 16.2 of the ACHR) and the freedom of movement and residence (Article 22.3 of the ACHR). For its part, the African Charter on Human and Peoples' Rights (ACHPR) allows restrictions based on national security grounds of the right to freedom of assembly and the right to freedom of movement (respectively Arts. 11 and 12.2). With regard to the International Covenant on Civil and Political Rights (ICCPR), under certain circumstances, this allows the restriction of the right to freedom of movement, the presence of the press and the public during trials, the right to hold opinions, the right to peaceful assembly and the right to freedom of association (respectively, Arts. 12.3; 14.1; 19.3(b); 21; and 22. 2) on national security grounds. Moreover, Article 13 of the ICCPR envisages an exception to the right to appeal a decision on the expulsion of an alien for compelling reasons of national security.

[2]Pion-Berlin (1988), pp. 382–407.

[3]Mendel (2013); Dycus and Kellman (2000), pp. 811–837.

2.1 *The Lack of Universally Accepted Definition of National Security as a Gateway to Potential Abuses*

As of today, there is no universally accepted definition of this expression in international law and most States do not have one in their domestic legislation either. *Per se*, the fact that this notion—whose application may have very serious ramifications—is so elusive, can be regarded as problematic and, indeed, for decades, scholars, policy makers, international organisations and civil society organisations have engaged in attempts to define or re-define it. If one is to draw a common denominator in the traditional understanding of national security, it is that of protecting States' territorial sovereignty from alleged threats, be they internal or from outside their jurisdiction. As Professor Scovazzi once put it in a conversation we had on the subject, it can be interpreted as "the protection of national territory from the enemy who is willing (or thought to be willing) to attack it" or "the protection of power from those who would like to replace those who currently hold it". In fact, "national security" is usually equated to "State security", where the State is both the "object" to be secured from external threats and the subject in charge of "protection".

After World War II,[4] the notion of national security became of crucial importance, especially in the domestic and foreign policy of the United States of America.[5] In August 1945, the United States' Senate fully embraced it, following the lead of Navy Secretary James Forrestal, who referred to it in terms of military preparedness after the conflict. Other governments followed a similar interpretation. Indeed, the notion is used worldwide, with variations in the understanding of its scope (which can be stretched to "global security") and the kind of "threats" at stake, which morph over time and today are certainly not limited to menaces that are military in nature. These different interpretations are construed around the equally wide—and hence vague—concepts of political and economic interests to be protected. The existence of so many nebulous notions floating around national security paves the way to its potential abuse and is what, arguably, led to the construction of an alleged inherent dichotomy with human rights.[6]

Whereas, as contended in this chapter, the said dichotomy does not necessarily have to exist—quite the opposite, actually—it is nevertheless indisputable that, in its ambiguity, the notion of national security lends itself to distortions and specious interpretations, which have led to the perpetration of gross human rights violations, often on a widespread or systematic scale. One prime example is that of the hundreds of thousands of crimes, including enforced disappearances, massacres, extra-judicial executions, torture, rapes and other forms of sexual violence perpetrated in Latin America in the 1970s and 1980s, specifically in the name of national security. Latin

[4]The notion was indisputably used even before World War II, but the historical affirmation of the concept goes beyond the scope of this chapter. Balzacq (2003), pp. 33–50.

[5]May (1991), p. 235.

[6]Burke-White (2004), pp. 249–280.

American governments justified these abuses and the subsequent attempts to cover them up (for instance, through the adoption of amnesty laws or pardons), by referring to their "national security doctrine".[7] The idea underlying such a "doctrine" was conceived in the 1940s, on the basis of French counter-insurgency concepts used in Algeria and Indochina, and it was later embraced and propelled throughout the Americas by the United States.[8] The latter trained the elites of the Latin American armies in the infamous "*school of the Americas*", located in Panama, and this prompted the application of the same repressive techniques across the continent and the establishment of *Operation Cóndor*, a code name given to the alliance of security forces and intelligence services of the Southern Cone dictatorships in their repression of, and fight against, individuals designated as "subversive elements".[9] The activities deployed as part of this Operation were coordinated by the military personnel of the countries involved, who, with the support of the Central Intelligence Agency (CIA), enhanced the clandestine coordination between the security forces, military personnel and intelligence services of the region.[10]

The doctrine of national security reflected the bipolar paradigm of the Cold War and was inherently anti-communist and combined with the defence of religion, tradition, and conservative values. Those who did not conform with—or were perceived as departing from—this "model" were automatically labelled as "internal enemies". The latter were deliberately depicted as a mortal threat to national security. Security forces—often backed by paramilitary groups—were provided with justification to resort to any means (including torture, secret detention, enforced disappearance and extra-judicial killings) to ensure the intimidation and, ultimately, the annihilation of the "internal enemy". This overly vague notion was voluntarily stretched to encompass anyone suspected of political opposition, from members of armed guerrilla groups, to human rights defenders, students and social workers, who were referred to as "subversives", "communists" and "terrorists".[11] The horrific consequences to which this ill-conceived interpretation of security can lead are well summarised in the statement attributed to the Argentine General Ibérico Saint Jean: "first we must kill all the subversives, then their sympathisers, then those who are indifferent, and finally, we must kill all those who are timid".[12]

The example of the application of the national security doctrine in Latin America shows how the relationship between this notion and human rights can be intricate, to

[7] Dulitzky (2019), pp. 436–437; Osorio et al. (2019); Dash (1989), pp. 67–85.

[8] McSherry (2005), pp. 16–17; Robin (2004), p. 183.

[9] Central Intelligence Agency (1953); Shlaudeman (1976), p. 3.

[10] See, among others, Inter-American Court of Human Rights (IACtHR), Case *Goiburú and others* v. *Paraguay*, judgment of 22 September 2006, Ser. C No. 153, para 61.6. See also Corte di Assise di Roma III Corte di Assise, Sent. n. 1/2017 Reg. Inserz. Sentenze N. 2/15 Reg. Gen. 17 January 2017 (Processo Condor); Corte di Assise di Roma II Corte di Assise N. 40/2000 Reg. Inserz. Sentenze N. 3/2000 Reg. Gen. 6 December 2000 (Processo Mason et al.); Corte di Assise di Roma, II Corte di Assise N. 12/06 Reg. Gen N. 5/07 Reg. Inserz. Sent. 14 March 2007 (Processo ESMA).

[11] Pion-Berlin (1988), pp. 382–407.

[12] Rosenberg (1991), p. 124.

say the least. It is indisputable that "in the name of security, human rights and fundamental freedoms were violated on a massive scale, and the rule of law and the democratic system damaged".[13] Yet, some of the main characters of the repression perpetrated in the name of national security were self-proclaimed fervent promoters of human rights. Among others, in his public speeches, the Argentine General Jorge Rafael Videla frequently portrayed the abuses committed as a means to defend human rights.[14] The very same General Videla who had a rather clear—albeit somewhat cynical—view on what could be justified in the (abused) name of national security, crystallised in his quote that "as many people as necessary must die in Argentina, so that the country will again be secure".[15] Domestic tribunals eventually gave this its correct name, which seemingly has nothing to do with security: "crimes against humanity".[16] Another accurate expression to describe it would be "State terrorism".[17] The tragic experience of Latin America is a testament to the fact that the notion of national security—with its conceptual ambiguities—can be interpreted on the basis of an immense distortion of the purposes of the State, departing from the rule of law and seeking to erase any limitations to its power. From this dystopic view, the State can be transformed into an end in itself,

> the final depositary of human freedoms, 'alpha and omega', justifying the excesses of nationalism with an emphasis on 'national security' and fascism [. . .], in the context of which grave human rights violations and successive atrocities were committed.[18]

---

[13] Special Rapporteur on Torture and Other Cruel, Inhuman or Degrading Treatment or Punishment, Special Rapporteur on the Promotion and Protection of Human Rights and Fundamental Freedoms while Countering Terrorism, Working Group on Arbitrary Detention (WGAD), and Working Group on Enforced or Involuntary Disappearances (WGEID), *Joint Study on Secret Detention*, UN Doc. A/HRC/13/42 of 19 February 2010, para 61. Hereinafter "Joint Study on Secret Detention".

[14] 'Human rights' were so frequently invoked by General Videla in his speeches that a few years ago one of Prof. Scovazzi's students, to his great astonishment, specifically chose a quote by Videla to open her thesis on the protection of human rights. She had thought he was a champion of human rights. The sombre irony of this unwarranted choice was not lost on Prof. Scovazzi, but caused quite the shock when the young lady learned what General Videla had actually done in the alleged name of human rights and to preserve national security.

[15] Statement by Jorge Rafael Videla in 1975, as quoted in Bernstein (2013).

[16] General Jorge Rafael Videla was involved in multiple trials for his crimes and sentenced on two occasions to life imprisonment and once to 50 years imprisonment. See Cámara Federal de Apelaciones en lo Criminal, Case No. 13/84 *Videla and others*, verdict of 9 December 1985; Tribunal Oral Federal No. 1 Córdoba, Case No.63/2010 *Videla and others*, verdict of 22 December 2010; and Tribunal Oral en lo Criminal Federal No. 6 de la Capital Federal, Case *Franco Rubén O. and others s/sustracción de menores de diez años* No. 1351, verdict of 5 July 2012.

[17] IACtHR, Case *Goiburú and others*, supra note 10, paras 66-67 and separate opinion of Judge A.A. Cançado Trindade, paras 9–25.

[18] Ibidem, para 12.

2.2 Attempts to Close the Gate and Define National Security

The above-described conceptual distortions and their far-fetched ramifications prompted international initiatives to better define, if not the very notion of national security, at least its repercussions on the limitation of certain human rights, and especially the right to freedom of information. These initiatives were launched by civil society organisations, experts and scholars, thus culminating in the adoption of soft law principles. Among others,[19] the so-called "Siracusa Principles" must be recalled.[20] Adopted as the result of an initiative convened by prominent NGOs, with the participation of several human rights experts,[21] the Principles were circulated in 1984 as an official document of the UN Economic and Social Council. They concern the limitation and derogation provisions in the International Covenant on Civil and

---

[19] Although they will not be analysed in the present chapter, two other global initiatives worth mentioning are the so-called 'Johannesburg Principles' and the 'Tshwane Principles'. With regard to the former, they were drawn up in 1995 by NGOs and international human rights experts and they concern 'National Security, Freedom of Expression and Access to Information" (integral text available at: https://www.article19.org/wp-content/uploads/2018/02/joburg-principles.pdf). Principle 2 of the Johannesburg Principles establishes that

> (a) A restriction sought to be justified on the ground of national security is not legitimate unless its genuine purpose and demonstrable effect is to *protect a country's existence or its territorial integrity against the use or threat of force*, or its capacity to respond to the use or threat of force, whether from an *external source, such as a military threat, or an internal source, such as incitement to violent overthrow of the government.* (b) In particular, a restriction sought to be justified on the ground of national security is not legitimate if its genuine purpose or demonstrable effect is to protect interests unrelated to national security, including, for example, to protect a government from embarrassment or exposure of wrongdoing, or to conceal information about the functioning of its public institutions, or to entrench a particular ideology, or to suppress industrial unrest (emphasis added).

With regard to the Tshwane Principles, their adoption was promoted in 2011 by several UN Special Procedures and civil society organisations. The initiative culminated in 2013, with the adoption of the "Global Principles on National Security and the Right to Information". https://www.justiceinitiative.org/uploads/bd50b729-d427-4fbb-8da2-1943ef2a3423/global-principles-national-security-10232013.pdf. This document delves in particular into the relationship between national security and the public's right to know and on State secrecy. On this subject, see *infra* Sect. 4. The Tshwane Principles do not define 'national security', although Principle 2 (c) points out that "it is good practice for national security, where used to limit the right to information, to be defined precisely in a country's legal framework in a manner consistent with a democratic society". The Tshwane Principles have been officially endorsed by the Special Rapporteur for Freedom of Expression of the Inter-American Commission on Human Rights in the report on "*National Security and Right to Information*", OEA/Ser.L/V/II/CIDH/RELE/INF.24/20 of July 2020.

[20] United Nations Economic and Social Council, *Principles on the Limitation and Derogation Provisions of the International Covenant on Civil and Political Rights*, UN Doc. E/CN.4/1985/4 of 28 September 1984 (hereinafter, "the Siracusa Principles").

[21] The American Association of the International Commission of Jurists played a crucial role. See the introductory note and reconstruction of the work of the group of experts at the conference held in Siracusa from 30 April to 4 May 1984 at: https://www.icj.org/wp-content/uploads/1984/07/Siracusa-principles-ICCPR-legal-submission-1985-eng.pdf.

Political Rights (ICCPR).[22] Pursuant to the latter, as recalled above,[23] under certain circumstances, "national security" constitutes a valid reason to restrict the enjoyment of the liberty of movement, the right to hold opinions, the right to peaceful assembly and the right to freedom of association (respectively Arts. 12, 19, 21 and 22 of the ICCPR). Moreover, "compelling reasons of national security" can be invoked to justify the expulsion of an alien lawfully residing in the territory of a State party to the ICCPR (Article 13) and for the exclusion of the public and the press from all or part of a trial (Article 14). Arguably, pursuant to the ICCPR, national security can play a significant role in limiting and restricting the enjoyment of various fundamental freedoms and rights enshrined therein. Since their introduction, the Siracusa Principles stress that

> there is a *close relationship between respect for human rights and the maintenance of international peace and security*; indeed the *systematic violation of human rights undermines national security* and public order and may constitute a threat to international peace (emphasis added).

This principle offers a persuasive answer to the question of what truly ensures the security of a State.

Principles 29 to 32 deal with "national security" as a limitation clause to the enjoyment of some of the rights and freedoms guaranteed under the ICCPR. Accordingly,

> national security may be invoked to justify measures limiting certain rights only when they are taken *to protect the existence of the nation, its territorial integrity or political independence against force or threat of force*. National security cannot be invoked as a reason for imposing limitations to prevent merely local or relatively isolated threats to law and order (Principles 29 and 30, emphasis added).

Without defining the notion of "national security", the Siracusa Principles promote its narrow interpretation. In this regard, Principle 31 adds that

> *national security cannot be used as a pretext for imposing vague or arbitrary limitations* and may only be invoked when there exist adequate safeguards and effective remedies against abuse (emphasis added).

Furthermore, the fundamental importance of linking the notion of "national security" with the full respect and guarantee of human rights (more than with their potential limitation) is stressed anew by Principle 32:

> the systematic violation of human rights undermines national security and may jeopardize international peace and security. A State responsible for such violation shall not invoke national security as a justification for measures aimed at suppressing opposition to such violation or at perpetrating repressive practices against its population.

Pursuant to the Siracusa Principles, there can be no security (national or international) without respect for human rights and abuses and violations of the latter cannot

[22] International Covenant on Civil and Political Rights, New York, 16 December 1966, entered into force on 23 March 1976, 999 UNTS 171.

[23] Supra note 1.

be committed by invoking (in vain) national security justifications. Under this perspective, it is the State that must serve the higher purpose of the promotion and protection of human rights and not the other way around. Indeed, the interpretation of national security enshrined in the Principles has been fully embraced by the UN Human Rights Committee, which also referred to the Siracusa Principles in its recent General Comment on the right to peaceful assembly, affirming that

> the "interests of national security" may serve as a ground for restrictions if such restrictions are necessary to preserve the State's capacity to *protect the existence of the nation, its territorial integrity or political independence against a credible threat or use of force*. This threshold will only exceptionally be met by assemblies that are "peaceful". Moreover, *where the very reason that national security has deteriorated is the suppression of human rights, this cannot be used to justify further restrictions*, including on the right of peaceful assembly.[24]

Whilst the proposed reading of national security is certainly sensible and shows a clear awareness that States are not inherently benign entities and have not refrained—and do not refrain—from neglecting and violating human rights in the very name of national security, the latter seems to be construed in extremely broad—and precisely because of this, leaving them open to manipulation—terms, and based on an entirely State-centred view. Likely, this is at the origin of many ill-conceived applications of national security and gross violations of human rights and international crimes perpetrated in its name. Were this analysis conducted in the post-Westphalian world, it could probably stand. However, Westphalia is well past and the very notion of the State, its aims and the limitations to its powers can and should be revisited. This is arguably the first step to interpreting and applying the notion of national security in a way that is grounded in international law and, ultimately, which is most conducive to the full respect of fundamental human rights and freedoms.

3 Setting the Roles Straight: Who Is the Villain?

As aptly noted by Professor Scovazzi, "having no head, arms, legs (nor paws) or other organs, the State exists only as an abstract entity"[25] and as such it must be regarded, i.e. in a way that puts aside any (inexistent) sacredness and which assumes that the abstract entity called the State is not almighty and moreover that it has an impassable limit: human dignity. In one of its first judgments, often quoted by Professor Scovazzi, the Inter-American Court of Human Rights ("IACtHR") masterfully summarised this idea:

> without question, the State has the right and duty to guarantee its security. It is also indisputable that all societies suffer some deficiencies in their legal orders. However,

---

[24] Human Rights Committee, *General Comment No. 37 – Right to Peaceful Assembly,* UN Doc. CCPR/C/GC/37 of 23 July 2020, para 42 (emphasis added).

[25] Scovazzi (2014), p. 116 (translation by the author).

> regardless of the seriousness of certain actions and the culpability of the perpetrators of certain crimes, the power of the State is not unlimited, nor may the State resort to any means to attain its ends. The State is subject to law and morality. Disrespect for human dignity cannot serve as the basis for any State action.[26]

Along the same lines, the IACtHR also addressed the relationship between security and human rights, holding that

> the exercise of public authority has certain limits which derive from the fact that human rights are inherent attributes of human dignity and are, therefore, superior to the power of the State.[27]

Nevertheless, States—which unfortunately have repeatedly shown in a multitude of ways that they are anything but benign entities—seem quite keen on solving the equation between their own powers and human rights in their favour. Here lies what Professor Scovazzi regards as a paradox: how can individuals representing the State protect human rights, if the latter are essentially aimed at limiting the privileges and immunities enjoyed by individuals representing the State?[28] If national security is construed as a tool to defend at all costs—and without any limitation—the State (and hence the privileges and immunities of those representing it), it is bound to incur the same paradox; and, when the State—as frequently happens—is not after all benevolent, but rather is the "villain of the piece", it can end up perpetrating the worst crimes in the very name of national security. To fully appreciate this, it may be useful to describe specific cases and the corresponding relevant facts, which, in Professor Scovazzi's words, "prove how the so-called sovereign States can engage themselves in the most disgusting behaviours".[29] The judgments rendered respectively by the European Court on Human Rights ("ECtHR") and the IACtHR in three landmark cases can serve this purpose. In his lectures and writings on international human rights law, Professor Scovazzi often refers to these cases, focusing his attention on the persons involved and those directly affected by the States' criminal behaviours, usually emphasising their higher dignity and morality compared to the respondents' worthlessness.

In the case *McCann and others* v. *the United Kingdom*,[30] the use of lethal force by security forces led to the arbitrary deprivation of the lives of Mr. Daniel McCann, Ms. Mairéad Farrel and Mr. Sean Savage. British soldiers who believed that the three were terrorists of the Irish Republican Army (IRA) about to set off a car bomb in Gibraltar, instead of arresting them at the border upon arrival, "took the risk" of letting them reach the place where the terrorist attack would allegedly occur, and then opened fire. On 6 March 1988, Mr. McCann was hit by 5 bullets, Ms. Farrell by 8 and Mr. Savage by 16. When, after the shooting, the bodies of the three suspects

---

[26] IACtHR, Case *Godínez Cruz v. Honduras*, Ser. C No. 5, judgment of 20 January 1989, para 162.

[27] Ibidem, para 174.

[28] Scovazzi (2014), p. 117. In the same sense, Cassese (1994), p. 115.

[29] Scovazzi (2020b), p. xxii.

[30] ECtHR, Case *McCann and others* v. *United Kingdom*, Appl. No. 18984/91, judgment of 27 September 1995.

were searched, no weapons, explosive devices or detonators were discovered. When, after the death of Ms. Farrell, Mr. Savage and Mr. McCann, the area was searched, no explosive device or bomb was found. Yet, the United Kingdom held that the use of force by its State agents was "no more than absolutely necessary in defence of the people of Gibraltar from unlawful violence".[31] Although national security is not expressly invoked here, the facts described equally raise the question of how far the State (through its agents) is allowed to go with its actions and whether it has any limitations.

Notably, Article 2 of the European Convention on Human Rights ("ECHR")—although the United Kingdom had advocated for the opposite[32]—does not mention "national security" among the reasons that may justify the use of lethal force by State agents. However, national security considerations can play a role in the decision to use lethal force, for instance in defence of any person from unlawful violence (Article 2.2.a, ECHR).

The ECtHR rejected the interpretation put forward by the United Kingdom (which was rather liberal in assessing the existence of potential limitations to its powers and to the actions of its own agents), and held that, in establishing whether the use of force is "no more than absolutely necessary", a stricter and more compelling test of necessity must be employed from that normally applicable when determining whether State action is necessary in a democratic society.[33] Moreover, the force used must be strictly proportionate to the achievement of the aims set out in sub-paragraphs (a), (b) and (c) of paragraph 2 of Article 2 of the ECHR, taking into consideration not only the actions of the agents of the State who actually administer the force, but also all the surrounding circumstances, including such matters as the planning and control of the actions under examination.[34] In the *McCann and others*' case, the State ignored its responsibilities and twice purported not to have any limitations. First, when it considered the lives of three people less important than an alleged—and not duly verified—threat. Second, when it failed to thoroughly investigate the events and to hold its agents accountable for the arbitrary killings. The judgment of the ECtHR is a landmark in spelling out the limitations to the State's actions and powers, especially vis-à-vis significant security threats. Notwithstanding that, the ECtHR was not fully consistent when drawing upon the consequences of its own findings. In fact, the ECtHR declared that the United Kingdom had violated Article 2.2, of the ECHR, but it nonetheless dismissed the applicants' claim for damages, not considering it appropriate to make an award, "having regard to the fact that the three terrorist suspects who were killed had been intending to plant a bomb in Gibraltar".[35] The conclusion reached by the ECtHR is surprising to say the least, in that it seems to ignore the presumption of innocence,

---

[31] Ibidem, para 143.

[32] *Travaux préparatoires*, vol. III, p. 186.

[33] ECtHR, Case *McCann and others,* supra note 30, para 149.

[34] Ibidem, para 150.

[35] Ibidem, para 219.

the right to an effective remedy and the prohibition of discrimination,[36] somewhat suggesting that, as long as the lives unlawfully taken by State agents are those of suspected terrorists, they could justifiably be regarded as worthless. Put another way, in its judgment, the ECtHR showed how the State could be the villain. However, with its findings on reparations, it held that, as long as this happens against suspected terrorists, then the State nevertheless does not have to pay. Leaving aside any considerations on the legal soundness and moral standing (or lack thereof) of this reasoning, this is a missed opportunity, because it is precisely in determining and designing adequate measures of reparation that the roles of the villain and the innocent can be re-established, and dignity restored.[37]

In the case *McCann and others,* the State chose to be the villain for a cause: that cause—saving lives—was legitimate, the means and the manner chosen to achieve it, less so. There are other instances where the State has lowered itself, even to the level of a swindler, going so far as to cheat a child and his illiterate parents. In the case *Vargas Areco* v. *Paraguay,*[38] adjudicated by the IACtHR on 26 September 2006, the respondent State recruited 15-year-old Gerardo Vargas Areco into military service in the Paraguayan Armed Forces by deception. In Paraguay, one-year military service is mandatory for all male citizens aged 18 to 50 and the minimum age for enlisting in active service is the age of 18. However, the recruitment of people under this age is possible, subject to approval by the parents of the minor and the authorisation of a Juvenile Court. Whilst these legal requirements are often not fulfilled, the recruitment of children into the armed forces is a deep-rooted tradition in Paraguay and there is a heroic narrative revolving around the figure of the "soldier children sacrificed to the flag".[39] For several years, it has been a common practice to illegitimately obtain signed authorisations for the recruitment of minors from poor families, where the parents are illiterate.[40] This is what happened in the case at stake, where, as a matter of fact, Gerardo Vargas Areco was certainly not keen to sacrifice himself for the flag. So much so that, having been recruited, whenever he obtained leave to visit his family, he sought not to return to military post. Nevertheless, each time he did so, a zealous officer retrieved him and brought him back, subsequently and inevitably punishing him for the failure to comply with the rules. On his third attempt to escape, Gerardo Vargas Areco was brought back and, when trying to flee from his post and escape punishment, he was shot dead from behind by another zealous officer. Other equally earnest State agents then sought to cover up the events and returned a coffin to the family of Gerardo which had been welded closed,

[36] Scovazzi and Citroni (2013), p. 183.

[37] Scovazzi (2013), pp. 93–109.

[38] IACtHR, Case *Vargas Areco* v. *Paraguay*, judgment of 26 September 2006, Ser. C No. 155.

[39] Ibidem, expert report No. 4 and paras 124–134. The common nature of forced recruitment of minors in Paraguay is confirmed by the fact that the IACtHR has recently been called upon to rule again on the subject: IACtHR, Case *Noguera and others* v. *Paraguay*, judgment of 9 March 2020, Ser. C No. 401.

[40] IACtHR, Case *Vargas Areco*, expert report No. 4 and paras 124–134.

ordering them not to open it. Beginning to understand that the State is not always a trustworthy counterpart, Gerardo's parents did not comply and, upon opening the coffin, were forced to see the clear marks of torture on their son's body: an eye was out of its socket and one arm showed signs of burns. Other State authorities ensured that the authors of these heinous crimes could enjoy virtual impunity. It took more than 17 years for the case to reach the IACtHR and only then did the State recognise—albeit in rather ambiguous terms—its responsibility. It is therefore particularly relevant that, besides declaring Paraguay internationally responsible for the violation of several provisions of the American Convention on Human Rights, among various measures of reparation, the IACtHR also ordered the State to hold a ceremony to publicly acknowledge its responsibility, in the presence of the relatives of Gerardo Vargas Areco and representatives of the State's civil and military authorities, in the community where the family resides. During the said ceremony, the State was required to affix a plaque (whose text and wording had to be agreed upon with the relatives of Gerardo Vargas Areco), to preserve his memory and prevent the repetition of similar events and the authorities were required to publicly apologise to the family.[41] Measures of reparation such as public apologies are all but symbolic, in that they set the roles straight between the villain (who can occasionally also be a swindler) and the innocent, whose dignity has been trampled on, thus posing the question of whose interests and security should be protected and from which threats.

Any doubts on whether States are the sovereign subjects whose security should be protected at all costs and to whom *carte blanche* should be given for such purposes, become even more pressing where the State acts as a bully, exercising pure savagery against the most vulnerable, such as street children. The sadly notorious case of *Villagrán Morales and others* v. *Guatemala*[42] is a powerful reminder of how ruthless a State can be.[43] Agents of the Guatemalan National Police Force abducted, tortured and extra-judicially killed four street youths, namely Henry Giovanni Contreras (18 years old), Federico Clemente Figueroa Túnchez (20 years old), Julio Roberto Caal Sandoval (15 years old) and Jovito Josué Juárez Cifuentes (17 years old). Their mutilated bodies were left on the outskirts of Ciudad de Guatemala, exposed to the elements and were attacked by wild animals. When another street child, Anastraum Villagrán Morales (17 years old), tried to report what had happened to his friends and who those responsible were, he was also extra-judicially killed. As established by the IACtHR, these were not isolated incidents:

---

[41] Ibidem, para 157. The public ceremony took place on 15 December 2008 in the city where the family of Gerardo Vargas Areco lives and was chaired by the Minister of National Defence, who publicly apologised. On the same occasion, the commemorative plaque was unveiled. See IACtHR, Resolution of 24 November 2010, paras 16–17.

[42] IACtHR, Case *Villagrán Morales and others* v. *Guatemala*, judgment on the merits of 19 November 1999, Ser. C No. 63; and judgment on reparations and costs of 26 May 2001, Ser. C No. 77.

[43] Citroni and Scovazzi (2006), pp. 616–635.

> at the time the events occurred, there was a common pattern of illegal acts perpetrated by State security agents against "street children"; this practice included threats, arrests, cruel, inhuman and degrading treatment and homicides as a measure to counter juvenile delinquency and vagrancy.[44]

This seemingly explains why the abduction, torture and killing of the five street youths by State agents was not subjected to a thorough and effective investigation and the perpetrators could enjoy impunity. The State—in its entirety—gave up its role: police officers acted as bullies and criminals instead of protecting the most vulnerable, and prosecutors and judges did not regard this as attention-worthy. The IACtHR noted and denounced the particularly grave "betrayal" of the fundamental State's function, recalling that where there are minors—and particularly on top of that, those who are vulnerable—the State is expected to take special measures of protection (and not to abduct, torture, kill them and then cover up these disgusting crimes).[45] Guatemala failed these children and youth twice. In the impeccable words of the IACtHR:

> [...] the Court wishes to record the particular gravity of the fact that a State Party to this Convention can be charged with having applied or tolerated a systematic practice of violence against at risk children in its territory. When States violate the rights of at-risk children, such as "street children", that makes them victims of a double aggression. First, such *States do not prevent them from living in misery, thus depriving them of the minimum conditions for a dignified life and preventing them from the 'full and harmonious development of their personality', even though every child has the right to harbor a project of life that should be tended and encouraged by the public authorities so that it may develop this project for its personal benefit and that of the society to which it belongs*. Second, they violate their physical, mental and moral integrity and even their lives.[46]

Arguably, a State where a child's right to a dignified life is not protected, tended and encouraged is not a secure one. In that sense, it is highly disputable whether the interests of such a State are worthy of protection at any cost, or whether instead the State constitutes the real threat, from which protection shall be offered to a different subject in order to eventually attain security.

Although the cases recalled in this section seemingly have no direct relationship with national security, by exposing the disgusting behaviours certain States can shamelessly engage in, they are meant to call into question the underlying premises

---

[44] IACtHR, Case *Villagrán Morales,* supra note 42, para 79 of the judgment on the merits. See also para 190.

[45] Ibidem, para 146.

[46] Ibidem, para 191 (emphasis added). In this case, among other measures of reparation, the IACtHR ordered Guatemala to

> designate an educational center with a name allusive to the young victims in this case and to place in this center a plaque with the names of Henry Giovanni Contreras, Federico Clemente Figueroa Túnchez, Julio Roberto Caal Sandoval, Jovito Josué Juárez Cifuentes and Anstraum Aman Villagrán Morales. This will contribute to raising awareness in order to avoid the repetition of harmful acts such as those that occurred in the instant case and will keep the memory of the victims alive (IACtHR, *Villagrán Morales,* supra note 42, para 103 of the judgment on reparations).

of a mostly State-centered notion. A move in this direction, beginning in the 1990s, was the suggestion put forward by international organisations, civil society associations, scholars and some States to refer to "human security" rather than "national security".[47] Without going into detail on the nuances of the notion of human security,[48] the fundamental idea is to shift from the protection of the security of a territorial State to that of the people. The latter should not replace the former, but rather should give it a purpose. The protection of territorial integrity and that of human rights are not incompatible, but interdependent. Indeed, being the State does not equate to being almighty. Sovereignty comes with responsibilities,[49] the first one being to protect and not to violate the fundamental human rights of those under the State's jurisdiction. A close second would be to avoid the use of pretexts and excuses in the attempt to do so with impunity.

4 No Excuses: When National Security Is Invoked in Vain (Again)

As they say, old habits die hard and, in a world where threats (old and new, real and perceived) thrive, national security—in its traditional State-centered interpretation and its often abusive application—does not seem to go out of fashion. In this regard, 2001 marked a turning point in the sense that national and international policies in this area appear to have somehow regressed by 30 years. As observed by Judge Cançado Trindade in his separate opinion in the case of *Goiburú and others*,

> in the 1970s, it was the "war [sic] against subversion," today it is the "war [sic] against terrorism." *In both cases, for the perpetrators of grave human rights violations, the ends justify the means, and anything is allowed, outside the law.* As an advocate of the current "war [sic] on terrorism," stated recently, "those who are not with us are against us," exactly as the members of the Army, all Heads of State, engaged in "Operation Condor" affirmed in the 1970s in order to sow terror and try to justify State crimes.[50]

"Subversives" (or those alleged to be) have been replaced by "terrorists" (or those alleged to be) as enemies against whom everything is permitted, in the name of

[47] The document regarded as foundational for the definition of the notion of 'human security' is the Human Development Report issued by the United Nations Development Programme in 1994.

[48] Bindenagel Šehović (2018); Thakur (2016), pp. 79–107; Gasper and Gómez (2015), pp. 100–116; Shani (2013), pp. 5–24; MacFarlane and Foong Kong (2006). Others have argued that it would be preferable to acknowledge the existence of five complementary dimensions of security, namely human, national, transnational, environmental, and transcultural. This theory—on which Al-Rodhan (2007) writes extensively—will not be analysed in further detail in the present chapter.

[49] Nolte (2005), pp. 389–392.

[50] IACtHR, Case *Goiburú and others*, supra note 10, separate opinion of Judge A.A. Cançado Trindade, para 55.

national security.[51] No one can deny the existence of terrorism and the imperative to defeat it. What is more questionable, is that in achieving such a crucial goal, States should have no restrictions, including in relation to the respect for human rights, and are able to invoke "national security" as a shield for any behaviour (however disgusting and/or criminal) and as an excuse to cover up abuses. On the one hand, as this section outlines, States consistently struggle to manage the "privilege" of invoking national security when they are called upon to justify the limitation of fundamental rights and freedoms (including the right to access to information and the right to know the truth), often through State secrecy.[52] On the other hand, as the next section of this chapter illustrates, there have been even more blunt and wholly unacceptable attempts to suggest that, in the (abused) name of national security, peremptory norms of international law such as the prohibition of torture can be derogated from.

An episode in which Professor Scovazzi was directly involved shows how efforts to maintain "national security" as a loophole to justify or cover up some of the most heinous crimes under international law can be particularly underhand. It also shows the need for human rights defenders to remain vigilant in the face of these recurring challenges. As described above in Sect. 2, enforced disappearance was perpetrated on a widespread and systematic basis in Latin America during the 1970s and 1980s, specifically in the name of national security. One might therefore expect that, when trying to provide effective legal remedies vis-à-vis this crime under international law and complex human rights violation, if "national security" is mentioned at all, it should only be to flag it as an example of an unacceptable justification invoked in the past for such a practice and, as such, as an absolutely unacceptable pretext. Surprisingly, this was not the case during the negotiations that led to the adoption of the International Convention on the Protection of All Persons from Enforced Disappearance ("ICPED"),[53] which Professor Scovazzi participated in.

Article 1 of the ICPED establishes that no one shall be subjected to enforced disappearance and specifies that

> no exceptional circumstances whatsoever, whether a state of war or a threat of war, internal political instability or any other public emergency, may be invoked as a justification for enforced disappearance.

Whilst "national security" is certainly encompassed within the "exceptional circumstances whatsoever' wording above, there is no explicit reference to it within the provision, despite the fact that this is precisely where it would have made the most sense to have such a notion mentioned in a treaty on enforced disappearance. Indeed, during the negotiations multiple references were made to "national security" and its

---

[51] Posner and Vermeule (2007); Golder and Williams (2006), pp. 43–62.

[52] For a comprehensive analysis of the intricate relationship between State secrecy and human rights, see: Carpanelli (2019); Scovazzi (2009a), pp. 959–992; Scovazzi (2009b), pp. 885–900.

[53] International Convention on the Protection of All Persons from Enforced Disappearance (ICPED), adopted on 20 December 2006, opened for signature in Paris on 6 February 2007 and entered into force on 23 December 2010.

inclusion in the ICPED was repeatedly called for, although mostly with a view to restricting access to information arising from investigations and on persons deprived of their liberty. Before analysing the attempts to have national security included among the potential just causes which would permit the denial of access to information and Professor Scovazzi's fierce opposition to them, it is worth recalling that "the refusal to acknowledge the deprivation of liberty or the concealment of the fate or whereabouts of a disappeared person" are among the constitutive elements of this crime (Article 2 ICPED). Access to information is therefore crucial, on the one hand, to prevent legal arrests and detentions from turning into enforced disappearance, and, on the other hand, to put an end to the anguish of the relatives of the disappeared persons for not knowing the fate and whereabouts of their loved ones, which *per se* amounts to a form of ill-treatment.

The draft text initially discussed during the negotiations contained a provision[54] aimed at guaranteeing the right of persons having a legitimate interest (e.g. relatives of the disappeared and their counsel or legal representative) to be kept informed on the progress and the findings of, investigations conducted against someone suspected of having committed an act of enforced disappearance, who might therefore be in a position to elucidate the fate and whereabouts of the person who had disappeared. It is in this context that national security was put forward, as part of a proposal to restrict access to such information for the "needs of national security".[55] On this first occasion, the proposal was rejected by the person chairing the negotiations (Ambassador Bernard Kessedjian), who emphasised that "the right to be informed of progress in and the findings of an investigation was crucial and must not be worded in a way that would leave room for abuses"[56] or compromise the prevention of enforced disappearance. Notwithstanding this, in a subsequent session of the negotiations, the call to expressly include national security as a valid reason to withhold information was reiterated. In this case, some delegations proposed that access to documents and other information useful in the context of the investigation of an alleged enforced disappearance "should be subject to judicial authorization and to certain restrictions having chiefly to do with national security".[57] This proposal generated a harsh criticism and debate, as other delegations found it unacceptable given it suggested that information vital to determining the fate and whereabouts of a disappeared person, and therefore to put an end to a crime and to the suffering of the relatives of the disappeared person, could be kept secret in the name of national security, *de facto* condemning the disappeared person never to be found and his or her loved ones to be kept between hope and despair. Consensus on the issue could

---

[54] The provision became Article 12 in the approved text of the ICPED.

[55] Report of the Intersessional Open-ended Working Group to elaborate a draft legally binding normative instrument for the protection of all persons from enforced disappearance, UN Doc. E/CN.4/2004/59 of 23 February 2004, para 106.

[56] Ibidem, para 107.

[57] Report of the Intersessional Open-ended Working Group to elaborate a draft legally binding normative instrument for the protection of all persons from enforced disappearance, UN Doc. E/CN.4/2005/66 of 10 March 2005, para 63.

not be found over two more sessions of the negotiations, showing how challenging and controversial this subject remains. In the final text of the provision, reference to potential prior authorisation of a judicial authority was retained, specifying that it shall rule promptly on the matter (Article 12.3.b ICPED). However, any mention of national security was dropped.

During the same session of the negotiations, whilst discussing what would later become Article 16 of the ICPED, which enshrines the principle of *non-refoulement* where there are substantial grounds for believing that a person would be in danger of being subjected to enforced disappearances, the delicate issue of derogating from this principle if the person concerned is regarded as a danger to the security of the country emerged.[58] In other words, in line with a troublesome trend,[59] some States insinuated that if someone is regarded as a potential threat to national security, then this person would be less deserving of protection from enforced disappearance. These proposals were rejected and there is no trace of them in the text of the article as enshrined in the treaty.

The ICPED contains several provisions aimed at preventing enforced disappearance, including by setting forth guarantees for all persons deprived of their liberty, especially in the sense of ensuring access to a minimum set of information in relation to their physical integrity, legal situation and whereabouts to be provided to those with a legitimate interest, including their relatives and counsels (Arts. 17–19 and 21 of the ICPED). When drafting these provisions, the necessity to foresee the possibility of invoking national security as a valid reason to withhold information on persons deprived of their liberty was repeatedly put forward,[60] seemingly disregarding that this is the exact justification used, among others, by military regimes and dictatorships in Latin America to abduct and forcibly make thousands of women and men labelled as internal enemies that would allegedly threat national security disappear. The debate around this subject was heated and led to the inclusion of Article 20 in the ICPED, whose convoluted wording is a testament to the contrasting positions which emerged during the negotiations. Paragraph 1 of Article 20 establishes that

> only where a person is under the protection of the law and the deprivation of liberty is subject to judicial control may the right to information referred to in article 18 be restricted, on an exceptional basis, where strictly necessary and where provided for by the law, and if the transmission of the information would adversely affect *the privacy or safety of the person, hinder a criminal investigation, or for equivalent reasons* in accordance with the law, and in conformity with applicable international law and with the objectives of this Convention. In no case shall there be restrictions on the right to information referred to in article 18 that could constitute conduct defined in article 2 or be in violation of article 17, paragraph 1 (emphasis added).

[58] Ibidem, paras 73–74.

[59] *Infra* Sect. 5.

[60] UN Doc. E/CN.4/2005/66, supra note 57, para 90; and Report of the Intersessional Open-ended Working Group to elaborate a draft legally binding normative instrument for the protection of all persons from enforced disappearance, UN Doc. E/CN.4/2006/57 of 2 February 2006, para 18.

While exceptional circumstances to withhold the information on persons deprived of their liberty were eventually foreseen, national security does not appear among them and this is due to the firm opposition led by Professor Scovazzi, who openly remarked that including those very words in such a context would be contrary to the spirit of the treaty, to the right to truth which the ICPED is meant to protect and, ultimately, a mockery in the face of thousands of victims of enforced disappearance and their relatives.[61]

The episodes relating to the negotiations of the ICPED show a recurring tendency among States: they may formally condemn certain crimes and practices (e.g. enforced disappearance and secret detention), but they are not so ready to accept an obligation to fully disclose information, especially when it may concern the very perpetration of such crimes and practices. "National security", in its broad and vague meaning, remains a common justification for withholding information or, to put it more bluntly, a wide carpet under which dirty secrets could be swept.

The concepts of "national security" and "State secrecy" tend to go hand in hand and it is not uncommon for States to use the latter to cover some of the worst crimes they perpetrated in the (abused) name of the former. There are unfortunately many examples that could be recalled, including that—which has been the subject of many of Professor Scovazzi's writings[62] and much of his indignation—of the abduction and extra-ordinary rendition of the imam Hassan Mustafa Osama Nasr, also known as Abu Omar.[63] The imam, an Egyptian citizen with the status of political refugee in Italy, was suspected of involvement in terrorist activities. On 17 February 2003, he was abducted in broad daylight in Milan in the context of an operation that involved several CIA agents. He was taken to Egypt via the military airbases of Aviano (Italy) and Ramstein (Germany). Once there, he was held *incommunicado* and subjected to torture until his liberation in 2004. Over this period, his wife did not know his fate and whereabouts, thus qualifying the facts as an enforced disappearance. The Public Prosecutor of Milano opened a criminal investigation upon the complaint lodged by the wife of Abu Omar, pressing charges against 26 CIA agents and diplomatic representatives of the United States of America in Italy and 6 Italian citizens who were members of the intelligence services. In the course of the ensuing proceedings, the executive (no matter its political affiliation) consistently invoked State secrecy to prevent the use in court of documents concerning the relationships between Italian and United States intelligence services, alleging that this was imperative in the interest of national security. Even the highest Italian judicial authorities endorsed as valid the invocation of State secrecy, *de facto* hampering the outcome of the criminal proceedings against those responsible and contributing to their impunity.

---

[61] UN Doc. E/CN.4/2006/57, supra note 60, para 23.

[62] Scovazzi (2020a), pp. 165–180; Scovazzi (2018), pp. 239–252; and Scovazzi (2016), pp. 157–184.

[63] On this case there have been numerous judgments rendered by various Italian courts, including the Constitutional Court and the Cassation Court, as well as one by the ECtRH, Case *Nasr and Ghali v. Italy*, Appl. 44883/09, judgment of 23 February 2016.

Among the many questionable aspects of this not exactly remarkable page of the Italian executive and judiciary, Professor Scovazzi denounced as especially disturbing the attempt to justify the withdrawal of crucial information invoking national security as he considered this a perversion of the notion and its underlying aims. Indeed, what was unacceptable in Professor Scovazzi's view, was that national security was construed as such an absolute and dominant value that it would take precedence over any other interest and value enshrined in the Italian Constitution, going as far as to justify the failure to establish the truth on one of the worst human rights violations.[64] In his words,

> it is never permissible for a State to refuse to give information on the fate of people forcibly disappeared, on the pretext that such information would be harmful to national security. Instead, the opposite is true, namely that the most elementary foundation of national security lies precisely in the fact that people never run the risk of being subjected to enforced disappearance at the hands or with the connivance of State agents.[65]

5 Holding the Ground: No Room for Exceptions

The examples referred to in the previous section relate to the not infrequent attempts that States have made to invoke national security as a legitimate ground to withhold sensitive information and to refuse its disclosure to judicial authorities, the public, and other subjects (including relatives of victims of gross human rights violations). Besides being problematic, such attempts are also subtle in that they are construed as potential exceptions to the right to access to information, which, at the end of the day, is not an absolute one. An even more troublesome trend consists in bluntly affirming that, in the name of national security, even peremptory norms, such as the absolute prohibition of torture, could be derogated from and overrode.

The prohibition of torture amounts to *jus cogens* and it does not allow for any exception whatsoever.[66] That is the case even if national security is allegedly at stake. It is also the case even if the target is an alleged threat to such national security (be it a subversive, a terrorist, a criminal, or in the most recent trend, which will be illustrated below, a migrant). The rule is crystal-clear and, it being customary, it should not be questioned nor raise any doubt: the unconditional nature of the prohibition of torture and inhuman or degrading treatment or punishment implies that national security can never be relied upon to justify a violation of the rule and the ensuing obligations. Unfortunately, this is not the case, as shown by the recurrent attempts to relativize this absolute principle and to bypass a rule that does not foresee any exception. The referred challenges emerge especially in three domains, namely anti-terrorism measures and policies, proposed derogations to the principle of

[64] Scovazzi and Citroni (2013), pp. 79–82.

[65] Scovazzi (2014), p. 117 (translation by the author).

[66] Scovazzi (2006), pp. 905–947.

non-refoulement, and, lately, relating to the latter, and on a massive scale, migration laws and policies.

Terrorism can—and should—be legitimately regarded as a threat to security, interpreted in its broader sense (i.e. not only of a sovereign entity, but of every person). However, "terrorism", as well as "national security", pertains to those expressions that are equally heavy (bearing in mind the consequences they trigger) and vague (in the sense of a lack of precise and unanimously agreed definition), thus lending themselves to abuse, especially where those who have the authority to use them may be villains, swindlers or bullies. The crimes perpetrated in the name of national security after 11 September 2001 speak for themselves. No one can deny that the horrific terrorist attacks called for a firm, effective and collective response, but authorising the use of torture in interrogations through the notorious "torture memos",[67] systematically using secret detention, and setting up the infamous programme of extra-ordinary renditions (all in the—clearly abused—name of national security) arguably was neither an acceptable nor a successful reply.[68] An appalling number of reports and documents—and, as shown in the previous section, judgments rendered by international courts amidst unprecedented obstacles and attempts to cover up the crimes perpetrated—prove that the notion of national security was purportedly abused, among other reasons, to circumvent the absolute prohibition of torture. A comprehensive analysis goes beyond the scope of this chapter, but a lesson that should be retained is that, even when faced with unprecedented challenges and risks, States have a choice on the means to be used and some are and shall remain forbidden. This is masterfully captured in an episode recalled in the prologue of the report "Never Again!", issued by the Argentine National Commission on the Disappearance of Persons:

> Italy, for example, has suffered for many years from the heartless attacks of Fascist groups, the Red Brigades, and other similar organisations. Never at any time, however, did that country abandon the principles of law in its fight against these terrorists, and it managed to resolve the problem through the normal courts of law, guaranteeing the accused all their rights of a fair hearing. When Aldo Moro was kidnapped, a member of the security forces suggested to General Della Chiesa that a suspect who apparently knew a lot be tortured. The general replied with the memorable words: "Italy can survive the loss of Aldo Moro. It would not survive the introduction of torture".[69]

Unfortunately, as attested by post 9/11 policies and events, the temptation to ignore the principles of law in the name of national security is a recurrent trend. Indeed, the perverse effects that such a departure from the aims of a State and such a crass abandonment of its fundamental obligations may generate are well summarised in a speech on national security delivered on 21 May 2009 by the then President of the United States of America, Barak Obama:

[67] Greenberg (2009), pp. 5–12.

[68] See, among many others, Joint Study on Secret Detention, paras 103 and 282.

[69] National Commission on Disappeared Persons (1984), prologue.

> [. . .] time and again, our values have been our best national security asset - in war and peace; in times of ease and in eras of upheaval. [. . .] After 9/11, we knew that we had entered a new era - that enemies who did not abide by any law of war would present new challenges to our application of the law [. . .] all too often our government made decisions based on fear rather than foresight; that all too often our government trimmed facts and evidence to fit ideological predispositions. [. . .] Now let me be clear: We are indeed at war with al Qaeda and its affiliates. We do need to update our institutions to deal with this threat. But we must do so with an abiding confidence in the rule of law and due process; in checks and balances and accountability. [. . .] I know some have argued that brutal methods like waterboarding were necessary to keep us safe. I could not disagree more. [. . .] What's more, they undermine the rule of law. [. . .] Indeed, the existence of Guantanamo likely created more terrorists around the world than it ever detained. So the record is clear: Rather than keeping us safer, the prison at Guantanamo has weakened American national security.[70]

However, it is especially unfortunate that this acknowledgment was not followed by the enforcement of the promises made in the speech, which contained a phrase that, alone, should have rung alarm bells, namely the reference to the need to "turn the page", announcing that the President of the United States of America would continue withholding certain information for the sake of national security. Usually, and the speech here quoted is no exception, this formula translates into impunity for perpetrators and eventually in more torture and a further departure from the rule of law. Torture is a crime, not merely an unfortunate political choice. Acknowledgment without accountability is an empty promise, unlikely to produce any meaningful and lasting effects unless and until the absolute legal prohibition of torture is fully re-established; national security cannot serve as a pretext to circumvent accountability and, then, to hide the crime.[71]

Another realm where States' attempts to side step and erode an absolute principle in the name of national security are frequent is that of *non-refoulement.*[72] While refugee law—and notably the 1951 Convention relating to the Status of Refugees—allows exceptions, especially due to national security considerations, to the principle of *non-refoulement,*[73] pursuant to international human rights law, *non-refoulement* vis-à-vis the risk of being subjected to torture or ill-treatment is an absolute and non-derogable principle.[74] Yet, over the years, States have challenged this principle on a regular basis, often in the name of national security. Several instances come to mind from the jurisprudence of, among others, the ECtHR. In the landmark case of

---

[70] The integral text of President Obama's speech on national security of 21 May 2009 is available at https://www.nytimes.com/2009/05/21/us/politics/21obama.text.html?pagewanted=print.

[71] In the same sense see, among others, Parliamentary Assembly, *Abuse of State Secrecy and National Security: Obstacles to Parliamentary and Judicial Scrutiny of Human Rights Violations,* 2011 (Rapporteur Mr. Dick Marty), Report Doc. 12714 of 16 September 2011.

[72] *Supra* Sect. 4.

[73] See Article 33.2 of the Convention relating to the Status of Refugees, adopted in Geneva on 28 July 1951, entered into force on 22 April 1954. See also Articles 9 and 32.2 therein.

[74] In this sense, see, among others, Article 3 of the Convention against Torture and other Cruel, Inhuman or Degrading Treatment or Punishment (adopted in New York on 10 December 1984 and entered into force on 26 June 1987); and Article 16 of the ICPED, referred to *supra* in Sect. 4.

Chahal v. *the United Kingdom*,[75] the respondent State had served Mr. Chahal, an advocate of the Sikh separatist cause, suspected of involvement in terrorist activities with a deportation order on the grounds of national security. Mr. Chahal alleged that, were he to be deported to India, he faced a real risk of ill-treatment. The United Kingdom tried to persuade the ECtHR to relativize the prohibition of torture, arguing that the threat posed by an individual to the national security of a State should be weighted in the balance when considering alleged violations of Article 3 ECHR.[76] The ECtHR resolutely rejected this attempt:

> Article 3 enshrines one of the most fundamental values of democratic society. The Court is well aware of the immense difficulties faced by States in modern times in protecting their communities from terrorist violence. However, even in these circumstances, the Convention prohibits in absolute terms torture or inhuman or degrading treatment or punishment, irrespective of the victim's conduct. Unlike most of the substantive clauses of the Convention and of Protocols Nos. 1 and 4, Article 3 makes no provision for exceptions and no derogation from it is permissible under Article 15 even in the event of a public emergency threatening the life of the nation.[77]

The ECtHR added that

> the prohibition provided by Article 3 against ill-treatment is equally absolute in expulsion cases. Thus, whenever substantial grounds have been shown for believing that an individual would face a real risk of being subjected to treatment contrary to Article 3 if removed to another State, the responsibility of the Contracting State to safeguard him or her against such treatment is engaged in the event of expulsion. In these circumstances, the activities of the individual in question, however undesirable or dangerous, cannot be a material consideration. The protection afforded by Article 3 is thus wider than that provided by Articles 32 and 33 of the United Nations 1951 Convention on the Status of Refugees.[78]

The crystal-clear stance of the ECtHR evidently clashes with States' political interests and it is likely to be difficult to digest for them, so that they cyclically fall back. For instance, in the case *Saadi* v. *Italy,*[79] the United Kingdom intervened as a third party, alleging that, where an applicant presents a threat to national security, stronger evidence must be adduced to prove that, if expelled, returned or extradited, he or she would face a risk of ill-treatment.[80] The ECtHR held the ground and confirmed that

> such an approach is not compatible with the absolute nature of the protection afforded by Article 3 either. It amounts to asserting that, in the absence of evidence meeting a higher standard, protection of national security justifies accepting more readily a risk of ill-treatment for the individual. The Court therefore sees no reason to modify the relevant standard of proof, as suggested by the third-party intervener, by requiring in cases like the

[75] ECtHR, Case *Chahal* v. *the United Kingdom*, Appl. No. 22414/93, judgment of 15 November 1996.

[76] Ibidem, para 76.

[77] Ibidem, para 79.

[78] Ibidem, para 80.

[79] ECtHR, Case *Saadi* v. *Italy*, Appl. No. 37201/06, judgment of 28 February 2008.

[80] Ibidem, para 122.

> present one that it be proved that subjection to ill-treatment is "more likely than not". On the contrary, it reaffirms that for a planned forcible expulsion to be in breach of the Convention it is necessary – and sufficient – for substantial grounds to have been shown for believing that there is a real risk that the person concerned will be subjected in the receiving country to treatment prohibited by Article 3.[81]

It is worth reaffirming that, as Professor Scovazzi often points out, when faced with the question of whether a State can torture an individual—or accept exposing him or her to such risk in case of *refoulement*—and the four answers that are in abstract admissible (i.e. "yes, always"; "yes, but in some cases no"; "no, but in certain cases yes"; "no, never"), the answer is only one: no, never (and certainly not on national security grounds).[82] This correct answer also holds true with regard to the new trend in terms of attempts to dodge the prohibition of torture: after subversives and terrorists, the latest category to be increasingly depicted as a threat to national security are migrants. This happens in the public discourse of certain political exponents, is often reflected in the language used in the media to refer to migration, and has been incorporated in domestic laws and policies. The consequences are far reaching, as effectively illustrated by the UN Working Group on Enforced or Involuntary Disappearances:

> [. . .] The discourse and language used to address the issue of migration and, in particular, to associate migrants, notably those with undocumented status, with security threats and/or criminality places them in a situation of increased vulnerability, which in turn further exposes them to violence and to becoming victims of human rights violations,[83]

including enforced disappearances, which are, *per se*, violations of the prohibition of torture. Along the same lines, the Special Rapporteur on Extrajudicial, Summary or Arbitrary Executions observed that

> in a global environment where refugees and migrants are demonized, and their movements criminalized, countries around the world have designed policies based on deterrence, militarisation and extraterritoriality which implicitly or explicitly may tolerate the risk of migrant deaths as part of an effective control of entry. Deterrence policies are punitive, including policies ranging from securing the more accessible border entry points — thereby purposefully funnelling the migration flows into more hazardous terrain — to the imposition of strict detention and return policies.[84]

In addition, referring to policies and laws that criminalise those who try to assist and save migrants at risk, often justified as responses to perceived threats to national security, the Special Rapporteur emphasised that

---

[81] Ibidem, para 140.

[82] Scovazzi and Citroni (2013), p. 25.

[83] WGEID, *Report on Enforced Disappearances in the Context of Migration*, UN Doc. A/HRC/36/39/Add.2 of 28 July 2017, para 52.

[84] Special Rapporteur on Extrajudicial Killings, Summary or Arbitrary Executions (Special Rapporteur on Executions), *Unlawful Death of Refugees and Migrants,* UN Doc. A/72/335 of 15 August 2017, para 10.

> acts prohibiting or otherwise impeding humanitarian services violate the obligation of States to respect the right to life. Any death linked to such prohibition would constitute an arbitrary deprivation of life.[85]

One may add that any act of torture linked to such policies and laws is attributable to the States that put in place those policies and adopted such laws in the first place.

In the (once more abused) name of national security, to allegedly protect their borders and themselves from a new "mortal threat", States—with the blessing of certain international organisations and economic and political unions of States—are erecting fences and walls; militarising borders and, in some cases, even authorising the use of lethal force to prevent migrants from crossing borders.[86] They are letting vessels with thousands of people on board sink, without even attempting to provide them assistance and rescue them; keeping hundreds of persons—including children and pregnant women—for several days waiting outside ports in conditions that can only be described as inhumane, refusing their right to disembark; and pushing back thousands of other people despite knowing without a doubt that they will be exposed to torture and indescribable suffering. It is *per se* very much in question as to whether this succeeds in making a State truly secure. What is certain is that it makes the State—again—an inhumane and arrogant villain which has given up all its prerogatives and has recklessly trampled its duties. Yet, as rightly remarked, being humane and secure would not take so much:

> States can effectively control their borders in a rights-based and protection sensitive manner. This includes abiding by the principle of *non-refoulement* and international norms on the use of lethal force as well as the rights to life and bodily integrity in the implementation of border policies.[87]

Once again, security and human rights' protection should not be seen as opposites, but rather as complementary and mutually reinforcing and this should be borne in mind also by international human rights courts, when called upon to evaluate these new efforts to relativize the absolute prohibition of torture. Unfortunately, recent rulings of the ECtHR—such as the shameful judgment of the Grand Chamber on the case of *N.D. and N.T.* v. *Spain,* which *de facto* legitimizes collective push-backs of migrants, affirming that *non-refoulement* would not apply where the individuals concerned maintained a "culpable conduct" and are seen as "endangering public safety"[88]—seem to go in the opposite direction and are a source of concern,[89] in that they depart from the longstanding principle that the rights guaranteed—

---

[85] Special Rapporteur on Executions, *Saving Lives Is Not A Crime,* UN Doc. A/73/314 of 7 August 2018, para 26.

[86] Basaran (2011); Sorel (2014), pp. 131–141.

[87] Special Rapporteur on Executions, *Unlawful Death of Refugees and Migrants,* supra note 84, para 35.

[88] ECtHR, Case *N.D. and N.T.* v. *Spain*, Appl. No. 8675/15 and 8697/15, Grand Chamber judgment of 13 February 2020.

[89] Mussi (2020); Hakiki (2020); and Carrera (2020).

considerations of national security notwithstanding—must not be theoretical or illusory, but practical and effective.[90]

6 Conclusions

> "When I use a word," Humpty Dumpty said, in rather a scornful tone, "it means just what I choose it to mean—neither more nor less." "The question is," said Alice, "whether you can make words mean so many different things." "The question is," said Humpty Dumpty, "which is to be master—that's all."
>
> (Lewis Carroll, *Through the Looking-Glass and What Alice Found There,* 1871)

Words matter and some weigh more than others. "National security" and "threat", for instance, carry loaded meaning and entail potentially far-reaching consequences. They should be used carefully and parsimoniously and their meaning, as well as the corresponding applicable rules and limitations, should be defined with the utmost precision. Instead, they are ubiquitous and, at the same time, extremely elusive. On the one hand, they are used as buzzwords to justify almost everything States do, be it in the context of counter-terrorism or migratory policies. On the other hand, their vague nature lends itself to the abusive interpretation of their meaning, which, in turn, can lead to the perpetration of gross human rights violations, usually followed by impunity. The lack of a clear definition becomes even more problematic because those called upon to interpret and apply such influential notions are ultimately those who hold the power and do not like to see themselves as anything less than almighty, persuaded that they are entitled to use all means, including the extremely powerful and shady "State secret", at their whim. This is especially troublesome, bearing in mind that to be master does not necessarily mean to be good. Among masters, such as among States, there are villains, swindlers and bullies. If they are those who have to interpret and apply what their own "national security" means, and what "threats" they are entitled to fight with *carte blanche*, the outcome cannot be anything other than poor.

Recurring trends and challenges concerning national security call for a paradigm shift, where the notion of security—and the corresponding threats—are clearly defined and interpreted not through purely State-centred lenses, but through the rule of law and international human rights law.

Most of Professor Scovazzi's writings[91] or lectures on international human rights law—no matter the specific issue they deal with—contain references to the judgment

[90] In this sense, *infra* Sect. 6 and, in a seminal judgment specifically concerning migrants, ECtHR, Case *Hirsi Jamaa and others* v. *Italy*, Appl. No. 27765/09, judgment of 23 February 2012, para 175. Similarly, for an example of sound jurisprudence, which upholds the absolute nature of certain rights in cases, involving migrants (consideration of national security notwithstanding), see, IACtHR, Case of *Nadege Dorzema and others* v. *Dominican Republic*, judgment of 24 October 2012, Ser. C No. 251.

[91] Scovazzi and Arcari (2018), pp. 127–129; Scovazzi and Citroni (2013), pp. 93–95.

delivered by the ECtHR on the case *Artico* v. *Italy*[92] and, on many occasions, I jokingly told him that it was not the *alpha* and the *omega* of the jurisprudence or of the subject in general. Hence, when we did discuss national security, his interpretation of such a notion and the relevant literature, he ironically observed that, much to his regret, he has never dealt with this very issue in his "few" contributions on the *Artico* case.

True as it is that the case has, in principle, no link whatsoever with national security (it concerns the right to free legal aid), the reasons that Professor Scovazzi always quotes it actually do. The poor—to say the least—arguments put forward by Italy during the proceedings before the ECtHR, show once more that a State can be the villain of the piece and, with its despicable procedural behaviour, highlight the superior dignity of the applicant, albeit the latter is a convicted habitual offender who, nevertheless, has a better understanding of the true meaning of human rights. As the ECtHR affirmed in its judgment, human rights treaties, such as the ECHR, are intended to "guarantee not rights that are theoretical or illusory but rights that are practical and effective".[93] States should therefore refrain from quibbles and legal technicalities, clearly define notions and terms (such as "national security" and "threat") which, if construed too broadly, can have unwarranted ramifications, and embrace a similarly straightforward interpretation of international human rights law and their corresponding obligations. National security and human rights are not opposites and the relationship between the two must be set straight.

To set the foundations of the definition of security and its link with human rights, and to identify the boundaries that States must respect, one can quote the former Deputy High Commissioner for Human Rights of the United Nations:

> individual security must be the basis for national security, and national security grounded in individual security must be the basis of international security. National security and international security cannot be achieved without respect for individual security in the form of respect for human rights and fundamental freedoms.[94]

It must be added that "national security" can never equate to *carte blanche* for States' behaviours, as they must adhere to limiting principles that reflect the values of individual rights, constitutionalism and accountability.

Once I asked Professor Scovazzi how he would define national security and he sharply replied "the very protection of human rights – practical and effective – for all". I would add to this full accountability, without excuses or exceptions, when such rights are violated. I reckon, after all, naïve as it may sound, that this is what a State truly secure makes.

Acknowledgment The author is extremely grateful to the editors of the book and to Dr. Elena Carpanelli and Dr. Luca Gervasoni for their invaluable comments on an earlier version of this chapter. This is likely the first time that Prof. Tullio Scovazzi has not commented one of my

[92] ECtHR, Case *Artico* v. *Italy*, Appl. No. 6694/74, judgment of 13 May 1980.

[93] Ibidem, para 33.

[94] Ramcharan (2004), p. 40.

writings. I am sure that his cutting remarks and clever intuitions would have greatly enriched the quality of this chapter, but "secrecy" was required to ensure that this book came as a true surprise. I hope he will understand and I reassure him that I will continue pestering him with requests for reviews in the future.

References

Al-Rodhan N (2007) The five dimensions of global security – proposal for a multi-sum security principle. Palgrave Macmillan, London

Balzacq T (2003) Qu'est-ce que la sécurité nationale? Revue internationale et stratégique 25(4): 33–50

Basaran T (2011) Security, law and borders: at the limits of liberty, Routledge studies in liberty and security. Routledge, London

Bernstein A (17 May 2013) Jorge Rafael Videla, ruthless Argentine junta leader, dies at 87. The Washington Post

Bindenagel Šehović A (2018) Reimagining state and human security beyond borders. Palgrave MacMillan, London

Burke-White W (2004) Human rights and national security: the strategic correlation. Harv Human Rights J 17:249–280

Carpanelli E (2019) State Secrecy and International Human Rights Law. Giappichelli, Torino

Carrera S (2020) The Strasbourg Court Judgement N.D. and N.T. v Spain A Carte Blanche to Push Backs at EU External Borders?. EUI Working Paper. Available at https://www.cadmus.eui.eu/bitstream/handle/1814/66629/RSCAS%202020_21.pdf?sequence=1

Cassese A (1994) I diritti umani nel mondo contemporaneo. Laterza, Roma-Bari

Central Intelligence Agency (1953) A Study of Assassination. Langley. Available at https://www.cia.gov/library/readingroom/docs/DOC_0000135832.pdf

Citroni G, Scovazzi T (2006) Vos vas a aparecer muerto como aparecieron tus amigos, los demás. In: Pineschi L (ed) La tutela internazionale dei diritti umani: norme, garanzie, prassi. Giuffrè, Milano, pp 616–635

Dash R (1989) US Foreign Policy, National Security Doctrine, and Central America. Latin Am Persp 16(4):67–85

Dulitzky A (2019) The Latin American flavor of enforced disappearance. Chinese J Int Law 19(2): 423–489

Dycus S, Kellman B (2000) International law and national security. Int Legal Dev Rev 35(2): 811–837

Gasper D, Gómez O (2015) Human security thinking in practice 'personal security', 'citizen security' and comprehensive mappings. Contemp Polit 21(5):100–116

Golder B, Williams G (2006) Balancing national security and human rights: assessing the legal response of common law nations to the threat of terrorism. J Comp Policy Anal Res Pract 8(1): 43–62

Greenberg KJ (2009) What the torture memos tell us. Glob Polit Strategy 51(3):5–12

Hakiki H (2020) N.D. and N.T. v. Spain: Defining Strasbourg Position on Push Backs at Land Borders?. Available at https://strasbourgobservers.com/2020/03/26/n-d-and-n-t-v-spain-defining-strasbourgs-position-on-push-backs-at-land-borders/

MacFarlane N, Foong Kong Y (2006) Human security and the UN: a critical history. Indiana University Press, Bloomington and Indianapolis

May E (1991) National security in American history. In: Allison GT, Treverton G (eds) Rethinking America's security: beyond cold war to new world order. Norton, New York, pp 230–260

McSherry JP (2005) Predatory states: operation condor and covert war in Latin America. Rowman & Littlefield Publishers, Lanham

Mendel T (2013) Defining the Scope of National Security: Issues Paper for the National Security Principles Project. Available https://www.right2info.org/resources/publications/mendel-on-defining-national-security
Mussi F (2020) La sentenza N.D. e N.T. della Corte Europea dei Diritti Umani: uno "schiaffo" ai diritti dei migranti alle frontiere terrestri?. SIDI Blog. Available at http://www.sidiblog.org/2020/03/19/la-sentenza-n-d-e-n-t-della-corte-europea-dei-diritti-umani-uno-schiaffo-ai-diritti-dei-migranti-alle-frontiere-terrestri/
National Commission on the Disappearance of Persons (1984) Never again! [English edition] Faber & Faber Ltd., London
Nolte G (2005) Sovereignty as responsibility? Proc Am Soc Int Law Annual Meeting 99:389–392
Osorio C, Tandeciarz S, Weech J (eds) (2019) Inside Argentina's killing machine: US intelligence documents record gruesome human rights crimes of 1976-1983. National Security Archive, Washington
Pion-Berlin D (1988) The National Security Doctrine, military threat perception, and the "Dirty War" in Argentina. Comp Polit Stud:382–407
Posner E, Vermeule A (2007) Terror in the balance: security, liberty and the courts. OUP, Oxford
Ramcharan B (2004) Human rights and human security. Disarmament Forum 39–47
Robin MM (2004) Escadrons de la Mort: L'école Français. La découverte, Paris
Rosenberg T (1991) Children of Cain: violence and the violent in Latin America. William Morrow & C, New York
Scovazzi T (2006) Tortura e formalismi giuridici di basso profilo. Rivista di diritto internazionale 89(4):905–947
Scovazzi T (2009a) La Repubblica riconosce e garantisce i diritti inviolabili della segretezza e delle relazioni tra i servizi informativi italiani e stranieri? Rivista di diritto internazionale 4:959–992
Scovazzi T (2009b) Considerazioni in tema di segreto di Stato e gravi violazioni dei diritti umani. In: Venturini G, Bariatti S (eds) Diritti individuali e giustizia internazionale – Liber Fausto Pocar. Giuffrè, Milano, pp 885–900
Scovazzi T (2013) Le forme di riparazione non pecuniaria dovute alle vittime di gravi violazioni ai diritti umani. I sentieri della ricerca 16:93–109
Scovazzi T (2014) Il lato oscuro dei diritti umani: aspetti di diritto internazionale. In: Meccarelli M, Palchetti P, Sotis C (eds) Il lato oscuro dei diritti umani – Esigenze emancipatorie e logiche di dominio nella tutela giuridica dell'individuo. Ed. Universidad Carlos III, Madrid, pp 115–136
Scovazzi T (2016) Segreto di Stato e diritti umani: il sipario nero sul caso Abu Omar. Diritti umani e diritto internazionale 10(1):157–184
Scovazzi T (2018) Il segreto di Stato nel caso Abu Omar: un sorprendente conflitto tra poteri dello Stato. In: Forni L, Vettor T (eds) Sicurezza e libertà in tempi di terrorismo globale. Giappichelli, Torino, pp 239–252
Scovazzi T (2020a) Il caso 'Abu Omar': Corte EDU, Nasr e Ghali c. Italia (IV sezione, 23 febbraio 2016). In: Ríos Vega E, Spigno I (eds) La crisi dei diritti umani – La visione della giustizia regionale. Editoriale Scientifica, Napoli, 165–180
Scovazzi T (2020b) Foreword. In: Carcano A (ed) Notable cases of the European Court of Human Rights on the rights to life. Giappichelli, Torino, pp xi–xii
Scovazzi T, Arcari M (2018) Corso di diritto internazionale – parte I. Giuffrè, Milano
Scovazzi T, Citroni G (2013) Corso di diritto internazionale – parte III. Giuffrè, Milano
Shani G (2013) From national to human security? Reflection on post 3.11 Japan. J Soc Sci 76:5–24
Shlaudeman H (1976) ARA Monthly Report (July), The "Third World War" and South America. The National Security Archive. Available at https://nsarchive2.gwu.edu/NSAEBB/NSAEBB125/condor05.pdf
Sorel JM (2014) Is the wall soluble into international law? In: Vallet E (ed) Borders, Fences and Walls: state of insecurity? Routledge, London, pp 131–141
Thakur R (2016) Human security and human rights. In: The United Nations, peace and security: from collective security to the responsibility to protect. CUP, Cambridge, pp 79–107
United Nations Development Programme (1994) Human Development Report. OUP, Oxford

Starvation and Humanitarian Assistance in Time of Armed Conflicts

Matteo Fornari

Abstract The recent practice (i.e. the conflicts in Syria and Yemen) shows that civilians are very often intentionally starved by the belligerents, often on the basis of mere suspicion that being a part of the civilian population means that they would sympathize with a belligerent. This is in sharp contrast with the normative body prohibiting the tactics of starvation of the civilian population as a method of war, provided for in the 1977 Geneva Protocols and by customary law. The attention of this chapter will focus on how this method of war is put into practice, through the destruction of objects indispensable for the survival of the civilian population and of siege warfare. An interesting development around this issue is the amendment of the International Criminal Court Statute, introducing the crime of starvation of civilians in non-international armed conflicts; and UN Security Council (UNSC) Resolution 2417 (2018), in which the UNSC stressed for the first time, in general terms, the direct impact of armed conflicts on food security.

1 Introduction

In December 2019 the International Criminal Court (ICC) Assembly of States Parties adopted by consensus an amendment to Article 8 of the Rome Statute, proposed by Switzerland, introducing the crime of starvation of civilians in non-international armed conflicts.[1] In May 2018, the UN Security Council (UNSC) adopted Resolution 2417,[2] in which it emphasised the direct impact of armed conflicts on food security. In particular, it underlined that "using starvation of civilians as a method of warfare may constitute a war crime" (preamble) and

[1]ICC Assembly of States Parties, Resolution on Amendments to Article 8 of the Rome Statute of the International Criminal Court, 6 December 2019, ICC-ASP/18/Resolution5.

[2]UNSC Resolution 2417 (2018), 24 May 2018.

M. Fornari (✉)
University of Milano-Bicocca, Milan, Italy
e-mail: matteo.fornari@unimib.it

M. Arcari et al. (eds.), *Trends and Challenges in International Law*,
https://doi.org/10.1007/978-3-030-94387-5_4

condemned both "the use of starvation as a method of warfare in a number of conflict situations" (paragraph 5) and "the unlawful denial of humanitarian access and depriving civilians of objects indispensable to their survival" (paragraph 6).

These facts show, on one hand, that the use of starvation is a constant of armed conflicts throughout history, notwithstanding an express prohibition of this method of warfare provided for by treaty instruments, such as the two 1977 Additional Protocols to the Geneva Conventions of 1949—Article 54 of I Protocol (AP I) and Article 14 of II Protocol (AP II);[3] on the other hand, the legal vacuum created by the absence of a provision criminalizing starvation in internal conflict has only recently been filled. This despite the fact that, in relation to the protection of civilians, the distinction between international and non-international armed conflicts no longer has any real basis.[4]

Armed conflicts present a range of methods used to defeat the enemy (irrespective of whether these actions are lawful or not), from direct attacks against enemy forces and military positions, to involvement in the conflict of the adverse civilian population. Given that food is an essential condition for life, even the recent practice of conflicts shows that starvation continues to be a method of warfare often applied by belligerents to break down the resistance of the enemy. But if there is little doubt regarding the legality of starving enemy combatants,[5] the starvation of civilians as a method of warfare is prohibited by the current law of armed conflict.[6]

[3]Protocol I, Article 54 (Protection of objects indispensable to the survival of the civilian population): "1. Starvation of civilians as a method of warfare is prohibited. 2. It is prohibited to attack, destroy, remove or render useless objects indispensable to the survival of the civilian population, such as foodstuffs, agricultural areas for the production of foodstuffs, crops, livestock, drinking water installations and supplies and irrigation works, for the specific purpose of denying them for their sustenance value to the civilian population or to the adverse Party, whatever the motive, whether in order to starve out civilians, to cause them to move away, or for any other motive. 3. The prohibitions in paragraph 2 shall not apply to such of the objects covered by it as are used by an adverse Party: a) as sustenance solely for the members of its armed forces; or b) if not as sustenance, then in direct support of military action, provided, however, that in no event shall actions against these objects be taken which may be expected to leave the civilian population with such inadequate food or water as to cause its starvation or force its movement. 4. These objects shall not be made the object of reprisals. 5. In recognition of the vital requirements of any Party to the conflict in the defence of its national territory against invasion, derogation from the prohibitions contained in paragraph 2 may be made by a Party to the conflict within such territory under its own control where required by imperative military necessity". Protocol II, Article 14 (Protection of objects indispensable to the survival of the civilian population): "Starvation of civilians as a method of combat is prohibited. It is therefore prohibited to attack, destroy, remove or render useless, for that purpose, objects indispensable to the survival of the civilian population, such as foodstuffs, agricultural areas for the production of foodstuffs, crops, livestock, drinking water installations and supplies and irrigation works".

[4]Prosecutor v. Dusko Tadić—Decision on the Defence Motion for Interlocutory Appeal on Jurisdiction, 2 October 1995, para 97.

[5]See infra, Sect. 3.

[6]Supra, fn 3.

Nevertheless, there are countless cases of starvation of civilians in armed conflicts throughout history.[7] By way of example, a notorious case where starvation was used as a method of warfare was Biafra's war of secession from Nigeria (1967–1970). Having difficulties stopping the armed actions of the rebel forces operating in the south-eastern provinces, the Federal Nigerian Army laid siege to the Biafran area and blocked humanitarian relief to the civilian population;[8] the Nigerian government claimed that the starvation of civilians was a legitimate form of warfare.[9] During the Geneva diplomatic conference on the reaffirmation and development of international humanitarian law (hereinafter: the Geneva conference), the delegate from the Democratic Republic of Vietnam stressed "the vital importance of dykes in agricultural countries", saying that "aggressors always tended to attack them in order to starve the civilian population".[10] In 1987, the 4 month siege of Palestinian camps in Lebanon by Amal Shiite Moslem forces forced inhabitants to eat rats so as not to starve. The same year, Sri Lanka forces blocked the Jaffna Peninsula, controlled by the Tamil rebels, causing a serious food shortage.[11] In Somalia in 1992 the parties to the conflict deliberately impeded the delivery of essential food and medical supplies. During the siege of the enclaves in Bosnia and Herzegovina, civilians were systematically deprived of assistance that was necessary for their survival.[12]

More recently, serious humanitarian crises have occurred during armed conflicts in Syria, South Sudan and Yemen. In 2012, Syrian government forces attacked bakeries in Aleppo province, killing numerous civilians waiting for bread: it was a clear tactic designed to spread terror among civilians so that they were afraid to get food.[13] Again, since July 2013, Syrian government forces have prevented all food, medicine and other supplies from entering Yarmouk, a district south of Damascus,

---

[7] For the medieval era, see Settia (2009), p. 109 ss.; Luisi (2017), pp. 167 ff.

[8] Mertens (1969), pp. 191 ff.

[9] Allen (1989), p. 5.

[10] According to the Vietnamese representative, during the war in Viet-Nam "561 sections of dyke had been either damaged or destroyed… the bombing of the dykes in North Viet-Nam, carried out systematically with explosive and penetration bombs, could have effects comparable to those of a hydrogen bomb: flooding of the delta, destruction of the summer and autumn rice harvest and the death of two or three million inhabitants by drowning or starvation": Official Records of the Diplomatic Conference on the Reaffirmation and Development of International Humanitarian Law Applicable in Armed Conflicts, Geneva (1974–1977), Volume XIV, 161.

[11] Provost (1992), p. 633.

[12] Report of the Secretary-General to the Security Council on the Protection of Civilians in Armed Conflict (1999). UN Doc. S/1999/9578, para 19.

[13] Human Rights Watch (2012); Report of the Independent International Commission of Inquiry on the Syrian Arab Republic, UN Doc. A/HRC/34/64, 2 February 2017, para 41: "Repeated attacks against markets, bakeries and other food sources indispensable for civilian life have been a hallmark of the prolonged siege laid to eastern Aleppo city, violating the right to regular, permanent and unrestricted access to sufficient food…The total number of markets and bakeries attacked from the air during the period under review is indicative of a pattern on the part of pro-Government forces of intentionally violating this right by targeting civilian infrastructure in order to compel the surrender of armed groups".

exposing the inhabitants to rampant malnutrition, leading to scores of deaths from starvation, as well widespread illness.[14] In addition, as stated by the United Nations Secretary-General, the conflict in Yemen has created "the world's worst humanitarian crisis",[15] in which

> 24 million people – 80 per cent of the population – need humanitarian aid and protection... Twenty million people cannot reliably feed themselves or their families. And almost 10 million are just one step away from famine.[16]

Again, as stressed by a report of Human Rights Council released in October 2020, in some areas of South Sudan

> [t]here has been a discernible spike in food insecurity... which is linked directly to the conflict and therefore almost entirely human-induced. Pervasive human rights violations, including deliberate strategies on the part of both Government and opposition forces to use starvation as a method of warfare, have contributed to the food insecurity,[17]

creating a situation with more than 290,000 children currently suffering from severe acute malnutrition, and more than one million children suffering from moderate acute malnutrition.[18]

This contribution starts with a brief analysis on the meaning of "starvation as a method of warfare" (Sect. 2); then, after having considered if and how the fighters can be starved (Sect. 3), attention will be focused on the customary value of the prohibition of starvation (Sect. 4), and how this method of war is put into practice against civilians, through the destruction of objects indispensable for the survival of the civilian population (Sect. 5) and siege warfare (Sect. 6). The prevention of starvation through humanitarian assistance is an important aspect of this issue (Sect. 7). Finally, it seems of interest to analyze the action of the UNSC on humanitarian assistance, in the light of the latest (Sect. 8).

---

[14] Amnesty International (2014), pp. 10–11: "For months residents survived scouring the area for anything that might be edible, including cactus leaves, dandelion leaves and other plants. Hunger has driven many to expose themselves to government snipers while searching for food".

[15] Secretary-General's remarks to the Pledging Conference on Yemen (3 April 2018). www.un.org/sg/en/content/sg/statement/2018-04-03/secretary-generals-remarks-pledging-conference-yemen-delivered.

[16] Secretary-General's remarks to the Pledging Conference for Yemen (26 February 2019). www.un.org/sg/en/content/sg/statement/2019-02-26/secretary-generals-remarks-the-pledging-conference-for-yemen-delivered-%C2%A0.

[17] "There is Nothing Left for Us": Starvation as a Method of Warfare in South Sudan. UN Doc A/HRC/45/CRP.3, 5 October 2020, para 6.

[18] Integrated Food Security Phase Classification (IPC) (February 2020) Acute Food Insecurity and Acute Malnutrition Analysis, January 2020–July 2020, p. 7. www.ipcinfo.org/fileadmin/user_upload/ipcinfo/docs/IPC_SouthSudan_AFI_AMN_2020Jan2020July.pdf.

2 Starvation as a Method of Warfare

The term "starvation" is generally understood as "the action of subjecting people to famine, which is in turn defined as extreme and general scarcity of food, or severe lack of food"; it is worth noting that famine is also a question of access to food, not only an issue of food availability. Defined as extreme suffering or death caused by the lack of food, the term starvation does not necessarily imply death.[19]

As for the objects considered indispensable to the survival of the civilian population, the 1977 Protocols adopted an illustrative approach, as the list of these objects contained in Article 54 of AP I and Article 14 of AP II is not exhaustive. As observed by the United States ambassador who participated in the Geneva negotiations, "the list given (all relating to food and drink) includes every item that could be identified as *always* indispensable".[20] But starvation is not necessarily restricted to deprivation of food and water; it can be caused by the deprivation of other essential things or something necessary to live, such as medical supplies, clothing, shelter in certain climatic conditions, or the destruction or damage of objects needed to harvest and process food.[21] For instance, with regard to starvation caused by deprivation of water as a method of war, the Commission of inquiry on Darfur ascertained that the Janjaweed militias poisoned water by dropping the carcasses of cattle into the wells of the attacked villages.[22]

Under the law of armed conflict, Article 54 of the I Protocol (AP I) refers to starvation as a method of warfare—or method of combat, as stressed by Article 14 of the II Protocol (AP II)—used "to annihilate or weaken the population".[23] "Methods of warfare" refers to the way weapons are used in war; in particular, this notion refers to the way and manner in which the weapons are used; and any specific, tactical or strategic, ways of conducting hostilities that are not particularly related to weapons and that are intended to overwhelm and weaken the adversary.[24] Used as a weapon,

---

[19]Report of the Detailed Findings of the Group of Eminent International and Regional Experts on Yemen. Situation of Human Rights in Yemen, including Violations and Abuses since September 2014, UN Doc. A/HRC/42/CRP.13, September 2019, para 739.

[20]Aldrich (1981), p. 779.

[21]Triffterer and Ambos (2016), para 768–769; Dörmann (2004), p. 363. See Akande and Gillard (2019), pp. 758 f. At the Geneva Conference proposals to add other items, such as communication systems for food distribution and fuel reservoirs, were rejected, as such items were considered to be often, if not always, important military objectives: Official Records of the Diplomatic Conference on the Reaffirmation and Development of International Humanitarian Law Applicable in Armed Conflicts. Geneva (1974–1977), Vol. XIV, 1978, p. 142, para 7, p. 146, para 21. In this respect, Additional Protocol II considers food and medical supplies as objects indispensable to the survival of the civilian population, while Additional Protocol I also mentions clothing, bedding and means of shelter: Article 18, para 2, of AP II and Article 69 of AP I.

[22]Report of the International Commission of Inquiry on Darfur to the United Nations Secretary-General, 25 January 2005, para 305.

[23]Sandoz et al. (1987), para 2090.

[24]Gaggioli and Melzer (2020), p. 237.

starvation weakens the enemy's war capability and demoralizes the population. This implies that the prohibition of starvation may be violated in different manners, by attacking objects indispensable to the survival of the population, siege warfare, or arbitrary denial of access of humanitarian aid to civilians in need.

Hence, starvation can be considered as an attack when the action of depriving of food or essential goods causes harmful consequences and effects to the enemy which are similar in gravity to an armed attack. This seems to be confirmed by Article 17 of the Lieber Code, which stresses that "[war] is not carried on by arms alone". It is lawful to starve the hostile belligerent, armed or unarmed, so that it leads to the speedier subjection of the enemy.

The two additional Protocols do not include the adjective "armed" when referring to attacks—defined as "acts of violence against the opponent" (Article 49 of I Protocol)—conducted by a belligerent party.[25] Such absence has the consequence of widening the content of the notion of "attack", so as to include those unarmed hostile actions which also cause the destruction of enemy forces (or of the civilian population of the enemy belligerent). For example, the opening of a dam, resulting in the release of a large quantity of water to cause the drowning of enemy military forces or the flooding and destruction of crops located downstream of the dam. This is obviously an unarmed action, but it can be considered an attack against the enemy due to the consequences produced. During the Geneva Conference, the example of the use of defoliants as an act of destruction was made, even if it might not perhaps be considered an armed attack.[26] Attention to characterizing a hostile action against enemy forces should be paid not so much to the fact that it is "armed", but rather to the harmful consequences for the enemy (and the civilian population of the enemy belligerent).

Moreover, it is worth noting that the notion of "method of warfare" is to be understood in a broad sense, that is irrespective of the permissibility or legality of the particular manner of using weapons or conducting hostilities. As stated by Article 54, para 2, of AP I, the prohibition of starvation applies "whatever the motive" of the attacking belligerent. It means that starvation certainly covers starvation aimed at gaining a military advantage, such as to pressure the enemy to accept certain conditions or other aims; but to qualify starvation as a "method of warfare", the belligerent is not required to obtain a military advantage on the battlefield. Using starvation to obtain other objectives, such as ethnic cleansing of an area, to force civilians to abandon their homes or simply to annihilate a civilian population, would

---

[25] AP II does not define the term "attack", but it is generally assumed that this term considered in Article 49 of AP I "has the same meaning in Protocol II": Sandoz et al. (1987), para 4783; Schmitt et al. (2006), p. 7.

[26] Official Records of the Diplomatic Conference on the Reaffirmation and Development of International Humanitarian Law Applicable in Armed Conflicts. Geneva (1974–1977), Vol. XIV, 1978, p. 136, para 41.

fall within the prohibition as incompatible with the general principle of protecting the civilian population.[27]

3 Starvation of Fighters

In both an international armed conflict (IAC) and a non-international armed conflict (NIAC), whomever participates in hostilities is a legitimate military objective. Where the certainty exists that only fighters are present in a theatre of war, the belligerent has no duty to observe certain restraints on the conduct of hostilities, such as the principles of distinction and proportionality. As these principles must be taken into account in the planning and execution of an attack where there is a risk of involving civilians in this action, the proportionality rule is only to be applied when civilians or civilian objects are at risk of harm from attacks on military objectives. As a consequence, the law of war does not impose any limit on the degree of force directed against enemy forces.[28]

Applying this consideration to the question of the starvation of fighters, the legality of this method of war may be inferred. Hence, starvation is justified for the purpose of forcing the enemy to surrender.[29] For example in 1952–1954, during the campaign against communist guerrillas in Malaya, the British, after having forced the insurgents to withdraw from populated areas into deep jungle to cultivate their own food, used to spray food crops affecting their ability to survive.[30]

The legality of starving belligerent enemies is in line with treaty law. The destruction of enemy property—such as, for example, foodstuffs intended *exclusively* for enemy military forces—is permitted if "imperatively demanded by the necessities of war" (Article 23(g) of the 1907 Hague Regulations). In addition, the AP I provides for a derogation from attacking or destroying objects indispensable to

[27] See Sandoz et al. (1987), para 2089 f.; Triffterer and Ambos (2016), para 794 f.; Akande and Gillard (2019), p. 765.

[28] See United States Department of Defense (2015), para 5.12.1.

[29] See the Instructions for the Government of Armies of the United States in the Field, General Order No. 100 (Lieber Code), 24 April 1863, Article 15: "military necessity . . . allows . . . of all withholding of sustenance or means of life from the enemy; of the appropriation of whatever an enemy's country affords necessary for the subsistence and safety of the army"; Article 17: "It is lawful to starve the hostile belligerent, armed or unarmed, so that it leads to the speedier subjection of the enemy".

[30] Buckingham (1982), pp. 4 f. More questionable, for the violations of the principle of distinction, seems to be the massive use of defoliants and herbicides by the United States in the Vietnam War, even if the US Law of War Manual stresses that during this conflict "the VC [Viet Cong] had suffered serious personnel losses due to the lack of food. Troops normally used in fighting had to be detailed to crop raising, and in one case the 95th North Vietnamese Army (NVA) regiment had to fast for one or two days on several occasions due to a lack of food. The overall conclusion... was that crop destruction was 'an integral, essential and effective part of the total effort in South Vietnam'": United States Department of Defense (2015), para 5.20.1, fn 610.

the survival of the civilian population (such as foodstuffs, agricultural areas or drinking waters installations) if these resources are used by an adverse Party "as a sustenance *solely* for the members of its armed forces" (Article 54, paragraph 3a),[31] or if they are used

> in direct support of military action, provided, however, that in no event shall actions against these objects be taken which may be expected to leave the civilian population with such inadequate food or water as to cause its starvation or force its movement (Article 54, paragraph 3b).[32]

By way of example, the expression "direct support of military action" could refer to a food-producing area used by the enemy to advance hidden through it, or a food-storage barn used by the enemy forces for cover or as an arms depot.[33] In these scenarios, these objects could be lawfully destroyed by military necessity, provided that such destruction does not starve the civilian population.

However, it seems that it is not always easy to establish whether some resources or foodstuffs are used *exclusively* by armed forces.[34] During the Secession War and the Boer Wars, the Union Army and the British Army destroyed crops used by the enemy forces, but it is not clear if these resources were also used for the subsistence of the civilian population. Some authors have been indulgent about the destruction of these crops, assuming that this conduct was dictated by military necessity and concerned only the *surplus* consumed by enemy armed forces.[35] As regards the Vietnam War, it has been observed that the use of herbicides against rice fields in the regions under the control of the Viet Cong was to be condemned, given that it was unlikely in the extreme that the harvests of rice in these fields were intended only for

---

[31] Italics added by the author. As observed during the diplomatic conference on international humanitarian law, this derogation "was intended to apply only to those objects which clearly are assigned solely for the sustenance of the armed forces": Official Records of the Diplomatic Conference on the Reaffirmation and Development of International Humanitarian Law Applicable in Armed Conflicts, Geneva (1974–1977) Vol. XV, CDDH/215/Rev.l, para 76, p. 280.

[32] This exception is set forth in several military manuals of several States, such as Australia, Belgium, Canada, Israel, Netherlands, New Zealand, Spain, Sweden and Yugoslavia and in the legislation of Spain. See also the statements of Colombia and United States: Henckaerts and Doswald-Beck (2005), Vol. II Practice, Part. 1, para 313 ff.

[33] Sandoz et al. (1987), para 2110. During World War II, German fat imports were considered a direct support to military action because fats were used to make explosives: Provost (1992), p. 606.

[34] According to the 1956 United States manual of warfare, it is not prohibited to adopt measures "to dry up springs, to divert rivers and aqueducts from their courses, or to destroy, through chemical or bacterial agents harmless to man, crops intended solely for consumption by the armed forces (if that fact can be determined)": The Law of Land Warfare, FM 27-10, July 1956, para 37.

[35] According to Spaight (1911), p. 138, "[i]f there is a war right to destroy the enemy's food supplies, and if, under such peculiar conditions as existed in the Confederate States and in South Africa, the course of events has brought it about that the enemy depends for his supplies on the surplus of cereals, etc., held by the noncombatant population, then a commander is justified by the necessities of war in destroying or seizing that surplus... and it must be remembered that the Boer farmers were well compensated for the destruction of their farms and crops at the close of the war".

the feeding of the Vietcong fighters and that this destruction therefore deliberately affected the civilian population.[36]

Moreover, it is worth noting that with regard to non-international armed conflicts, Article 14 of AP II does not provide for the exceptions envisaged in Article 54, paragraph 3, of the AP I and there is no practice supporting it. Accordingly, it would be doubtful whether those exceptions apply to internal conflicts.[37]

Having said that, one should bear in mind that the "freedom" to starve enemy forces should be assessed in the light of the general limit according to which the right of belligerents to adopt means of injuring the enemy is not unlimited, as stressed by the Hague Regulations of 1907 (Article 22) and AP I (Article 35, paragraph 1).[38] If the final goal is to win the war, weakening the military forces of the enemy without causing unnecessary suffering (1868 Saint Petersburg Declaration; Article 35, paragraph 2 of AP I),[39] it follows that the object of starving combatants is to induce them to capitulate or surrender, not to starve them to death.

Lastly, the starvation of fighters is to be assessed in the light of Article 50, paragraph 3, of AP I. In accordance with the principle of distinction (the "basic rule" as defined by Article 48 of AP I) this article stresses that "[t]he presence within the civilian population of individuals who do not come within the definition of civilians does not deprive the population of its civilian character". In other words, the presence of members of enemy forces among a civilian population does not deprive civilians of immunity from attacks.[40] It follows that it is prohibited to resort to starvation against these soldiers if such a tactic will cause the starvation of civilians, since consequences similar to those resulting from an indiscriminate attack would likely be produced.

[36] Meyrowitz (1985), p. 190. Another very objectionable destruction of products and instruments essential for the subsistence of civilians was the destruction of the properties of the Russian fishermen by the English cruisers in the sea of Azoff during the Crimean War. It can hardly be maintained that the destruction of fish-stores, fisheries, nets, boats, and even the homesteads of these fishermen was essential to the defeat of the Russian Army: Nolan (1857), p. 598.

[37] Henckaerts and Doswald-Beck (2005), Vol. I Rules, p. 192.

[38] Article 35, para 1, of the I Protocol: "In any armed conflict, the right of the Parties to the conflict to choose methods or means of warfare is not unlimited".

[39] Article 35, para 2, of the I Protocol: "It is prohibited to employ weapons, projectiles and material and methods of warfare of a nature to cause superfluous injury or unnecessary suffering".

[40] See Prosecutor v. Dusko Tadić. Opinion and Judgment 7 May 1997, para 638: "it is clear that the targeted population must be of a predominantly civilian nature. The presence of certain non-civilians in their midst does not change the character of the population".

4 Prohibition of Starvation as a Customary Rule of International Law

As anticipated above, the 1977 Protocols prohibit starvation of the civilian population (Article 54, paragraph 1, of AP I and Article 14, first sentence, of AP II). This prohibition can be seen as a development of the previous discipline focused on the protection of civilians which was introduced by the IV Geneva Convention on the protection of civilian persons in time of war. At the Geneva Conference, the view was expressed that the scope of the introductory paragraph of Article 54 would be defined by the remainder of the provision and by the other relevant articles of the Protocol, particularly those dealing with relief actions and humanitarian assistance.[41]

Article 14 of AP II reproduces almost literally paragraph 1 of Article 54 of AP I, with the difference that, while the provision dedicated to IACs prohibits starvation as a "method of warfare", Article 14 prohibits starvation as a "method of combat". During the Conference, States preferred the expression "methods of warfare" to be applied to IACs, because the term "combat" could be given a narrower interpretation than the word "warfare" and because it was considered inappropriate to refer to warfare in a Protocol dedicated to NIACs.[42] Be that as it may, international humanitarian law strictly prohibits starvation of the civilian population as a method of warfare, in both international and non-international armed conflicts, as enshrined in treaty law and now recognised under customary international humanitarian law.[43] Moreover, the prohibition of starvation binds both States and non-State armed groups and does not provide for any exception in the case of imperative military necessity.[44]

As a new rule introduced in the Protocols, it is not totally clear whether before its adoption, the prohibition of starvation had already acquired customary value.[45] During the United States Secession War, the blockade of southern States through

[41] Official Records of the Diplomatic Conference on the Reaffirmation and Development of International Humanitarian Law Applicable in Armed Conflicts, Geneva (1974–1977), Vol. XV, CDDH/264/Rev.1, p. 348 f. Ibidem, CDDH/215/Rev.1, p. 279, para 73: "Paragraph 1 was accepted after considerable discussion as a useful statement of the basic principle from which the rest of the article flows and as an important addition to the law protecting civilians. The scope of the principle will be defined by the remainder of the article and by the other relevant articles in the Protocol, particularly those dealing with relief actions". On the question of the humanitarian assistance see *infra*, Sect. 7.

[42] Official Records of the Diplomatic Conference on the Reaffirmation and Development of International Humanitarian Law Applicable in Armed Conflicts, Geneva (1974–1977), Vol. XV, CDDH/215/Rev.l, p. 267, para 20; CDDH/236/Rev.l, p. 394, para 57.

[43] Henckaerts and Doswald-Beck (2005), Vol. I Rules, Rule 53.

[44] Situation of human rights in Yemen, including violations and abuses since September 2014—Report of the detailed findings of the Group of Eminent International and Regional Experts on Yemen, UN Doc. A/HRC/42/CRP.1, 3 September 2019, para 738.

[45] According to Solf (1986), p. 133: "By prohibiting the starvation of civilians as a method of warfare, article 54 establishes a substantially new principle which is not yet customary international law".

the destruction of railroads lines was in part aimed at starving the Confederacy, and Union troops deliberately destroyed food supplies and farm machinery. As Sherman said: "We are not only fighting hostile armies but a hostile people".[46] During the Franco-Prussian War (1870–1871), Metz and Paris were reduced to submission partly by bombardment and partly by starvation; Bismarck stated that it was uncertain which of starvation and bombardment was the more humane. According to him, both were legitimate methods of war for overcoming the enemy.[47] On the other hand, during the First World War the Anglo-French blockade was criticized by Germany on the ground that its aim was to reduce the civil population to starvation. The Imperial Chancellor, Bethmann Hollweg, in 1916 declared it to be contrary to international law, because the blockade sought "to starve [German people] out and to extend the war to the entire German nation, to... women and... children".[48] As regards the Biafra's war of secession from Nigeria, characterized also by the use of starvation as a method of war by Nigerian armed forces, on 7 July 1969 British Foreign Secretary, Michael Stewart, declared before the House of Commons: "We must accept that, in the whole history of warfare, any nation which has been in a position to starve its enemy out has done so"; however, it is not clear whether the Foreign Secretary was referring only to the starvation of enemy fighters or also of the civilian population.[49] And in 2005, in the case of the bombardment of the Harsile reservoir, the Eritrea-Ethiopia Claims Commission, observed that

> Article 54 represented a significant advance in the prior law when it was included in the Protocol in 1977, so it cannot be presumed that it had become part of customary international humanitarian law more than 20 years later.[50]

However, since then, national and international practice has shown the affirmation of a corresponding customary rule. Numerous examples of national legislation and military manuals, including those of States not party to APs I and II, prohibit starvation of the civilian population;[51] for example, the Law of War Manual of the

[46] Liddell Hart (1958), p. 358. According to Article 17 of the Lieber Code (*supra*, fn. 23), "[i]t is lawful to starve the hostile belligerent, armed or unarmed, so that it leads to the speedier subjection of the enemy". The term "unarmed" could be intended to also include the civilians; but, on the other hand, the Lieber Code is generally considered to be the first example of a legal text underlying a narrow application of military necessity (Article 16: "Military necessity does not admit of cruelty") and the principle of distinction (Article 22: "The principle has been more and more acknowledged that the unarmed citizen is to be spared in person, property, and honor as much as the exigencies of war will admit"): Allen (1989), pp. 33 f.

[47] Garner (1920), p. 337.

[48] Ibidem, p. 336.

[49] https://hansard.millbanksystems.com/commons/1969/jul/07/nigeria#S5CV0786P0_19690707_HOC_196.

[50] Eritrea-Ethiopia Claims Commission—Partial Award: Western Front, Aerial Bombardment and Related Claims—Eritrea's Claims 1, 3, 5, 9–13, 14, 21, 25 & 26, 19 December 2005 (2009). Reports of International Arbitral Awards, Vol. XXVI, para 104.

[51] Henckaerts and Doswald-Beck (2005), Vol. II Practice, pp. 1123 ff.

United States (not party to the 1977 Protocols) recognises that starvation is prohibited both in IACs and NIACs.[52] The national and international jurisprudence upholds the customary value of this prohibition. For example, the Eritrea-Ethiopia Claims Commission in the case of the bombardment of the Harsile reservoir, observed that none of the States Parties to the AP I had made any reservation or statement of interpretation rejecting or limiting the binding nature of this prohibition[53] and concluded that

> a treaty provision of a compelling humanitarian nature that has not been questioned by any statements of reservation or interpretation and is not inconsistent with general State practice in the two decades since the conclusion of the treaty may reasonably be considered to have come to reflect customary international humanitarian law.[54]

The conflict in the former Yugoslavia also seems to confirm the existence of a customary norm that prohibits starvation, since the belligerents committed themselves not to resort to this practice against civilians.[55] In addition, the Commission of experts established pursuant to UNSC Resolution 780 (1992) observed, in its final report, that "the use of starvation as a method of war, regardless of the modalities used, is also contrary to the customary law applicable in international armed conflicts".[56]

5 Starvation of Civilians: The Destruction of Objects Indispensable to the Survival

5.1 Recent Practice on the Destruction of Objects Indispensable to the Survival

In the ongoing Yemeni civil war, the Group of Experts established by the United Nations High Commissioner for Human Rights ascertained that "all parties to the conflict have used starvation as a method of warfare in Yemen by attacking objects indispensable to the survival of the population" (other than "imposing blockades or

---

[52] United States Department of Defense (2015), para 5.20.

[53] Eritrea-Ethiopia Claims Commission—Partial Award: Western Front, Aerial Bombardment and Related Claims—Eritrea's Claims 1, 3, 5, 9–13, 14, 21, 25 & 26, 19 December 2005 (2009). Reports of International Arbitral Awards, Vol. XXVI, para 104.

[54] Ibidem, para 105.

[55] Memorandum of Understanding on the Application of International Humanitarian Law between Croatia and the SFRY, 27 November 1991, para 6 (in https://casebook.icrc.org/case-study/former-yugoslavia-special-agreements-between-parties-conflicts); Agreement on the Application of IHL between the Parties to the Conflict in Bosnia and Herzegovina, 22 May 1992, para 2.5.

[56] Final Report of the Commission of Experts Established Pursuant to Security Council Resolution 780 (1992), UN Doc. S/1994/674, 27 May 1994, para 69.

using siege-like tactics, and impeding the delivery of humanitarian assistance"),[57] and "[a]ll parties to the conflict... used and conducted attacks impacting objects indispensable to the survival of the civilian population".[58] In particular, between June 2015 and 2019, the Saudi-led coalition air strikes systematically destroyed farms and agricultural land, water facilities and essential port infrastructure, following a strategy of hitting the infrastructure of rural life to cause starvation.[59] This war tactic by the anti-Houthi coalition is a clear example of a violation of the prohibition against the destruction of goods and infrastructure indispensable for the survival of the civilian population.

The civil war in Yemen is the most recent example of conflict characterized by the deliberate destruction of objects indispensable for the survival of the civilian population, but one can cite several examples of belligerent action clearly and solely intended to destroy the means of sustenance for civilians.

As for the internal conflict in South Sudan, in its report of 31 January 2020, the Commission on Human Rights ascertained that

> both government and opposition forces attacked, destroyed and rendered useless objects indispensable to the survival of the population and used starvation of civilians as means to achieve military objectives,

and

> deliberate policies pursued in both government and opposition forces-controlled areas to destroy and loot primary means of livelihood such as fresh crops, livestock, and ready harvest on which civilians were dependent for their survival.[60]

---

[57] Report of the Detailed Findings of the Group of Eminent International and Regional Experts on Yemen. Situation of Human Rights in Yemen, including Violations and Abuses since September 2014, UN Doc. A/HRC/42/CRP.1, 3 September 2019, para 747.

[58] Ibidem, para 760.

[59] Ibidem, para 752 ff. See also Mundy (2018).

[60] Report of the Commission on Human Rights in South Sudan, UN Doc. A/HRC/43/56, 31 January 2020 p. 35, para 42. During the civil war in Angola in the 1990s, both the National Union for the Total Independence of Angola (UNITA), the opposition guerrilla force, and the Angolan Armed Forces were responsible for methods of warfare deliberately aiming at starving the civilian population. On the one hand, UNITA were responsible for mining footpaths and fields around some urban centres to make difficult or impede rummaging for food by the residents, attacking operations of humanitarian assistance, sabotaging road transportation and capturing or killing those who took care of their fields; on the other, the government forces were responsible for bombing airstrips to block humanitarian aid from reaching UNITA-controlled zones. Since it was an internal conflict, Article 14 of AP II is relevant and mining of fields is a clear example of rendering "useless" objects indispensable to the survival of the civilian population: Human Rights Watch (1994), pp. 109 f. During the Diplomatic Conference for the adoption of the APs, the delegate of Vietnam declared that "[i]n the war in Viet-Nam, the imperialist aggressor had systematically attacked and destroyed foodstuffs, crops livestock, water supplies, irrigation works, forests and so forth for the purpose of starving the civilian population and forcing them to become refugees": Official Records of the Diplomatic Conference on the Reaffirmation and Development of International Humanitarian Law Applicable in Armed Conflicts, Geneva (1974–1977) Vol. XIV, CDDH/III/SR.17, p. 143, para 9.

A deliberate policy seeking to prevent the permanent and unrestricted access to sufficient food for the civilian population has also been denounced by the Commission of Inquiry on the Syrian conflict. In particular, during hostilities in Aleppo, between 21 July and 22 December 2016, "[r]epeated attacks against markets, bakeries and other food sources indispensable for civilian life have been a hallmark of the prolonged siege laid to eastern Aleppo city", at that time controlled by anti-Government forces; "[t]he total number of markets and bakeries attacked from the air... is indicative of a pattern on the part of pro-Government forces of intentionally violating this right by targeting civilian infrastructure".[61] In addition, the denial of food as a military strategy in some agricultural area, such as Dumah or eastern Ghouta, began in July and August 2013, when crops and farms were shelled and burned.[62]

In the on-going armed conflict in the Sudanese Darfur region, extensive destruction of villages, crops and objects indispensable to the survival of the population has been applied as a war strategy, very often by the pro-government militia of Janjaweed, independently or in combination with Government forces. As stressed by the Commission of Inquiry on Darfur,

> [t]he destruction was targeted at the areas of habitation of African tribes...; [t]he targets of destruction during the attacks under discussion were exclusively civilian objects; and objects indispensable to the survival of civilian population were deliberately and wantonly destroyed,[63]

> [s]uch a pattern of destruction can only be interpreted as having the objective of driving out the population through violence and preventing their return by destroying all means of survival and livelihood...; a number of villages previously inhabited by [African tribes] are now being populated by Arab tribes.[64]

[61] Report of the Independent International Commission of Inquiry on the Syrian Arab Republic, UN Doc. A/HRC/34/64, 2 February 2017, p. 10, para 41. To mention another less recent case of deliberate deprivation of food from civilians, it is worth recalling the Beirut siege of 1987 by Amal Shiite forces, provoking starvation of the Palestinians living in refugee camps. In this case the Amal, after having announced that women would be allowed to leave the camp to get food and supplies, made the women themselves targets for snipers: Boustany N, Syrians Enter Beirut Camp; Refugees Describe Horrors. The Washington Post, 8 April 1987, 1. See also Canada Immigration and Refugee Board, Lebanon: Treatment of Old Women by Amal, 1 February 1990: "There are numerous reports that the Shiite Amal militia shot women as they tried to leave Palestinian camps for food, between November 1986 and April 1987. The Palestinian camps of Shatila and Bourj al-Baranej in Beirut, were under siege and blockaded by Amal during that time. Reports of starvation were common"; in www.refworld.org/docid/3ae6ab3668.html.

[62] Report of the independent international commission of inquiry on the Syrian Arab Republic, UN Doc. A/HRC/25/65, 12 February 2014, para 133.

[63] Report of the International Commission of Inquiry on Darfur to the United Nations Secretary-General, 25 January 2005, para 315.

[64] *Ibidem*, para 312. See also UNEP (2007), Sudan. Post-Conflict Environmental Assessment, p. 75; in https://postconflict.unep.ch/publications/UNEP_Sudan.pdf. For other less recent examples see Conley and de Waal (2019), pp. 707 f.

These examples show how starvation through the destruction of indispensable objects can be carried out for various purposes—such as the punishment of civilians for their alleged aiding and abetting of enemy forces; to force the civilian population to abandon their homes; or to carry out a real policy of ethnic cleansing. But "whatever the motive, whether in order to starve out civilians, to cause them to move away, or for any other motive"—as stressed by Article 54, paragraph 2, of AP I—this method of war is always prohibited.

5.2 The Prohibition of Destruction of Objects Indispensable to the Survival (Article 54, Paragraph 2, of AP I; Article 14, Second Sentence, of AP II)

As regards the destruction of objects indispensable for the survival of the population, Article 54, paragraph 2, of AP I and Article 14, second sentence, of AP II are relevant. The prohibition against attacking these objects develops the principle prohibiting starvation by pointing out the most usual ways in which starvation may be applied. The close relationship between the prohibition of starvation and the prohibition against attacking objects indispensable to the survival of the civilian population is highlighted by the second sentence of Article 14 of AP II, which begins with the expression "is therefore prohibited".[65]

As a corollary of the general rule concerning the prohibition of starvation, the rule prohibiting attack against objects indispensable for the survival of civilians can also be deemed to reflect a customary norm of international law.[66] As stressed by the Eritrea-Ethiopia Claims Commission in the case of the bombardment of the Hersile reservoir,

> the provisions of Article 54 that prohibit attack against drinking water installations and supplies that are indispensable to the survival of the civilian population for the specific

[65] Sandoz et al. (1987), paras 2098 and 4800.

[66] In a letter of 20 May 1863, Francis Lieber asked Henry Wagner Halleck, General-in-Chief of the Union Armies, to issue an order recalling the Code and prohibiting the destruction of private properties and objects useful for sustenance; such a practice "annihilates wealth irrevocably and makes a return to a state of peace and peaceful minds more and more difficult. Your order... might be written, with reference to the Code, and pointing out the disastrous consequences of reckless devastation, in a manner that it might not furnish our reckless enemy with new arguments for his savagery": Letter from Francis Lieber to General Henry W. Halleck, in Hartigan (1983), p. 108 f. Also, Islamic international law prohibits unnecessary destruction of properties, devastation of harvest and cutting fruitful trees: Hamidullah (1945), p. 196; Zawati (2015), pp. 285 f. Respect for human life and personal property is a fundamental principle of the Shari'ha; even the first Caliph, Abu Bakr (573–674), prohibited the destruction of palm trees and the cutting of cut any fruitful tree: Schwartz (1991), p. 650.

> purpose of denying them for their sustenance value to adverse Party had become part of customary international humanitarian law by 1999.[67]

Numerous military manuals, included those of States not party to the AP I and II, prohibit the attack or destruction of objects indispensable for the survival of civilian population.[68] For example, the Law of War Manual of the United States prohibits attacks against means of sustenance for civilians expressly recalling Article 54, paragraph 2,[69] and Article 14.[70] That today there is a general acceptance of the obligation not to disrupt public utilities and not to destroy objects indispensable to the survival of civilians is also demonstrated by the condemnation of this practice by the UNSC, for example with respect the conflict in Bosnia[71] and in the Democratic Republic of Congo.[72] As for internal conflicts, in the *Perisić and Others* Case a Croatian district court in 1997 convicted several members of the Yugoslav Army for ordering the shelling of the city of Zadar, violating, *inter alia*, Article 14 of AP II.[73]

The APs explicitly introduce the prohibition of starvation—and the destruction of objects indispensable for the survival of civilian population—for the first time, but wanton destruction was considered unlawful by previous convention instruments. The Annex to the Hague Convention (IV) respecting the laws and customs of war on land of 1907 prohibited the destruction or seizure of enemy property unless such actions was imperatively demanded by military necessity (Article 23 (g)).[74] The effect of this prohibition was to limit the destruction of civilian food supplies and to lower the risk of starvation; nevertheless, a total prohibition on depriving civilians of goods indispensable for their survival was not yet recognised. The Hague Regulation

---

[67] Eritrea-Ethiopia Claims Commission—Partial Award: Western Front, Aerial Bombardment and Related Claims—Eritrea's Claims 1, 3, 5, 9–13, 14, 21, 25 & 26, 19 December 2005 (2009). Reports of International Arbitral Awards, Vol. XXVI, para 105.

[68] Henckaerts and Doswald-Beck (2005), Vol. I Rules, p. 190.

[69] United States Department of Defense (2015), para 5.20.4.

[70] *Ibidem*, para 17.9.2. See also Annotated Supplement to the Commander's Handbook on the Law of Naval Operations (1989). Washington, para 8.1.2.

[71] With a presidential statement of 22 July 1993, the UNSC condemned the Bosnian Serb military or paramilitary force offensive aimed at isolating Sarajevo and demanded "an end to the disruption of public utilities (including waters, electricity, fuel and communications) by the Bosnian Serb party and to the blocking of, and interference with, the delivery of humanitarian relief by both the Bosnian Serb and the Bosnian Croat parties": Note by the President of the Security Council, UN Doc. S/26134, 22 July 1993.

[72] Through a presidential statement of 31 August 1998, the UNSC "[r]ecall[ed] the unacceptability of the destruction or rendering useless of objects indispensable to the survival of the civilian population, and in particular of using cuts in the electricity and water supply as a weapon against the population": Statement by the President of the Security Council, UN Doc. S/PRST/1998/26, 31 August 1998.

[73] Judgment against 19 soldiers tried in absentia for war crimes, Zadar District Court, 24 April 1997, in https://ihl-databases.icrc.org.

[74] A similar provision is contemplated by Article 23 of the IV Geneva Convention, which prohibits "[a]ny destruction by the Occupying Power of real or personal property... except where such destruction is rendered absolutely necessary by military operations".

allowed a belligerent to starve an enemy civilian population if the means of subsistence served both civilians and combatants.[75] By way of example, during the American Civil War, the so-called Sherman March through Georgia applied a scorched earth policy, destroying food supplies, burning mills and crops and killing cattle and farm animals. This method of war was justified because the food supplies were also military supplies, hence the military necessity justified a food shortage among the civilian population.[76] As observed, "the Hague Law provided few special protection against starvation of civilians in general and devastation of the population's objects of sustenance in particular",[77] and also the provisions of the IV Geneva Convention—as it does not pay particular attention to the means and methods of warfare—did not specifically improve the protection afforded to items of sustenance for the civilian population, leaving the issue of civilian sustenance "in the fog of the "military necessity" concept".[78]

The Protocols adopt an opposite approach. Unlike The Hague Regulation, as a general rule the Protocols do not permit any derogation of the prohibition to attack objects indispensable to the survival of the civilian population for military necessity. It is still permitted to destroy the means indispensable to survival used by both the enemy belligerent and its civilians, but only to the extent that it does not deprive civilians of all means of survival; hence, paragraph 2 of Article 54 of AP I disallows indiscriminate starvation measures under the notion of military necessity in scenarios where both civilians and military forces might consequently suffer.[79] It means that, even if the enemy may benefit from the destruction of objects indispensable to survival, it is prohibited to destroy or attack them. In other words, it is not relevant the nature of the dual use object; in this case the "civilian" nature of the object indispensable to survival of the civilian population should prevail.[80] This is the meaning of the expression "for the specific purpose of denying them for their sustenance value" introduced in paragraph 2 of Article 54 (adopted by consensus after lengthy discussions at the Conference[81]). The denial of items is prohibited, if it aims at denying the goods for the sole reason that these are indispensable for the survival of the civilian population. As specified by the same rule, the motive of destruction is irrelevant ("whatever the motive, whether in order to starve out civilians, to cause them to move away, or for any other motive"), and it is not necessary that these attacks produce any *de facto* effect on the food supplies of the

[75] Cassese (1984), p. 92.

[76] Spaight (1911), p. 133.

[77] Allen (1989), p. 38.

[78] Ibidem, p. 60.

[79] Ibidem, p. 62.

[80] As stressed by Cassese, "one cannot starve civilians as a consequence of starving enemy combatants": Cassese (1984), p. 92.

[81] Official Records of the Diplomatic Conference on the Reaffirmation and Development of International Humanitarian Law Applicable in Armed Conflicts, Geneva (1974–1977) Vol. XV, CDDH/215/Rev.l, p. 279, para 74; *ibidem*, Vol. VI, CDDH/SR.42, p. 208, para 19.

civilian population, only the specific purpose being relevant.[82] Humanitarian law covers the unfortunate possibility that civilians are involved in hostilities (that is where collateral damage is produced by an action against the enemy forces), but the discipline examined here is characterized by the specific intention of deliberately target foodstuffs or objects indispensable to the survival of civilians with the sole or primary purpose of reducing civilians to hunger.[83] This determines the characterization of this violation as a war crime.

The intention of using starvation as a method of weapon to attack the civilian population may not be easy to prove, as most armies are unlikely to admit this intention. However, intention may be inferred from the circumstances of the military campaign. For example, particularly relevant in the assessment of intention is that the attacker takes into account the duty of distinction between civilians and military targets and to avoid harming civilians by choosing means of attack less harmful to civilians. If the attacker does not comply with these duties, and food shortages result, an intention to attack civilians by starvation may be inferred. The more indiscriminate the measures adopted which result in food shortages, when other less restrictive means of combat are available, the more likely the real intention is to attack the civilian population through food deprivation.[84]

5.3 The Exceptions to the Prohibitions to Destroy Objects Indispensable to Survival (Article 54, Paragraph 3, of AP I)

The third paragraph of Article 54 AP I specifies two situations in which objects, otherwise protected under paragraph 2, may be subject to attack, destruction or removal. It means that there are two exceptions that mitigate the prohibition against attacking objects indispensable to the survival of the civilian population. Based on the consideration that there are particular situations where these objects qualify as military objectives, these exceptions determine their loss of immunity from attacks. This is the case if the objects are used by the adverse party as sustenance solely for its armed forces (Article 54, paragraph 3a). It means that, with the qualifier "solely", to be attacked, these objects shall be used only by combatants;[85] in other words, the

[82] Provost (1992), p. 604.

[83] As stressed by the Group of Experts on Yemen, "[i]n order to violate the prohibition related to objects indispensable to the survival of the civilian population, these attacks must have been conducted with the objective to deprive the civilian population of the sustenance value of these objects, whatever the motive": Report of the Detailed Findings of the Group of Eminent International and Regional Experts on Yemen. Situation of Human Rights in Yemen, including Violations and Abuses since September 2014, UN Doc. A/HRC/42/CRP.13, September 2019, para 760.

[84] Human Rights Watch (1994), p. 157.

[85] At the Geneva Conference, the delegate of the International Committee of the Red Cross "drew attention to the fact that no mention was made of the purpose of the objects in question;

destruction of items used by both civilians and armed forces is always prohibited. This is a matter of enhanced protection, in the sense that, as for objects indispensable to the sustenance of civilians, a dual-use object cannot be attacked.[86]

This first exception to the prohibition against attacking items indispensable for the sustenance of civilians should apply only to supplies already in hands of the enemy's armed forces, since only in this situation could one be able to determine that they are intended for exclusive use by the enemy armed forces.[87] This is the point where the principle of precaution should come in. In fact, those who are responsible for planning and executing attacks necessarily have to reach a decision, in good faith and with due diligence, on the basis of information available to them from all sources at the relevant time.[88] Hence, taking all feasible precautions would allow them to ascertain whether certain items were being used only by armed forces.

The second exception (paragraph 3b) permits attack or destruction of items used "in direct support of military action", provided, however, that in no event shall actions against these objects leave the civilian population with inadequate food or water so as to cause starvation. It means that the fact that these supplies can serve to sustain the armed forces is not sufficient justification to allow their destruction, as it is necessary that such destruction does not cause starvation. By way of example, the destruction of supplies, objects or infrastructures used in direct support of military action can be the bombardment of a food-producing area to prevent the enemy from advancing through it, the attack of a food-storage barn used by the enemy for cover or as an arms depot, the attack of a water tower used as an observation post, the devastation of a cornfield or an orchard used as cover for the infiltration of an attacking force, the attack of an irrigation canal used as a defensive position.[89]

To sum up, from the joint reading of paragraph 2 with paragraph 3b of Article 54, it can be argued that, in the first case (paragraph 2), the prohibition applies to acts carried out for the specific purpose—that is, with the intention—of starving the civilian population, no matter the reason for this purpose and no matter the dual-use nature of the object attacked (this, for example, is what is happening in Syria and

consequently, it was forbidden to attack or destroy them even if the army of the adverse party derived benefit from them. An exception should no doubt be made for objects which were definitely earmarked for consumption by the army": Official Records of the Diplomatic Conference on the Reaffirmation and Development of International Humanitarian Law Applicable in Armed Conflicts, Geneva (1974–1977) Vol. XIV, CDDH/III/SR.16, p. 136, para 42. The delegate of the United States "raised the question of objects such as food intended solely for military consumption, which should not be entitled to any degree of protection": ibidem, p. 138, para 52. Ibidem, Vol. XV, CDDH/215/Rev.1: "Paragraph 2 (a) was intended to apply only to those objects which clearly are assigned solely for the sustenance of the armed forces".

[86] The 1987 Commentary to the Protocols stressed that this exception "is undoubtedly concerned with foodstuffs and the agricultural areas producing them, crops, livestock and supplies of drinking water, but not with installations for drinking water or irrigation works": Sandoz et al. (1987), para 109.

[87] Bothe et al. (2013), para 2.4.1.

[88] On the principle of precaution, see Henckaerts and Doswald-Beck (2005), Vol. I Rules, pp. 54 ff.

[89] Sandoz et al. (1987), para 2110; Allen (1989), p. 66; Conley and de Waal (2019), pp. 381 ff.

Yemen). In the second case (paragraph 3b), there is no intention to starve civilians, but only the intention to hit a military objective (which produces goods indispensable for survival). In other words, this object is not attacked because it produces food, but for its importance for the enemy (such as a cornfield where the enemy forces are hiding: in this case the field provides a "direct support of military action"). But this attack is in any case prohibited if such action could result in the starvation of civilians.[90] From this the problem arises of establishing or predicting whether the attack will actually starve the civilian population (to follow the above example, if only one cornfield among many is shelled, starvation is unlikely to occur). Also in this case a correct observance of the precautionary principle by the attacker will be of fundamental importance.

Finally, it is worth noting that the concise formulation of Article 14 of AP II—even if intended to preserve the essence of Article 54 of AP I[91]—may present some key points. From a strict interpretation of this rule, it might be inferred that, in internal conflicts, the prohibition of the destruction of goods only covers those dedicated exclusively to the civilian population; hence, Article 14 would not prohibit the destruction of objects for their sustenance value to both the armed forces and the civilian population. This interpretation contradicts the intent of the Geneva discipline. However, this "unfortunate formulation"[92] of Article 14 could be remedied by taking into account the Martens clause, included in the Preamble of AP II,[93] which makes it possible to apply the principle of proportionality to the whole Protocol. Hence, this principle

> would restrict denial actions against objects having sustenance value for both the armed forces and the civilian population to those whose effects on civilians are not disproportionate to the military advantage anticipated.[94]

Moreover, it is worth noting that the approach taken by Article 54 of AP I has been essentially confirmed by Article 14 of the Commentary of the IRCR, according to

---

[90] At the Geneva Conference it was observed that "[t]he term "civilian population" referred to in paragraph 2 (b) was not intended to mean the civilian population of a country as a whole, but rather of an immediate area, although the size of the area was not defined": Official Records of the Diplomatic Conference on the Reaffirmation and Development of International Humanitarian Law Applicable in Armed Conflicts, Geneva (1974–1977) Vol. XV, CDDH/215/Rev.1, p. 280, para 76. As observed by Aldrich (1981), p. 779: "the prohibition of starvation is really a prohibition of certain acts intended to result in starvation, not a prohibition of acts that may produce starvation but are done and are justifiable on other grounds".

[91] Official Records of the Diplomatic Conference on the Reaffirmation and Development of International Humanitarian Law Applicable in Armed Conflicts, Geneva (1974–1977) Vol. XV, CDDH/236/Rev.1, p. 400, para 79; Report of the Detailed Findings of the Group of Eminent International and Regional Experts on Yemen. Situation of Human Rights in Yemen, including Violations and Abuses since September 2014, UN Doc. A/HRC/42/CRP.13, September 2019, para 759.

[92] Hutter (2015), p. 213.

[93] AP II, Preamble: "in cases not covered by the law in force, the human person remains under the protection of the principles of humanity and the dictates of the public conscience".

[94] Bothe et al. (2013), p. 783.

which it is prohibited to destroy or attack objects indispensable for survival, even if the adversary may benefit from them. However, the objects used for military purposes becomes a military objective, and therefore a target, but only provided that such attack does not risk causing starvation of the civilian population.[95]

A final consideration regarding the prohibition of destroying or rendering objects unusable to the civilian population may be added. It has been suggested by some authors that if civilians are reduced to starvation as a result of an attack against an object used in direct support of military action, "relief consignments may have to be undertaken".[96] This conclusion seems to be questionable. The Geneva discipline clearly states that attacks against goods used in direct support of military action are prohibited if these actions may cause starvation (Article 54, paragraph 3b). Inferring from this that it would be possible, in the scenario sub paragraph 3b, to provide humanitarian assistance to civilians seems to bypass the prohibition against attack, granting the belligerent a certain discretion in acting. In other words, according to this conclusion, a belligerent would be allowed to attack in any case, knowing that humanitarian aid will subsequently be provided in the event of starvation (notwithstanding the difficulties involved in providing humanitarian assistance in such circumstances). Accepting this reasoning would mean denying the enhanced protection regime of objects indispensable for the survival of the civilian population.

6 Starvation of Civilians: Siege Warfare

What just said above leads us to consider the other method of starving the civilian population, namely the cutting off of a population from its supply of food by siege. Siege warfare is a military operation through which enemy forces surround a place (such as a fortress or an inhabited area), isolating it and cutting off essential supplies in order to force those inside to surrender.[97]

---

[95] Sandoz et al. (1987), para 4806 f.

[96] Dinstein (2016), p. 253.

[97] According the United Nations Office for the Coordination of Humanitarian Affairs (UN OCHA), "a 'besieged area' is an area surrounded by armed actors with the sustained effect that humanitarian assistance cannot regularly enter, and civilians, the sick and wounded cannot regularly exit the area": UN OCHA, 2015 Humanitarian Needs Overview: Syrian Arab Republic, November 2014. Similar to the siege is the blockade, that is an operation that seals off a place by force, preventing the movement of people and goods from entering or leaving and depriving the population from food supplies. While these two methods of war can produce the same result—the starvation of the civilian population—they are different, in that a blockade is usually directed at isolating an entire region or country, rather than a more limited space as a fortress or a town: Kraska (2009); Heintschel von Heinegg (2015); Hutter (2015), p. 224. In World War II, the United Kingdom maintained that naval blockades did not differ from sieges in land warfare in which the responsible commander was under no duty to allow food and other goods to pass into the town: Heintschel von Heinegg (2000).

As even the recent practice seems to show, siege warfare continues to be applied in armed conflicts. In the Bosnian War, the Serbian forces used a siege strategy against Bosnian Muslims, for example laying siege to the capital Sarajevo from 1992 to 1996,[98] and during the siege of the enclaves in Bosnia and Herzegovina, civilians were systematically deprived of assistance necessary for their survival.[99] These sieges were condemned by individual Member States of the UNSC,[100] by the UNSC itself[101] and by the General Assembly.[102]

Throughout Syria, brutal sieges have remained the primary method of warfare employed by parties to the conflict;[103] in particular, in 2012 pro-Government forces began laying sieges in a coordinated and planned manner, aimed at forcing populations, collectively, to starve or surrender.[104] As the siege was tightened, government forces blocked access roads and systematically confiscated food, fuel and medicine at checkpoints; soldiers at checkpoints harassed anyone caught

[98] As observed by the Prosecutor of the International Criminal Tribunal for the Former Yugoslavia (ICTY), the siege of Sarajevo "was an episode of such notoriety in the conflict in the former Yugoslavia that one must go back to World War II to find a parallel in European history. Not since then had a professional army conducted a campaign of unrelenting violence against the inhabitants of a European city so as to reduce them to a state of medieval deprivation in which they were in constant fear of death. In the period covered in this Indictment, there was nowhere safe for a Sarajevan, not at home, at school, in a hospital, from deliberate attack": Prosecutor v. Stanislav Galić, Judgment 5 December 2003, para 2.

[99] Report of the Secretary-General to the Security Council on the Protection of Civilians in Armed Conflict, UN Doc. S/1999/957, 8 September 1999, para 19.

[100] Albania stated that "[m]any cities in Bosnia and Herzegovina have been besieged for several months, and their population is under constant artillery fire and left without food, electricity, water supply and medicine. All this will certainly leave a scar on the population for several generations, and the evil is beyond remedy": UN Doc. S/PV/3136, 16 November 1992, para 50. Pakistan declared that "we have witnessed with mounting horror and revulsion... the use of siege and the cutting off of supplies of food and other essentials to civilian population centres": UN Doc. S/PV/3191, 31 March 1993, para 30.

[101] UNSC Resolution 761, 29 June 1992, preamble; Resolution 764, 13 July 1992, preamble; Resolution 859, 24 August 1993, preamble.

[102] General Assembly Resolution 48/88, 20 December 1993, para 6; Resolution 49/10, 3 November 1994, para 4, Resolution 49/196, 23 December 1994, para 7.

[103] Independent International Commission of Inquiry on the Syrian Arab Republic, Siege as a Weapon of War: Encircle, Starve, Surrender, Evacuate. 29 May 2018, para 1. The longest siege was that in eastern Ghouta, which lasted for over five years (2013–2018): *ibidem*, para 2. See also United Nations Human Rights Office of the High Commissioner, Living under Siege. The Syrian Arab Republic, February 2014; in www.ohchr.org/Documents/Countries/SY/LivingUnderSiege.pdf.

[104] Independent International Commission of Inquiry on the Syrian Arab Republic, Siege as a Weapon of War: Encircle, Starve, Surrender, Evacuate. 29 May 2018, para 9. The first long-term sieges started in mid-2012, as checkpoints were strategically emplaced by government forces to regulate the flow of goods and people into and out of targeted opposition-controlled areas. By mid-2013, communities in Eastern Ghouta, the southern Damascus Suburbs, parts of Western Ghouta, the northern Homs countryside, and the Old City of Homs were completely cut off: Pax (2019), p. 15.

carrying food and destroyed it on the suspicion that they were "aligned with the opposition".[105] Nearly all documented cases of starvation were in areas besieged by the Syrian government forces and its allies.[106] However, anti-government forces have also laid siege to certain localities, where the civilian communities were also eventually subjected to forced transfers in July 2018.[107] At the beginning of 2016, due to the sieges throughout Syria, nearly 400,000 vulnerable civilians were trapped inside densely populated districts where food, water, medicine and electricity were scarce.[108]

It should be recalled that the Independent International Commission of Inquiry on the Syrian Arab Republic, established on 2011 by the Human Rights Council, found that since February 2012 a non-international armed conflict has arisen, caused by the intensity and duration of the fighting combined with the increased organizational capabilities of anti-Government armed groups.[109] Syria is party to the Geneva Conventions of 1949—therefore obliged by common Article 3—but has not ratified AP II (while it is party to AP I). However, the principles relating to the conduct of hostilities listed in AP I and confirmed in AP II represent customary international law and, as such, apply not only to Syrian government armed forces, but also to non-State organized armed groups operating in the conflict. For example, the prohibition of starvation as a method of warfare of ICRC Rule 53 is reflected by Article 14 of AP II, as well as ICRC Rule 55 governing access to humanitarian relief to civilians, which is enshrined in Article 18 of AP II.[110]

In the past, the legality of siege warfare has never been questioned and it has been a tactic used for centuries; but the civilians involved in these sieges, from antiquity to

[105] Report of the independent international commission of inquiry on the Syrian Arab Republic, UN Doc. A/HRC/25/65, 12 February 2014, para 133.

[106] Report of the independent international commission of inquiry on the Syrian Arab Republic, UN Doc. A/HRC/25/65, 12 February 2014, para 13: "As part of their strategy aimed at weakening the insurgents and breaking the will of their popular base, government forces besieged several localities, a strategy reinforced by prolonged shelling campaigns. Partial sieges aimed at expelling armed groups turned into tight blockades that prevented the delivery of basic supplies, including food and medicine, as part of a "starvation until submission" campaign..."; para 132: "The Government employs siege warfare, instrumentalizing basic human needs for water, food, shelter and medical care, as part of its military strategy. Sieges have been imposed on towns across the Syrian Arab Republic... The denial of humanitarian, including food aid, has been protracted in many areas, leading to malnutrition and starvation".

[107] Pax (2019), p. 21. See also Report of the independent international commission of inquiry on the Syrian Arab Republic, UN Doc. A/HRC/25/65, 12 February 2014, para 141 ff.; Independent International Commission of Inquiry on the Syrian Arab Republic, Siege as a Weapon of War: Encircle, Starve, Surrender, Evacuate. 29 May 2018, para 14 ff.

[108] Report of the independent international commission of inquiry on the Syrian Arab Republic, UN Doc. A/HRC/31/68, 11 February 2016, para 118, p. 17.

[109] Report of the independent international commission of inquiry on the Syrian Arab Republic, UN Doc. A/HRC/21/50, 16 August 2016, p. 1.

[110] Power (2016), p. 8; Report of the independent international commission of inquiry on the Syrian Arab Republic, UN Doc. A/HRC/21/50, 16 August 2012, para 12.

the present day,[111] have always been the first victims[112] of a practice that the Commission of Inquiry on Syria qualified as "a medieval form of warfare".[113] It is well recognized that, in reality, in case of shortages caused by armed conflict, when it comes to available sustenance materials, the highest priority is assigned to combatants to the detriment of civilians.[114] During the Second World War, for example, this circumstance was essentially accepted as an inevitable consequence of the war, and in particular of a siege, where a certain solidarity between civilians and soldiers was taken for granted;[115] consequently, the use of a protracted siege to starve occupants of a city, both combatants and non-combatants alike, to force them into submission gained widespread acceptance as a method of warfare.[116] Moreover, the idea was accepted that the besieging forces could impede the evacuation of civilians—"useless mouths",[117] and as such a burden for the besieged forces—and drive them back so as to hasten the surrender of the city. As stated by a United States Military Tribunal in 1948 at Nuremberg,

> [a] belligerent commander may lawfully lay siege to a place controlled by the enemy and endeavour by a process of isolation to cause its surrender. The propriety of attempting to

---

[111] See Corfis and Wolfe (1995); Campbell (2006); Settia (2009). Among the best known examples of sieges of a city it is worth mentioning the siege of Jerusalem during the First Crusade (Kostick 2009); the siege of Strasbourg during the 1870 Franco-Prussian War (see Chrastil 2014); the siege of Petersburg during the American Civil War (Field 2009); the siege of Leningrad during the II World War (Glantz 2001). During the siege of Leningrad, more than one million Russians died of starvation; as observed by Walzer (2006), p. 160, "[m]ore civilians died in the siege of Leningrad than in the modernist infernos of Hamburg, Dresden, Tokyo, Hiroshima and Nagasaki, taken together".

[112] As observed by Mayer (1968), p. 83, past wars make clear that "the food shortage will strike first and hardest the children, the elderly, and pregnant and lactating women; last and least at adult males, and least of all at soldiers".

[113] Independent International Commission of Inquiry on the Syrian Arab Republic, Siege as a Weapon of War: Encircle, Starve, Surrender, Evacuate. 29 May 2018, para 5.

[114] "[I]t was inevitably the civilian population that suffered first. The soldiers were the last to be without food": Official Records of the Diplomatic Conference on the Reaffirmation and Development of International Humanitarian Law Applicable in Armed Conflicts, Geneva (1974–1977), Vol. XIV, CDDH/III/SR.17, p. 145, para 18. This is also demonstrated by the siege of Eastern Aleppo by the Syrian government forces, when "[s]hortly after the siege was laid, some armed groups began to confiscate and hide food items that had previously been available throughout most districts... Some armed groups distributed food and aid preferentially to those within their ranks, their family members and confidants over civilians. For the remaining population, minimal food assistance was occasionally circulated": Report of the Independent International Commission of Inquiry on the Syrian Arab Republic, UN Doc. A/HRC/34/64, 2 February 2017, para 63.

[115] In Spaight's words, "[t]he solidarity between the troops and the inhabitants of a fortified town... may almost be said to deprive the latter, temporarily, of their non-combatant character": Spaight (1911), p. 171.

[116] Waxman (1999), pp. 407 f. See Article 18 of the 1863 Lieber Code, according to which "when a commander of a besieged place expels the noncombatants, in order to lessen the number of those who consume his stock of provisions, it is lawful, though an extreme measure, to drive them back, so as to hasten on the surrender".

[117] Rosenblad (1979), p. 109.

> reduce it by starvation is not questioned. Hence the cutting off of every source of sustenance from without is deemed legitimate. It is said that if the commander of a besieged place expels the non-combatants, in order to lessen the number of those who consume his stock of provisions, it is lawful, though an extreme measure, to drive them back, so as to hasten the surrender... We might wish the law were otherwise, but we must administer it as we find it.[118]

Since World War II, the increased concern for the respect of humanitarian law and to minimize civilian suffering in armed conflicts has called into question the legitimacy of specific practices such siege warfare. But even today, siege warfare is not expressly prohibited by APs. This is confirmed, for example, by the ICTY in the *Galić* case: where he was tried and convicted as the commander of the Bosnian Serb forces that besieged Sarajevo, but where the siege of the city itself was not included among the charges against him.[119]

Also the IV Geneva Convention seems to accept the legality of siege warfare, by providing rules aimed at protecting certain categories of civilians situated within besieged areas;[120] and the study of the ICRC on the customary international humanitarian law recognizes that "[t]he prohibition of starvation as a method of warfare does not prohibit siege warfare as long as the purpose is to achieve a military objective and not to starve a civilian population".[121] This is the guiding principle that belligerents should today take into account. This principle clearly comes directly, although implicitly, from the 1977 Geneva discipline prohibiting starvation as a method of warfare and from the corresponding customary rule, and is confirmed by various national military manuals. This implies, first, that belligerents should conclude agreements permitting the passage of food and means of sustenance for the civilian population under siege;[122] second, that today the practice of impeding the evacuation of civilians is totally illegal, and that the besieging belligerent shall

---

[118]Law Reports of Trials of War Criminals (1949), Vol. XII. The German High Command Trial. London, p. 84. The same principle was adopted by the 1956 Law of War Manual of the United States: "if a commander of a besieged place expels the noncombatants in order to lessen the logistical burden he has to bear, it is lawful, though an extreme measure, to drive them back, so as to hasten the surrender": United States Department of the Army (1956), The Law of Land Warfare. FM 27-10, p. 20.

[119]Prosecutor v. Stanislav Galić, Judgment 5 December 2003, para 609: "There is no dispute between the parties that General Galić, as Corps commander, was in charge of continuing the planning and execution of the military encirclement of Sarajevo... In itself, that encirclement is not directly relevant to the charges of the Indictment".

[120]Article 17 of the IV Geneva Convention. Gaggioli (2019).

[121]Henckaerts and Doswald-Beck (2005), Vol. I: Rules, p. 188. Article 27 of the 1907 Hague Regulation permits siege as a method of warfare, stressing that "all necessary steps must be taken to spare, as far as possible, certain categories of buildings and persons, such as buildings dedicated to religion or art, hospitals and places where the sick and wounded are collected". As observed by Van Shaack (2016), "[s]iege warfare remains lawful under contemporary law so long as it is directed only at combatants and those directly participating in hostilities, and only in so far as other provisions of the law are adhered to – a major challenge when both combatants and civilians depend on the same necessities". See also Gaggioli (2019).

[122]Henckaerts and Doswald-Beck (2005), Vol. II: Practice, Part I, pp. 1139 ff.

permit non-combatants to leave a besieged city to seek shelter and better living conditions elsewhere.[123]

However, these conditions were not respected as regards the Syrian conflict. Pro-Government forces accepted the evacuation of civilian residents who were suffering in certain besieged areas only after armed groups surrendered.[124] Belligerents should also come to an agreement to evacuate as a minimum and at the earliest opportunity those civilians presenting with critical health issues. On the contrary, the pattern of evacuations carried out throughout the country seems to be based not so much on humanitarian grounds as on the intention to produce a political change in the area or in the city under siege, through a *de facto* expulsion of that part of citizenship considered adverse to the besieging forces. Moreover, in no instance did the warring parties carrying out the evacuation ensure that civilians had satisfactory conditions of safety, nutrition, health, or hygiene; rather they moved civilians to overcrowded camps lacking basic services and which were not adequate to receive them.[125]

Starvation can be produced by a positive action, such as the destruction of objects indispensable to the survival of civilians, but also by an omission, through a deliberate decision not to take measures to supply the population with objects indispensable for its survival. This often happens during sieges. As stated previously, siege warfare is not necessarily unlawful, as its prohibition is not covered by the APs; but this method of warfare can conflict with the prohibition of starvation when civilians are involved. It can be true that, to be effective, a siege must lead to a deprivation of food, but this obviously conflicts with the general prohibition of the starvation of civilians. This contrast makes it "very difficult for a commander to conduct a siege that is both successful and lawful";[126] but the present reality of humanitarian law seems to prevent, from a legal point of view, the use of the siege if civilians are affected. In other words, owing to the 1977 discipline, when civilians are involved, siege "in the old meaning and function of the term" seems to be prohibited.[127]

---

[123] See, for example, the 1998 Israel's Manual of the Law of War: "Until recently there were no rules relating to this method of warfare, and it was allowed to exploit the suffering of the local population in order to subdue the enemy. Following the Second World War, a provision was set in the Additional Protocols of 1977, forbidding the starvation of a civilian population in war. This provision clearly implies that the city's inhabitants must be allowed to leave the city during a siege": *ibidem*, p. 1140, para 137. See also United States Department of Defense (2015), para 5.19.4.1: "In the past, it was permissible, but an extreme measure, to refuse to allow civilians to leave a besieged locality and to use force to drive any who attempted to flee back to the besieged locality. However, such actions would now be prohibited because they would not be consistent with the duty to take feasible precautions for the protection of civilians".

[124] Independent International Commission of Inquiry on the Syrian Arab Republic, Siege as a Weapon of War: Encircle, Starve, Surrender, Evacuate. 29 May 2018, para 10.

[125] Ibidem, para 24 f.

[126] Riordan (2010), p. 150.

[127] Detter (2000), p. 298. For a critical position of these considerations, see Dinstein (2016), pp. 255 f.; Rogers (2012), pp. 140 ff.

7 Humanitarian Assistance to Civilians to Prevent Starvation

Since methods of warfare such as siege or blockade often result in dramatic shortcomings in the delivery of food and goods essential for their survival to civilians, one of the most delicate and thorny issues related to the prohibition of starvation concerns the question of offers of humanitarian assistance to the civilian population affected by the conflict and, most importantly, those offers being accepted. As practice shows, during an armed conflict access to humanitarian assistance is often deliberately impeded as a tactic of warfare. In the Syrian war, on several occasions States, the United Nations and non-governmental organisations engaged in the protection of human rights have called on both the Syrian authorities and organized armed groups to allow humanitarian organizations and agencies unfettered access to all areas to assist the civilian population without discrimination.[128]

The reference legislation on humanitarian assistance to civilian victims of armed conflict is Article 70 of AP I for international conflicts and Article 18 of AP II for non-international conflicts.[129] These rules shall be considered jointly with the prohibition of starvation,[130] in the sense that when a belligerent is confronted with a situation where the survival of a civilian population is under threat because of the inadequate supply of goods, its denial to permit a humanitarian relief operation amounts to a violation of the prohibition of starvation of the civilian population as a method of warfare under Article 54 of AP I and Article 14 of AP II.

According to Article 70,[131] "relief actions... shall be undertaken" as soon as the civilian population is not adequately provided with essential supplies for survival

[128] Amnesty International (2014), p. 6. On 22 February 2014, the UNSC passed Resolution 2139, the first to address the humanitarian situation in Syria, calling on the parties to the conflict to immediately lift sieges of populated areas, end violations of human rights and international humanitarian law, and allow rapid, unhindered and safe access for humanitarian agencies to reach people in need (para 5 ff.). A Presidential Statement of the UNSC issued on 2 October 2013 stressed that "the magnitude of the humanitarian tragedy caused by the conflict in Syria requires immediate action to facilitate safe and unhindered delivery of humanitarian assistance in the whole country, including in areas and districts where humanitarian needs are especially urgent", it condemned "all cases of denial of humanitarian access," and recalled "that arbitrarily depriving civilians of objects indispensable to their survival, including wilfully impeding relief supply and access, can constitute a violation of international humanitarian law": UN Doc. S/PRST/2013/15, 2 October 2013.

[129] Article 69 of AP I is dedicated specifically to humanitarian assistance of the civilian population in occupied territories.

[130] Sandoz et al. (1987), paras 2808 and 4885; Pejic (2001), p. 1103.

[131] The discipline contained in Article 70 is an improvement compared to the previous Article 23 of the IV Geneva Convention, insofar as it extends the relief actions to the whole of the affected civilian population. Article 23, indeed, allows distribution of essential foodstuffs, clothing and medicines, only to children under fifteen, expectant mothers, and maternity cases: Sandoz et al. (1987), para 2814.

(para. 1). However, humanitarian assistance is "subject to the agreement of the Parties concerned" (para. 2).[132]

Article 70 seems vaguely worded, causing interpretative uncertainties on a first reading ("relief actions... shall be undertaken, subject to the agreement of the Parties"). It would seem that a duty to provide humanitarian assistance would exist only after an agreement among Parties on such an issue is concluded; but it would not seem that the article lays down an obligation to conclude such an agreement. Absent any obligation to conclude this agreement, humanitarian assistance would therefore not be provided. This interpretation would obviously deprive the humanitarian assistance mechanism of its effectiveness. It should also be noted that at the Geneva conference on international humanitarian law it was clearly stated that the clause requiring the agreement

> did not imply that the Parties concerned had absolute and unlimited freedom to refuse their agreement to relief actions. A Party refusing its agreement must do so for valid reasons, not for arbitrary or capricious ones.[133]

Hence, the parties concerned do not have unfettered discretion to refuse the agreement.

Paragraph 1 of Article 70 sets the conditions which trigger the duty to give consent and conclude an agreement on humanitarian assistance. This duty exists when the relief is really necessary, that is the civilian population is not adequately provided with essential supplies and the party with the responsibility to meet its needs fails to provide assistance. Second, this relief action shall be humanitarian (not political) and impartial, in the sense that it must not be designed to give an undue advantage to one side. If these conditions are met and there is a real need for humanitarian assistance to the civilian population, there is a clear duty to agree and facilitate relief actions and consent may not be arbitrarily withheld.[134] A State may invoke a credible situation of military necessity, but only to restrict humanitarian assistance temporarily and within specific geographical limits, not to definitively prohibit the relief operations of an impartial humanitarian organization or third party.[135]

[132]The consent condition was added during the Diplomatic Conference, because States wanted to maintain their national sovereignty; a balance was then reached between the needs of the civilian population and the interests of the States: Spieker (2011), p. 13; Hutter (2015), p. 239.

[133]Official Records of the Diplomatic Conference on the Reaffirmation and Development of International Humanitarian Law Applicable in Armed Conflicts, Geneva (1974–1977), Volume XII, Doc. CDDH/III/SR.87, p. 336, para 27.

[134]Meyrowitz (1985), pp. 281 f.; Sandoz et al. (1987), pp. 844 f.; Akande and Gillard (2016), pp. 492 f. As observed by these authors, the consent "is withheld arbitrarily if it is withheld in circumstances that violate a party's other obligations under international law with respect to the civilian population in question; if it violates the principles of necessity and proportionality; or if it is withheld in a manner that is unreasonable, unjust, lacking in predictability or otherwise inappropriate": *ibidem*, p. 494.

[135]Right to Food. Note by the Secretary-General, UN Doc. A/72/188, 21 July 2017, para 77.

It is worth noting that the fact that relief is given only to one side does not deprive the actions of its impartiality. This is clearly stated by paragraph 2 of Art. 70, according to which transit of the humanitarian mission through the territory of a State shall be granted "even if such assistance is destined for the civilian population of the adverse Party".[136]

Paragraph 1 of Article 70 has twofold purposes. A humanitarian one, since it specifies that the relief goes, as a priority, to the weakest parts of the population, that is those persons who "are to be accorded privileged treatment or special protection", such as children or expectant and nursing mothers. But this clarification also has a military aspect, as it is intended to prevent that civilian war labour forces working with the Armed Forces may benefit from priority in terms of distribution, which would affect the legitimate military interests of an adverse Party.[137] Once an agreement is reached on consignment of goods essential for survival, the warring State is obliged to permit "rapid and unimpeded" transit through its territory to reach the civilians affected by the armed conflict (paragraph 2). This duty has to be understood in a broad sense, namely that the transit state must not only allow such transit, but that it must facilitate the passage providing, where appropriate, active help.[138] As important as permitting free passage, States are also required to protect relief consignments and facilitate their rapid distribution (paragraph 4).

Even if not explicitly stated in Article 70, it can be argued that transit States have the right to control the goods transiting through its territory[139] and ascertain whether the relief action respects the condition of impartiality and is conducted without discrimination. In any case, it has the right to prescribe the technical arrangements under which the passage is permitted, but in no way can it divert relief consignments nor delay their forwarding, except in cases of urgent necessity in the interests of the civilian population concerned (paragraph 3). For example, a belligerent could deny relief consignments containing goods used in direct support of military actions, as was the case with fats during the British blockade of Germany in both world wars. Clearly, in no case can belligerents deny relief assistance due to a desire to deprive the civilian population of sufficient foodstuffs, as this is in clear violation of the prohibition of starvation stated by Article 54 of AP I.[140]

As for non international armed conflicts, the reference norm is Article 18 of AP II. One of the most hotly debated articles of Protocol II during the Diplomatic Conference, it merely sets out the fundamental principles of the relief actions, without elaborating in detail how they are to be implemented. This article is the result of the conciliation of two opposing positions. On the one hand, critics of adopting an international discipline in relation to internal conflicts, and in particular focusing on the question of relief, considered that the actions of humanitarian

---

[136] Bothe et al. (2013), pp. 485 f., para 2.4 f.

[137] *Ibidem*, p. 486, para 2.8.

[138] *Ibidem*.

[139] Henckaerts and Doswald-Beck (2005), Vol. II Practice, Part. 1, p. 197.

[140] Provost (1992), p. 612.

assistance constituted a foreign intervention in their internal affairs. On the other hand, traditional donor countries stressed that relief for affected civilian population is above all essential in internal conflicts, as the Biafra conflict showed at that time and as recent conflicts also show.[141]

As reflected in the preparatory work, what has been said regarding Article 70 of AP I also applies to Article 18 of AP II. According to its paragraph 2, relief actions shall be undertaken subject to the consent of the "High Contracting Party concerned", in the event that the civilian population is suffering undue hardship owing to a lack of the supplies essential for its survival. If necessary, this action must take place. As in Article 70 of AP I, the expression "shall be undertaken" refers to the requirement of consent, and the withholding of consent to humanitarian access that leads to starvation is considered arbitrary, hence unlawful.[142] Therefore, the failure of the Syrian government to respond to repeated requests by humanitarian actors to enter various towns under siege around Damascus[143] is contrary to international humanitarian law. The same conclusion applies to the thwarting of aid efforts made by the United Nations and non-governmental entities since September 2013 in Yarmouk, near Damascus. In this case, convoys of food and medical aid have repeatedly been turned back from checkpoints. In January 2014, the High Commissioner for Human Rights strongly condemned the repeated obstruction of convoys trying to bring supplies to the besieged population, stressing that "impeding humanitarian assistance to civilians in desperate need may amount to a war crime".[144]

The State concerned has no unfettered discretion to refuse the agreement—better, the "consent" as specified in paragraph 2 of Article 18[145]—where such assistance is of an "exclusively humanitarian and impartial nature" and conducted without any adverse distinction. The inclusion in Article 18 of AP II of the adverb "exclusively" (not present in the corresponding Article 70 of AP I) seems to further restrict the possibility of carrying out relief actions in a scenario of internal conflict. This seems also to be in line with the resistance that emerged during the Diplomatic Conference

[141] Bothe et al. (2013), p. 799, para 2.1 f.; Sandoz et al. (1987), para 4870.

[142] Report of the Detailed Findings of the Group of Eminent International and Regional Experts on Yemen. Situation of Human Rights in Yemen, including Violations and Abuses since September 2014, UN Doc. A/HRC/42/CRP.13, September 2019, para 745.

[143] United Nations Human Rights Office of the High Commissioner, Living under Siege. The Syrian Arab Republic, February 2014, p. 5; in www.ohchr.org/Documents/Countries/SY/LivingUnderSiege.pdf.

[144] Ibidem, p. 7. A denial of access to humanitarian assistance by the Sudanese authorities has also been stressed by the Human Rights Committee, Concluding Observations on the Fourth Periodic Report of the Sudan The Committee, UN Doc. CCPR/C/SDN/CO/4, 19 August 2914, para 8: "State party authorities have at times arbitrarily denied the timely access of life saving humanitarian assistance for civilian populations in some conflict-affected areas, particularly those controlled by rebel groups".

[145] As for the form in which the "consent" of the State in whose territory the humanitarian mission passes must be expressed, Article 18 does not specify if the consent must be express and public. The word used in Article 18 would imply implies less formality than the word "agreement" used in Article 70 of AP I: Bothe et al. (2013), p. 801.

to accepting the intervention of third parties in the internal affairs of States in the case of non-international armed conflicts.

Be that as it may, the State concerned may refuse the humanitarian assistance only for valid reasons, not for arbitrary and capricious ones.[146] Thus, the denial of consent for carrying out humanitarian action may justify possible actions and pressures intended to stigmatize it. For example, the Parliamentary Assembly of the Council of Europe (CoE) condemned the opposition of the Russian Federation to permitting the delivery of humanitarian aid to the civilian population of Chechnya during the Second Chechen War (1999–2009). In particular, with Recommendation 1444 of 27 January 2000, the Assembly of the CoE requested Russia "to allow for the unhindered delivery of international humanitarian assistance and for the effective operation of international governmental and non-governmental humanitarian organisations in the region" (paragraph 16),[147] emphasising that failure to meet this requirement "will inevitably necessitate... a review of Russian continued membership of, and participation in, the Assembly's work and in the Council of Europe in general" (paragraph 18).[148] Following this pressure, the Russian Federation allowed a humanitarian convoy to reach the capital of Chechnya.[149] Even in Syria, in some cases government forces and the armed opposition groups have reached a deal to allow humanitarian access to trapped civilians.[150] Nevertheless, in general, both Government and armed opposition groups have been in clear violation of international humanitarian law, failing to allow and facilitate rapid and unimpeded passage

[146] See the intervention on this point of Belgium and the Federal Republic of Germany during the Geneva Conference: Official Records of the Diplomatic Conference on the Reaffirmation and Development of International Humanitarian Law Applicable in Armed Conflicts, Geneva (1974–1977), Volume VII, Doc. CDDH/SR.53, pp. 156 f.

[147] Parliamentary Assembly of the Council of Europe Recommendation 1444, 27 January 2000, para 16.

[148] Ibidem, para 18. Following Recommendation 1444, Russia allowed an Ad Hoc Committee of the CoE to go to Chechnya. In Grozny, the capital of Chechnya, the Committee found that "[t]he centre of the city has been totally and systematically destroyed. We did not see a single building intact... some 15 000 inhabitants have remained in Grozny (out of a population of some 400 000 in 1991). In the centre of the city it has been estimated that there are only some 1 000 to 1 500 people left, and they are living in conditions of total privation. The Russian authorities have declared Grozny a "closed city" until 1 May 2000": Conflict in Chechnya—Implementation by Russia of Recommendation 1444 (2000) Report, Doc. 8697, 4 April 2000, in http://assembly.coe.int/nw/xml/XRef/X2H-Xref-ViewHTML.asp?FileID=8902&lang=EN.

[149] Parliamentary Assembly of the Council of Europe Recommendation 1444, 27 January 2000, para 42.

[150] On 25 December 2013, government forces and the armed opposition groups reached a deal to allow humanitarian access to civilians in al-Muadhamiya. The agreement involved raising the Syrian official flag over the area for 72 h in exchange for food supplies. In a second phase, armed opposition groups committed to hand over their heavy weaponry, while Government forces would remain outside of the area. In a third and final phase, displaced persons would be allowed to return to their homes without reprisal and the checkpoints around the area would be removed: United Nations Human Rights Office of the High Commissioner, Living under Siege. The Syrian Arab Republic, February 2014, p. 6.www.ohchr.org/Documents/Countries/SY/LivingUnderSiege.pdf.

of humanitarian relief for civilians in need, to ensure access to essential goods which are indispensable to the survival of the civilian population, and to allow safe passage to persons protected out of the besieged area.[151]

The fact that paragraph 2 of Article 18 requires only the consent of the State concerned without mentioning the consent of anti-government or rebel forces may give rise, as a matter of practice, to some problems. Indeed, it is not clear how humanitarian assistance should be provided in cases in which the relief does not pass through the territory controlled by the government armed forces, but through that controlled by rebel forces. In other words, the question is open of how to convince (or oblige) the rebel forces—which did not evidently ratify the AP II—to accept the transit of a humanitarian mission through a territory controlled by them.[152] Moreover, it is worth nothing that AP II makes reference only to an armed conflict between the armed forces of a State and dissident armed forces or other organized armed groups (Article 1, paragraph 1), but does not consider a scenario of armed conflict between organized armed groups on a territory of a State without the intervention of government armed forces.[153] Such an internal conflict is not uncommon: a good example is provided by the situation in Somalia in the 1990s, where various organized armed factions began to fight each other for the control of the country after having overthrown the government of Siad Barre in 1991,[154] or by the Lebanese civil war (1975–1990), where various militias fought each other after the central government authority dissolved.[155] Hence, in many cases it may not be clear which part is the established or legitimate government and which are the anti-government or rebel forces. Rather, as a determining element it would be better to take into account who has effective control of that part of territory through which the relief action must transit or where relief consignments shall be distributed.[156]

Having said that, it must be stressed that the obligation on the parties to a conflict to allow and facilitate the rapid and unimpeded passage of humanitarian relief has to be considered as a customary norm applicable in both international and non international conflicts. Since the prohibition of starvation is a customary norm, it can be

---

[151] Ibidem, pp. 9 f.

[152] This issue was not fully clarified during the Conference: Bothe et al. (2013), pp. 696 f. On this question, see Momtaz (2001), pp. 9 ff.

[153] In the *Tadić* Case, the ICTY broadened the notion of non-international armed conflict to include this kind of conflict: Prosecutor v. Dusko Tadić, 2 October 1995, para 70: "an armed conflict exists whenever there is a resort to armed force between States or protracted armed violence between governmental authorities and organized armed groups *or between such groups within a State*" (italic of the a.).

[154] Annual Human Rights Reports Submitted to Congress by the U.S. Department of State, 1996, Vol. 21, pp. 249 ff.; Clark (1992), pp. 109 ff. During the Somali armed conflict, the international humanitarian assistance was the target of constant attacks as a tactic of war by these armed groups fighting each other: Report of the Secretary-General to the Security Council on the Protection of Civilians in Armed Conflict, UN Doc. S/1999/957, 8 September 1999, para 19.

[155] International Center for Transitional Justice (2013).

[156] Bothe et al. (2013), p. 802, para 2.4.1.

inferred that the implementing rules of this general principle also have a customary value. The practice of States and international organisation, such as the United Nations, confirm this conclusion.[157]

8 Prohibition of Starvation and Denial of Humanitarian Assistance: The Recent Practice of the Security Council

In recent years, the practice of the UNSC has assumed a significant importance for the reaffirmation of the prohibition of the starvation of the civilian population in armed conflicts and, in particular, in relation to humanitarian aid to civilians.

Resolution 2417 (2018) is a first of its kind and represents a watershed, as the UNSC did not focus on a particular conflict, but for the first time reasoned in more general terms, stressing "the vicious cycle between armed conflict and food insecurity" and "recognising that armed conflict impacts of food security can be direct".[158] For the first time a cause-effect relationship between armed conflict and food insecurity is recognized. In this sense, Resolution 2417 is a point of arrival of a long process of the work of the UNSC on humanitarian assistance to civilians, determined by the belligerents' non-compliance with the prohibition of starvation, the destruction of the means of survival and the denial of humanitarian relief. In particular, these practices had been condemned by the UNSC in previous resolutions, such as Resolution 2139 (2014), 2165 (2014), 2258 (2015) on the Syrian conflict, Resolution 2179 (2014) on the conflict between Sudan and South Sudan; and also through various presidential statements, such as the statement of the President of the UNSC, of 9 August 2017, through which he expressed "its grave concern about the unprecedent level of humanitarian needs and the threat of famine... in Yemen, Somalia, South Sudan and northeast Nigeria".[159]

From an analysis of these resolutions, it is possible to outline some salient points. First, the UNSC usually reiterates the primary responsibility of the State's authorities for ensuring access to food for the civilian population during an armed conflict, as well as its main responsibility to guarantee humanitarian assistance to civilians affected by war. This responsibility is usually related to the principle of sovereignty

[157] Many military manuals contain the obligation to allow and facilitate access of humanitarian relief to civilians in need during an international or a non international conflict, and the UNSC on many occasions has called for unimpeded access for humanitarian relief efforts in various war scenarios: Henckaerts and Doswald-Beck (2005), Vol. II Practice, Part. 1, pp. 193 ff. The role of the United Nations is particularly important in putting the warring parties in contact and encouraging them to enter into agreements to provide humanitarian assistance to the civilian population. For example, during the armed conflict in Angola, the government approved the United Nations plan on relief operations in late July 1993 and UNITA did so on September 3 after a special meeting with the United Nations representatives in Kinshasa: Human Rights Watch (1994), p. 111.

[158] UNSC Resolution 2417 (2018), 24 May 2018, preamble.

[159] UN Doc. S/PRST/2017/14, 9 August 2017.

and territorial integrity of the State in which the conflict takes place.[160] Second, the UNSC "recalls" that starvation of civilians as a method of combat is prohibited by international humanitarian law.[161] With the word "recalls", it refers to a pre-existing situation, confirming the customary character of the prohibition of starvation,[162] also in relation to internal conflicts.[163]

Third, the deliberate starvation and the denial of humanitarian assistance is defined by the UNSC as a threat to international peace and security (together with other serious violations of humanitarian law and human rights law, such as indiscriminate shelling, targeting of civilians, taking of hostages, rapes and kidnappings).[164] By determining this as a threat to peace, the UNSC may act on the basis of Chapter VII of the Charter, adopting *inter alia* "measures not involving the use of armed force ... to give effect to its decisions" (Article 41).

As is well known, in addition to the measures expressly provided for in this article ("complete or partial interruption of economic relations and of rail, sea, air, postal, telegraphic, radio, and other means of communication, and the severance of diplomatic relations"), the UNSC may also adopt resolutions containing "atypical" measures, that are not expressly listed in Article 41. For example, in the *Tadić* Case, this article has been considered to be the legal basis for the creation of the *ad hoc* Tribunal for the Former Yugoslavia.[165]

From this perspective, Resolution 2165 (2014) on the Syrian conflict is relevant, because with this document the UNSC introduces elements of novelty in addressing the issue of humanitarian assistance to the civilian population due the inactivity of state authorities. The premise of what is decided in this resolution is previous

---

[160] Resolution 2139 (2014), second paragraph of the preamble, and UN Doc. S/PV.7116, p. 3; Resolution 2165 (2014), second and twelfth paragraph of the preamble, and UN Doc. S/PV. 7216, p. 10; Res 2258 (2015), second and eighth paragraphs of the preamble; Right to Food. Note by the Secretary-General, UN Doc. A/72/188, 21 July 2017, para 45.

[161] Resolution 2165 (2014), para 7.

[162] Zimmermann (2017), p. 17.

[163] See Resolution 2191 (2014), with which the UNSC refers to the "Syrian domestic conflict", "recalling... [the] legal obligations [of the Parties] under international humanitarian law... as the use of starvation of civilians as a method of combat, including by the besiegement of populated areas" (fifth paragraph of the preamble); UN Doc. S/PV.7216, p. 11 ("The Syrian conflict... has become a global threat to international peace and security").

[164] Resolution 2165 (2014), eighteenth paragraph of the preamble; Resolution 2179 (2014), twenty-ninth paragraph of the preamble; Resolution 2258 (2015), twenty-sixth paragraph of the preamble; UN Doc.7216, p. 11: "The Syrian conflict... has become a global threat to international peace and security".

[165] *Prosecutor v. Dusko Tadić*, 2 October 1995: "the Security Council has a broad discretion in deciding on the course of action and evaluating the appropriateness of the measures to be taken" (para 31); "the International Tribunal matches perfectly the description in Article 41 of "measures not involving the use of force"" (para 34); "[i]t is evident that the measures set out in Article 41 are merely illustrative examples which obviously do not exclude other measures. All the Article requires is that they do not involve "the use of force""; "[i]n sum, the establishment of the International Tribunal falls squarely within the powers of the Security Council under Article 41" (para 35).

Resolution 2139 (2014), according to which the UNSC demanded that all parties, "in particular the Syrian authorities", promptly allow rapid, safe and unhindered access for United Nations humanitarian agencies in order to ensure humanitarian assistance to civilians affected by the conflict (paragraphs 6 and 7). The Council also expressed "its intent to take further steps in the case of non-compliance with this resolution" (paragraph 17). Although this resolution did not explicitly characterize the situation in Syria as a threat to peace, the statements made by the members of the UNSC after the adoption of Resolution 2139 (2014) would indicate its compulsory nature.[166]

As a result of an almost total failure to comply with what was required by this resolution, the UNSC decided to take "further steps" in adopting Resolution 2165 (2014), which expressly defined the deteriorating humanitarian situation in Syria as "a threat to peace and security in the region" (preamble).

In essence, if the UNSC determines that the parties to the conflict, "in particular the Syrian authorities" (paragraph 1), cannot or do not want to act effectively for the subsistence of civilians, it can take concrete action by authorizing

> the United Nations humanitarian agencies and their implementing partners... to use routes across conflict lines and the border crossings... in order to ensure that humanitarian assistance... reaches people in need (paragraph 2).

The interesting aspect of this authorization is that the crossing of Syrian borders is subject only to a mere notification to the Syrian authorities (paragraph 2). Therefore, in this specific case, there is an imposition on Syria to accept the entry into its territory of humanitarian missions of the United Nations, the will of the State thus being irrelevant.

Thus, in the management of a humanitarian emergency in the Syrian armed conflict, and in particular in providing humanitarian relief to the civilian population, under Resolution 2165 (2014) the UNSC bypassed the territorial State, adopting an approach opposed to that envisaged by the discipline of Geneva, which provides for the consent of the State in which the humanitarian crisis takes place. The UNSC imposed its decision on the State concerned, *de facto*, by merely notifying Syria of its obligation to allow the transit through its territory of UN humanitarian missions. According to this scheme, due to the failure of the Syrian government to comply

---

[166] See the statements by the delegates of Luxemburg ("The Council expresses its intent, in the case of non-compliance with the resolution, to take further steps to support the vital humanitarian efforts in Syria": *ibidem*, p. 3); Australia ("The resolution has made very clear the Council's expectations that its demands will be met and that there will be consequences for non-compliance": *ibidem*, p. 4); United States ("The resolution... has a clear demand for specific and concrete actions, and it is a commitment to act in the event of non-compliance": *ibidem*, p. 6); United Kingdom ("The Security Council will review the humanitarian situation... and, as the resolution makes clear, we fully intend to take further steps if the demands set out in the resolution are ignored": *ibidem*, p. 8); Chile ("the resolution... is a forceful message that obliges all parties to comply with international humanitarian and humanitarian rights law"; "[i]n he case of non-compliance, the Council should consider additional measures": *ibidem*, p. 12); Lithuania ("the Council should and must be ready to take necessary further steps in the event that parties to the conflict fail to heed the call of the resolution": *ibidem*, p. 14).

with Resolution 2139 (2014),[167] the UNSC has therefore excluded Syria from the humanitarian emergency management. Moreover, the humanitarian assistance afforded by this resolution is completed by a monitoring mechanism, under the authority of the UN Secretary-General, aimed at supervising the loading of the humanitarian relief consignments with the collaboration of the neighbouring countries (paragraph 3). Hence, even in this case the UNSC has excluded Syria from the control of humanitarian aid (whereas such control is provided for in the Geneva discipline).

It is worth noting that, with Resolution 2401 (2018), adopted on 24 February 2018, the UNSC qualified as a threat to peace and security in the region "the devastating humanitarian situation in Syria". In particular, the UNSC determined that the humanitarian situation "*continue[d]* to constitute a threat to peace", stressing that even well before the adoption of Resolution 2401 there was a threat to peace. Moreover, with this resolution the UNSC recalled that "States are obligated under Article 25 of the Charter of the United Nations to accept and carry out the Council's decisions".[168]

In light of the above, and considering the qualification of the Syrian situation as a threat to peace,[169] imposing the United Nations humanitarian missions and the related monitoring mechanism upon Syrian territory without the consent of Syria could be considered as an atypical enforcement measure based on Article 41 of the Charter. The sanctioning nature of the above measures may also be deduced both from the statements of some member States of the UNSC[170] and from the intention

[167] Report of the Secretary-General on the Implementation of Security Council Resolution 2139 (2014), UN Doc. S/2014/365, 22 May 2014, para 51: "The Government of the Syrian Arab Republic is failing in its responsibility to look after its own people. It is failing in that responsibility through its refusal to give consent to humanitarian organizations to use all means at their disposal, including the use of border crossings operated by opposition groups... Arbitrarily withholding consent for the opening of all relevant border crossings is a violation of international humanitarian law, and an act of non-compliance with resolution 2139 (2014)".

[168] UNSC Resolution 2401 (2018), 24 February 2018, preamble (italic of the a.).

[169] As stressed by Lithuania's delegate, "[t]he Syrian conflict is no longer a regional problem. It has become a global threat to international peace and security": UN Doc. S/PV.7216, 14 July 2014, p. 11.

[170] See the statement of Luxembourg ("The consent of the Syrian authorities will no longer be necessary. The monitoring mechanism... provides for a simple notification system... without interference from Damascus": *ibidem*, p. 3); United Kingdom ("Today's resolution authorizes the United Nations to use four additional border crossings to deliver life-saving humanitarian aid... without any opportunity for the Syrian regime to obstruct, impede or delay that assistance": *ibidem*, p. 5); United States ("the Council has opened four crossings... without the need for approval from the regime"; "the Syrian regime, which is systematically denying cross-line humanitarian assistance, must heed that obligation": *ibidem*, p. 6 f.); France ("the resolution innovates by introducing a convoy inspection mechanism so that the Syrian regime will no longer be able to object to the work of humanitarian actors on its territory": *ibidem*, p. 11).

of the UNSC to "take further measures in the event of non compliance with this resolution or resolution 2139 (2014) by any Syrian party" (paragraph 12).[171]

The idea that the UNSC can impose sanctions for obstructing the delivery, access or distribution of humanitarian assistance is reiterated by Resolution 2417 (2018), the first thematic resolution focusing in general terms on hunger and armed conflict.[172] This landmark resolution—adopted unanimously[173] under the broader item "Protection of civilians in armed conflict"[174]—definitively overcomes the "fatalistic" approach according to which starvation is an inevitable consequence of armed conflict. In addition, for the first time the UNSC considers the issue of hunger in a thematic way, not merely with regard to a specific war scenario, as it had done previously.[175] Resolution 2417 (2014) can be considered as a framework resolution outlining guidelines to be taken into account in the event of a food shortage in future conflicts, based on three points. First, starvation is characterized as a war crime, which involves the necessity to put an end to the impunity of perpetrators of this crime (as well as for other crimes, such as genocide and crimes against humanity committed in armed conflicts) (preamble). To that end, States are required to conduct, urgently and in an independent manner, impartial and effective investigations into violations of international humanitarian law related to the use of starvation of civilians as a method of warfare, and to take action against those responsible in accordance with domestic and international law (paragraph 10). Second, as mentioned above, the UNSC can adopt sanctions against individuals or entities obstructing the delivery of humanitarian assistance (paragraph 9). Third, a monitoring system is put in place, asking the Secretary-General to provide information on the humanitarian situation dealt with by Resolution 2417 (2018). In particular, the Secretary-General is involved in three ways: providing a regular report on country-specific situations as regards the risk of famine and food insecurity during an armed conflict (paragraph 11); where necessary, reporting quickly to the UNSC when the risk of conflict-induced famine and food insecurity occurs in armed conflict (paragraph 12); submitting to the UNSC an annual report on the implementation of Resolution 2417 (2018) (paragraph 13).

Some final considerations can be advanced with regard to Resolution 2417 (2018). It presents at the same time some positive, but also questionable aspects.

[171] For the opinion according to which Resolution 2139 (2014) and 2165 (2014) are not based on Chapter VII of the United Nations Charter, see Zimmermann (2017), pp. 11 ff.

[172] See Zappalà (2019), pp. 881 ff.

[173] Resolution 2417 (2014) is a result of a conciliation between the position of those States (such as China, Ethiopia and Russia) showing a certain reluctance in discussing the thematic issue of hunger considered not strictly and exclusively related to the maintenance of peace and security, but essentially a development issue, and other States (such as Netherlands and United Kingdom) ready to stress the hunger as ordinary consequence of armed conflict: Security Council to adopt a resolution on hunger in armed conflict, in www.whatsinblue.org/2018/05/security-council-to-adopt-a-resolution-on-hunger-in-armed-conflict.php.

[174] See UN Doc. S/PV.8267, 24 May 2018.

[175] Zappalà (2019), pp. 889 f.

On the one hand, in confirming the scaffolding of the rules on the prohibition of starvation and its modalities (siege and destruction of objects indispensable to the civilian population), the resolution widens the categories of goods whose deprivation causes starvation. In fact, it calls on all parties to an armed conflict not only not to attack or destroy objects that are indispensable to the survival of the civilian population, as requested by the 1977 Protocols ("such as foodstuffs, crops, livestock, agricultural assets, drinking water installations and supplies, irrigation work"), but also not to attack "objects necessary for food production and distribution, such as farms, markets, water systems, mills, food processing and storage sites, and hubs and means for food transportation" (paragraph 1).

On the other hand, it is regrettable the way in which Resolution 2417 (2014) deals with the question of the criminalization of starvation. It is true that it condemns the use of the starvation of civilians as a method of warfare in a number of conflict situations (paragraph 5); however, it qualifies starvation as a war crime and stresses the necessity to ensure accountability for war crimes only in its preambular part. It would have been better and more desirable to put all the parts concerning the criminalization of starvation in the operative part of resolution, in such a way as to give more "importance" (and credibility?) to the criminal consequences of starvation.[176] Moreover, an important step towards the effective prosecution of the crime of starvation would have been a reference to the competence of the ICC, as a "closing mechanism" to prevent the impunity of those responsible for this crime. The lack of any explicit mention is, however, understandable if one considers the presence in the UNSC of States that have always opposed the jurisdiction and functioning of the ICC.[177] That is why the resolution pays particular attention to the need for Member States to conduct an effective investigation "within their jurisdiction" into violations of humanitarian law related to the use of starvation of civilians (paragraph 10).

Another interesting aspect of Resolution 2417 (2018) is that it does not distinguish between IACs and NIACs, and confirms that the prohibition of denying humanitarian access applies "in situations of armed conflict" (paragraph 6). The position of the UNSC on this matter is in line with the proposal of Switzerland that,

[176] While, for example, in Resolution 794 (1992) on the situation in Somalia, the individual responsibility of who committed or ordered to commit the deliberate impeding of the delivery of food and medical supplies essential for the survival of the civilian population was put in the operative part (para 5). See Zappalà (2019), p. 900.

[177] That is the reason why, for example, China and Russia vetoed a draft resolution according to which the UNSC decided to refer the situation in Syria, which is not party to the Statute of the ICC, to the Prosecutor of the ICC, to ascertain any responsibility for war crimes and crimes against humanity committed during the conflict: UN Doc. S/2014/348, 22 May 2014, para 2; UN Doc. S/PV.7810, 22 May 2014. Among the permanent member States of the UNSC, China, Russia and the United States are not parties to the Statute of the ICC. Russia (https://treaties.un.org/doc/Publication/CN/2016/CN.886.2016-Eng.pdf) and the United States (https://treaties.un.org/doc/Publication/CN/2002/CN.434.2002-Eng.pdf) expressly stated their intention not to become a party to the Rome Statute of the International Criminal Court.

as said at the beginning of this contribution, promoted the inclusion in the statute of the crime of starvation of civilians also in relation to internal conflicts.[178]

9 Concluding Remarks

Despite the existence of an overall satisfactory normative body prohibiting the starvation of the civilian population as a method of war, even the recent practice (i.e. the conflicts in Syria and Yemen) shows that civilians are very often intentionally starved by the belligerents. While not actively participating in hostilities, nor providing indirect support, the mere suspicion that a part of the population would sympathize with a belligerent is considered a valid reason to starve these civilians or deprive them of essential goods for survival.

The prohibition of starvation must be considered in the light of the fundamental rule of the conduct of hostilities, namely the obligation of distinction (the "Basic rule" provided for in Article 48 of the AP I). In this sense, for the protection of civilians there is no difference, for the consequences produced, between the prohibition of indiscriminate bombings and starvation; the act of intentional starvation is analogous to that of terror bombardment.

Having said that, it is worth noting that some recent developments could improve the effectiveness of the ban on starvation. These developments are, on the one hand, the inclusion of the crime of starvation of civilians in non-international armed conflicts, through an amendment of the Rome Statute; on the other, the adoption by the UNSC of Resolution 2417 (2018). For the first time, the UNSC considered the issue of starvation in a thematic way, not merely with regard to a specific war scenario, stressing the direct impact of armed conflicts on food security. The next few years will show if Resolution 2417 (2018) will have the important distinction of putting the question of starvation at the centre of the UNSC's attention. In this respect, it is worth noting that this framework resolution has already been invoked as regards certain conflicts, such the ones in Somalia[179] and Yemen.[180] But the UNSC

---

[178] *Supra*, fn. 1.

[179] With Resolution 2431 (2018) on Somalia, based on Chapter VII of the Charter, the UNSC, *inter alia*, recalled Resolution 2417 (2018) in expressing grave concern at the ongoing humanitarian crisis in Somalia, condemning the increase in attacks against humanitarian workers and calling on all parties to respect and protect humanitarian personnel, facilities and assets.

[180] During a meeting of the UNSC, the Netherlands delegate, after having stressed that "Yemen is a clear example of the relationship between conflict and hunger", recalled that Resolution 2417 (2018) "commits the Council to address man-made crises with man-made solutions": International Community Must Take Action to Stop Catastrophic Famine in Yemen, Top Humanitarian Affairs Official Tells Security Council, 23 October 2018; www.un.org/press/en/2018/sc13550.doc.htm. Also the Swedish delegate, invoking Resolution 2417 (2018), called for safe and unhindered humanitarian access and respect for international humanitarian law, and a durable ceasefire, stressing that only a negotiated political solution can end "this futile war": *ibidem*; Swedish Statement at the UN Security Council Briefing on Yemen, 23 October 2018; www.government.

did not adopt specific measures and concrete consequences due to this resolution have not been produced.

Moreover, two problematic issues show and confirm the difficulty in concretely implementing the prohibition of starvation. First, the question of involving and empowering certain armed groups to respect humanitarian law, such as ISIS. As the recent practice showed, this is a thorny and very problematic issue: how to convince these particularly cruel fighters to act inside an accepted regulatory framework? The trial and conviction of these fighters for war crimes committed during an armed conflict, even by the ICC, will in any case be subsequent to the commission of the crime. The second question relates to the *mens rea* requirement; it is in fact necessary to show that the perpetrator intended to starve the civilians as a method of warfare.[181] During armed conflicts, in particular those non-international, a shortage of food and the difficulty of reaching the civilian population with relief consignments may well be "only" an incidental consequence of the hostilities. Although there may exist a serious situation for civilians, this would not be enough to determine that there had been the commission of the crime of starvation. The problematic issue is to establish with certainty whether starvation of civilians is caused by the intention of a belligerent to deliberately cause hunger among civilians.[182]

se/statements/2018/10/swedish-statement-at-the-un-security-council-briefing-on-yemen/. Likewise, the United Nations Special Advisor on Genocide Prevention, Adama Dieng, referred to Resolution 2417 (2018) in condemning the attack against the Yemeni port of Hudaydah, under control of Houthi fighters, launched by pro-government forces backed by Saudi Arabia and United Arab Emirates: "[s]tarvation of civilians as a method of war is a war crime and was condemned by the Security Council in resolution 2417 of 24 May 2018. It seems that the first test of this resolution is Yemen: the Yemeni port of Hudaydah is a lifeline for the delivery of aid and the Coalition's air strikes can kill many more people over time through famine and hunger when damaging such civilian infrastructure": Note to Correspondents: Statement by Adama Dieng, United Nations Special Adviser on the Prevention of Genocide, on the situation in Hudaydah, Yemen, 14 June 2018.www.un.org/sg/en/content/sg/note-correspondents/2018-06-14/note-correspondents-statement-adama-dieng-united-nations.

[181] See Dörmann (2004), pp. 363 ff. "[W]hat is clear is that that Article 8(2)(b)(xxv) [of the ICC Statute] does not allow prosecutions for inadvertent consequences, such as societal mismanagement or otherwise failures to generally live up to internationally promoted standards of good governance": Can We Prosecute Starvation? Briefing paper, May 2018, p. 4; in https://sites.tufts.edu/wpf/files/2018/09/Can-we-prosecute-starvation-20180501-LA_bc.pdf.

[182] See World Peace Foundation (2019). A useful toll to tackle situations of starvation caused by armed conflicts could be the Integrated Food Security and Humanitarian Phase Classification (IPC). See www.fao.org/3/i0275e/i0275e.pdf. It is a programme created in 2004 by the Food and Agriculture Organization (FAO) to analyze the problem of food (in)security in Somalia owing the collapse of this State, through the identification of five levels of food scarcity (from "minimal" to "famine"), but it could be also useful on a wider scale. For example, the IPC was used to analyze situations of food shortage or starvation in various provinces of Yemen, following the current conflict, in such a way as to enable the donor agencies and donor States to act in a timely and more effective manner for providing assistance to the civilian population: Yemen: Integrated Food Insecurity Phase Classification Snapshot. October 2020–June 2021, www.ipcinfo.org/fileadmin/user_upload/ipcinfo/docs/IPC_Yemen_Acute_Food_Insecurity_2020Oct2021June_Snapshot.pdf.

References

Akande D, Gillard EC (2016) Arbitrary withholding of consent to humanitarian relief operations in armed conflict. Int Law Stud 92:483–511

Akande D, Gillard E (eds) (2019) Conflict-induced food insecurity and the war crime of starvation of civilians as a method of war. J Int Crim Just 17(4):753–779

Aldrich GH (1981) New life for the laws of war. Am J Int Law 75(4):764–783

Allen C (1989) Civilian starvation and relief during armed conflict: the modern humanitarian law. Georgia J Int Comp Law 19(1):1–85

Amnesty International (2014) Squeezing the life out of Yarmouk. War crimes against besieged civilians. www.amnesty.org/en/documents/MDE24/008/2014/en/

Bothe M, Partsch KJ, Solf WA (2013) New rules for victims of armed conflicts. Commentary on the two 1977 protocols additional to the Geneva Conventions of 1949. Nijhoff, Leiden

Buckingham W (1982) Operation Ranch Hand. The Air Force and Herbicides in Southeast Asia 1961–1971. Office of Air Force History, Washington

Campbell D (2006) Besieged. Siege warfare in ancient world. Osprey, Oxford

Cassese A (1984) The Geneva protocols of 1977 on the humanitarian law of armed conflict and customary international law. UCLA Pacific Basin Law J 55(3):55–118

Chrastil R (2014) The siege of Strasbourg. Harvard University Press, Cambridge

Clark J (1992) Debacle in Somalia. www.foreignaffairs.com/articles/somalia/1992-01-01/debacle-somalia

Conley B, de Waal A (2019) The purposes of starvation. Historical and contemporary uses. J Int Crim Just 17(4):699–722

Corfis I, Wolfe M (eds) (1995) The Medieval City under siege. Boydell and Brewer, New York

Detter I (2000) The law of war. Cambridge University Press, Cambridge

Dinstein Y (2016) The conduct of hostilities under the law of international armed conflict. Cambridge University Press, Cambridge

Dörmann K (2004) Elements of war crimes under the Rome Statute of the International Criminal Court. Sources and commentary. Cambridge University Press, Cambridge

Field R (2009) Petersburg 1864–65. The longest siege. Osprey, Oxford

Gaggioli G (2019) Are sieges prohibited under contemporary IHL? EJIL Joint Blog Series on International Law and Armed Conflict. www.ejiltalk.org/joint-blog-series-on-international-law-and-armed-conflict-are-sieges-prohibited-under-contemporary-ihl/#more-16877

Gaggioli G, Melzer N (2020) Methods of warfare. In: Saul B, Akande D (eds) The Oxford guide to international humanitarian law. Oxford University Press, Oxford

Garner J (1920) International law and the World War, vol II. Longmans, Green and Co., London

Glantz D (2001) The Siege of Leningrad 1941–1944. 900 days of terror. Brown Partworks, Staplehurst

Hamidullah M (1945) Muslim conduct of state. Kashmiri Bazar, Lahore

Hartigan RS (1983) Lieber's code of the law of war. Precedent Publishing, South Holland

Heintschel von Heinegg W (2015) Blockade. https://opil.ouplaw.co

Heintschel von Heinegg W (2000) Naval blockade. Int Law Stud 75:203–230

Henckaerts JM, Doswald-Beck L (eds) (2005) Customary international humanitarian law, vol I and II. Cambridge University Press, Cambridge

Human Rights Watch (1994) Angola. Arms trade and violations of the laws of war since the 1992 elections. New York. https://www.hrw.org/reports/ANGOLA94N.PDF

Human Rights Watch (2012) Syria: government attacking bread lines. www.hrw.org/news/2012/08/30/syria-government-attacking-bread-lines

Hutter S (2015) Starvation as a weapon. Nijhoff, Leiden

International Center for Transitional Justice (2013) Lebanon's legacy of political violence. A mapping of serious violations of international human rights and humanitarian law in Lebanon, 1975–2008. https://www.ictj.org/sites/default/files/ICTJ-Report-Lebanon-Mapping-2013-EN_0.pdf

Kostick C (2009) The Siege of Jerusalem. Crusade and Conquest in 1099. Continuum, London
Kraska J (2009) Siege. https://opil.ouplaw.com
Liddell Hart B (1958) Sherman: soldier, realist, American. Da Capo Press, Boston
Luisi R (2017) Scudi di pietra. I castelli e l'arte della guerra tra Medioevo e Rinascimento. Odoya, Bologna
Mayer J (1968) Starvation as a weapon. In: Rose S (ed) CBW. Chemical and biological warfare. Beacon Press, Boston
Mertens P (1969) Les modalités de l'intervention du Comité International de la Croix Rouge dans le conflit du Nigéria. Annuaire français de droit international 15:183–209
Meyrowitz H (1985) Le Protocole additionel I aux Conventions de Genève de 1949 et le droit de la guerre maritime. Revue générale de droit internationale public 89:243–298
Momtaz D (2001) Le droit international Humanitaire applicable aux conflits armés non internationaux. Recueil des cours de l'Académie de droit international 292:9–145
Mundy M (2018) The strategies of the coalition in the Yemen War: aerial bombardment and food war. World Peace Foundation at The Fletcher School of Law and Diplomacy
Nolan E (1857) History of the war against Russia, vol II. London
Pax (2019) Siege Watch: Final Report. Out of sight, out of mind: the aftermath of Syria's Sieges. https://reliefweb.int/sites/reliefweb.int/files/resources/pax-siege-watch-final-report.pdf
Pejic J (2001) The right to food in situations of armed conflict: the legal framework. Int Rev Red Cross 83(844):1097–1109
Power S (2016) Siege warfare in Syria: prosecuting the starvation of civilians. Amsterdam Law Forum 8(2):1–22
Provost R (1992) Starvation as a weapon: legal implications of the United Nations blockade against Iraq and Kuwait. Columbia J Transnatl Law 30:577–639
Riordan KJ (2010) Shelling, sniping and starvation: the law of armed conflict and the lessons of the Siege of Sarajevo. Victoria Univ Wellington Law Rev 41:149–178
Rogers APV (2012) Law on the battlefield. Manchester University Press, Manchester
Rosenblad E (1979) International humanitarian law of armed conflict. Henri Dunant Institute, Geneva
Sandoz Y, Swinarski C, Zimmermann B (eds) (1987) Commentary on the additional protocols of 8 June 1977 to the Geneva Conventions of 12 August 1949. Nijhoff, Geneva
Schmitt MN, Garraway CHB, Dinstein Y (eds) (2006) The manual on the law of non-international armed conflict. With commentary. International Institute of Humanitarian Law, Sanremo
Schwartz D (1991) International terrorism and Islamic law. Columbia J Transnatl Law 29(3): 629–652
Settia A (2009) Rapine, assedi, battaglie. Laterza, Bari
Solf W (1986) Protection of civilians against the effects of hostilities under customary international law and under protocol I. Am Univ J Int Law Policy 1:117–136
Spaight JM (1911) War rights on land. Macmillan, London
Spieker H (2011) The right to give and receive humanitarian assistance. In: Heintze HJ, Zwitter A (eds) International humanitarian law and humanitarian assistance. Springer, Berlin
Triffterer O, Ambos K (eds) (2016) The Rome Statute of the International Criminal Court. H. Beck/ Hart/Nomos
United States Department of Defense (2015) Law of war manual
Van Shaack B (2016) Siege warfare and the starvation of civilians as a weapon of war and war crime. www.justsecurity.org/29157/siege-warfare-starvation-civilians-war-crime/
Walzer M (2006) Just and unjust wars. Basic Books, New York
Waxman MC (1999) Siegecraft and surrender: the law and strategy of cities as targets. Virginia J Int Law 39(2):353–423

World Peace Foundation (2019) The crime of starvation and methods of prosecution and accountability. https://reliefweb.int/sites/reliefweb.int/files/resources/Legal%20Paper%20Starvation.pdf
Zappalà S (2019) Conflict related hunger, "Starvation Crimes" and UN Security Council Resolution 2417 (2018). J Int Crim Just 17(4):881–906
Zawati H (2015) Theory of war in Islamic and public international law. In: Shah NA (ed) Islam and the law of armed conflict. Edward Elgar, Cheltenham
Zimmermann B (2017) Humanitarian assistance and the Security Council. Israel Law Rev 50(1): 3–23

Part II
Cultural Heritage Law

Underwater Cultural Heritage and Salvage Law

Angelo Merialdi

Abstract At an early stage of underwater cultural heritage exploration, the maritime law doctrines of salvage and finds were relied upon by US Courts in granting treasure seekers' property rights over historical objects recovered from the bottom of the sea, to the detriment of the concurrent claims of the interested State. This caused a public outcry amongst archaeologists and conservationists, who developed the general perception that not only did the recovery of historical objects amount to looting, but also that the traditional maritime law concepts of finds and salvage were in any case incompatible with the purpose of the preservation of underwater cultural heritage. Since then, a complex legal framework has developed to ensure that activities directed to underwater cultural heritage are carried out in an orderly manner, protecting the public interest in the preservation of historical sites, respecting the right of States and persons having an interest or title thereupon and avoiding the disturbance of human remains. The law of finds, being focused on the finder's appropriation of recovered historical objects, does not appear to be compatible with the developing legal framework for the protection of underwater cultural heritage. Conversely, the law of salvage, which as a rule does not involve the private appropriation of salved objects, has demonstrated the ability to evolve beyond its original purpose of the preservation of property at sea and to adapt to concerns having a public nature. In the current legal framework, a good application of the law of salvage is not necessarily antithetical to the duty to protect underwater cultural heritage for the public benefit.

1 Introduction

The bottom of our oceans hosts an immense number of shipwrecks having an historic or archaeological value. Unlike sites on land, often these have the benefit of not having been corrupted by the interaction of human activities intervening in the

A. Merialdi (✉)
Genoa, Italy
e-mail: a.merialdi@siccardibregante.it

M. Arcari et al. (eds.), *Trends and Challenges in International Law*,
https://doi.org/10.1007/978-3-030-94387-5_5

following eras. As such they are regarded as "time capsules": snapshots of the era when the sinking occurred. It is in the interest of mankind to preserve these sites.

On the other hand, men, throughout the centuries, whether driven by sincere archaeological interest or motivated by profit have not been able to resist the impulse to bring the remains of shipwrecks and their cargo, which in some cases may retain considerable economic value, to the surface. Subsequent to World War II, technological advances have made seabed exploration at considerable depths and in international waters feasible. The early seventies witnessed the beginning of a "gold rush" especially in waters that are in close proximity to the coasts of the United States, where sunken galleons together with their precious cargoes, have been laying on the floor of the ocean undisturbed for centuries. In this early period, activities in relation to sunken shipwrecks were often conducted by treasure seekers whose behaviour had little or no regard at all for the historical value of underwater archaeological sites and the public interest in their preservation. To make things worse, competing salvage enterprises often appeared on the scene of discovered wrecks, each claiming priority rights vis à vis the others in relation to the recovery of objects. In these circumstances, US Courts were called upon by treasure hunters seeking judicial orders to affirm their priority/exclusive rights to exploration and recovery. In doing so, treasure seekers relied on the long established commercial maritime law concepts of salvage and the law of finds. In turn, historically the US Courts had relied upon these concepts to grant the requested relief, in some cases recognizing that treasure seekers had property rights over the recovered objects.[1]

These facts were looked at with utmost concern by archaeologists and institutions dedicated to the protection of underwater cultural heritage. The general perception spread among them, is that not only does the recovery of historical objects amount to looting, but also that the traditional commercial maritime law concepts of finds and salvage were in any case incompatible with the purpose of the preservation of underwater cultural heritage.[2]

Since then, the need to ensure that activities directed at underwater cultural heritage are carried out in an orderly manner, *i.e.* protecting the public interest in the preservation of historical sites, respecting the right of States and persons having an interest or title thereupon and avoiding the disturbance of human remains, to the detriment of the action of unauthorized looters, has prompted States and the international community as a whole to develop a new and complex body of rules for the protection of underwater cultural heritage. Case law has also evolved accordingly.

Whether and to what extent, the ancient laws of salvage and finds may still have a role in the developing legal regime of protection of underwater cultural heritage

---

[1]The most notable US judicial cases affirming salvors' title over the recovered material, to the detriment of the concurrent claims of the State of Florida, are *Nuestra Señora de Atocha* and *Cobb Coin*: see Scovazzi (2019), pp. 247–261.

[2]See McQuown (2000), pp. 289–326; Dromgoole (2013), p. 173. This negative perception persists today, see *e.g.*: Scovazzi (2019), pp. 280–283.

represents one of the most debated and interesting topics in the analysis of this regime.

2 Salvage and Law of Finds

2.1 Salvage

2.1.1 The Essence of Salvage

Salvage is a traditional maritime law concept, which is universally shared by civil law and common law countries. Even if there is no unanimously recognized definition, it can be said to occur whenever assistance is rendered to a ship at sea which is in such a dangerous position that in all human probability, she will not be able to extricate herself by her unassisted effort.[3] The aforementioned concept also includes assistance efforts in relation to the onboard cargo, as well as in respect to the preservation of or contribution to freight payments.

In a vast number of cases salvors act in pursuance of a salvage contract with the owners of the salved property. Traditionally this is done by way of an open contract, where the salvage remuneration is to be determined at the end of salvage operation in the light of its outcome, although different arrangements are possible, for instance whereby the salvor and the owner agree that remuneration will not exceed an agreed limit. But a pre-existing contractual arrangement is not a necessary condition for salvage and the law of salvage applies irrespectively. Under certain circumstances, the rules of salvage may even apply when a salvage operation is undertaken in spite of the prohibition by the owner of the property.[4]

The essential ground for salvage is that of danger. This is intended not only as the danger for property of being lost at sea. It extends to the danger of suffering additional significant damage and deterioration.

Different from the typical common law concept of law of finds (see Sect. 2.2 below), as a rule salvors do not acquire ownership of the salved property. The purpose of salvors is to return imperilled property to the respective owner and obtain a remuneration from the latter. The salvor's claim for salvage remuneration is assisted by a lien on salved property.[5] The lien operates as security for the payment of salvage remuneration. When the owner of salved property does not spontaneously abide by an enforceable judicial decision or arbitration award issued in favour of the salvor, the lien can ultimately be enforced by judicial sale of the said property.

---

[3] Baughen (2019), p. 291; Rose (2017), para 1-016.

[4] See infra, Sect. 2.1.4.

[5] See Article 4 of the International Convention on Maritime Liens and Mortgages, 1993 and Article 2 of the International Convention for the Unification of Certain Rules of Law relating to Maritime Liens and Mortgages, 1926. On common law maritime lien for salvage reward see Rose (2017), paras 14-028 *et seq.*

It is suggested that something similar to salvage was already present in the Rhodian Maritime Code (900 BC) where volunteer salvors were entitled to a reward for their services to imperilled ships[6] and that the subsequent *Corpus Juris Civilis* (ancient Roman law 533),[7] Marine Ordinance of Trani (1063), the Law of Oleron (1189), the Code of Hanseatic League (1597) and the Marine Ordinances of Louis XIV (1681) all contained similar principles.[8] Some have also expressed the view that the roots of salvage go back to the Roman law concept of *negotiorum gestio*.[9]

Although the accuracy of some or all of the above theories on the ancient origins of salvage has been questioned,[10] it is not in dispute that the need to give fair remuneration to those with the skill and bravery to endure risky salvage operations for the purpose of salvaging property in danger at sea, in order to return it to their owners is a concept which has generally long been accepted by all maritime nations. It is not surprising, then, that the codification of the law of salvage was taken up by the *Comité Maritime International* as a priority task after the foundation of this institution, resulting in the adoption in 1910 of the Convention for the Unification of Certain Rules of Law with respect to Assistance and Salvage at Sea (hereinafter the "1910 Convention").[11]

The distinct and fundamental feature of this Convention was that salvage remuneration was recognized to be strictly due on a "no cure no pay" basis, which means that salvors are remunerated only to the extent that they are successful in salving property, otherwise no remuneration is due by the respective owner.

The performance of salvage operations on modern ships often occurs in situations where pollution caused by the cargo or by the contents of the bunker of the attended vessel is already present or threatens to become an issue. Salvors focusing exclusively on the preservation of property would often neglect the need to preserve the environment, in some cases their actions could also aggravate the risk of pollution. The growing concern for the environmental implications of salvage led maritime nations to believe that the traditional no cure no pay regime of the 1910 Convention was no longer sustainable and that a new, more environmentally sensitive, regime needed to be set in place.

This resulted in the adoption in 1989 of the International Convention on Salvage (hereinafter the "1989 Convention"),[12] which, already in its preamble, acknowledges

---

[6]Reeder (2012), paras 1-12.

[7]See *The Calypso* (1828) 166 ER 221 (HCA) 224.

[8]Reeder (2012), paras 1-13. See also *RMS Titanic, Inc v Haver*, 171 F 3d 943, p. 960 (1999).

[9]*The Calypso* (1828) 166 ER 221 (HCA) 224.

[10]Scovazzi (2017), pp. 511–512. The link to the roman *negotiorum gestio* is questioned by the editors of *Brice on Maritime Law of Salvage*, see Reeder (2012), paras 1-12.

[11]The 1910 Convention was adopted in Brussels on 23 September 1910 and entered into force on 1 March 1913. It was amended by the Protocol to amend the Convention for the Unification of Certain Rules of law relating to Assistance and Salvage at Sea Signed at Brussels on 23 September 1910, Brussels, 27 May 1967, which entered into force on 15 August 1977.

[12]The 1989 Convention was adopted on 28 April 1989. It has been ratified by 75 States (see Status of IMO Treaties 15 September 2020 https://wwwcdn.imo.org/localresources/en/About/

the major contribution that salvage may give to the protection of the environment, in addition to the safety of property at sea.

Under Article 1 (a) the 1989 Convention applies to salvage defined as "any act or activity undertaken to assist a vessel or any property in danger in navigable waters or in any other waters whatsoever". Danger for property at sea represents the essential ground for salvage and salvage remuneration. The wording "any other property" is very broad and covers the cargo of the ship, its bunker and freight, aircraft or in general any other object owned by a person or entity, to the extent the same are not "permanently and intentionally attached to the shoreline".[13]

The main change compared to the 1910 Salvage Convention is the introduction of provisions dealing with the protection of the environment.

While Article 12 affirms that—in principle—salvage remuneration remains subject to the condition of a useful result, under Article 13 "the skill and efforts of the salvors in preventing or minimizing damage to the environment" are listed (in the second place) among the criteria for fixing salvage remuneration, just after the criterion of "salved value of the vessel and other property" and before a number of additional traditional criteria, including: the measure of success obtained by the salvor; the nature and degree of the danger; the skill and efforts of the salvors in salving the vessel, other property and human life.

Article 14 goes further by introducing the concept of special compensation for the protection of the environment. The peculiarity of this special compensation is that it is not awarded on a "no cure no pay" basis. The principle under Article 14 is that if salvors fail to obtain adequate remuneration—or obtain no remuneration at all—under Article 13, in respect of a vessel that by itself or its cargo threatened damage to the environment, they are at least entitled to special compensation covering the expenses incurred in the operation, which is increased if salvors were successful in preventing or minimizing damage to the environment. Conversely, salvors may be deprived of the whole or part of any special compensation, when they are deemed negligent and thereby failed to prevent or minimize damage to the environment.

In the actual salvage practice, and specifically pursuant to the widely used contractual form known as the Lloyd's Open Form (LOF),[14] Article 14 is systematically replaced by the more flexible contractual regime of the Special Compensation Protection and Indemnity Club (SCOPIC) Clause, whereby salvors are afforded the possibility to cover expenses incurred in salvage operations irrespective of the conditions set out under Article 14.[15]

The above environmental provisions of the 1989 Convention are of importance for the present analysis because they show that salvage law has been capable of

Conventions/StatusOfConventions/StatusOfTreaties.pdf) and has entered into force at the international level on 14th July 1996.

[13] Article 1 (c) of the 1989 Convention.

[14] On LOF see Rose (2017), Ch 9. S 4; Reeder (2012), Ch 8.

[15] On SCOPIC see Rose (2017), Ch 9 S. 9; Reeder (2012), paras 8-240–8-301.

evolving beyond its original scope and purpose, *i.e.* the preservation of property at sea, so as to embrace other interests having a public nature.

2.1.2 Does the 1989 Convention Apply to Underwater Cultural Heritage?

The question of whether the 1989 Convention also applies to wrecks and more generally to underwater cultural heritage is a much debated one.

Pursuant to Article 1 (b) of the 1989 Convention "vessel means any ship or craft, or any structure capable of navigation" whereas under Article 1 (c) "property means any property not permanently and intentionally attached to the shoreline and includes freight at risk". It is true that neither definition expressly refers to wrecks. Some authors suggest that the expression "capable of navigation" in the definition of "vessel" only applies to "structures" and not to the words "ship or craft" which would imply that wrecks are included in the "vessel" definition.[16] In any case the definition of "property" is very broad and there is no indication that sunken property, such as shipwrecks and the cargo they may still contain, should be excluded.

The fact that—either because they qualify as a "vessel" or "property"—the 1989 Convention also contemplates salvage of wrecks and respective cargo is confirmed by the reservation of Article 30(1)(d), reading

> Any State may, at the time of signature, ratification, acceptance, approval or accession, reserve the right not to apply the provisions of this Convention: (. . .) (d) when the property involved is maritime cultural property of prehistoric, archaeological or historic interest and is situated on the sea-bed.[17]

Further support for the inclusion of wrecks can be drawn from the Travaux Préparatoires of the Convention on Salvage 1989.[18] The proposal of the Spanish delegation to include an additional reservation in Article 30 so that sunken vessels would in principle not be covered was rejected due to opposition by the British, Swedish, Japanese and Dutch delegations. In particular the United Kingdom and Sweden thought that no clarification was needed as they "*(. . .)* have always taken the view that sunken vessels and wrecks are included in the term 'property'". Therefore this reservation was not added to the final version of Article 30.

---

[16] Berlingieri (2009), p. 473; Reeder (2012) paras 4-23; 4-15; 4-35.

[17] Berlingieri (2009), p. 467. Reservations pursuant to Article 30.1(d) have been made by Australia, Bulgaria, Canada, China, Croatia, Ecuador, Estonia, Finland, France, Germany, Islamic Republic of Iran, Jamaica, Mexico, Netherlands, New Zealand, Norway, Poland, Russian Federation, Saudi Arabia, Spain, Sweden, Tunisia, Turkey, Ukraine and United Kingdom see Status of IMO Treaties 15 September https://wwwcdn.imo.org/localresources/en/About/Conventions/StatusOfConventions/Status%20-%202021.pdf.

[18] *Travaux Préparatoires of the Convention on Salvage 1989*, p. 101, https://comitemaritime.org/wp-content/uploads/2018/05/Travaux-Preparatoires-of-the-Convention-on-Salvage-1989.pdf. On this point see more in detail Berlingieri (2009), p. 474.

It is often suggested that shipwrecks lying on the bottom of the sea after a while reach a state of equilibrium and as such that they are not exposed to an imminent danger of suffering further damage, which would make salvage law not applicable to them.[19] The opposite view is expressed by some authors suggesting either "the fact that the property lays immobilised on (. . .) the seabed is a sufficient 'danger'" or that the notion of "danger" in the case of shipwrecks should be read as "danger of permanent loss".[20] The concept of danger in salvage has been held to apply to shipwrecks in a number of common law judicial decisions.[21]

The truth is that danger cannot be discarded as a matter of principle. In many cases underwater cultural heritage may not be exposed to an imminent danger of deterioration due to natural causes. But in a residual number of cases, especially in waters in proximity to the coast, such a risk may also exist due—for instance—to extreme meteorological phenomena that may upset the environmental conditions in the area where the wreck is located.

In addition, for the purpose of traditional salvage, danger does not derive from natural causes only. It may also derive from human activities,[22] including for instance collisions,[23] groundings, fires accidentally caused by the crew and piracy.[24] By way of analogy this implies that with respect to underwater cultural heritage, danger for the purposes of salvage may arise out of illegal activities, such as possible interference by unauthorised salvors or looters, but also legitimate activities, such as drilling, dredging and cable and pipe laying.

As discussed, salvage is traditionally aimed at the preservation of property at sea. This implies that the existence of identifiable owners is a condition for the application of the law of salvage. This should not be an absolute obstacle to the application of law of salvage to underwater cultural heritage, either, considering that in many cases the owner of the shipwreck and respective cargo remains identifiable and where this is not so, for instance in relation to ancient shipwrecks and respective

---

[19] Juvelier (2018), pp. 1038–1041.

[20] Alexander (1989), pp. 14–17: Berlingieri (2009) p. 468; Brice (1996), p. 339. Brice argues that in the case of salvage of a wreck, danger should be presumed.

[21] In the United States see *e.g. Treasure Salvors, Inc v Unidentified, Wrecked and Abandoned Sailing Vessel*, 569 F2d 330, p. 337 (5th Cir 1978); *Platoro Ltd, Inc v The Unidentified Remains of a Vessel*, 614 F2d 1051, p. 1055-56 (5th Cir 1980); *Cobb Coin Co v Unidentified, Wrecked and Abandoned Sailing Vessel*, 549 F Supp 540, 561, 557 (SD Fla 1982). *Contra*: *Subaqueous Exploration & Archaeology Ltd v The Unidentified, Wrecked and Abandoned Vessel*, 577 F Supp 597 (D Md 1983). In England and Wales see *The Calypso* See *The Calypso* (1828) 166 ER 221; *The HMS Thetis* 166 ER 312; *The Tubantia* [1924] p. 78, where the danger inherent in the salvage of wrecks was taken for granted. For a brief overview of case law on danger see also Reeder (2012) paras 4-66-4-69.

[22] Sweeney (1999), p. 190.

[23] See *e.g.* the English cases *The Port Caledonia and The Anna* [1903] p. 184; *The Ovre and the Conde de Zubiria* (1920) 2 Ll L Rep 21.

[24] See *The Calypso* See *The Calypso* (1828) 166 ER 221 HCA p. 224 and Rose (2017) para 5-008.

cargo, ownership may often be attributed to the coastal State based on its domestic legislation.[25]

A possible restriction to the application of the 1989 Convention to underwater cultural heritage is represented by the "State-owned vessels exception" pursuant to Article 4, which states that

> this Convention shall not apply to warships or other non-commercial vessels owned or operated by a State and entitled, at the time of salvage operations, to sovereign immunity under generally recognized principles of international law unless that State decides otherwise.

However, the effect of this exception for the purpose of the salvage of underwater cultural heritage is limited in several respects. First, Article 4 seems to have a merely declaratory value, in that it simply re-affirms the principle of sovereign immunity of State-owned ships, which as such is recognized by Public International Law.[26] Second, as expressly provided by Article 4 itself, the protection of sovereign immunity may be waived by the interested flag State.[27] Third, Article 4 only refers to vessels and this implies that the exception does not apply to other State-owned property, like aircraft and cargo.[28]

Salvage of State-owned cargo, in fact, is specifically governed—in permissive terms—by Article 25 of the 1989 Convention, reading:

> (. . .) no provision of this Convention shall be used as a basis for the seizure, arrest or detention by any legal process of, nor for any proceedings in rem against, non-commercial cargoes owned by a State and entitled, at the time of the salvage operations, to sovereign immunity under generally recognized principles of international law.

This refers to the usual salvors' practice of seizing salved property as security for payment of salvage remuneration. The prohibition of seizure and similar remedies

---

[25] In the United Kingdom see s. 241 of the Merchant Shipping Act 1995 (hereinafter the "MSA 1995") stating that

> Her Majesty and Her Royal successors are entitled to all unclaimed wreck found in the United Kingdom or in United Kingdom waters except in places where Her Majesty or any of Her Royal predecessors has granted the right to any other person;

in the United States s. 6 of the Abandoned Shipwreck Act:

> (a) The United States asserts title to any abandoned shipwreck that is — (1) embedded in submerged lands of a State; (2) embedded in coralline formations protected by a State on submerged lands of a State; or (3) on submerged lands of a State and is included in or determined eligible for inclusion in the National Register;

in Italy Article 91 D.Lgs. 42/2004 states that shipwrecks found on the seabed of territorial waters are owned by the Italian State.

[26] The same principle is also expressly preserved by the Convention on the Protection of the Underwater Cultural Heritage, see infra Sect. 3.2.3.

[27] For example, the United Kingdom stipulated an exclusive salvage agreement with the US based company Odyssey Marine Exploration Inc. for the salvage of *SS Gairsoppa*, a British cargo vessel enlisted in the service of the United Kingdom for the Ministry of War Transport during World War II. Generally, on the salvage of *SS Gairsoppa* see Symmons (2012), pp. 635–646.

[28] Camarda (2006), p. 83.

clearly implies that under Article 25 the salvage of State-owned cargo as such is in principle admitted.

2.1.3 Duties of the Salvor in Relation to Underwater Cultural Heritage

If, based on the above analysis, it appears that salvage law, and in particular the salvage regime of the 1989 Convention is also applicable to underwater cultural heritage, this is still subject to a number of specific duties which must qualify the salvage activity.

Article 8 imposes on salvors a duty to the owner of the vessel or other property in danger to carry out salvage operations with due care.[29] This provision is very important for the salvage of wrecks as it means that salvors are required not to damage the wreck and/or its cargo during salvage operations. Whenever this duty is breached a salvor is adversely affected in three ways: first, he is liable to pay damages; second, the size of the salved fund, in respect of which he is to be remunerated, will be diminished; third, the salvage reward will be reduced by his negligence.[30]

Under Article 8 the duty of due care is not limited to the property itself, being specifically provided that the same is also true in relation to preventing and minimizing damage to the environment.[31] Failure to exercise due care in protecting the environment may expose the salvor to liability and adversely impact on their right to obtain remuneration under Article 13 or special compensation under Article 14.

Article 18, titled "The effect of salvor's misconduct", further provides that

> A salvor may be deprived of the whole or part of the payment due (. . .) to the extent that the salvage operations have become necessary or more difficult because of fault or neglect on his part or if the salvor has been guilty of fraud or other dishonest conduct.

There is no reason why salvor's misconduct under Article 18 should not apply to the salvage of underwater cultural heritage. This is not contradicted by the fact that attempts were made in the past, on the initiative of one of the most prominent scholars of salvage law, to promote the adoption of a "Draft Protocol to the Salvage Convention 1989" (also known as the "Brice Protocol") to amend Article 18 of the 1989 Convention so that—in relation to the salvage of wrecks—misconduct would expressly include a failure to comply with the reasonable requirements of the appropriate scientific, archaeological and historical bodies and organizations, as well as with the reasonable and lawful requirements of the governmental authorities having a clear and valid interest in the wreck.[32]

---

[29] Under Article 8.1: "The salvor shall owe a duty to the owner of the vessel or other property in danger: (a) to carry out the salvage operations with due care".

[30] Rose (2017), para 12-046.

[31] See Article 8.1 (b) reading: "in performing the duty specified in subparagraph (a), to exercise due care to prevent or minimize damage to the environment".

[32] The text of the Brice Protocol is reproduced in CMI Yearbook 2000 Singapore I, pp. 412–414.

Salvors' misconduct, in similar terms to Article 18 of the 1989 Convention, has been considered in salvage of wreck cases by United States courts, with it being affirmed that reckless or grossly negligent conduct in salvage—and even more so salvors' illicit behaviour—may also lead to diminution or denial of a salvage remuneration.[33] In *RMS Titanic, Inc v The Wrecked and Abandoned Vessel*[34] the competent court affirmed the principle that "if a salvor comes to the court with unclean hands, its award may be reduced or entirely forfeited, depending on the level of misconduct".[35]

2.1.4 The Reasonable Prohibition by the Owner to Carry Out Salvage in the Case of Underwater Cultural Heritage

Article 19 of the 1989 Convention reads:

> Services rendered notwithstanding the express and reasonable prohibition of the owner or master of the vessel or the owner of any other property in danger which is not and has not been on board the vessel shall not give rise to payment under this Convention.

This provision is of interest for the present analysis in that, thereunder, salvage operations in relation to a wreck will not give rise to remuneration when this is done with the express and reasonable prohibition of the owner. In relation to the salvage of ships, traditionally, the reasonableness of the prohibition is to be evaluated on a case by case basis on the ground of a nautical analysis.[36] This test does not adapt to the specific instance of the salvage of wrecks, but it is interesting to note that in the *Vrow Maria* case, a Finnish court affirmed the State's right—claiming ownership of a wreck pursuant to its domestic legislation—to prohibit a private company from carrying out a salvage operation on that wreck, on the ground that it was not in real danger.[37] The decision of the Finnish court was challenged by the salvors before the European Court of Human Rights, which in its decision held that the State, as owner, had the right to prohibit salvage.[38]

---

[33] Sweeney (1999), p. 193. *The Bello Corrunes*, 19 U.S. (6 Wheat) 152, pp. 173-75 (1821); *The Cape Race*, 18 F 2d 79, 1927 AMC 628 (2d Cir 1927); *Klein v Unidentified, Wrecked and Abandoned Sailing Vessel*, 758 F 2d 1511 (11th Cir. 1985), where the Court denied a salvage award in a case where the "unscientific removal of the artifacts did more to create a marine peril than to prevent one".

[34] *RMS Titanic, Inc v The Wrecked and Abandoned* Vessel, 742 F. Supp. 2d 784, p. 803.

[35] See also Dromgoole (2013), p. 196.

[36] See *The Auguste Legembre* [1902] p. 123 suggesting that it is "(. . .) a nautical question whether, having regard to the circumstances of the case, and what might be anticipated at that time of year and in that locality, it was reasonably prudent and necessary (. . .)" for the vessel to receive assistance. This approach was confirmed in other subsequent cases. See *The Kangaroo* [1918] P 227; *The Pretoria* (1920) 5 Ll L Rep 112; *The Rosa Luxemburg* (1934) 49 Ll L Rep 292; *The Flore* (1929) 34 Ll L Rep 172.

[37] Dromgoole (2013), pp. 182–184.

[38] *Koivusaari and others v. Finland* (dec.), no. 20690/06, 23 February 2010, p. 10.

As we shall see below, the prevailing view, as codified by the UNESCO Convention on the protection of the underwater cultural heritage (hereinafter also the "UCH Convention"),[39] is that for the purpose of the protection of underwater cultural heritage *in situ* preservation has priority over recovery and this suggests that the owner's refusal to perform salvage operations would, at least *prima facie*, be considered as reasonable and justified for the purpose of Article 19 of the 1989 Convention.

2.2 *Law of Finds*

The law of finds (informally known as "finders keepers") can be broadly defined as the right of a person who finds lost or abandoned goods to acquire their property.[40] This is a typical common law principle originating from general property law.[41] It requires that the goods have been lost or abandoned.[42] The basis of the acquisition of ownership is that the goods were abandoned and hence no longer have an owner—and that the finder took their possession.[43]

In the United Kingdom, the application of the law of finds in the maritime context is not undisputed. Traditionally under English law the law of finds has been limited by numerous exceptions, mostly in favour of the rights of the sovereign on abandoned wrecks (also known as the "English Rule").[44] This approach was codified into s. 241 of the Merchant Shipping Act 1995 (hereinafter the "MSA 1995") stating that

> Her Majesty and Her Royal successors are entitled to all unclaimed wreck found in the United Kingdom or in United Kingdom waters except in places where Her Majesty or any of Her Royal predecessors has granted the right to any other person.[45]

The States' claim to unclaimed wrecks does not extend to beyond United Kingdom territorial waters, where the law of finds may in principle find residual application.[46]

In the United States, in a number of instances, for some time courts have consistently applied the law of finds in its classic form, declaring an abandoned

[39] See Sect. 3.2 below.

[40] Dromgoole (2013), pp. 171–172.

[41] Lipka (1970), pp. 97–110; Dromgoole (2013), p. 171. See *e.g. Armory v Delamirie* (1722) 93 ER 664.

[42] Dromgoole (2013), p. 172.

[43] Dunlap (2018), p. 426.

[44] Lipka (1970), pp. 98–102; Dunlap (2018), p. 426. See also Reeder (2012) paras 4-28–4-30.

[45] Gaskell, Forrest (2019), p. 247.

[46] In *Pierce v Bemis (The Lusitania)* [1986] QB 384 (QB) pp. 400–401 Sheen J held that a wreck found outside of the United Kingdom territorial waters and brought into the United Kingdom was not subject to the Crown's right and that the finder had good title to that property, unless someone was able to prove to be the true owner.

wreck to be *res nullius* until reduced to the possession of a finder who would be then declared to be its owner (also known as the "American Rule").[47] These decisions held that the prerogative of the sovereign to the wreck had not been inherited from English law and thus was not a part of US law.[48] In 1956, for the first time, an American court awarded ownership of a sunken vessel to the State of Florida.[49] Subsequently, a general limit on the application of the law of finds to wrecks was introduced in 1987 through the Abandoned Shipwreck Act (hereinafter the "ASA"), which transferred title to the States of the United States in whose waters the wrecks were found.[50] This left some residual room for the application of the law of finds to wrecks lying in international waters. However, in more recent times, United States courts have further reduced the scope of application of the law of finds to wrecks, defining it as "a disfavoured common-law doctrine rarely applied to wrecks and then only under limited circumstances"[51] or placing a harsh burden of proof on the claimant in relation to the condition of abandonment, by requiring evidence of the owner's positive relinquishment of his rights.[52]

The enactment of legislation whereby title on derelict historical wrecks is acquired by the coastal State, coupled with the increasing disfavour of judges towards the appropriation by private parties, have progressively and substantially eroded the scope of application of the law of finds in the two main common law jurisdictions where these concepts originated. The trend appears to be clearly set and prospects for the application of the law of finds to wrecks appear to be coming to an end.

---

[47] Lipka (1970), pp. 102–103; Dunlap (2018), p. 426.

[48] Gaskell and Forrest (2019), p. 247. *United States v Tyndale,* 116 F 820 (1st Cir 1902); *Thompson v United States,* 62 Ct Cl 516 (1926); *Murphy v Dunham,* 38 F 503 (ED Mich 1889); *Treasure Salvors Inc v The Unidentified, Wrecked and Abandoned Sailing Vessel* [1978] AMC 1404 (*Salvors I*), [1981] AMC 1529 (*Salvors II*), [1981] AMC 1857 (*Salvors III*); *Cobb Coin Co v Unidentified, Wrecked and Abandoned Sailing Vessel,* 549 F. Supp. 540, p. 561 (Sd Fla 1982).

[49] *State ex rel Erin v Massachusetts Co*, 95 So 2d 902 (Fla 1956).

[50] 43 USC sec. 2015(a):

> The United States asserts title to any abandoned shipwreck that is — (1) embedded in submerged lands of a State; (2) embedded in coralline formations protected by a State on submerged lands of a State; or (3) on submerged lands of a State and is included in or determined eligible for inclusion in the National Register.

[51] *RMS Titanic, Inc v The Wrecked and Abandoned Vessel,* 435 F3d 521, p. 530 (4th Cir 2006).

[52] *Columbus-America Discovery Group v Atlantic Mut Ins Co,* 974 F 2d 450, p. 464 (4th Cir (Va) Aug 26, 1992).

3 Protection of Underwater Cultural Heritage

Compared to the law of salvage and the law of finds, the law for protection of cultural heritage has relatively recent origins. In relation to underwater cultural heritage its development has been driven by technological advances in underwater exploration and excavation and the concern this has brought in relation to the possible unauthorized removal and appropriation of historic artifacts by private persons.

3.1 UNCLOS

While the 1958 Law of the Sea Conventions did not contain any reference to underwater cultural heritage, this issue was raised during the conference leading to the adoption of the United Nations Convention on the Law of the Sea (UNCLOS) 1982, although only at a late stage of the works and receiving little attention.[53] This resulted in the adoption of two provisions covering the protection of underwater cultural heritage.

The most important provision in UNCLOS is represented by Article 303, positioned in Part XVI "General provisions" of the Convention.

Under the first paragraph of Article 303 "States have the duty to protect objects of an archaeological and historical nature found at sea and cooperate for this purpose". The duty of protection and co-operation is formulated in generic terms. It is addressed to all States, without setting a priority between coastal States and States that may have a concurrent interest, *i.e.* primarily the flag State. It does not provide any precise guidance for the qualification of "objects of an archaeological and historical nature".

The role of the coastal State is somewhat specified in paragraph 2, reading:

> In order to control traffic in such objects, the coastal State may, in applying Article 33, presume that their removal from the seabed in the zone referred to in that article without its approval would result in an infringement within its territory or territorial sea of the laws and regulations referred to in that article.

The language of paragraph 2 is cumbersome. It recognizes the coastal States' right to prevent the unauthorized removal of objects of an archaeological and historical nature within the contiguous zone[54] as defined under Article 33, *i.e.* in the area

---

[53] Gaskell and Forrest (2019), p. 325.

[54] Under Article 33 of UNCLOS (Contiguous zone)

> In a zone contiguous to its territorial sea, described as the contiguous zone, the coastal State may exercise the control necessary to: (a) prevent infringement of its customs, fiscal, immigration or sanitary laws and regulations within its territory or territorial sea; (b) punish infringement of the above laws and regulations committed within its territory or

adjacent to the outer limit of the territorial sea, extending no further than 24 nautical miles from the baseline. However, this is done by stretching and adapting the scope and purpose of the general regime of the contiguous zone, rather than providing for a specific jurisdiction of the coastal State in the matter of protection of underwater cultural heritage.[55]

Paragraph 2 does not refer to the regime of internal waters and territorial sea. But the right of the coastal State to protect underwater cultural heritage in these areas is implied by the sovereignty exercised thereupon by the coastal State.[56]

UNCLOS does not contain any provision allowing the coastal State to exercise its jurisdiction either in the exclusive economic zone (EEZ) and Continental shelf in matters of cultural heritage. In these areas, under UNCLOS coastal States do not exercise their sovereignty. They are only afforded with a functional jurisdiction recognized for specific purposes which do not specifically adapt to the protection of cultural heritage. It has been observed that in view of this legal vacuum, the principle of freedom of the sea may prevail to the detriment of the protection of cultural heritage.[57]

Paragraph 3 reads "nothing in this article affects the rights of identifiable owners, the law of salvage or other rules of admiralty".[58] According to an authoritative opinion, the wording of paragraph 3 is unfortunate because it suggests that in case of a conflict, the law of salvage prevails on the duty to protect and cooperate under paragraph 1.[59] It may be argued, however, that the fact that salvage is "not affected" does not necessarily mean that it should prevail on the aforesaid duty to protect. Other authors have in fact offered a different reading of this provision, whereby under paragraph 3, read in context with paragraph 1, the protection of underwater cultural heritage and the law of salvage—at least under certain circumstances—may coexist.[60] In the light of subsequent international legal practice this latter reading of paragraph 3 appears to be consistent with the following paragraph 4, clarifying that Article 303 (in its entirety) is "without prejudice to other international agreements

---

territorial sea. 2. The contiguous zone may not extend beyond 24 nautical miles from the baselines from which the breadth of the territorial sea is measured.

[55] Strati (2006), pp. 29–30 refers to paragraph 2 of Article 303 of UNCLOS as a "legal fiction".

[56] Scovazzi (2017), p. 505.

[57] Ibidem p. 510; Strati (2006), pp. 31–32.

[58] Interestingly, paragraph 3, while generally preserving in addition to the "law of salvage" the application of "other rules of admiralty", does not specifically refer to the law of finds.

[59] Scovazzi (2017), p. 512.

[60] Varmer and Blanco (2018), p. 410 suggesting that "A contextual reading of Article 303 and, particularly, subsections (1) and (3) together, clarifies that the duties to protect and cooperate on UCH may well be accomplished through the law of salvage". A restrictive reading of Article 303 paragraph 3 is proposed by Strati (2006), p. 32 at footnote 30:

> In the writer's view, the reservation of the law of salvage under Article 303(3) of the LOS Convention should be interpreted to refer to cases in which archaeological and historical objects are not involved, i.e. recent objects which do not possess historical value and which are eligible for salvage.

and rules of international law regarding the protection of objects of an archaeological and historical nature". Although at the time of the adoption of UNCLOS no specific international law instruments existed for the protection of underwater cultural heritage, read today, paragraph 4 requires that the UCH Convention be taking into account,[61] at least in terms of the relations between States that are Parties to this convention and UNCLOS. As we shall see in the next section of this chapter, the UCH Convention contains provisions whereby salvage is contemplated, although on a residual basis only, as a possible option in the protection of underwater cultural heritage.[62]

The other provision of UNCLOS dealing with archaeological and historical objects is Article 149, which is positioned in Part XI, titled "The Area". The Area is defined under Article 1of UNCLOS as "*the sea-bed and ocean floor and subsoil thereof, beyond the limits of national jurisdiction*".

Under Article 149:

> All objects of an archaeological and historical nature found in the Area shall be preserved or disposed of for the benefit of mankind as a whole, particular regard being paid to the preferential rights of the State or country of origin, or the State of cultural origin, or the State of historical and archaeological origin.

In providing that historical objects in the Area must be "preserved or disposed of", this provision suggests that *in situ* preservation is not the only envisaged option and that recovery is also a viable one, provided this is done in the interest of mankind.

3.2 *The 2001 UNESCO Convention on the Protection of Underwater Cultural Heritage (UCH Convention)*

The UNESCO Convention on the protection of underwater cultural heritage was adopted in Paris on 2 November 2001 and entered into force at the international level on 2 January 2009. Although the UCH Convention has been widely ratified[63] and further ratifications, including that of the Netherlands,[64] are expected in the near future, the list of States Parties still does not include a number of States having an important maritime tradition, such as the United States and the United Kingdom.

The UCH Convention consists of a preamble, of 35 Articles and of an Annex titled "Rules concerning activities directed at underwater cultural heritage" (the "Rules").

[61] See Sect. 3.2 below.

[62] The 2001 UNESCO Convention on the protection of underwater cultural heritage and in particular its provisions on salvage are covered below in the following Sect. 3.2.

[63] The UCH Convention has been ratified by 71 States, https://pax.unesco.org/la/convention.asp?KO=13520&language=E&order=alpha. On the UCH Convention see Strati (2006), pp. 38–59; Garabello and Scovazzi (2003); Dromgoole (2003), pp. 59–108.

[64] Roberts (2018), p. 853.

3.2.1 Defining Underwater Cultural Heritage

Article 1 of the UCH Convention defines as underwater cultural heritage

> all traces of human existence having a cultural, historical or archaeological character which have been partially or totally under water, periodically or continuously, for at least 100 years, such as:
>
> (i) sites, structures, buildings, artefacts and human remains, together with their archaeological and natural context;
> (ii) vessels, aircraft, other vehicles or any part thereof, their cargo or other contents, together with their archaeological and natural context; and
> (iii) objects of prehistoric character.

The definition represents a compromise between the different views expressed by States during the negotiation of the Convention. While some States preferred the adoption of a blanket inclusion of "all traces of human existence remaining under water for at least 100 years", others advocated the addition of a significance criterion, which was eventually included with the wording "having a cultural, historical or archaeological character", which leaves some room for the discretional evaluation of State Parties as to what is deemed significant for the purpose of the Convention.[65]

This list of examples clarifies that the Convention affords protection not only to specific historic objects but also to their archaeological and natural context.

3.2.2 Objective and General Principles, the "Rules"

Article 2 sets out the objectives and general principles of the UCH Convention. These include: the duty of co-operation of States for the protection of underwater cultural heritage, *in situ* protection as a preferred option, conservation of recovered underwater cultural heritage in a manner ensuring its long term preservation.

The focus of the Convention is represented by the regulation of activities directed at underwater cultural heritage, which are defined under Article 1.6 as "activities having underwater cultural heritage as their primary object and which may, directly or indirectly, physically disturb or otherwise damage underwater cultural heritage".[66] In relation to activities incidentally affecting underwater cultural heritage,[67] such as for instance trawling, cable and pipeline laying and seabed exploration and

---

[65] Gaskell and Forrest (2019), p. 333.

[66] See Roberts (2018), p. 841:

> The Convention makes no mention of protecting individual sites. Rather, it takes an activity-based approach. This means that the aim of the Convention is not protecting UCH by designating all sites that fall within the definition; it is to protect UCH by regulating activities directed at UCH.

[67] Under Article 1.7: activities incidentally affecting underwater cultural heritage "means activities which, despite not having underwater cultural heritage as their primary object or one of their objects, may physically disturb or otherwise damage underwater cultural heritage".

drilling for the purpose of exploitation of natural resources, Article 5 generally provides that "each State Party shall use the best practicable means at its disposal to prevent or mitigate any adverse effects that might arise from activities under their jurisdiction".

In furtherance to the provisions under Article 2 of the UCH Convention, the Annex sets out the Rules concerning activities directed at underwater cultural heritage. This is a body of regulations setting out the best archaeological practice for the protection of underwater cultural heritage.

Rule 1 re-affirms the principle that *in situ* preservation shall be considered as the first option. Recovery is contemplated under Rule 4 only to the extent that it is "necessary for the purpose of scientific studies or for the ultimate protection of the underwater cultural heritage", but still "the methods and techniques used must be as non-destructive as possible and contribute to the preservation of the remains".

Rule 2 affirms the principle that underwater cultural heritage cannot be subject to commercial exploitation.

Rule 5 provides that activities directed at underwater cultural heritage shall avoid unnecessary disturbance of human remains or venerated sites.

3.2.3 Protection of Underwater Cultural Heritage in the Coastal Areas and in the Area

In furtherance of the concise and generic provisions of Article 303 of UNCLOS, the UCH Convention contains a set of detailed rules governing the jurisdiction of States for the regulation and authorization of activities directed at underwater cultural heritage in their coastal zones. As specified under Article 3 of the UCH Convention, these provisions are without prejudice of

> the rights, jurisdiction and duties of States under international law, including the United Nations Convention on the Law of the Sea. This Convention shall be interpreted and applied in the context of and in a manner consistent with international law, including the United Nations Convention on the Law of the Sea.

Internal Waters, Archipelagic Waters and Territorial Sea

Under Article 7 of the UCH Convention, paragraph 1, in their internal waters, archipelagic waters and territorial sea, which under UNCLOS are subject to the sovereignty of the coastal State, States Parties have the exclusive right to regulate and authorize activities directed at underwater cultural heritage. This right does not appear to be unlimited, in that, under paragraph 2, States shall require that the Rules are applied "[w]ithout prejudice to other international agreements and rules of international law regarding the protection of underwater cultural heritage". This proviso suggests that the coastal State can apply standards other than the Rules, only pursuant to other international law instruments. Hence, this cannot be done through the unilateral adoption of domestic legislation.

Moreover, under paragraph 3, the coastal State,

> with a view to cooperating on the best methods of protecting State vessels and aircraft, should inform the flag State Party to this Convention and, if applicable, other States with a verifiable link, especially a cultural, historical or archaeological link, with respect to the discovery of such identifiable State vessels and aircraft.

State vessels and aircraft are defined under Article 1.8 as

> warships, and other vessels or aircraft that were owned or operated by a State and used, at the time of sinking, only for government non-commercial purposes, that are identified as such and that meet the definition of underwater cultural heritage.

Paragraph 3 met with criticism from certain States, including the United Kingdom and the United States, on the ground that it also recognizes exclusive jurisdiction to the coastal State in relation to State owned ships and aircraft, irrespective of the fact that these would continue to enjoy flag State sovereign immunity after their sinking, combined with the fact that the coastal State only "should", rather than "shall", inform the flag State of the discovery.[68] However, it is suggested that this is a misplaced concern in the light of the fact that the principle of sovereign immunity of State owned wrecks is preserved by Article 2.8 of the Convention, whereby

> Consistent with State practice and international law, including the United Nations Convention on the Law of the Sea, nothing in this Convention shall be interpreted as modifying the rules of international law and State practice pertaining to sovereign immunities, nor any State's rights with respect to its State vessels and aircraft.

Based on this reading, in relation to State owned wrecks the action of the coastal State would still be subject to the flag State consent.[69]

Contiguous Zone

Under Article 8 of the UCH Convention, States parties may regulate and authorize activities directed at underwater cultural heritage within their contiguous zone. This is "without prejudice and in addition to Articles 9 and 10", [70] dealing with the protection of underwater cultural heritage in the EEZ and continental shelf "and in accordance with Article 303, paragraph 2 of the United Nations Convention on the Law of the Sea". This latter proviso affirms the intention not to grant to the coastal State powers exceeding those recognized by UNCLOS. Still, Article 8 seems to

---

[68] Gaskell and Forrest (2019), p. 338.

[69] Roberts (2018), p. 850.

[70] The meaning of reference to arts. 9 and 10 is somewhat obscure. According to Strati (2006), p. 44, this does not mean that the consultation procedures envisaged for the EEZ and continental shelf are also to apply in the contiguous zone and should rather be interpreted

> as simply accommodating the "interests" of State parties with a cultural, historical or archaeological verifiable link to the underwater cultural heritage concerned and not affecting the otherwise applicable jurisdiction of the coastal State.

extend the scope of the powers granted to the coastal State under Article 303(2) of UNCLOS. In fact, while the latter only refers to the removal of objects, Article 8 (like Article 7) envisages extended powers to "regulate and authorize activities directed at underwater cultural heritage".[71]

Similar to Article 7 in relation to internal waters, territorial sea and archipelagic waters, State Parties, in authorizing and regulating activities in their contiguous zone, shall require that the Rules be applied.

EEZ and Continental Shelf

On the ground that the regimes of exclusive economic zones and the continental shelf to a large extent coincide, the activities directed at underwater cultural heritage in these two areas are jointly regulated by the UCH Convention under Article 10.

The content of Article 10 represents a compromise between the positions expressed during the negotiation of the Convention by those States who were ready to extend the jurisdiction of the coastal State in these areas and those who expressed concern that by doing so the balance set by UNCLOS between the costal State jurisdiction and freedom of the sea would be upset.

As a result, under Article 10.2, the rights of the coastal State to prohibit or authorize activities are restricted to the case where this is done "to prevent interference with its sovereign rights or jurisdiction as provided for by international law including the United Nations Convention on the Law of the Sea". Considering that under Article 56 of UNCLOS the sovereign rights of the coastal State in its EEZ are limited to the exploration and exploitation of "natural resources", a concept that hardly adapts to underwater cultural heritage, and that jurisdiction is limited to specific activities which also have no clear connection therewith,[72] the scope for unilateral action of the coastal State under Article 10.2, if any, appears to be very limited.

In the intention of the Convention, the objective of the protection of underwater cultural heritage in the EEZ and continental shelf is instead pursued through a complex system of co-operation between the coastal State and other interested States, with the assistance of the Directorate General of UNESCO.

The system is based on the principles of reporting and consultation.

Under Article 9.1(a) States Parties must require their nationals or vessels flying their flag to report activities or discoveries located in their EEZ or the continental shelf.

[71] Dromgoole (2003), p. 79 also suggests that compared to Article 303 (2) of UNCLOS Article 8 "does make it easier to defend the exercise of legislative rather than merely enforcement jurisdiction".

[72] Scovazzi (2017), p. 510. The prevailing view is that Article 10.2 has a declaratory nature only and does not afford the coastal State with any jurisdictional power in excess of those envisaged by UNCLOS: see Roberts (2018), p. 850.

When the activities are located in the EEZ or continental shelf of another State Party, under Article 9.1(b):

> (i) States Parties shall require the national or the master of the vessel to report such discovery or activity to them and to that other State Party;
> (ii) alternatively, a State Party shall require the national or master of the vessel to report such discovery or activity to it and shall ensure the rapid and effective transmission of such reports to all other States Parties.[73]

States Parties who receive reports of discoveries or activities as above in turn have the duty to notify the Director General of UNESCO, who will then promptly make that information available to all State Parties.

This enables the interested State Parties to declare to the State Party in whose EEZ or continental shelf the cultural heritage is located, their interest in being consulted on how to ensure the effective protection of the cultural heritage. The declaration must be based on a verifiable cultural, historical or archaeological link.

The purpose of the reporting phase is to allow, pursuant to Article 10, consultation between the interested States, which in turn leads to the implementation of protection measures and the granting of necessary authorizations.

Consultations are coordinated by the State where the discovery or the activity is located, acting as Coordinating State, unless this State expressly declares its intention not to do so, in which case States having declared their interest shall designate another Coordinating State.

The purpose of consultation is for the consulting Parties to agree the protection measures to be adopted, which will be implemented or authorized as necessary by the Coordinating State or another State so designated by the consulting Parties.

Under Article 10.4 of the UCH Convention, the Coordinating State is also vested with the power to take urgent measures of protection, pending the consultation, to prevent any immediate danger to the underwater cultural heritage, whether arising from human activities or any other cause, including looting. In doing so the Coordinating State may request the assistance of other States Parties.[74]

The principle that the actions taken by the Coordinating State under Article 10 does not imply any jurisdictional claim not specifically provided by international

[73] Article 9.1 (b) is ambiguous. It says that "States Parties" shall require the national or the master of a vessel to report the discovery or activity. It does not refer to, as Article 9.1 (a) does, to the vessel flying the flag of the captioned State Party. The question then arises as to whether the duty to require reporting applies only to the flag State or rather to the coastal State. The second construction would be perceived as granting to the coastal States a jurisdiction in its EEZ and continental shelf not envisaged by UNCLOS. According to Roberts (2018), pp. 855–859, the correct reading would be that the duty to require reporting under Article 9.1 (b) is addressed to the flag State.

[74] See Scovazzi (2017), p. 515:

> The right of the coordinating State to adopt urgent measures is an important aspect of CPUCH regime. It would have been illusory to subordinate this right to the final outcome of consultations that are normally expected to last for some time. It would also have been illusory to grant this right to the flag State, considering the risk of activities carried out by vessels flying the flag of non-parties or flag of convenience.

law and UNCLOS is clearly stated in Article10.6, which also clarifies that the Coordinating State “shall act on behalf of the States Parties as a whole and not in its own interest”.

Finally, under para. 7, Article 10 also contains a special reservation applicable to State vessels and aircraft, in the sense that no activity directed at this underwater cultural heritage shall be conducted without the agreement of the respective flag State.

So far, the consultation and co-operation mechanism envisaged by Article 10 has been activated on only one occasion. In 2018 Italy notified UNESCO of the discovery of submerged archaeological vestiges on Skerki Banks, located in an area of the continental shelf of Tunisia, between Tunisia, Sicily and Sardinia. The historical objects resting in the area include shipwrecks from ancient history, as well as shipwrecks from the second world war. Following the Italian notification, four States Parties declared their interest in participating in the consultation process, namely, Italy itself, France, Spain and Tunisia. Periodical consultation meetings among these States for the adoption of protection measures are ongoing, with Tunisia acting as Coordinating State in view of the fact that the area is located in the Tunisian continental shelf.[75]

The Area

In relation to the Area, Arts.11 and 12 set out a system of reporting and consultation similar to the one envisaged for EEZ and continental shelf, with the difference that, in the absence of a coastal State, the Coordinating State shall in all cases be appointed by the interested States.

3.2.4 Provisions on Implementation and Effectiveness

Arts. 14 to 22 of the UCH Convention set out a number of measures that State Parties are required to take in order to ensure the proper implementation and effectiveness of the Convention, namely: preventing the entry into their territory, the dealing and possession of underwater cultural heritage recovered in violation of the UCH Convention; prohibiting the use of territory in support of activities which are not in conformity with the UCH Convention; ensuring that their nationals and ships flying their flag comply with the UCH Convention; providing adequate sanctions for the violation of the UCH Convention, seizing objects recovered in violation of the UCH Convention, cooperating and sharing of information, raising public awareness, cooperating in training in underwater technology and conservation techniques, establishing or reinforcing of domestic competent authorities.

[75] Information available on https://en.unesco.org/news/cooperation-international-maters-protection-skerki-banks.

3.2.5 UCH Convention and Salvage

The application of the law of salvage and law of finds to underwater cultural heritage is governed by Article 4 of the UCH Convention, reading:

> Any activity relating to underwater cultural heritage to which this Convention applies shall not be subject to the law of salvage or law of finds, unless it:
>
> (a) is authorized by the competent authorities, and
> (b) is in full conformity with this Convention, and
> (c) ensures that any recovery of the underwater cultural heritage achieves its maximum protection.

The wording of Article 4 represents the compromise between the conflicting views expressed during the negotiation of the UCH Convention by some States who sought a clear-cut and total exclusion of salvage and finds, and those who advocated the preservation of these concepts.[76]

The first paragraph states clearly that, as a rule, the laws of salvage and finds do not apply to the activities related to underwater cultural heritage. But the rule is followed by an exception, whereby the laws of salvage and finds will still be applicable when authorized, in full conformity with this Convention and to the extent that recovery ensures the maximum protection of underwater cultural heritage.

This must be read in conjunction with the principles of Rules 2 and 4, whereby the recovery of historical objects is allowed when necessary for scientific or protection purposes, albeit always subject to the principle of no commercial exploitation.

It is suggested by a number of authors that the laws of salvage and finds must be excluded because, by definition, they would be inconsistent with the principles of non-commercialization and good archaeological practice contained in the Rules.[77]

Being focused on the appropriation of recovered derelict objects by private persons who find and recover it, the law of finds is hardly consistent with the non-commercialization principle of Rule 2.

Salvage, on the other hand, deserves a more articulated analysis. Salvage presupposes the existence of a legitimate owner of the recovered object. The salvor does not act with the intent of acquiring the ownership of the recovered object. Quite to the contrary, it acts for the benefit of the owner, from whom he is entitled to obtain remuneration.[78]

---

[76] Dromgoole (2013), pp. 201–202.

[77] Dromgoole (2003), pp. 66–67 and more extensively Dromgoole (2013), pp. 202–204. At p. 204 Dromgoole expresses the view that "there is nothing to prevent a state party to the UNESCO Convention going further than the terms of Article 4 and excluding the application of salvage and finds laws from UCH falling within the scope of the Convention" but the legal basis for this exclusion are not clear: under Article 29 of the UCH Convention "with the exception of Article 29, no reservations may be made to this Convention". See also Forrest (2009), pp. 28–31; Garabello (2004), pp. 194–195.

[78] Camarda (2006), pp. 386–391.

Rule 2 itself does not seem to exclude salvage in absolute terms, in that, under paragraph 2 letter (b), it clarifies that the non-commercialization principle is without prejudice to

> the deposition of underwater cultural heritage, recovered in the course of a research project in conformity with this Convention, provided such deposition does not prejudice the scientific or cultural interest or integrity of the recovered material or result in its irretrievable dispersal; is in accordance with the provisions of Rules 33 and 34; and is subject to the authorization of the competent authorities.[79]

Salvage activities falling within the scope of the UCH Convention need to be authorized and regulated either by the coastal State or by a Coordinating State[80] and in a substantial number of cases the owner of the underwater cultural heritage site will be a State, which will be entitled to require salvors to operate pursuant to sensible, approved procedures.

Unauthorized activities carried out in violation of the UCH Convention will likely qualify as salvors' misconduct for the purposes of Article 18 of the 1989 Salvage Convention with the result that salvors will be deprived of the right to salvage remuneration. Such activities would be subject to sanctions and restrictions under the enforcement system established by Arts. 14 to 19 of the UCH Convention, which include seizure of the recovered material pursuant to Article 18, with the consequent unenforceability of salvors' lien.[81]

Hence, the recovery option does not seem to be necessarily antithetical to the scope and purpose of the UCH Convention. There may be cases where the balance of concurring interests, coupled with the assurance by salvors of responsible and technically proficient conduct, the recovery option becomes a viable one. In this respect, the practice followed by non-party common law States offers an interesting open perspective. In the recent past, the United Kingdom Government entered into contracts with private salvage companies for the purpose of the recovery of parts of State-owned shipwrecks and the respective cargo.[82] In the United States, the ASA, while disapplying the laws of salvage and finds to wrecks falling within its scope,

---

[79] Rule 33 reads

> The project archives, including any underwater cultural heritage removed and a copy of all supporting documentation shall, as far as possible, be kept together and intact as a collection in a manner that is available for professional and public access as well as for the curation of the archives. This should be done as rapidly as possible and in any case not later than ten years from the completion of the project, in so far as may be compatible with conservation of the underwater cultural heritage.

Under Rule 34 "The project archives shall be managed according to international professional standards, and subject to the authorization of the competent authorities".

[80] See Sect. 3.2.3 above.

[81] See Sect. 2.1.3 above.

[82] See above footnote 27 on the salvage of *SS Gairsoppa.* On salvage contracts entered into by the United Kingdom government with private salvors see Gaskell and Forrest (2019), pp. 331–332. For a critical analysis on the *HMS Sussex* salvage operation and respective agreement see Garabello (2004), pp. 189–195.

still includes "appropriate public and private sector recovery of shipwrecks consistent with the protection of historical values and environmental integrity of the shipwrecks and the sites" among the permitted management options for the interested States.[83] In relation to the case of the wreck of RMS Titanic, which was not subject to ASA, the US Courts applied the law of salvage, introducing "the degree to which salvors have worked to protect the historical and archaeological value of the wreck and the items salvaged" as a criterion for determining the salvage remuneration and making salvor's rights conditional upon the undertaking that recovered items would be held in trust for the public, conserved as one collection in conformity with archaeological standards and for the benefit of the public.[84]

The good application of salvage law, coupled with the protection mechanism of the UCH Convention, offer a legal framework where the scope for looting and obscure salvage operations should be substantially reduced.

4 Conclusion

Protection of underwater cultural heritage under the UCH Convention is based on the principles of primacy of the option of *in situ* preservation and non-commercialization.

It is often argued that the UCH Convention leaves little room, if any at all, for the application of the law of finds and the law of salvage, as these would both contradict the above fundamental principles.

The law of finds, which is a typical common law concept, involves appropriation by the finder. As such it is inconsistent with the scope and purpose of the UCH Convention and in general with the public interest of the preservation of underwater cultural heritage. As a matter of fact, this remedy has met with increasing disfavour in the case law of the common law jurisdictions which in the past have applied it to the recovery of underwater cultural heritage.[85]

Salvage is different. The law of salvage has demonstrated the ability to evolve beyond its original purpose of the preservation of property at sea and to adapt to concerns having a public nature. The environmental protection rules in the 1989 Convention are an example of this. Court decisions applying salvage to shipwrecks have also shown how salvage may adapt to the specific needs required in relation to activities directed at underwater cultural heritage.[86] Salvors are exposed to liability

---

[83] Dromgoole (2013), pp. 188–189; Varmer and Blanco (2018), p. 416.

[84] Varmer and Blanco (2018), pp. 420–422; Dromgoole (2013), pp. 191–193.

[85] See Sect. 2.2 above.

[86] See the analysis of the *Titanic* and *Central America* cases in Dromgoole (2013), pp. 190–193. On the other hand, decisions granting salvors property rights on recovered material to the detriment of the States' interest in preserving underwater cultural heritage for the public benefit, like in the *Atocha* and *Conception* cases, are not likely to occur today, see Scovazzi (2019), p. 273. For a review of the evolution of US case law whereby the traditional principles of salvage and finds have

when they act negligently and acting outside the law may result in their inability to obtain salvage remuneration. Considering the enormous investment that a recovery operation may require, in terms of the means and personnel deployed, for a duration that may not be easily predictable at its onset, the traditional salvage law no cure no pay principle may represent an economically viable solution for operations that the owner or the interested States may be otherwise reluctant to undertake, especially when the prospects of recovery are uncertain.

In contrast to finds, as a rule salvage does not involve appropriation. It presupposes the existence of a legitimate owner and it is aimed at returning the endangered property to the latter. In a large number of cases, underwater cultural heritage is in the ownership either of a private person or of a State, be it the coastal State, pursuant to its domestic legislation, or the flag State in case of State-owned vessels, aircraft and cargo. Under the law of salvage, the owner is entitled to object to salvage operations when these are not deemed to be reasonable or fairly undertaken. As shown in the Finnish court case of the "*Voruw Maria*",[87] this also applies when salvage is directed at historical objects.

The risk of unregulated salvage operations is mitigated by the ongoing development and implementation of a complex legal framework for the protection of underwater cultural heritage. Both in territorial and international waters the room for "freedom of salvage", as advocated in the past by pro-salvors authorities,[88] is bound to become more and more restricted by virtue of the reporting, co-operation, authorization and sanctioning systems provided by the UCH Convention and it is certainly desirable that more non-party States, especially those having a maritime tradition, ratify this instrument in the near future.[89] It is the responsibility of States who are not yet party to the UCH Convention to ensure that areas and persons under their jurisdictions are subject to rules and standards in pursuance of the duty to protect underwater cultural heritage under Article 303 of UNCLOS.

The UCH Convention does not rule out the salvage option, to the extent that the operation is authorized and necessary. The necessity of salvage may arise when the permanence of underwater cultural heritage on the bottom of the sea is no longer safe. This may be caused by the effect of natural elements, but also by possible unauthorised actions by looters or due to interference by legitimate activities such as fishing, drilling, dredging and cable and pipeline laying. In some circumstances, States may find that recovery is necessary for scientific purposes. In assessing the possible option of recovery, States may also consider that not all submerged objects qualifying as underwater cultural heritage necessarily have the same historical value: the need for *in situ* preservation of a cargo of precious metal stored in the holds of a

been gradually adapted so as to take into account the public interest of preservation as well as the possible concurrent claims of interested States see Nafziger (2003), pp. 251–270.

[87] See supra, Sect. 2.1.4.

[88] Bederman (1998), pp. 99–129.

[89] See Roberts (2018), pp. 833–865 for a review of the issues that have so far prevented the United Kingdom, but also other maritime States, from ratifying the UCH Convention.

ship sunk in World War I, for instance, may not be as pressing as in the case of the remains of an ancient Phoenician ship.

The techniques for the salvage of underwater cultural heritage have also evolved to meet the growing public concern for its preservation. The time where salvors would open their way to sunken cargo with the use of explosives has gone. The salvage industry is capable of deploying sophisticated technological means that can be put at the service of the cause of the protection of underwater cultural heritage.[90]

Underwater cultural heritage will always be threatened by the unauthorized actions of looters. But this does not mean that the law of salvage should be discarded as a whole and the UCH Convention itself contains a valuable set of rules allowing States to tackle and discourage illegal recovery actions.

Today this remains a divisive subject. For some, when referring to underwater cultural heritage, salvage is still seen as tantamount to looting. Others see the practical advantages that the long-established law of salvage may bring in this domain. But the increasing number of States ratifying the UCH Convention and the growing awareness—also within non-ratifying States – of the need to protect and preserve submerged historical sites for the public benefit may eventually have the effect of substantially reducing the scope remaining for undesirable practices of private appropriation, and to create the conditions for a more common understanding that the law of salvage and cultural heritage protection may go together.[91]

Acknowledgment The author wishes to express his gratitude to the editors for their valuable and constructive suggestions during the planning and development of this work and to Mr. Fabio Cerasuolo for his assistance in researching and collecting the bibliography.

References

Alexander B (1989) Treasure salvage beyond the territorial sea: an assessment and recommendations. J Maritime Law Commerce 20(1):1–19

Baughen S (2019) Shipping law, 7th edn. Informa Law, London

[90] Cottrell (1993): while advocating the exclusion by coastal States of the laws of finds and salvage from underwater cultural heritage, the author still suggests that

> experts in the field of marine archaeology including archaeologists and professional salvagers could negotiate to develop the best possible approach to preserving shipwrecks found in international waters for the public benefit.

[91] Nafziger (2003), p. 269, concludes his analysis on the evolving attitude of US admiralty courts on salvage of historic wrecks by saying that "The law of salvage and finds will nevertheless continue to be important. A redefinition of this body of law to include shared rules and principles in international law governing underwater cultural heritage poses no serious threat to responsible salvage or to the normal practice of salvage law, particularly if the salvage is conducted with the consent of the interested states. Commercial incentives can contribute to a responsible management of historic wreck. The core principle in simply "preservation for the benefit of humanity"".

Bederman D (1998) Historic salvage and the law of the sea. Univ Miami Inter-Am Law Rev 30(1): 99–129
Berlingieri F (2009) Le convenzioni internazionali di diritto marittimo e il codice della navigazione. Giuffré Editore, Milano
Brice G (1996) Salvage and the underwater cultural heritage. Marine Policy 20:337–342
Camarda G (2006) Il soccorso in mare. Profili contrattuali ed extracontrattuali. Giuffré Editore, Milano
Cottrell A (1993) The law of the sea and international marine archaeology: abandoning admiralty law to protects historic shipwrecks. Fordham Int Law J 17(3):666–725
Dromgoole S (2003) 2001 UNESCO convention on the protection of the underwater cultural heritage. Int J Mar Coast Law 18(1):59–108
Dromgoole S (2013) Underwater cultural heritage and international law. Cambridge University Press, Cambridge
Dunlap W (2018) Ownership of underwater cultural heritage. J Maritime Law Commerce 49:425–439
Forrest C (2009) Historic wreck salvage. Tulane Maritime Law J 33(1):1–33
Garabello R (2004) Sunken Warships in the Mediterranean in Scovazzi T (ed) La protezione del patrimonio culturale sottomarino nel Mare Mediterraneo. Giuffré Editore, Milano, pp 171–202
Garabello R, Scovazzi T (eds) (2003) The Protection of the underwater cultural heritage before and after the 2001 UNESCO Convention. Martinus Nijhoff Publishers, Leiden
Gaskell N, Forrest C (2019) The law of Wreck. Informa Law, London
Juvelier B (2018) "Salvaging" history: underwater cultural heritage and commercial salvage. Am Univ Int Law Rev 32(5):1023–1045
Lipka J (1970) Abandoned property at sea: who owns the salvage "finds"? William & Mary Law Rev 12:97–110
McQuown T (2000) An archaeological argument for inapplicability of admiralty law in the disposition of historic shipwrecks. William Mitchell Law Rev 26(2):289–326
Nafziger J (2003) The evolving role of admiralty courts in litigation related to historic wrecks. Harv Int Law J 44(1):251–270
Reeder J (2012) Brice on maritime law of salvage, 5th edn. Sweet & Maxwell, London
Roberts H (2018) The British ratification of underwater heritage convention: problems and prospects. Int Comp Law Q 67(4):833–865
Rose F (2017) Kennedy and Rose on the law of salvage, 9th edn. Sweet & Maxwell, London
Scovazzi T (2017) The relationship between two conventions applicable to underwater cultural heritage. In: Crawford J et al (eds) The international legal order: current needs and possible responses. Brill-Nijhoff, Leiden, pp 504–518
Scovazzi T (2019) Sunken Spanish ships before American courts. Int J Marine Coast Law 34:245–290
Strati A (2006) Protection of the underwater cultural heritage: from the shortcoming of the convention on the law of the sea to the compromises of the UNESCO convention. In: Strati A, Gavouneli M, Skourtos N (eds) Unresolved issues and new challenges to the law of the sea: time before and time after. Martinus Nijhoff Publishers, Leiden, pp 21–62
Sweeney J (1999) An overview of commercial salvage principles in the context of marine archaeology. J Maritime Law Commerce 30:185–203
Symmons C (2012) Current legal developments Republic of Ireland, recent off-shore treasure-seeking incidents relating to wrecks in Irish waters. Intl J Marine Coast Law 27:635–646
Varmer O, Blanco C (2018) The case for using the law of salvage to preserve underwater cultural heritage: the integrated marriage of the law of salvage and historic preservation. J Maritime Law Commerce 49(3):401–424

Lights and Shadows of the EU Regulation 2019/880 on the Introduction and the Import of Cultural Goods

Sabrina Urbinati

Abstract Crisis, conflict situations and wars increase the illicit trafficking of cultural objects for several reasons. Besides States, several international organisations are also engaged in the fight against this illicit trafficking, such as the United Nations, UNESCO and the European Union. Following the relevant resolutions of the UN Security Council, the EU has adopted Regulation No 1210/2003 concerning Certain Specific Restrictions on Economic and Financial Relations with Iraq and Regulation No 36/2012 concerning Restrictive Measures in View of the Situation in Syria, where issues related to the illicit trafficking of cultural property are addressed. Beside these regulations, the relevant existing EU legal framework is composed of other instruments: some articles of the Treaty on the Functioning of the European Union concerning the free movement of goods and Council Regulation No 116/2009 on the Export of Cultural Goods. Recently, this legal framework has been completed by Regulation No 2019/880 on the Introduction and the Import of Cultural Goods. The main purpose of this chapter is to analyse the EU legal framework in light of the introduction of this latest regulation, in order to assess whether it can effectively contribute to the fight against the illicit trafficking of cultural property, especially when it comes from situations of conflicts.

1 Introduction

At the end of June 2000, I was a young graduate in law at the University of Urbino (Italy), with a dissertation on the UNESCO World Heritage Convention, and I had just left my country in order to pursue my international studies in Paris (France). There, I met Professor Tullio Scovazzi at UNESCO, during one of the meetings for the negotiation of the Convention on the Protection of the Underwater Cultural Heritage. Since then, I have had the honour of collaborating and working with Professor Scovazzi principally either at the University of Milano-Bicocca, as a Research Fellow, or within the Italian Delegation at UNESCO, as a Legal Expert,

S. Urbinati (✉)
University of Milano-Bicocca, Milan, Italy

M. Arcari et al. (eds.), *Trends and Challenges in International Law*,
https://doi.org/10.1007/978-3-030-94387-5_6

on many issues concerning the protection of cultural heritage. Therefore, it was with great pleasure that I accepted the very kind proposal of the editors to take part in this book with a contribution on the fight against the illicit trafficking of cultural property.

Since 2014 the Western World has been shocked by the wilful destruction of, in particular, Syrian and Iraqi cultural heritage, such as the archaeological sites of Palmira,[1] as well as several monuments, mosques and churches in the Niniveh province, Mosul and Nimrud[2] which has been perpetrated by ISIL and Al-Qaida. Beyond these situations, there has not only been the will to destroy the evidence of other cultures and religions or other interpretations of the Muslim one, but also the desire to generate income from the illicit trafficking of cultural property to finance the activities of the above-mentioned terrorist groups.[3]

Furthermore, the increased illicit trafficking of cultural property following situations of crisis has two other reasons that warrant mentioning. First, the already existing looting and smuggling of cultural property, conducted by local and transnational criminal organisations, increases exponentially to take advantage of crisis or conflict situations. Second, people escaping such situations may easily take with them cultural property in order to finance their journey.[4] Some of the cultural property, stolen from their countries of origin in these ways, emerge in the Western art market, especially in Europe, and others will no doubt do so over the next 10 or 20 years.

Several international and regional organisations are engaged in the fight against the damage, destruction and illicit trafficking of cultural heritage. Among them, there are the Organisation of the United Nations (UN), the United Nations Educational, Scientific and Cultural Organisation (UNESCO), the International Criminal Court (ICC), Interpol and the European Union (EU). For instance, the United Nations Security Council (UNSC) has adopted several resolutions especially dedicated to Iraqi and Syrian situations, such as Resolution 1483 (2003), concerning the Situation between Iraq and Kuwait,[5] (Resolution 1483) and Resolution 2199 (2015), devoted

[1] See, i.e., the cases of the destructions of the Temple of Bel, the Arch of Triumph, the Tetrapylon and the Roman Theatre.

[2] See, i.e., the cases of the destruction of the Mosque of the Prophet Yunus, the Shrine of Imam Yahya ibn al-Qaasim, the Mosque of Prophet Seth, the Mosque al-Khidr and the Mosul museum.

[3] See, amongst other reports, Geneva Call, *Culture Under Fire: Armed Non-State Actors and Cultural Heritage in Wartime* (2018).

[4] For more information see, amongst other documents, the World Custom Organisation's annual reports on illicit trade (i.e. WCO, *Illicit Trade Report* (2019) (2018) (2017) etc.) and the documents of the meetings of the relevant Governing Bodies of UNESCO's legal instruments concerning the fight against the illicit trafficking of cultural property at www.unesco.org. As regards the European context, see in particular the document European Commission, *Impact Assessment. Accompanying the Document: Proposal for a Regulation of the European Parliament and of the Council on the Import of Cultural Goods* (2017).

[5] *Resolution on the Situation between Iraq and Kuwait*, UN Doc. S/RES/1483 (2003).

to Threats to International Peace and Security Caused by Terrorist Acts,[6] (Resolution 2199). These resolutions are characterised by the fact that they concern the general situations of conflict in Iraq and Syria and the protection of cultural property is taken into account amongst other issues.[7] The growing importance of and concern of the International Community around the protection of cultural property in armed conflict is evidenced through the latest UNSC Resolution 2347 (2017),[8] devoted to the Maintenance of International Peace and Security. Unlike previous resolutions, it is specifically dedicated to the protection of cultural property in the event of armed conflict.

In accordance with UNSC Resolutions 1483 and 2199, the EU has adopted two regulations: Council Regulation (EC) No 1210/2003 of 7 July 2003 concerning Certain Specific Restrictions on Economic and Financial Relations with Iraq[9] (Regulation 1210) and Council Regulation (EU) No 36/2012 of 18 January 2012 concerning Restrictive Measures in View of the Situation in Syria[10] (Regulation 36). Like the relevant UNSC resolutions, these regulations concern not only the fight against the illicit trafficking of cultural property, but also other issues related to the Iraqi and Syrian situations of armed conflict.[11]

Besides Regulations 1210 and 36, the existing EU legal framework to fight against the illicit trafficking of cultural property is composed of other legal instruments having a more general scope of application: the Treaty on the Functioning of the European Union[12] (TFEU), which includes some provisions concerning the free movement of goods (Arts. 28 to 30 and 34 to 36) within the territory of the EU and Council Regulation (EC) No 116/2009 of 18 December 2008 on the Export of Cultural Goods[13] (Regulation 116). Furthermore, in this legal framework there is also Directive 2014/60/EU of the European Parliament and of the Council of 15 May 2014 on the Return of Cultural Objects Unlawfully Removed from the Territory of a

[6] *Resolution on Threats to International Peace and Security Caused by Terrorist Acts*, UN Doc. S/RES/2199 (2015).

[7] Another Resolution on this same topic that warrants mentioning is *Resolution on Threats to International Peace and Security Caused by Terrorist Act*, UN Doc. S/RES/2253 (2015).

[8] *Resolution on the Maintenance of International Peace and Security*, UN Doc. S/RES/2347 (2017).

[9] Council Regulation (EC) No 1210/2003 of 7 July 2003 *concerning Certain Specific Restrictions on Economic and Financial Relations with Iraq*, OJ L 169 (2003), p. 6.

[10] Council Regulation (EU) No 36/2012 of 18 January 2012 *concerning Restrictive Measures in View of the Situation in Syria*, OJ L016 (2012), p. 1.

[11] On the UNSC resolutions and the EU regulations, mentioned in this text, see, amongst others: Urbinati (2019); Frigo (2018), pp. 1165–1181; Urbinati (2018); Hausler (2018); Jakubowski (2018); Kretschmer (2016), pp. 308–333; Mackenzie, Scott (2016), pp. 211–236; Roodt (2015); Scovazzi (2015), pp. 25–90; Jakubowski and Jakubowski (2014), pp. 305–353; Urbinati (2013); Carducci (2009).

[12] Treaty on the Functioning of the European Union, OJ 326 (2012), pp. 1–390.

[13] Council Regulation (EC) No 116/2009 of 18 December 2008 *on the Export of Cultural Goods*, OJ L 39 (2009), pp. 1–7.

Member State[14] (Directive 60). Nevertheless, since this directive concerns only "[...] the return of cultural objects classified or defined by a Member State as being among national treasures, which have been unlawfully removed from the territory of that Member State',[15] it does not apply to cultural property coming from third States, such as those from Iraq and Syria and from other countries in situations of armed conflict. In 2019, this legal framework has been completed through Regulation (EU) No 2019/880 of the European Parliament and of the Council of 17 April 2019 on the Introduction and the Import of Cultural Goods[16] (Regulation 880).

Since the EU is essentially an economic organisation, it should theoretically strictly pursue the promotion of the free trade of goods amongst its Member States, without paying attention to what happens outside its territory and all the more so in a situation of conflict external to its boundaries. Nevertheless, its ambitions to expand its competences outside its economic purpose are well known and, seen in this light, it is clear that the EU intends, via the regulations mentioned above, to deal with the protection of cultural property of third countries—States that are not EU Members—in situations of armed conflict, such as in Iraq and Syria.

The main purpose of this chapter is to analyse the EU legal framework[17] as enhanced by Regulation 880. The analysis will allow for an assessment of whether the EU legal framework can effectively contribute to the fight against the illicit trafficking of cultural property coming from situations of conflict. In order to achieve this purpose, the chapter first examines the existing EU legal framework, which, as mentioned above, is composed of the TFEU provisions on the free movements of goods within the territory of the EU and Regulations 116, 1210 and 36. Second, the chapter analyses Regulation 880.

---

[14] Directive 2014/60/EU of the European Parliament and of the Council of 15 May 2014 *on the Return of Cultural Objects Unlawfully Removed from the Territory of a Member State*, OJ L 159 (2014), pp. 1–10.

[15] Article 1 Directive 60. In order to better delineate the scope of application of this instrument, see also some definitions included in Article 2: '[...] (1) "cultural object" means an object which is classified or defined by a Member State, before or after its unlawful removal from the territory of that Member State, as being among the "national treasures possessing artistic, historic or archaeological value" under national legislation or administrative procedures within the meaning of Article 36 TFEU; (3) "requesting Member State" means the Member State from whose territory the cultural object has been unlawfully removed; (4) "requested Member State" means the Member State in whose territory a cultural object, which was unlawfully removed from the territory of another Member State, is located'.

[16] Regulation (EU) No 2019/880 of the European Parliament and of the Council of 17 April 2019 *on the Introduction and the Import of Cultural Goods*, OJ L 151 (2019), pp. 1–14 entered into force on 28 June 2019.

[17] See, amongst others, Jakubowski et al. (2019), Frigo (2015), Mackenzie and Scott (2016), Quadri (2014), Jakubowski and Jakubowski (2014), Scovazzi (2014).

2 The TFEU Provisions on the Free Movement of Goods Within the Territory of the European Union

The TFEU provides that cultural goods[18] located on the territory of the EU are considered in the same way as any other common good. This means that cultural property can move freely among the borders of the EU internal market, because custom duties and quantitative restrictions on imports and exports, as well as all changes and measures having equivalent effect are prohibited among Member States.[19] This encompasses all cultural property, including that coming from third countries[20] once it enters the EU's customs territory.

The substantial equivalence between common goods and cultural property (or "cultural goods"—the only expression used in the EU legal framework to indicate such a heritage) is a specific part of the EU legal framework[21] and is in contrast with the approach adopted by other international organisations such as UNESCO. This equivalence has been criticised on several occasions, at the very least by some EU Member States (i.e. Italy and Greece) without success, because it does not sufficiently take into consideration the cultural character of the heritage at stake[22] and, as a consequence, means that cultural property is not protected to the extent it deserves.

This situation has been, only partially, mitigated by Article 36 TFEU, where an exception to the prohibition of quantitative restrictions on imports and exports, as well as of measures having equivalent effect is established. This exception is applicable for "[...] the protection of national treasures possessing artistic, historic or archaeological value [...]". This exception is the only means that an EU Member State, with a remarkable cultural heritage, has to limit and try to avoid the loss of its cultural property. Following the wording of Article 36,[23] it is clear, and the doctrine

---

[18] In the EU legal framework there are only references to 'cultural goods', and the expression of 'cultural property' is never employed. Nevertheless, these two expressions have to be considered synonyms. In this chapter both expressions, as well as that of cultural object, will be utilised with an equivalent meaning.

[19] Articles 28 to 30 and 34 to 36 TFEU.

[20] Article 28(2) The provisions of Article 30 and of Chapter 3 of this Title shall apply to products originating in Member States and to products coming from third countries which are in free circulation in Member States.

[21] The same approach has been adopted in the GATT. It is important to underline also that the EU has only a subsidiary competence in the field of culture in respect of its Member States. Thus, the EU interventions in the field of the cultural objects' circulation have been carried out by the DG Taxation and Custom Union and by the DG Internal Market of the EU Commission. This, partially, explains the reason of the approach of the EU.

[22] On this point see CJEU, 10 December 1968, *Commission of the European Communities v Italian Republic*, Case 7-68, ECLI:EU:C:1968:51.

[23] Article 36 TFEU, The provisions of Articles 34 and 35 shall not preclude prohibitions or restrictions on imports, exports or goods in transit justified on grounds of public morality, public policy or public security; the protection of health and life of humans, animals or plants; the protection of national treasures possessing artistic, historic or archaeological value; or the protection

has never expressed doubt on this interpretation, that the expression "national treasures"[24] refers only to EU Member States' cultural property and it is therefore not applicable to the cultural heritage of third countries. Thus, as mentioned at the beginning of this paragraph, this implies that once third countries' cultural goods enter in the EU internal market, they may freely circulate like any other good without any control. This is very dangerous, because it allows the illicit trafficking of cultural property coming from third countries to flourish. In fact, the EU, along with North America, is well known as one of the most important markets for stolen and illegally exported cultural goods.[25]

3 Regulation 116 on the Export of Cultural Goods

Regulation 116 has a general scope of application and takes into consideration all the exports of cultural goods from the EU to a third country: "The export of cultural goods outside the customs territory of the Community shall be subject to the presentation of an export licence".[26]

Categories of cultural property covered by Regulation 116 are listed in its Annex I.[27] Among these categories, there are some which are considered particularly

---

of industrial and commercial property. Such prohibitions or restrictions shall not, however, constitute a means of arbitrary discrimination or a disguised restriction on trade between Member States.

[24] For more on the difficulties arising from this expression see Frigo (2015), pp. 307 et ss.

[25] See for example the European Commission, *Impact Assessment. Accompanying the Document: Proposal for a Regulation of the European Parliament and of the Council on the Import of Cultural Goods* (2017).

[26] Article 2(1).

[27] A.1. Archaeological objects more than 100 years old which are the products of:—excavations and finds on land or under water;—archaeological sites;—archaeological collections; 2. Elements forming an integral part of artistic, historical or religious monuments, which have been dismembered, of an age exceeding 100 years; 3. Pictures and paintings, other than those included in categories 4 or 5, executed entirely by hand in any medium and on any material; 4. Watercolours, gouaches and pastels, executed entirely by hand on any material; 5. Mosaics in any material executed entirely by hand, other than those falling in categories 1 or 2, and drawings in any medium executed entirely by hand on any material; 6. Original engravings, prints, serigraphs and lithographs with their respective plates and original posters; 7. Original sculptures or statuary and copies produced by the same process as the original (1), other than those in category 1; 8. Photographs, films and negatives thereof; 9. Incunabula and manuscripts, including maps and musical scores, singly or in collections; 10. Books more than 100 years old, singly or in collections; 11. Printed maps more than 200 years old; 12. Archives, and any elements thereof, of any kind or any medium which are more than 50 years old; 13. (a) Collections and specimens from zoological, botanical, mineralogical or anatomical collections; (b) Collections of historical, paleontological, ethnographic or numismatic interest; 14. Means of transport more than 75 years old; 15. Any other antique items not included in categories A.1 to A.14 (a) between 50 and 100 years old toys, games, glassware, articles of goldsmiths' or silversmiths' wares, furniture, optical, photographic or cinematographic apparatus, musical instruments, clocks and watches and parts thereof, articles of wood, pottery, tapestries, carpets, wallpaper, arms, (b) more than 100 years old. The cultural objects in

sensitive as potential objects of illicit trafficking coming from countries in situations of armed conflict. These categories, regardless of their value, include: archaeological objects, more than 100 years old, which are products of excavations and found on land or under water; archaeological sites and archaeological collections; elements forming an integral part of artistic, historical or religious monuments which have been dismembered, of an age exceeding 100 years; incunabula and manuscripts, including maps and musical scores, singly or in collections.

Article 2(2) provides that the export licence has to be requested for all cultural objects (a) lawfully and definitively located on a Member State territory on 1 January 1993, and (b) lawfully and definitively dispatched from another Member State, or imported from a third country, or re-imported from a third country after lawful dispatch from a Member State.

Thus, currently, on the basis of Regulation 116, the EU seems to be able to control the exit from its territory of cultural goods, even if they come from third countries. Since cultural property corresponds to cultural objects imported from a third country, Regulation 116 has to be considered applicable to them.

Nevertheless, it seems that the possibility of controlling the export of a third country's cultural property is hardly achievable, since the only provided restriction on the release of an export licence is applicable when "[...] cultural goods are covered by legislation protecting national treasures of artistic, historical or archaeological value in the Member State concerned".[28] On this basis, even if a licence is required to export third country cultural goods outside the EU territory, in actual fact, there are hardly any restrictions on the issuance of the relevant export licence for those objects. In this way, limitations on the export of third countries' cultural property could be provided only by the domestic law of each EU Member State. This means that in this field there may be a significant lack of uniformity amongst the EU Member States, with the result that new illicit routes of trafficking of cultural objects from third countries will develop through the countries with the least effective domestic legislation.

categories A.1 to A.15 are covered by this Regulation only if their value corresponds to, or exceeds, the financial thresholds under B. B. Financial thresholds applicable to certain categories under A (in euro). Value: Whatever the value: — 1 (Archaeological objects); — 2 (Dismembered monuments); — 9 (Incunabula and manuscripts); — 12 (Archives); 15,000: — 5 (Mosaics and drawings); — 6 (Engravings); — 8 (Photographs); — 11 (Printed maps). 30,000: — 4 (Watercolours, gouaches and pastels). 50,000: — 7 (Statuary); — 10 (Books); — 13 (Collections); — 14 (Means of transport); — 15 (Any other object). 150,000: — 3 (Pictures).

[28] Article 2(2).

4 Regulations 1210 and 36 Concerning Restrictions on Economic and Financial Relations with Iraq and Syria

Regulations 1210 and 36 have been adopted to fight against the financing of terrorist groups located in Iraq and Syria. Thus, these regulations contain, in addition to provisions concerning the fight against the financing of terrorist groups, some provisions combating the illicit trafficking of cultural property illegally removed from these countries. In other words, in these regulations the fight against the illicit trafficking of cultural property is considered as a means, amongst others, to stop the financing of terrorist groups and their activities.

In particular, Article 3, Regulation 1210 provides that:

1. The following shall be prohibited:

   (a) the import of or the introduction into the territory of the Community of,
   (b) the export of or removal from the territory of the Community of, and
   (c) the dealing in, Iraqi cultural property and other items of archaeological, historical, cultural, rare scientific and religious importance including those items listed in Annex II, if they have been illegally removed from locations in Iraq, in particular, if:

      (i) the items form an integral part of either the public collections listed in the inventories of Iraqi museums, archives or libraries' conservation collection, or the inventories of Iraqi religious institutions, or
      (ii) there exists reasonable suspicion that the goods have been removed from Iraq without the consent of their legitimate owner or have been removed in breach of Iraq's laws and Regulations.

2. These prohibitions shall not apply if it is shown that either:

   (a) the cultural items were exported from Iraq prior to 6 August 1990; or
   (b) the cultural items are being returned from Iraq institutions in accordance with the objective of safe return as set out in paragraph 7 of the UNSC Resolution 1483 (2003).

Following the wording of this article it is possible to underline that the protection of cultural property is pursued only indirectly, as the purpose of this provision is to prohibit a series of activities, concerning these objects, which may contribute to the financing of terrorist groups. This point is confirmed by Article 11- *quater*, Regulation 36, which provides that:

1. It shall be prohibited to import, export, transfer, or provide brokering services related to the import, export or transfer of, Syrian cultural property goods and other goods of archaeological, historical, cultural, rare scientific or religious importance, including those listed in Annex XI, where there are reasonable grounds to suspect that the goods have been removed from Syria without the consent of their legitimate owner or have been removed in breach of Syrian law or international law, in particular if the goods form an integral part of either the public collections listed in the inventories of the conservation collections of Syrian museums, archives or libraries, or the inventories of Syrian religious institutions.
2. The prohibition in paragraph 1 shall not apply if it is demonstrated that:

   (a) the goods were exported from Syria prior to 15 March 2011; or
   (b) the goods are being safely returned to their legitimate owners in Syria.

In order to assess the above provisions, two elements have to be taken into consideration: firstly, the categories of cultural property envisaged and, secondly, the activities these instruments apply to.

As regards the first element, Regulations 1210 and 36 are applicable to the same objects: cultural property and other goods of archaeological, historical, cultural, rare scientific and religious importance, including those listed in the annexes to these regulations.[29] The contents of these annexes are identical.[30] In particular, these regulations are applicable to those cultural goods which form an integral part of either the public collections listed in the inventories of Iraqi and Syrian museums, archives or libraries' conservation collection, or the inventories of Iraqi religious institutions.[31]

Moreover, both regulations require that the removal of cultural property from Iraqi or Syrian territories has to be illegal. This concept is defined in two different ways. On one hand, a removal is deemed illegal when there is reasonable suspicion that the goods have been removed from Iraq or Syria without the consent of their legitimate owner. On the other hand, a removal is illegal when there is reasonable suspicion that the goods have been removed in breach of the laws and regulations of these countries, as well as of international law.[32]

As regards the second element (the activities to which the EU regulations here considered are applicable), it is possible to affirm that they concern a wide range of activities. Regulation 1210 aims to prevent (1) the import of or the introduction into the territory of the EU; (2) the export of or the removal from this same territory, and also (3) the dealing in Iraqi cultural property.[33] Regulation 36 aims to prevent a more specific range of activities, inasmuch as besides the import and export activities it takes into account the transfer and the brokering services[34] related to export and import.[35]

Even though these two legal instruments entered into force several years ago, it is very difficult to assess whether they have produced positive results. In fact, it is possible to find on many of the websites of the customs and Ministries of Culture of the EU Member States details of provisions and measures aimed at complying with these instruments, as well as with Regulation 116; however no information is available on instances of restitutions that have taken place following the provisions of Regulation 1210 and 36. This situation is common to international legal

---

[29] Article 3(1)c Regulation 1210 and Article 11-*quater*(1) Regulation 36.

[30] They are also identical to the cultural property listed in the Annex to Regulation 116.

[31] Article 3(1)c i Regulation 1210 and Article 11-*quater*(1) Regulation 36.

[32] Article 3(1)c ii Regulation 1210 and Article 11-*quater*(1) Regulation 36.

[33] Article 3(1) Regulation 1210.

[34] In its Article 1b Regulation 36 defines the expression "brokering services" such as the 'negotiation or arrangement of transaction for the purchase, sale or supply of cultural objects' as well as 'selling or buying' in the process of illicit art trade: the attempts at trade, assisting in trading, the actual transaction itself, the handling of objects covered by the prohibition and the assisting in the handling with such objects.

[35] Article 11-*quater*(1) Regulation 36.

instruments. In fact, even though it is possible to find, not only in the report of the World Custom Organisation (WCO), but also on the UNESCO website and in other sources, information on cases of seizure or restitution, it is very hard to know on what basis or legal provisions these cases have been resolved.[36]

5 Regulation 880 on the Introduction and the Import of Cultural Goods

Before the entry into force of Regulation 880, the regulation of the entry of cultural property from third countries into the EU internal market was left to each Member State's domestic law. Nevertheless, this situation created a patchwork of legal norms, whereby some States (for example Germany, Italy and the Netherlands) adopted national measures to be applied in relation to the import of cultural property within their territories, while others did not enact specific provisions. Moreover, the existing national measures concerning import were often divergent. This patchwork allowed the development of illicit trafficking routes through the more vulnerable and unregulated EU Member States' borders, a phenomenon known as "port shopping". Anyone who wants to import cultural property into the EU territory might choose the EU Member State with the "most favourable" or "unregulated" domestic law.[37] Thus, cultural goods both legally or illegally exported from their country of origin might enter the EU and freely circulate within its territory. The only existing control in place was in the case of export, because it was necessary to ask for an export licence. Nevertheless, as mentioned before,[38] there is no provisions limiting the possibility of exporting third countries' cultural heritage.

The proposal for a new regulation in this field was foreseen in the Commission Action Plan for Strengthening the Fight against Terrorist Financing presented in 2016 and aimed at disrupting the sources of revenue used by terrorist organisations by targeting their capacity to raise funds. Moreover, this proposal responded to multiple calls for action on the part of other EU institutions and national governments to fight against the illicit trafficking of cultural property within the EU. In fact,

---

[36] On a restitution case where it was possible to determine that the applied law was the UNESCO Convention on the Means of Prohibiting and Preventing the Illicit Import, Export and Transfer of Ownership of Cultural Property see Urbinati (2014).

[37] The necessity of employing uniform import Regulations for cultural property is also underlined in recital 4 of the preamble of Regulation 880:

> In view of different rules in the Member States regarding the import of cultural goods into the customs territory of the Union, measures should be taken in particular to ensure that certain imports of cultural goods are subject to uniform controls upon their entry into the customs territory of the Union, on the basis of existing processes, procedures and administrative tools aiming to achieve a uniform implementation of [the Union Customs Code].

[38] See par. 3 in this Chapter.

in several EU documents concerns around the role played by the EU in situations of conflict in Iraq and Syria, as well as in the fight against terrorist financing and security issues, were raised. In others, the attention was concentrated on the role of the EU in relation to culture and on the protection of Iraqi and Syrian cultural heritage. In all these documents, the EU noted that the illicit trafficking of cultural property—especially that coming from Iraq and Syria—had, due to the situation of conflict, increased substantially. Furthermore, in these documents this illicit trafficking was determined to be a threat to Iraqi and Syrian cultural heritage, as well as a source of income for terrorist groups involved in the conflicts. Thus, the EU noted two main purposes for the fight against the illicit trafficking of Iraqi and Syrian cultural property: on the one hand, it is necessary to protect the relevant cultural heritage, on the other, it seeks to stop the financing of terrorist groups.[39]

On these bases, the EU Commission presented the draft regulation on 13 July 2017 and on 17 April 2019 Regulation 880 was adopted. It entered into force on 28 June 2019.

There are two main purposes of Regulation 880: namely, the safeguard of humanity's cultural heritage and the prevention of the illicit trade in cultural goods, in particular where it may contribute to terrorist financing.[40] On this basis, Regulation 880 fits and enlarges the purposes of the relevant policy documents previously adopted by the EU institutions[41]: the protection of cultural property and the fight against the terrorist financing.

Regulation 880 prohibits the introduction into the EU territory of cultural goods illegally removed from the country where they were created or discovered. This removal is considered illegal when it takes place in breach of the laws and regulations of the relevant country.[42]

The regulation in question applies to cultural goods, defined as: "any item which is of importance for archaeology, prehistory, history, literature, art or science as listed in the Annex".[43] However, Regulation 880 does not apply to cultural goods

[39] See, amongst others, these policy documents: European Commission, *Joint Communication to the European Parliament and the Council: Elements for an EU Regional Strategy for Syria and Iraq as well as the Da'esh Threat* (2015); European Commission, *Communication from the Commission to the European Parliament, the Council, the European Economic and Social Committee and the Committee of the Regions: the European Agenda on Security* (2015); *European Parliament Resolution of 30 April 2015 on the Destruction of Cultural Sites Perpetrated by ISIS/Da'esh* (2015); European Commission, *Joint Communication to the European Parliament and the Council: Towards an EU Strategy for International Cultural Relations* (2016); *European Parliament Resolution of 17 January 2019 on Cross-Border Restitution Claims of Works of Art and Cultural Goods Looted in Armed Conflicts and Wars* (2017).

[40] Article 1, This Regulation sets out the conditions for the introduction of cultural goods and the conditions and procedures for the import of cultural goods for the purpose of safeguarding humanity's cultural heritage and preventing the illicit trade in cultural goods, in particular where such illicit trade could contribute to terrorist financing. [. . .].

[41] See n. 39.

[42] Article 3(1).

[43] Article 2(1).

which were either created or discovered in the territory of the EU.[44] As in Regulation 116, the definition of cultural goods in Regulation 880 is specified in a list contained in its Annex.[45] Nevertheless, it has to be noted that the two lists do not include the same categories of cultural goods. They only partially overlap; in addition, the value and the age limit thresholds are different. Thus, it seems possible to argue that since the entry into force and complete implementation of Regulation 880, we are and will be faced with two different definitions of cultural goods in the EU legal framework: one that applies at the point of import and the other at the point of export.

The Annex to Regulation 880 contains the same categories of cultural property foreseen in Article 1 of the UNESCO Convention on the Means of Prohibiting and Preventing the Illicit Import, Export and Transfer of Ownership of Cultural Property (1970 UNESCO Convention) and in the Annex of the UNIDROIT Convention on Stolen or Illegally Exported Cultural Objects (1995 UNIDROIT Convention). The use of these already existing lists is justified in recital 7 of the Preamble to Regulation 880, where it is explained that many third countries and most EU Member States are familiar with these categories of cultural property contained in the international instruments mentioned above, to which a significant number of EU Member States is party.[46]

Following this development, it seems possible to argue that there is an improvement in the concept of "cultural good/property" as conceived until now in the EU legal framework. In fact, as argued in the second section of this contribution, while in the relevant provisions of the TFEU and in Regulation 116, cultural objects are treated essentially as common commercial goods, unless they fit into one of the

---

[44] Article 1(2).

[45] (a) Rare collections and specimens of fauna, flora, minerals and anatomy, and objects of paleontological interest; (b) property relating to history, including the history of science and technology and military and social history, to the life of national leaders, thinkers, scientists and artists and to events of national importance; (c) products of archaeological excavations (including regular and clandestine) or of archaeological discoveries on land or underwater; (d) elements of artistic or historical monuments or archaeological sites which have been dismembered; (e) antiquities more than one hundred years old, such as inscriptions, coins and engraved seals; (f) objects of ethnological interest; (g) objects of artistic interest, such as: (i) pictures, paintings and drawings produced entirely by hand on any support and in any material (excluding industrial designs and manufactured articles decorated by hand); (ii) original works of statuary art and sculpture in any material; (iii) original engravings, prints and lithographs; (iv) original artistic assemblages and montages in any material; (h) rare manuscripts and incunabula; (i) old books, documents and publications of special interest (historical, artistic, scientific, literary, etc.) singly or in collections; (j) postage, revenue and similar stamps, singly or in collections; (k) archives, including sound, photographic and cinematographic archives; (l) articles of furniture more than one hundred years old and old musical instruments.

[46] States Parties to the 1970 UNESCO Convention that are also EU Member States are: Austria, Belgium, Bulgaria, Croatia, Cyprus, Denmark, Estonia, Finland, France, Germany, Greece, Hungary, Italy, Latvia, Lithuania, Luxembourg, The Netherlands, Poland, Portugal, Romania, Slovakia, Slovenia, Spain, Sweden. States Parties to the 1995 UNIDROIT Convention that are also EU Member States are: Croatia, Cyprus, Finland, Greece, Hungary, Italy, Latvia, Lithuania, The Netherlands, Portugal, Romania, Slovakia, Slovenia, Spain, Sweden.

exceptions expressly provided for—being a "national treasure" of Member States–, in Regulation 880 the emphasis is placed on the cultural character of the relevant object. This is further confirmed by the content of recitals 2[47] and 3[48] of the Preamble.

The activities regulated by Regulation 880 are the introduction and import of cultural goods, as defined in Article 2:

> 2. "introduction of cultural goods" means any entry into the customs territory of the Union of cultural goods which are subject to customs supervision or customs control within the customs territory of the Union in accordance with [the Union Customs Code];
>
> 3. "import of cultural goods" means:
>
> (a) release of cultural goods for free circulation as referred to in Article 201 of [the Union Customs Code];[49] or

---

[47] The exploitation of peoples and territories can lead to the illicit trade in cultural goods, in particular when such illicit trade originates from a context of armed conflict, in this respect, *this Regulation should take into account regional and local characteristics of peoples and territories, rather than the market value of cultural goods.* (Emphasis added by the author).

[48] Cultural goods are a part of cultural heritage and are often of major cultural, artistic, historical and scientific importance. Cultural heritage constitutes one of the basic elements of civilization having, inter alia, symbolic value, and forming part of the cultural memory of humankind. It enriches the cultural life of all peoples and unites people through shared memory, knowledge and development of civilization. It should therefore be protected from unlawful appropriation and pillage. Pillaging of archaeological sites has always happened, but has now reached an industrial scale and, together with trade in illegally excavated cultural goods, is a serious crime that causes significant suffering to those directly or indirectly affected. The illicit trade in cultural goods in many cases contribute to forceful cultural homogenization or forceful loss of cultural identity, while the pillage of cultural goods leads, inter alia, to the disintegration of cultures. As long as it is possible to engage in lucrative trade in illegally excavated cultural goods and to profit therefrom without any notable risk, such excavations and pillaging will continue. Due to the economic and artistic value of cultural goods they are in high demand on the international market. The absence of strong international legal measures and the ineffective enforcement of any measures that do exist, lead to the transfer of such goods to the shadow economy. The Union should accordingly prohibit the introduction into the customs territory of the Union of cultural goods unlawfully exported from third countries, with particular emphasis on cultural goods from third countries affected by armed conflict. In particular where such cultural goods have been illicitly traded by terrorist or other criminal organisations. While that general prohibition should not entail systematic controls. Member States should be allowed to intervene when receiving intelligence regarding suspicious shipment and to take all appropriate measures to intercept illicitly exported cultural goods.

[49] 1. Non-Union goods intended to be put on the Union market or intended for private use or consumption within the customs territory of the Union shall be placed under release for free circulation. 2. Release for free circulation shall entail the following: (a) the collection of any import duty due; (b) the collection, as appropriate, of other charges, as provided for under relevant provisions in force relating to the collection of those charges; (c) the application of commercial policy measures and prohibitions and restrictions insofar as they do not have to be applied at an earlier stage; and (d) completion of the other formalities laid down in respect of the import of the goods. 3. Release for free circulation shall confer on non-Union goods the customs status of Union goods.

> (b) the placing of cultural goods under one of the following categories of special procedures referred to in Article 210 of [the Union Customs Code]:[50]
>
> (i) storage, comprising customs warehousing and free zones,
>
> (ii) specific use, comprising temporary admission and end-use,
>
> (iii) inward processing.

Regulation 880 provides for two different procedures to be followed when the holder[51] of cultural property belonging to a third EU country seeks to either introduce or import it into EU territory.[52] In the first procedure an import licence is required, while in the second one an importer statement is necessary. Some exceptions to these procedures are provided in Article 3(4)(5). These include: firstly, the import licence and the importer statement are not required when cultural goods of third countries, having originally been exported as EU goods from the customs territory of the Union, are returned to that territory within a period of three years and declared for release for free circulation upon application by the person concerned; secondly, when cultural goods are imported for the exclusive purpose of ensuring their safekeeping by, or under the supervision of, a public authority, with the intent to return these goods; thirdly, when cultural goods are temporarily admitted into the customs territory of the EU for educational, scientific, conservation, restoration, exhibition, digitization, performing arts, for the purpose of research conducted by academic institutions, or for the purpose of cooperation between museums or similar institutions, and finally, when cultural goods are temporarily admitted into the EU customs territory to be presented at commercial art fairs, where an importer statement has been provided.

The distinction, between the procedure when an import licence is required and the procedure when an importer statement is necessary, is based on the relevant category that the cultural property which is the object of the introduction or the import procedure falls into. Article 4 requires the release of an import licence when the relevant cultural goods belong to one of the categories listed in Part B of the Annex,[53] such as for example archaeological objects and elements of monuments. In this case, an import licence is required to introduce or import cultural property into EU territory. A request for an import licence has to be made to the "competent

[50] Goods may be placed under any of the following categories of special procedures: (a) transit, which shall comprise external and internal transit; (b) storage, which shall comprise customs warehousing and free zones; (c) specific use, which shall comprise temporary admission and end-use; (d) processing, which shall comprise inward and outward processing.

[51] The corresponding expression of the 'holder of the goods' is defined in Article 2(4) through a reference to Article 5(34) of the Union Customs Code as 'the person who is the owner of the goods or who has a similar right of disposal over them or who has physical control of them'.

[52] Article 3(2).

[53] (c) Products of archaeological excavations (including regular or clandestine) or of archaeological discoveries on land or underwater; (d) elements of artistic or historical monuments or archaeological sites which have been dismembered. For both categories the relevant good has to be more than 250 years old.

authorities"[54] by the holder of the relevant cultural property, through the electronic system foreseen in Article 8.[55] The requirement of an import licence for archaeological objects and elements of monuments is justified in recital 10 of the Preamble of Regulation 880, on the basis of the fact that these categories are particularly vulnerable to pillage and destruction.

The application for the import licence has to be supported by documents and information providing evidence[[56]] that the cultural goods in question have been exported from the country where they were created or discovered in accordance with the laws and regulations of that country, or providing evidence of the absence of such laws and regulations at the time they were taken out of its territory.[57]

Derogation to this rule is foreseen in two cases. Firstly, when the country where the cultural goods were created or discovered cannot be reliably determined; and secondly, when the relevant cultural goods left the country where they were created or discovered before 24 April 1972.[58] In both cases the application may be accompanied by supporting documents and information providing evidence that the cultural goods in question have been exported in accordance with the laws and regulations of the last country where they were located for a period of more than five years and for purposes other than temporary use, transit, re-export or transhipment.[59]

Once the application is received, the competent authority verifies whether it is complete and releases the import licence within 90 days. It may reject the application in four cases:

---

[54]This expression is defined in Article 2(5), as '[...] the public authorities designated by the Member States to issue import licences.'

[55]Article 8 (Use of an Electronic System) – 1. The storage and the exchange of information between the authorities of the Member States, in particular regarding import licences and importer statements, shall be carried out by means of a centralised electronic system. In the event of a temporary failure of the electronic system, other means for the storage and exchange of information may be used on a temporary basis. 2. The Commission shall lay down, by means of implementing acts: (a) the arrangements for the deployment, operation and maintenance of the electronic system referred to in paragraph 1; (b) the detailed rules regarding the submission, processing, storage and exchange of information between the authorities of the Member States by means of the electronic system or by the other means referred to in paragraph 1. Those implementing acts shall be adopted in accordance with the procedure referred to in Article 13(2) 28 June 2021. Article 9 (Establishment of an electronic system)—The Commission shall establish the electronic system referred to in paragraph 1. Those implementing acts shall be adopted in accordance with the examination procedure referred to in Article 13(2) by 28 June 2021.

[56]The evidence may consist of "export certificates or export licences where the country in question has established such documents for the export of cultural goods at the time of the export" Article 4(5). The nature of the evidence is further specified in recital 12 of the Preamble of Regulation 880 with a reference to ownership titles, invoices, sales contracts, insurance documents, transport documents and expert's appraisals.

[57]Article 4(4).

[58]This date corresponds to the entry into force of the 1970 UNESCO Convention.

[59]Article 4(4) second part.

(a) it has information or reasonable grounds to believe that the cultural goods were removed from the territory of the country where they were created or discovered in breach of the laws and regulations of that country;
(b) the evidence required in paragraph 4 has not been provided;
(c) it has information or reasonable grounds to believe that the holder of the goods did not acquire them lawfully; or
(d) it has been informed that there are pending claims for the return of cultural goods by the authorities of the country where they were created or discovered.[60]

A decision to reject an application has to explain the reasons for that decision and to include information on the appeals procedure.[61] Each decision to reject has to be communicated to the other EU Member States and to the EU Commission via the electronic system foreseen in Article 8.[62]

The second import procedure concerns categories of cultural property listed in Part C of the Annex.[63] To introduce or import these categories, an importer statement has to be submitted[64] by the holder of the goods, via the electronic system foreseen in Article 8.[65] The importer statement has to be composed of two parts:

(a) a declaration signed by the holder of the goods stating that the cultural goods have been exported from the country where they were created or discovered in accordance with the laws and Regulations of that country at the time they were taken out of its territory; and
(b) a standardised document describing the cultural goods in question in sufficient detail for them to be identified by the authorities and to perform risk analysis and targeted controls.[66]

Derogation from the content of the holder declaration is foreseen in two cases: firstly, when the country where the cultural goods were created or discovered cannot be reliably determined; and secondly when the cultural goods left the country where

[60] Article 4(7).

[61] Article 4(8).

[62] Article 4(10).

[63] (a) Rare collections and specimens of fauna, flora, minerals and anatomy, and objects of paleontological interests; (b) property relating to history, including the history of science and technology and military and social history, to the life of national leaders, thinkers, scientists and artists and to events of national importance; (e) antiquities, such as inscriptions, coins and engraved seals; (f) objects of ethnological interest; (g) objects of artistic interest, such as: (i) pictures, paintings and drawings produced entirely by hand on any support and in any material (excluding industrial designs and manufactured articles decorated by hand); (ii) original works of statuary art and sculpture in any material; (iii) original engravings, prints and lithographs; (iv) original artistic assemblages and montages in any material: (h) rare manuscripts and incunabula; (i) old books, documents and publications of special interest (historical, artistic, scientific, literary, etc.) singly or in collections. For all categories the relevant good has to be of more than 200 years old.

[64] Article 5(1).

[65] Article 5(2). For the description of the electronic system see note n. 55.

[66] Ibidem.

they were created or discovered before 24 April 1972.[67] In these cases, the declaration may be that

> the cultural goods in question have been exported in accordance with the laws and regulations of the last country where they were located for a period of more than five years and for purposes other than temporary use, transit, re-export or transhipment [. . .].[68]

As regards the standardised document describing the cultural goods in question, in recital 15 of the Preamble a reference is made to the Object ID standard, which was elaborated by the Getty Information Institute in 1997. Nowadays, the International Council of Museums (ICOM) has the licenced right to promote the use of the Object ID standard, which is a well-recognized instrument in the fight against the illicit trafficking of cultural property. In fact, UNESCO generally recommends the use of this standard and the World Customs Organisation and Interpol base their work on it.

Finally, with regard to the legal instrument at stake, it has to be recalled that both during its drafting and when it was definitively adopted, the associations representing the main actors in the art market raised criticisms as to its content. In fact, they considered that it would have made their job more difficult and, in some cases, impossible. Nevertheless, as illustrated above, several exceptions to the application of Regulation 880 have been provided for. Such exceptions were the result of the remarks proposed during the drafting phase by the art market associations. One of these exceptions is the possibility provided for art dealers to present only the importer statement for cultural property which is to be shown at commercial art fairs. In fact, in such a case it would be sufficient to only provide an importer statement, irrespective of the nature of the relevant cultural object. Yet, other exceptions have been established providing that for Regulation 880 to apply, a minimum age and minimum financial value threshold should be met in relation to the relevant cultural property in question. Moreover, it has to be recalled that the regulation at stake provides for the participation of the associations representing the actors in the art market in the implementation process currently on-going. Finally, Article 14 states that, when Regulation 880 is entirely applicable, the EU Commission will be required to present periodic reports to the EU Parliament and to the EU Council on the implementation of the regulation at stake. Amongst the information and data, on which the EU Commission will have to report, there is also the impact of the regulation at stake on the Union's economic operators, particularly SMEs. Thus, it seems possible to affirm that the concerns of those in the art market have been taken into consideration and that several opportunities to continue a fruitful cooperation with the relevant EU institutions are foreseen in the implementation process of Regulation 880.

---

[67] This date corresponds to the entry into force of the 1970 UNESCO Convention.

[68] Article 5(2).

6 Critical Assessment of the EU Legal Framework as Completed by Regulation 880

In the previous sections, the process of the establishment of the existing EU legal framework designed to fight the illicit trafficking of cultural property has been described. Some critical issues concerning each one of the regulations composing the above-mentioned legal framework have already been illustrated in the relevant section. Now it is time to attempt a critical assessment of the EU legal framework as a whole.

Before the entry into force of Regulation 880, the entrance of third countries' cultural property into the EU internal market was left to each Member State's domestic law. Nevertheless, this situation created a patchwork of legal norms, that allowed the development of illicit trafficking routes through the more vulnerable and unregulated EU Member States' borders, a phenomenon known as "port shopping'.

Once they entered the EU internal market, third countries' cultural goods—unless they came illegally from Iraq and Syria—could circulate freely within the EU territory and were controlled only at their exit from the external EU custom borders, due to the requirement of an export licence. Nevertheless, it is important to underline that there are no established restrictions on obtaining an export licence, except in the event that there is a reasonable suspicion that Iraqi and Syrian cultural property has illegally entered into the EU territory. Otherwise, for any other third countries' cultural property, even for that coming from situations of armed conflict, such as Afghanistan, Libya, Mali, and Yemen, the release of the export licence might be required and obtained without any limitations.

The adoption and entry into force of Regulation 880 is a big step forward, because this sees a remarkable improvement in the EU legal framework concerning the fight against the illicit trafficking of cultural property. In fact, now a uniform approach has been established in relation to the control of the entry of third countries' cultural property within the EU territory, with a uniform customs Regulation replacing the previous patchwork of domestic legislation. Furthermore, the new EU legal framework has a larger scope of application, since it is applicable to cultural property whether it comes from third countries in a situation of peace or in a situation of armed conflict. Moreover, the EU legal framework is applicable not only to the illicit trafficking of cultural property carried out by terrorist groups to finance their activities, but in general to every kind of illicit trafficking, independent of who the subject carrying it out is.

In the previous section the development that Regulation 880 represents for the concept of "cultural good" has also been underlined. In fact, it seems that in the legal instrument at stake the cultural character of a cultural object is ultimately taken into account more than in the previous regulations. Hopefully, this development will soon be expanded to these latest. Only in this way will the consistency of the EU legal framework for the fight against the illicit trafficking of cultural property be safeguarded. A more comprehensive concept of cultural property, with the right level of equivalence between the commercial and economic dimension, on one side, and the cultural and artistic character, on the other, will allow the EU legal framework to be an effective one in the domain of our interest.

Nevertheless, enthusiasm for this new regulation has to be mitigated, because even though—as foreseen in Article 16 of Regulation 880—it immediately entered into force on 28 June 2019, a number of its pivotal provisions remain non-applicable for a considerable length of time. In fact, the import ban for the cultural goods listed in Part A of the Annex, i.e. those that are illegally removed from the territory of the country where they were created or discovered, entered into force on 28 December 2020, that is 18 months later the entry into force of Regulation 880. In the same vein, the entry into force of the requirements for an import licence and for an importer statement, as well as the establishment of the electronic system, are foreseen to be operational at the latest 6 years after the entry into force of the regulation at stake. Moreover, several EU Commission interventions are needed for the practical application of Regulation 880.[69] In this way, an in-depth assessment of this new EU legal framework will only be possible in about 10 years. Even though it is understandable that EU Member States and EU institutions have asked for some time in order to establish the necessary operational framework for the application of this new regulation, the time period of "at the latest six years" seems to be too long, especially because, as mentioned above, this instrument is supposed to provide a response to the already ongoing illicit trafficking of cultural property coming from situations of armed conflict, especially where this trafficking is one of the sources of terrorist groups' financing. Iraqi and Syrian cultural property are already protected by Regulations 1210 and 36, but there are also other countries where cultural objects are currently in danger because of an on-going armed conflict in which terrorist groups are operating. Thus, it is to be hoped that the EU Member States and institutions will work hard and diligently to make Regulation 880 concretely operational as soon as possible.

Two further issues have to be taken into account to improve the EU legal framework under examination. First, there are no provisions on what the national custom authorities may do in the event that they uncover an attempt to illegally introduce or export a third countries' cultural property, including that from Iraq and Syria. Do they have the power to seize the relevant cultural goods? Usually, national laws provide for the seizure of the relevant cultural property. Nevertheless, other questions remain on the table. Is the relevant EU Member State under the obligation to return the seized cultural property to their country of origin? When does this restitution have to take place? The only EU legal instrument taking this point into consideration is Article 3(1), specifically the second sentence, of Regulation 880, which provides that the "customs authorities and competent authorities shall take any appropriate measure when there is an attempt to introduce [illegally] cultural goods [listed in Part A of the Annex]". Even though it is understandable that agreement on this point had been very hard to achieve, it would have been

[69] An implementing regulation is under negotiation in the period of the writing of this chapter and has to be adopted by 28 June 2021, see Article 8(2) second sentence Regulation 880.

preferable to provide a more detailed provision. Thus, it has to be concluded that even if the export rules are common to all EU Member States, and the import rules are now common as well, the decision on what consequences are applicable to their violation is left, once again, to each Member State and hence a new patchwork of the relevant domestic legislations, with all the well-known consequences thereof, will appear soon.

Second, it seems possible to extend this reasoning to the penalties applicable to violations of Regulations 116, 1210, and 36, as well as to Regulation 880. Each regulation provides that each EU Member State shall establish penalties applicable for violations of their provisions. Thus, in some fashion, the patchwork situation mentioned above will continue. One person may decide to seek the import or export of cultural goods illegally coming from a third country via the competent custom authorities of the EU Member State with the least onerous measures and penalties for the violation of the relevant regulation. Nevertheless, while this situation is more understandable for penalties—because they concern criminal law, which does not fall within the EU competence—custom authorities' measures are also of an administrative nature and thus they fall within the EU competence.

7 Conclusion

Regulation 880 has undoubtedly enhanced the EU legal framework devoted to the protection of cultural heritage. Nevertheless, as illustrated in this chapter, several issues remain to be solved and ameliorated in order to make it more effective in the fight against the illicit trafficking of cultural property. After the United States, the EU is the second most important market in the world for cultural property. Thus, in order to limit as far as possible and to avoid the development of an illicit market of cultural property, the EU institutions have to act rapidly in resolving the above-mentioned controversial issues. Hopefully, the adoption of the regulation implementing Regulation 880, which is expected to be adopted at the end of June 2021, will be a good occasion to start this process.

References

Carducci G (2009) The growing complexity of international art law: conflict of laws, uniform law, mandatory rules, UNSC resolutions and EU regulations. In: Hoffman BT (ed) Art and cultural heritage: law, policy and practice. Cambridge University Press, Cambridge, pp 68–86

Frigo M (2015) Circulation des biens culturels, détermination de la loi applicable et methods de règlement des litiges. Recueil des Cours de l'Académie de Droit International de la Haye 375: 89–474

Frigo M (2018) Approaches taken by the security council to the global protection of cultural heritage: an evolving role in preventing unlawful traffic of cultural property. Rivista di diritto internazionale:1165–1181

Hausler K (2018) Cultural heritage and the security council: why resolution 2347 matters. Quest Int Law

Jakubowski A (2018) Resolution 2347: mainstreaming the protection of cultural heritage at the global level. Quest Int Law

Jakubowski A, Jakubowski O (2014) Export and import of cultural property: Poland. In: Nafziger JAR, Paterson RK (eds) Handbook on the law of cultural heritage and international trade. Edward Elgar, Cheltenham, Camberley, pp 305–353

Jakubowski A, Hausler K, Fiorentini F (eds) (2019) Cultural heritage in the European Union. A critical inquiry into law and policy. Brill, Leiden, The Netherlands

Kretschmer B (2016) Transnational organised crime and cultural property. In: Hauck P, Peterke S (eds) International law and transnational organised crime. OUP, Oxford, pp 308–333

Mackenzie R, Scott G (2016) The European Union's approach to trade restrictions on cultural property: a trendsetter for the protection of cultural property in other regions? SAACLR 2:211–236. https://doi.org/10.4467/2450050XSR.16.028.6136

Quadri S (2014) Il regime dell'Unione Europea in materia di restituzione dei beni culturali illecitamente esportati. In: Scovazzi T (ed) La restituzione dei beni culturali rimossi con particolare riguardo alla pratica italiana. Giuffré Editore, Milano, pp 211–247

Roodt C (2015) Private international law, art and cultural heritage. Edward Elgar, Cheltenham, Camberley

Scovazzi T (2014) La restituzione dei beni culturali rimossi con particolare riguardo alla pratica italiana. Giuffré Editore, Milano

Scovazzi T (2015) Evolutionary trends as regards the return of removed cultural property. In: Pérez-Prat Durbán L, Lazari A (eds) El tráfico de bienes culturales. Tirant lo Balch, Spain, pp 25–90

Urbinati S (2013) Improving the principle of cooperation against illegal movement of cultural property. Transnat Disp Manage

Urbinati S (2014) Brevi considerazioni su un caso di restituzione dall'Italia alla Bulgaria di reperti archeologici derivanti da scavi clandestini. In: Scovazzi T (ed) La restituzione dei beni culturali rimossi con particolare riguardo alla pratica italiana. Giuffré Editore, Milano, pp 331–338

Urbinati S (2018) The evolving role of the United Nations security council and the protection of cultural heritage in the event of armed conflict. Quest Int Law

Urbinati S (2019) La risoluzione 2347 (2017): Il Consiglio di sicurezza e la difesa dei beni culturali in caso di conflitto armato. Molto rumore per nulla?! In: Baroncini E (ed) Il diritto internazionale e la protezione del patrimonio culturale mondiale. AMS Acta, Bologna, pp 83–99

Part III
Environmental Law

The Breach of the Obligation to Prevent Environmental Harm and the Law of State Responsibility

Revisiting the Issue Against the Test of Judicial Application

Maurizio Arcari

Abstract International environmental law is rightly perceived as one of the most challenging fields for the secondary rules governing State responsibility. In particular, the conditions for establishing how the critical obligation of States to prevent environmental harm has been breached remain rather obscure. The Articles on the Responsibility of States for Internationally Wrongful Acts, adopted by the UN ILC in 2001, do not help to clarify the issue of whether preventive commitments of States in the field of environmental protection can be classified as obligations of conduct, of result, or otherwise. Considering the poor conceptualization of the matter in the ILC Articles, very little can be expected from the test of judicial application to which the same Articles are currently submitted. Nonetheless, recent international case law in environmental matters reveals that international judges are inclined to rest on the qualification of the States' obligations to prevent environmental harm as one of conduct or of due diligence and to elaborate about the conditions governing the breach of such obligation. The present contribution aims at revisiting the issue of the breach of the obligation to prevent environmental damage in light of recent international case law and to assess its relevance for the process of the codification of State responsibility.

M. Arcari (✉)
School of Law, University of Milano-Bicocca, Milan, Italy
e-mail: maurizio.arcari@unimib.it

M. Arcari et al. (eds.), *Trends and Challenges in International Law*,
https://doi.org/10.1007/978-3-030-94387-5_7

1 Introduction

It is commonplace to state that international environmental law represents a challenging field for the law of State responsibility.[1] This is so, not only due to the fragmentation of international environmental law, which contributes to making a general regime of State responsibility very problematic to apply.[2] One of the main difficulties around the matter lies in the scope and content of the basic obligation of States in the field of environmental protection, i.e., the obligation to prevent harm to the environment of other States or areas beyond national jurisdiction.[3] Besides the problems posed by the nature of the activities involved—which are not as such prohibited by international law and for the most part are carried out by private actors—other major complications also arise from the fact that the commitments of States concerning polluting activities are often couched not in terms of an absolute engagement to avoid harm to the environment, but as an obligation to do their best in order to prevent damage from occurring. Hence, the conclusion that "the doubts on the scope of the primary rules affect also the operation of the secondary rules on responsibility" appears appropriate in this regard.[4]

At the same time, one cannot fail to note the authoritative call put forward by Roberto Ago in his conclusion to a pioneering collective book on international responsibility for environmental harm. On that occasion, Ago made a strong case for framing the question of damage caused to the environment within the general scheme of State responsibility for internationally wrongful acts.[5] In particular, he insisted that, concerning environmental harm, lack of vigilance and the failure to prevent may generate an autonomous source of responsibility for the State.[6] If this

[1] See Scovazzi (2001), p. 43 ("[i]nternational responsibility for environmental harm is commonly considered to be a complex issue for its substantive, procedural, and even terminological intricacies").

[2] See recently Koskenniemi (2020), p. xi (holding, with reference to special regimes of international environmental law, that "State responsibility is a blunt tool. It has been impossible to apply it in a globally uniform way"). See also Nègre (2010), p. 804 ("International responsibility is thus not well-adapted to the environmental field").

[3] See *Trial Smelter Case* (United States of America v. Canada), Award of 16 April 1938, 11 March 1941, reprinted in 1950. *Reports of International Arbitral Awards* 3:1911, at p. 1965; Declaration of the United Nations Conference on the Human Environment, 16 June 1972, Principle 21, reprinted in 1972. *International Legal Materials* 11:1416, p. 1420. See also the International Court of Justice relevant case law, referred to *infra*, note 59.

[4] Scovazzi (2001), p. 46.

[5] Ago (1991), pp. 498:

> Il faut surtout –je sais que je me repète– faire entrer avec une nouvelle fermeté les atteintes portées à la preservation de l'environnement non plus dans le domaine des agissements tolérés comme licites, mais dans celui des faits ouvertements définis comme internationalement illicites.

[6] Ibidem, pp. 495–496: "Ce qu'on lui reproche [=à l'Etat] . . . c'est d'avoir négligé, par défaut de vigilance, de prévenir le dit fait. Cela crée à sa charge une source autonome de responsabilité internationale".

approach may well help to bring the matter back to the overall conceptual scheme governing State responsibility,[7] at the same time, it inescapably raises the question of how to clarify the conditions under which the obligation of States to prevent environmental damage is breached.

Notwithstanding the above call from one of the Special Rapporteurs on the topic, the question of the breach of preventive obligations finds a very poor conceptualization in the Articles on the Responsibility of States for internationally wrongful acts (hereinafter: the "Articles" or "ARSIWA") as definitively adopted in 2001 by the UN International Law Commission (ILC).[8] One essential distinction which would have a bearing on the issue at stake, i.e., the distinction between obligations of conduct and obligations of result, with the cognate sub-category of obligations to prevent a given event, was introduced by the ILC in 1977–1978[9] and retained until the 1996 first reading of the (then) Draft Articles.[10] However, the ILC eventually dropped the distinction during the second reading, on the understanding that it pertained more to a classification of primary obligations of States and therefore had no room in a codification concerned with the secondary rules of State responsibility.[11] In keeping with this approach, the ILC confined the issue to the context of the different topic of "Prevention of transboundary harm from hazardous activities". The latter was intended to codify the primary obligations of States concerning the authorization and regulation of activities that pose a risk of causing environmental damage.[12] On the other hand, a small remnant of the old classification can still be found in the current text of the ARSIWA, namely in Article 14, devoted to the

---

[7]Ibidem, p. 496: "[o]n revient ainsi à l'hypothèse de base de la responsabilité pour fait internationalement illicite, avec toutes les consequences de droit qui en découlent".

[8]See the text of the ARSIWA, with relevant commentaries, in Report of the International Law Commission on the work of its fifty-third session (23 April–1 June and 2 July–10 August 2001) [hereinafter ILC Report 2001], in YILC, 2001, vol. II, pt. 2, p. 26 ff. See also General Assembly Res. A/RES/56/83 of 12 December 2001, where the GA

> takes note of the articles on responsibility of States for international wrongful acts presented by the International Law Commission, the text of which is annexed to the present resolution, and commends them to the attention of Governments without prejudice to the question of their future adoption or other appropriate action (para 3).

[9]See, for Draft Articles 20 and 21, Report of the Commission to the General Assembly on the work of its twenty-ninth session", in Yearbook of the International Law Commission [hereinafter YILC], 1977, vol. II, pt. two, pp. 9–11; for Draft Article 23 "Report of the Commission to the General Assembly on the work of its thirtieth session", YILC, 1978, vol. II, pt. two [hereinafter "ILC Report 1978"] pp. 78–70.

[10]See Report of the Commission to the General Assembly on the work of its forty-eighth session, in YILC, 1996, vol. II, pt. two, pp. 60–61.

[11]See Report of the Commission to the General Assembly on the work of its forty-eighth session, in YILC, 1999, vol. II, pt. two, [hereinafter "ILC Report 1999"], pp. 50–63.

[12]The text of the Draft Articles on Prevention of transboundary harm from hazardous activities, adopted by the ILC in 2001, is annexed to GA Res. A/RES/62/68 of 6 December 2007, whereby the General Assembly "commended the articles . . . to the attention of Governments, without prejudice to any future action, as recommended by the Commission regarding the articles" (para 3).

extension in time of the breach of an international obligation. According to the third paragraph of the latter provision,

> The breach of an international obligation requiring a State to prevent a given event occurs when the event occurs and extends over the entire period during which the event continues and remains not in conformity with that obligation.[13]

As is widely known, for the time being, the ARSIWA retain a non-binding status. Pending a final determination by the General Assembly (GA) on the matter,[14] the Articles are currently submitted to the test of judicial application.[15] The expectation is that their reception in international case law will confirm their conformity with customary rules of State responsibility.[16] An overview of the compilations so far prepared by the UN Secretary-General on the decisions of international courts and tribunals referring to the Articles[17] reveals a very modest application of the provision which may be relevant for the question under review, i.e. Article 14(3), for which only three judicial decisions have been recorded.[18] Beyond the fact that these decisions do not deal with the prevention of environmental damage, it is evident that very little can be expected from the test of judicial application of the Articles, given the above-referred loopholes on the categorization of international obligations for the purpose of their breach.

However, an appraisal of the very recent judicial case law on environmental matters demonstrates that international judges are keen to construe the obligation of States to prevent environmental harm as one of conduct (or of "due diligence"), as well as to elaborate on the conditions governing its breach, even without referring to

[13] See the text in ILC Report 2001, p. 59.

[14] See recently GA Res. A/RES/74/180 of 18 December 2019, in which the General Assembly decided to postpone to its seventy-seventh session of 2022 "the question of a convention on responsibility of States for internationally wrongful acts or other appropriate action on the basis of the articles" (para 9).

[15] Ibidem, paras 4 and 5.

[16] For a recent stocktaking on the matter see Paddeu (2018), p. 83 ff.

[17] See the reports by the Secretary-General, Responsibility of States for internationally wrongful acts. Compilation of decisions of international courts, tribunals and other bodies, UN Doc. A/62/62 (1 February 2007) plus A/62/62/Add. 1 (17 April 2007); UN Doc. A/65/76 (30 April 2010); UN Doc. A/68/72 (30 April 2013); UN Doc. A/71/80 (21 April 2016) plus A/71/80/Add. 1 (20 June 2017); UN Doc. A/74/83 (23 April 2019).

[18] See UN Doc. A/62/62/Add.1, supra note 17, pp. 5–6 (referring to ICJ, *Application of the Convention on the Prevention and Punishment of the Crime of Genocide (Bosnia and Herzegovina v. Serbia and Montenegro)*, judgment 26 February 2007, in ICJ Reports, 2007, p. 43 [hereinafter *Genocide* case]); UN Doc. A/68/72, supra note 17, p. 22 (referring to Inter-American Court of Human Rights, *Castillo Gonzáles et al. v. Venezuela*, judgment 27 November 2012 and to European Court of Human Rights, *El-Masri v. The Former Yugoslav Republic of Macedonia*, App. no. 39630/09, judgment 13 December 2012). Among these decisions, one (the *Genocide* case) is particularly pertinent for framing the issue of the breach of obligations of prevention and, while not concerning environmental matters, will be considered *infra*, under Sect. 3.

the ILC Articles.[19] Considering two critical judgments recently pronounced by the International Court of Justice (ICJ) in cases involving the breach of States' obligations in preventing environmental damage,[20] one author has poignantly suggested that, although the Court did not invoke ILC Article 14(3), it was ultimately willing to struggle with the same underlying questions.[21]

The present contribution purports to elaborate on the suggestions presented above. To this end, the classification of obligations of conduct, result and prevention formerly enshrined in the ILC Articles will first be revisited, and the reasons that brought about their demise will be explored (Sect. 2). Second, this contribution will appraise the recent international case law broaching the question of the breach of the obligations of States to prevent environmental harm (Sect. 3). Finally, some concluding remarks will be made concerning the significance of the case law in light of the process of codification of the secondary rules on State responsibility (Sect. 4).

2 Obligations of Prevention in the ILC Work on State Responsibility

Considering that a number of different outstanding contributions have been devoted to the topic,[22] a re-appraisal of the process that brought the ILC to outline the classification of obligations of conduct, of result, and of prevention may appear rather trite. Nonetheless, such a step appears inescapable in assessing the recent international case law dealing with the breach of obligations of States in the

---

[19] See in particular: ICJ, *Pulp Mills on the River Uruguay (Argentina v. Uruguay)*, judgment of 20 April 2010, in ICJ Reports, 2010, p. 14 [hereinafter *Pulp Mills*], para 187; International Tribunal for the Law of the Sea, *Responsibilities and Obligations of States Sponsoring Persons and Entities with respect to Activities in the Area (Request for Advisory Opinion Submitted to the Seabed Disputes Chambers)*, Advisory Opinion of 1 February 2011, in ITLOS Reports, 2011, p. 10 [hereinafter *Responsibilities of States in the Area*], para 110; ICJ, *Certain Activities Carried Out by Nicaragua in the Border Area (Costa Rica v. Nicaragua) and Construction of a Road in Costa Rica along the San Juan River (Nicaragua c. Costa Rica)*, judgment of 16 December 2015, in ICJ Reports, 2015, p. 665 [hereinafter *Certain Activities/Construction of a Road*], para 104; Permanent Court of Arbitration, *South China Sea Arbitration (Republic of The Philippines v. People's Republic of China)*, Award of 12 July 2016, reprinted in 2020. *Reports of International Arbitral Awards* 33:155 [hereinafter *South China Sea*], para 944; Inter-American Court of Human Rights, *Environment and Human Rights (States Obligations in Relation to the Environment in the Context of the Protection and Guarantee of the Rights to Life and to the Personal Integrity: Interpretation and Scope of Articles 4(1) and 5(1) in relation to Articles 1(1) and 2 of the American Convention on Human Rights)*, Advisory Opinion OC-23/17 of 15 November 2017. www.corteidh.or.cr/docs/opiniones/seriea_23_ing.pdf. [hereinafter *Environment and Human Rights*], para 143.

[20] See ICJ, *Pulp Mills* and *Certain Activities/Construction of a Road* cases referred to in previous footnote.

[21] See Brunnée (2020), p. 155.

[22] See Combacau (1981); Dupuy (1999); Marchesi (2004); Economides (2010); Wolfrum (2010); Crawford (2013), pp. 219–232; Aust and Feihle (2020).

prevention of environmental harm. It is true that, in the recent decisions addressing the issue, judges seem to have largely ignored, when not altogether reversed, the abstract qualifications elaborated by the ILC. However, as will be seen later on, when establishing *in concreto* whether preventive obligations of States were breached, international judges have struggled with some of the theoretical hurdles addressed by the ILC in its treatment of the issue. With this in mind, the first part of this section will analyze the early work of the ILC concerning the distinction between obligations of conduct and obligations of result, as well as the special category of the obligation to prevent a given event (Sect. 2.1). In the same vein, the second part of the section will explore the reasons leading to the demise of this distinction in the latest phase of the ILC work on State responsibility (Sect. 2.2).

2.1 Obligations of Conduct, of Result and of Prevention in the Early Works of ILC on State Responsibility

As already mentioned, the issue of the breach of preventive obligations of States was the object of a specific provision included in Part one of the Draft Articles on State responsibility, dealing with the origin of international responsibility. The text of Draft Article 23 ("Breach of an international obligation to prevent a given event") provisionally adopted by the ILC in 1978, read as follows:

> When the result required of a State by an international obligation is prevention, by means of its own choice, of the occurrence of a given event, there is a breach of that obligation only if, by the conduct adopted, the State does not achieve that result.[23]

As suggested by its initial wording ("When the result required..."), the provision above is but a specification of the more general distinction between obligations of conduct and obligations of result introduced before the ILC in 1977 by the then Special Rapporteur Roberto Ago. Ago introduced the distinction in order to cope with the conditions governing a breach of an international obligation.[24] According to Ago, although all obligations placed upon a State under the rules of international law are directed towards a particular goal, they are structured differently with respect to the ways and means by which the State is expected to ensure their fulfilment.[25] In this respect, Ago distinguished obligations that call categorically for the use of specific means or a specific course of conduct and obligations that leave the State

[23] See text and related commentary in YILC, 1978, vol. II, pt. two, pp. 81–86.

[24] See R. Ago, Sixth Report on State Responsibility, UN Doc. A/CN.4/302 and Add. 1–3, in YILC, 1977, vol. II, pt. one, p. 3 ff., respectively pp. 8 and 20 for the text of Draft Articles 20 ("Breach of an international obligation calling for the State to adopt a specific course of conduct") and 21 ("Breach of an international obligation requiring the State to achieve a particular result") submitted by the Special Rapporteur.

[25] Ibidem, p. 4, para 2. See also on this distinction Ago (1939), pp. 506–511.

free to choose the means for attaining a specific result.[26] For Ago, the distinction impacted how a breach would accrue, the former category of obligations being violated if the conduct specifically required has not been adopted, the latter being violated only when the required result has not been attained.[27]

Although a detailed account of the complexities behind the distinction proposed by Ago is not advisable in this context, three related aspects are worth noting. First, in outlining his categorization Ago built upon the assumption that much of the distinction depended on the measure in which international law, by its commands, "intrudes" into the domestic order of States, either by imposing directly on State machinery the adoption of a very precise course of conduct, or by merely requiring the State to ensure a particular situation or result.[28] Second, Ago seemed to suggest that the "determinacy" of the conduct required by international law to the State can set the threshold for establishing whether a certain obligation was one of conduct or one of result.[29] Third, despite being aware that the distinction was not perfectly consistent with the notion of obligations of conduct and result usually adopted in domestic (civil) law systems, the Special Rapporteur underscored that the proposed meaning seemed "to correspond to typical aspects of the international community and its law".[30]

During the discussion on the two relevant draft provisions submitted by Ago (Draft Articles 20 and 21), some members of the ILC incidentally queried whether preventive engagements assumed by States under international law had to be classified as obligations of conduct or obligations of result.[31] In order to address

[26] See Ago, Sixth Report, supra note 24, p. 4, para 4.

[27] Ibidem, pp. 4–5, para 4 and p. 8, paras 14–15.

[28] Ibidem, p. 4, para 3:

> In the former case, the obligations are laid upon the State, requiring it to take or refraining from taking some specific action: for example, to adopt or to refrain from adopting a specific legislative, administrative or judicial act. In the latter case, international law, concerned with respect of the internal freedom of the State, merely requires the State to ensure a particular situation or result and leaves it free to do so by whatever means it chooses.

The approach above described is explicitly borrowed by Ago from Anzilotti (1906), p. 26, but it was shared among Italian scholars during the twentieth century: for an overview see Marchesi (2004), pp. 828–834.

[29] Ago, Sixth Report, supra note 24, p. 8, para 12:

> It might, however, be wiser to speak more precisely, with regard to the first category, of 'obligations of specific conduct', for even in the case of 'obligations of result' it is still the 'conduct' of the State which is required in order to ensure the required result.

[30] Ibidem, especially footnote 27. On this aspect see further *infra*, note 46 and accompanying text.

[31] In particular Paul Reuter, while basically endorsing the distinction proposed by the Special Rapporteur, suggested that a third category of obligations "at a lower degree of precision" can also be identified: referring to obligations which required of the State neither specific acts nor definite results, but an attitude conducive to a result which was not mandatory, Reuter made as a relevant example the general obligation to be vigilant. See Summary records of the twenty-ninth session, 9 May-29 July 1977, 1455th Mtg., in YILC, 1977, vol. I., p. 219, paras 8–9.

these remarks, in 1978 Ago introduced before the ILC a new provision (Draft Article 23) devoted to the "Breach of an international obligation to prevent a given event".[32] The Special Rapporteur pointed out that the specific object of these obligations was to prevent "the occurrence of certain events which might unduly harm foreign States or their representatives and nationals", and that the preventive action required of the State consisted "essentially of surveillance and vigilance with a view to preventing th[e] event, in so far as it is materially possible".[33] At the same time, he maintained that a breach of an obligation to prevent required two conditions to accrue:

> the event to be prevented must have occurred, and it must have made it possible by a lack of vigilance on the part of the States organs... [o]nly the combination of these two elements permits the conclusion that there has been such a breach.[34]

During the ensuing discussion before the ILC it became clear how difficult it was to frame under the general scheme so far proposed due diligence obligations. Some members of the Commission, explicitly referring to due diligence obligations of States in preventing transboundary pollution, questioned whether, in the event that the State had taken no measures to prevent the situation, it was really necessary to wait until the event actually came about before concluding that responsibility was engaged.[35] In his reply, the Special Rapporteur invited caution in drawing parallelism between Draft Article 23 and due diligence obligations. Ago pointedly warned that

> in the case the Commission was considering, where the obligation was to prevent the occurrence of some event, the obligation did not require that due diligence should be exercised in a particular form, but that care should be taken to ensure that the event did not occur, which was another matter.[36]

This seems to confirm that, according to Ago, the guiding criterion for classifying an obligation (including one qualified by "due diligence") was the determinacy of the conduct required of States by the international norm at stake.[37]

Be that as it may, the Commission eventually approved Draft Article 23 along the lines suggested by Ago.[38] The ILC commentary to that provision is prominent in

---

[32] Ago, Seventh Report on State Responsibility, UN Doc. A/CN.4/307 and Add. 1-2, in YILC, 1978, vol. II, pt. one, p. 31 ff, at 37 for the text of Draft Article 23 submitted by Ago.

[33] Ibidem, p. 32, paras 1 and 2.

[34] Ibidem, para 3.

[35] See Summary records of the thirtieth session, 8 May-28 July 1978, in YILC, 1978, vol. I, the statements by Reuter (1476th and 1478th Mtgs, respectively p. 7, paras 21–23 and 14, paras 6–7), Díaz González (1477th Mtg., p. 9, para 2), El-Erian (1478th Mtg., p. 15, para 9), Vallat (1478th Mtg., p. 9, para 14).

[36] Ibidem, 1478th Mtg., p. 18, para 36.

[37] In this respect, the Special Rapporteur unequivocally pointed out that "there were obligations of due diligence that were obligations of conduct, and which might therefore be said to have been breached by the mere fact that requisite due diligence had not been exercised" (ibidem).

[38] See ibidem, 1513th Mtg., pp. 206–208, in particular the report of the Chairman of the Drafting Committee on Draft Article 23 and the adoption of the text by the Commission.

underscoring that obligations falling under the article "are a special type of the general category of obligations of 'results'".[39] In fact, the non-occurrence of the event is singled out as the specific result requested of the State by the obligation to prevent, and the occurrence of the event is singled out as the key indicator that the obligation has not been fulfilled.[40] At the same time, the commentary required the existence of a "certain causal link" between the event and the conduct of the State: accordingly, the obligation is considered breached only when the means chosen by the State proved inadequate to prevent the occurrence of the event.[41] It is probably on the relationship between these two basic conditions that the ILC approach to the matter of prevention leaves more room for ambiguity. This is also revealed by the rather cryptic treatment of "due diligence" obligations, which are marginally addressed in a footnote of the commentary, stating that

> obligations requiring the prevention of given events are not the same as those that are commonly referred to by the blanket term 'obligations of due diligence'. The breach of the latter obligations often consists of an action or omission by the State and is not necessarily affected by the fact that an external event does or does not take place.[42]

In the following years, Draft Articles 21, 22 and 23 as approved by the ILC were not the object of substantial observations by States commenting the first part of the Draft on State responsibility. Some noteworthy remarks were made by a couple of States, which criticised the failure of the Commission to take into account the element of "due diligence" in Draft Article 23 and queried as to what may constitute an appropriate or inappropriate conduct with regard to the event to be prevented.[43]

As already mentioned, the three provisions ultimately passed unaltered during the first reading of the Draft Articles in 1996,[44] before being subject to a substantial revision on a second reading, during the ILC session of 1999.

2.2 *The Demise of the Distinction in the Final ILC Articles on State Responsibility*

Taking momentum from the criticism expressed by (a few) States in the written comments submitted on the eve of the ILC's second reading of the Articles on State

[39] See ILC Report 1978, p. 81, para 1 and p. 85, para 15.

[40] Ibidem, p. 82, para 4.

[41] Ibidem, pp. 82–83, para 6.

[42] Ibidem, p. 82, para 4, fn 397.

[43] See respectively the comment on Draft Article 23 made by Austria and Mali, Observations and comments of Governments on chapters I, II and III of part I of the Draft Articles on State responsibility for internationally wrongful acts, UN Doc. A/CN.4/328 and Add. 1-4, in YILC, 1980, vol. II, pt. one, respectively pp. 92–93 and p. 101.

[44] See supra note 10.

responsibility,[45] the new Special Rapporteur on the topic, James Crawford, questioned the opportunity and the practical utility of maintaining the general distinction between obligations of conduct and obligations of result enshrined in Draft Articles 20 and 21.

First, Crawford underscored that, at a theoretical level, in borrowing from the civil law the distinction between obligations of conduct and result, the ILC had nearly reversed its effect, thereby generating a source of terminological and conceptual confusion. In fact, under the ILC approach, obligations of conduct are more precise than obligations of results, which leave more leeway to the State. The contrary is true in domestic (in particular French) law, where obligations of conduct are meant to be less stringent, being in the nature of best effort obligations, as opposed to obligations of result, which impose an imperative outcome on the debtor of the obligation.[46] Second, the Special Rapporteur pointed out that although international case law had occasionally referred to the distinction between obligations of conduct and result as a means for the classification of international obligations, it had not done so with much consistency.[47] Third, Crawford maintained that obligations of conduct and result in practice present not a dichotomy but a spectrum, that the means and ends in performing an obligation can be combined in various ways and that, ultimately, whether a breach has accrued depends on the precise term of the obligation and the facts of the case.[48] Similar criticism was also extended to Draft Article 23.[49] Eventually, the new Special Rapporteur made a strong case for deleting Draft Articles 20, 21 and 23.[50]

Some ILC members appeared inclined to endorse the suggestions of the Special Rapporteur on three main accounts. First, the distinction between obligations of conduct and obligations of result pertained to the classification of substantive norms of international law, and its retention might lessen the separation between primary and secondary rules. Second, the distinction had not attained a level of universal acceptance that would have required codification. Third, the distinction had no special relevance regarding the consequences of the breach of international law.[51]

---

[45] See State responsibility. Comments and observations received from Governments, UN Doc. A/CN.4/488, in YILC, 1998, vol. I, pt. one, pp. 123–124, in particular the criticisms expressed by Denmark, on behalf of Nordic Countries (Finland, Iceland, Norway, Sweden and Denmark), Germany and France.

[46] See Crawford, Second report on State Responsibility, UN Doc. A/CN.4/498 and Add. 1-4, in YILC, 1999, vol. II, pt. one, 21–22, paras 57–58. This point is built on the famous argument developed by Combacau (1981), pp. 194–199. See also Dupuy (1999), pp. 374–378; Economides (2010), pp. 375–376. Compare the position of Ago referred to supra note 30 and accompanying text.

[47] Ibidem, pp. 22–24, paras 60–68.

[48] Ibidem, pp. 26–27, paras 26–27, paras 77–79.

[49] Ibidem, pp. 27–28, paras 81–87.

[50] Ibidem, p. 29, paras 90–91, for the Crawford conclusion that "the case for deletion is a formidable one". Alternatively, the Special Rapporteur suggested dealing with the issue at stake in a single, consolidated, provision (see ibidem, p. 44 for his proposal of a new Draft Article 20 dealing with "obligations of conduct and obligations of result").

[51] See ILC Report 1999, pp. 59–61, especially paras 147–150 and 163.

During the debate, interesting points were also raised concerning Draft Articles 23, with some members of the Commission questioning the presentation of the obligation to prevent a given event as a sub-category of the obligations of result. In this respect, it was pointed out that, especially under international treaties on the environment, such obligations were often obligations of conduct or due diligence obligations and not obligations of result.[52]

In the end, the Drafting Committee of the ILC proposed dropping from the second reading Draft Articles 20, 21 and 23 and incorporating the ideas and distinctions outlined by those provisions in the commentary to the Draft Articles.

As is well known, this solution was eventually retained in the second reading of the Articles on State responsibility adopted in 2001. "Old" Draft Articles 20, 21 and 23 disappeared, and the distinction between obligations of conduct and result is now indirectly covered by the commentary to current Article 12, i.e. the provision introducing in general term the conditions for the existence of a breach of an international obligation. This text recites that "[t]here is a breach of an international obligation by a State when an act of that State is not in conformity with what is required of it by that obligation, regardless of its origin *or character*".[53]

As explained in the relevant commentary, the italicised text is meant to suggest that the distinction between obligations of conduct and obligations of result may assist in ascertaining when a breach has occurred, but "it is not exclusive". The commentary then adds some examples from case law, which are intended to support the view that, even if occasionally adopted by international courts, the distinction above is not determinative of whether a breach has accrued or not.[54]

However, not all of the controversial distinctions discussed by the ILC during the seventies have been removed. As already noted, a trace of the past categorization remains in the current text of Article 14.[55] Although the provision as a whole is intended to cope with the extension in time of a breach of international law, its third paragraph deals explicitly with "the temporal dimension of a *particular category of breaches of international obligations*, namely the breach of obligations to prevent the occurrence of a given event".[56] The singling out of this special category of obligations cannot but renew some of the old (and odd) ambiguities attached thereto. On the one side, the text of paragraph 3 is pleonastic in stating that "the breach of an international obligation to prevent a given event *occurs when the event occurs...*", thereby confirming that the occurrence of the event is necessary for establishing the breach of the preventive obligation. On the other side, the commentary to the provision specifies that

---

52 See Summary records of the meetings of the fifty-first session 3 May-23 July 1999, in YILC, 1999, vol. I, 2571st Mtg., pp. 29–35, 2573rd Mtg., pp. 41–44, and 2574th Mtg., pp. 48–49, especially the statements of Rao (p. 33, para 43) and Yamada (p. 41, para 6).

53 See the text in ILC Report 2001, p. 54 (emphasis added).

54 Ibidem, pp. 56–57, para 11 of the commentary to Article 12.

55 See supra text accompanying note 13.

56 ILC Report 2001, p. 62, para 14 of the commentary to Article 14 (emphasis added).

> obligations of prevention are usually construed as best efforts obligations, requiring States to take all reasonable means or necessary measures to prevent a given event from occurring, *but without warranting that the event will not occur.*[57]

If this does not dispose definitively of the matter, it may perhaps provide the first hint for many of the persisting ambiguities that we will encounter in the ensuing case law.

3 The Test of Judicial Application: Hints from Recent International Case Law in Environmental Matters

As cursorily mentioned, one of the arguments supporting the ILC's choice to remove from the Articles on State responsibility the provisions concerning the breach of obligations of conduct, result, and prevention was that in international case law the underlying distinction was seldom applied and, when this happened, judges used it inconsistently.[58] However, an overview of the judicial practice of the last decade concerning the prevention of transboundary environmental harm seems to point to the opposite conclusion. Not only have international judges and arbitrators consistently classified preventive obligations of States as obligations of conduct or "due diligence"—a fact that *per se* would justify the reconsideration of the past theoretical classifications made by the ILC; they have also demonstrated readiness to elaborate upon the basic conditions governing the breach of the obligations at stake. In doing so, they have struggled with some of the conceptual alternatives considered by the ILC during its past attempt at codifying the "objective element" of international responsibility. For these reasons, it seems opportune to review the theoretical issues mentioned above in the context of their recent judicial application. For substantive and practical purposes, the case law discussed below is clustered based on the issuing jurisdiction and is not presented in strict chronological succession. Special attention will first be reserved to the case law of the ICJ (Sect. 3.1) since the latter has been used as a benchmark in subsequent decisions dealing with the prevention of environmental harm. Second, a cursory look at the relevant opinions and awards issued by other tribunals and courts will be provided (Sect. 3.2).

3.1 The International Court of Justice

Between 2010 and 2015 the ICJ rendered two critical decisions in which it elaborated upon its previous case law concerning the basic obligations of States in

[57] Ibidem (emphasis added).

[58] See references supra notes 47 and 54. See further ILC Report 1999, p. 59, paras 148–149 and p. 63, para 186.

environmental protection.[59] Both cases, confronting respectively Argentina and Uruguay (Sect. 3.1.2) and Costa Rica and Nicaragua (Sect. 3.1.3), are particularly relevant for the present purposes; they dealt precisely with the question of the breach of the obligation to prevent transboundary damage caused by planned activities of States on shared resources. However, just before these two critical cases, the Court took the opportunity to sketch a sort of general approach towards due diligence and preventive obligations of States in the 2007 judgment concerning the dispute between Bosnia and Serbia over the violation of the 1948 Genocide Convention.[60] Therefore, it is useful to commence this section devoted to the ICJ by recalling some of the relevant points of the reasoning developed in the latter judgment (Sect. 3.1.1).

3.1.1 Genocide Case (Bosnia and Herzegovina v. Serbia and Montenegro)

In its judgment of 2007, the ICJ considered the question of whether Serbia had complied with its obligation to prevent genocide under Article I of the 1948 Convention. The Court generally stated that the content of the duty to prevent varies from one instrument to another, according to the wording of the relevant provisions and depending on the nature of the acts to be prevented. Accordingly, the Court stressed that it did not purport in the case at hand to establish a general jurisprudence on the preventive obligations of States under international law.[61]

Having so defined its purpose, the Court provided a general qualification of the duty to prevent genocide, pointing out that

> the obligation in question *is one of conduct and not of result*, in the sense that a State cannot be under an obligation to succeed, whatever the circumstances, in preventing the commission of genocide: the obligation of State parties is rather to employ all means reasonably available to them so as to prevent genocide as far as possible.

The Court pushed things a step further, adding that "in this area, *the notion of 'due diligence'*, which calls for an assessment in concreto, is of critical importance", and

---

[59] See *Legality of the Threat of Use of Nuclear Weapons*, Advisory Opinion of 8 July 1996, ICJ Reports 1996, p. 226, at pp. 241–242 para 29 (considering that

> [t]he existence of the general obligation of States to ensure that activities within their jurisdiction and control respect the environment of other States or of areas beyond national control is now part of the corpus of international law relating to the environment);

Gabčíkovo-Nagymaros Project (Hungary v. Slovakia), Judgment of 25 September 1997, ICJ Reports 1997, p. 7, at p. 78, para 140 (holding that

> in the field of environmental protection, vigilance and prevention are required on account of the often irreversible character of damage to the environment and the limitations inherent in the very mechanism of reparation of this type of damage).

[60] See *Genocide*, supra note 18.

[61] Ibidem, p. 220, para 429.

then suggested some of the basic parameters which may serve to assess whether a State has duly discharged the obligation concerned.[62]

Despite the ICJ's stated intention not to provide an overall theory on the subject, one can hardly find a more explicit statement to the effect that obligations of prevention are *best effort* obligations, i.e. ones calling upon States to do their utmost to prevent something without burdening them with an absolute commitment to succeed. This approach can also explain the reference made by the Court to the "notion" of due diligence, presumably recalled here for its role of general principle injecting flexibility in the performance of international obligations.[63] If this is true, it is easy to see how far we are from the configuration of the obligation to prevent a given event as a sub-category of the obligations of result outlined by the ILC in its early work on (the former) Draft Article 23.

The otherwise irreproachable reasoning on the nature of the obligation to prevent genocide becomes problematic when the Court addresses the issue of establishing when the same obligation has been breached. The Court introduced the issue by stating that "a State can be held responsible for breaching the obligation to prevent genocide only if genocide was actually committed. It is at the time when the commission of the prohibited act (...) begins that the breach of an obligation of prevention occurs". Unexpectedly, the Court reinforced this finding with a full citation of the text of current Article 14(3) of the ARSIWA, referred to as "a general rule of the law of State responsibility".[64] As perspicuously noted by one commentator, there may be a slight contradiction between stating (as the Court does in the following) that the obligation of a State to prevent arises at the instant that the State learns of the existence of serious risk that genocide will be committed and the conclusion that the same obligation is breached only once genocide has been committed.[65] Beyond this point, it is evident the clash between a general presentation of the obligation to prevent genocide as one of due diligence (which is infringed when proven that a State has not exercised *in concreto* its best efforts towards prevention) and the requirement that the event must have materialised for considering the State responsible. Moreover, what seems questionable in the reasoning of the Court, is to have taken for granted the customary nature of a provision—Article 14(3) of the ARSIWA—which should be deemed, at a minimum, controversial in light of the drafting history referred to above. This could perhaps partly explain why the ICJ, in its subsequent case law concerning the prevention of environmental damage, abstained from any references to this provision.

[62] Ibidem, p. 220, para 430 (emphasis added).

[63] See on this function of due diligence in international obligations Pisillo Mazzeschi (1992), pp. 30, 38, 44–45; Besson (2020), pp. 209–216.

[64] *Genocide* pp. 221–222, para 431.

[65] Milanović (2007), p. 687. See Gattini (2014), pp. 36–37 and 45–46, holding that "the partial contradiction in which the ICJ entangles itself in the *Genocide* case of 2007... was due to the Court explicit qualification of the obligation at stake as an obligation of means". Also Crawford (2013), pp. 231–232, appears to note the apparent contradiction of the ICJ reasoning in the *Genocide* case.

3.1.2 Pulp Mills Case (Argentina v. Uruguay)

In this case decided by the ICJ in 2010, Argentina claimed the responsibility of Uruguay arising from its authorization of the construction and the commissioning of two pulp mills located along the banks of the river Uruguay, which were deemed to infringe various provisions of the 1975 Statute for the river Uruguay in force between the two States ("the 1975 Statute"). The Statute prescribed different obligations of both a procedural and substantive nature, aimed at attaining the optimum utilization of and preventing environmental harm to the shared watercourse.[66] Argentina alleged that procedural obligations were inextricably linked to the substantive obligations and that a breach of the former entailed the breach of the latter. Uruguay rejected this argument, asserting that the violation of the two categories of obligations had to be determined separately.[67]

On this critical point, the Court recognised that, as the 1975 Statute created a joint commission and established procedures intended to enable the parties to fulfil their substantive obligations,[68] a functional link "in regard to prevention" existed between the two categories of obligations enshrined in the 1975 Statute. However, this functional link did not prevent the States parties from being required to answer those obligations separately.[69] Accordingly, the Court developed a two-tiered inquiry for ascertaining the breach of procedural and substantive obligations. After separate analysis, the ICJ held that Uruguay had violated all of its procedural obligations under the 1975 Statute.[70] The Court then found that it lacked the decisive evidence to conclude that Uruguay had infringed the substantive rules concerning the protection and preservation of the aquatic environment and the prevention of pollution.[71]

Legal scholars have criticised the distinction made by the Court between procedural and substantive obligations labelling it artificial,[72] untenable,[73] or misleading as to the nature and scope of the general obligation to prevent environmental harm.[74]

---

[66] For a detailed account of the factual and legal background of the case see *Pulp Mills* case, pp. 31–40, paras 25–46.

[67] Ibidem, pp. 47–48, paras 67–74.

[68] Ibidem, p. 49, para 78.

[69] Ibidem, para 79.

[70] Ibidem, p. 58, para 111 (concerning the breach of the obligation to inform the joint commission before the issuing under domestic law of initial environmental authorizations for the two mills), p. 60, para 122 (concerning the breach of the obligation to notify Argentina through the joint commission about the planned measures), p. 68, para 149 (concerning the obligation to negotiate) and p. 70, para 158 (concerning the overall breach of procedural obligations by Uruguay).

[71] See in particular p. 86, para 214, and p. 101, para 265 (for the finding that there is no conclusive evidence that Uruguay has not acted with the requisite degree of due diligence or that the discharges from the mills had deleterious effects or caused damage).

[72] See Kerbrat (2018a), p. 11 ("La distinction... s'avère fragile").

[73] See Besson (2020), p. 326 ("cette distinction est largement intenable en soi").

[74] See the elaborate treatment of this point by Brunnée (2020), pp. 142–147.

An overview of the judgment indeed confirms this. The ICJ referred to "the principle of prevention [which], as a customary rule, has its origin in the due diligence that is required to a State in its territory" as a conceptual tool for substantiating the "functional link" between procedure and substance referred to above.[75] However, beyond these references to the backbone role of the principle of prevention, the Court was not successful in drawing a clear line between the procedural and substantive components of the principle and articulating the legal relationship between such components.[76]

A telling example is the oscillation of the Court in dealing with the obligation to undertake an environmental impact assessment (EIA) on activities expected to involve significant harmful effects. The Court first consider the EIA in the context of procedural obligations; it held that, under the relevant provisions of the 1975 Statute, the concerned party is required to notify the other of the EIA in order to enable the latter to participate in assessing the effects of a planned activity.[77] Having observed that the notification to Argentina of the EIAs concerning the two mills did not take place through the joint commission and that Uruguay transmitted the assessments only *after* the issuing of initial environmental authorizations for the mills, the Court concluded that Uruguay had failed to comply with its obligation to notify plans to Argentina.[78]

The EIA was then reconsidered at a later stage of the decision when the Court dealt with substantive obligations. The Court introduced the issue stating that the practice of undertaking an EIA for activities likely to cause significant adverse impacts "may now be considered a requirement under general international law". This statement was further reinforced by the finding that "due diligence, and the duty of vigilance and prevention it implies, would not be considered to have been exercised" if the planning State "did not undertake an environmental impact assessment on the potential effects of such works".[79] This being said, the Court observed

[75] *Pulp Mills*, pp. 55–56, para 101. This statement is included in the "procedural" part of the analysis made by the Court, concerning Uruguay's obligation to inform the joint commission. Similar expressions are found in the "substantive" part of the judgment, where it is stated that

> [a]n obligation to adopt regulatory or administrative measures either individually or jointly and to enforce them is an obligation of conduct. Both Parties are therefore called upon (. . .) to exercise due diligence in acting through the Commission for the necessary measures to preserve the ecological balance of the river (ibidem, p. 77, para 187);

and that

> the obligation to 'preserve the aquatic environment, and in particular to prevent pollution by prescribing appropriate rules and measures' is an obligation to act with due diligence in respect to all activities which take place under the jurisdiction and control of each party (ibidem, p. 79, para 197).

[76] Plakokefalos (2012), pp. 23–24.

[77] Ibidem, pp. 59–60, para 119.

[78] Ibidem, p. 60, paras 121–122.

[79] Ibidem, p. 83, para 204.

that neither the 1975 Statute nor general international law specifies the scope and content of an EIA. The Court argued that it is for each State to determine, through domestic legislation or during the authorization process for the project, the specific content of the EIA required in each case.[80] Accordingly, the Court concluded that Uruguay had not failed to exercise due diligence in conducting the EIA and, ultimately, in fulfilling its substantive obligations in that regard.[81]

To summarise this convoluted reasoning, Uruguay was blamed not for having undertaken an insufficient or inappropriate EIA, but for having provided notification of the results of its assessment at the wrong time (i.e. *after* having granted under its domestic law the initial environmental authorization for the two mills). One is left with the impression that if the whole analysis is predicated on the existence of a (unique) general obligation to exercise due diligence to prevent environmental harm, the breach of such an obligation depends on whether the EIA is considered in its procedural or substantive dimension. However, as aptly underscored by two dissenting judges of the Court,[82] it can be hard to accept the conclusion that these different dimensions have no effect on each other, especially when the EIA is proposed as a standard for measuring the diligent conduct of the State in preventing environmental harm.[83]

As a matter of fact, the ICJ treated procedural and substantive obligations differently when dealing with their respective breach. This differential treatment does not seem completely estranged from the consideration—incidentally inserted by the Court at the beginning of its decision—that "whereas the substantive obligations are frequently worded in broad terms, the procedural obligations are narrower and more specific".[84] It is for attentive readers to assess whether this reference echoes the old criterion of "determinacy" suggested by Ago as a benchmark for classifying international obligations. Be that as it may, one cannot exclude that the unsettled puzzle of obligations of conduct and result, together with the unmentioned ghost of Article 14(3) of the ARSIWA, has haunted the judges' reasoning in the *Pulp Mills* case.

3.1.3 Certain Activities (Costa Rica v. Nicaragua) and Construction of a Road (Nicaragua c. Costa Rica) Cases

In the context of a larger dispute involving several contentious issues, Costa Rica and Nicaragua alleged reciprocal violations of both procedural and substantial

[80] Ibidem, para 205.

[81] Ibidem, pp. 84–86 paras 207–214.

[82] See the joint dissenting opinion of judges Al-Khasawneh and Simma appended to the judgment in *Pulp Mills*, questioning that "the conclusion whereby non-compliance with pertinent procedural obligations has eventually no effect on compliance with the substantive obligations is a proposition that cannot easily be accepted" (ICJ Reports, 2010, p. 120, para 26).

[83] See reference supra note 79 and accompanying text.

[84] *Pulp Mills*, p. 49, para 77.

obligations (mostly arising under customary international law) concerning the prevention of transboundary harm in the common border area. In its judgment of 2015, the ICJ followed the path already explored in *Pulp Mills*, and approached violations concerning the procedure and those regarding substance separately.[85] On the procedural side, the Court considered that Nicaragua did not commit any breach in connection to the dredging activities executed to improve the navigability of the San Juan River. Contrarywise, it held that Costa Rica had failed to comply with its obligation to evaluate the environmental impact of the construction of a road along the same river.[86] On the substantive side, the Court concluded that, in the absence of evidence of detrimental effects caused by the activities under scrutiny, neither of the two States had violated obligations to prevent significant transboundary harm.[87]

One may dare to say that in the Costa Rica/Nicaragua case, the ICJ both clarified and complicated some of the outstanding legal issues inherited from *Pulp Mills*. No doubt, in the instant case, the Court successfully overcame the previous ambiguities concerning the treatment of the EIA by clearly filing the topic under the category of procedural obligations. The Court purportedly positioned in the "procedural" parts of the judgement its previous statements in *Pulp Mills* to the effect that an EIA is based on the principle of prevention and is a requirement under general international law.[88] On the other hand, because detailed treaty provisions were lacking in the case at hand, the ICJ also ventured into a comprehensive description of the procedural dimension of the principle of prevention and the role of the EIA in this context.

The Court depicted the EIA as an intermediate step in a chain of procedural obligations, all based on the due diligence obligation to prevent significant harm. Under this sequence, prior to undertaking an activity with potential adverse effects on the environment of another State, a planning State is under a duty to carry out a preliminary assessment to ascertain if there is a risk of significant transboundary harm. If that is the case, the obligation arises for the planning State to conduct a full EIA. Hence, if the EIA confirms the risk of significant transboundary harm, the planning State is required to notify and consult in good faith with the potentially affected State to determine the appropriate measures to prevent or mitigate the risk.[89]

In evaluating how this overly complicated process worked in the case at hand, the Court reserved special attention to the "preliminary assessment" of the risk made by the planning State. Concerning the dredging activities carried out by Nicaragua, the Court was substantially satisfied with the results of a study conducted by that country on the impact that the dredging programme would have on its environment; the latter

[85] See *Certain Activities/Construction of a Road*, respectively p. 705, para 100 (introducing the section devoted to Nicaragua violations arising from dredging activities) and p. 718, para 145 (introducing the section on the alleged breaches by Costa Rica in connection with the construction of a road).

[86] See ibidem, respectively p. 710, para 112, and pp. 725–726, para 173.

[87] See ibidem, respectively p. 712, para 120, and p. 737, para 217.

[88] See ibidem, respectively p. 706, para 104 (concerning "certain activities"), and p. 720, para 153 (concerning "construction of a road").

[89] Ibidem.

stated that the programme would not have significant environmental impacts. Given the absence of the risk of significant harm, the Court concluded that Nicaragua was not required to carry out a full EIA;[90] consequently, that State was not under the obligation to notify, or consult with, Costa Rica.[91] Conversely, concerning the position of Costa Rica in respect of the construction of a road, the ICJ found that Costa Rica "did not adduce any evidence that it actually carried out such a preliminary assessment".[92] This brought the Court to consider that, given the "nature and magnitude of the project and the context in which it was to be carried out", the construction of a road involved a risk of significant harm; therefore, the threshold for triggering the obligation to evaluate the environmental impact was met.[93] Ultimately, the Court concluded that Costa Rica had not complied with its obligation under general international law to carry out an EIA concerning the construction of the road.[94]

The reasoning of the ICJ in this case has been praised for having contributed to injecting some objective standards into the content of the EIA and having clarified that this content is not completely dependent on the domestic legislation of a planning State.[95] However, it is a matter of contention whether the Court was really successful in its attempt of "objectivizing" the standards of diligent conduct required of States to fulfil their procedural obligations.[96] With regard to the "triggering" layer of the procedure described above, the legitimate impression is that States are only committed to a minimum achievement, namely to provide some form of preliminary assessment under their domestic law of the risk of transboundary harm involved in planned activities. This is even more so if one considers the reminder inserted on this point by the Court, to the effect that "to conduct a preliminary assessment of the risk posed by an activity *is one of the ways* in which a State can ascertain whether the proposed activity carries a risk of significant transboundary harm".[97] On the other hand, it is frankly difficult to understand why an obligation to notify and consult would be triggered only when the EIA has confirmed the existence of a risk of significant transboundary harm associated with certain activities. Likewise, one fails to see why due diligence might not require the concerned State to enter in

---

[90] Ibidem, p. 707, para 105.

[91] Ibidem, p. 708, para 108.

[92] Ibidem, p. 720, para 154.

[93] Ibidem, pp. 720–721, para 155–156.

[94] Ibidem, pp. 722–723, para 161.

[95] See the separate opinion of Judge Donoghue appended to the judgement (ibidem, p. 786, para 15). See also Bendel and Harrison (2017), p. 14.

[96] It can be contested whether this purpose can be served by a reminder in the sense that "[d] etermination of the content of the environmental impact assessment should be made in light of the specific circumstances of each case": noteworthily, this reminder is followed by the full quotation of the paragraph of *Pulp Mills* underscoring that it is for each State to determine in its domestic legislation the specific content of EIA (see *Certain Activities/Construction of a Road* p. 707, para 105 and supra note 80 and accompanying text).

[97] *Certain Activities/Construction of a Road* p. 720, para 154.

consultation with its neighbours during the initial phases of the planning of such activities.[98]

Be that as it may, it is a fact that the whole reasoning developed by the Court on the implementation of procedural obligations had no bearing on the ascertainment of the breach of substantial obligations.[99] As already recalled, the Court concluded that neither State had violated the obligation to prevent significant damage in the border area.[100] In particular, the Court held that Costa Rica had not proved that the dredging programmes carried out by Nicaragua caused harm, considering as conclusive that "a causal link between this reduction [in the flow of the Colorado River] and Nicaragua's dredging programme has not been established".[101] The ICJ made similar findings concerning the absence of a demonstrated causal link between the construction of the road by Costa Rica and significant harm caused to the morphology and navigability of the rivers in the border area,[102] or river ecosystems and water quality.[103] In other words, in assessing this point the Court was driven by the idea that, lacking any harmful event or a causal link between the harm and the conduct of the State, no breach of the rule to prevent significant damages can be established.[104] There is no need to emphasise here how much this approach comes close to the reconstruction of the obligation to prevent a given event that was covered by the "old" Article 23 of the first reading of the Draft on State responsibility.[105]

3.2 *Other International Courts and Tribunals*

The substantial amount of attention given to the ICJ's case law, especially with reference to the *Pulp Mills* and *Certain Activities/Construction of a Road* affairs, is justified by its ground-breaking character in outlining the general contours of the preventive obligations of States in environmental protection. In fact, the

[98] See on this point the separate opinion of Judge Donoghue (ibidem, p. 787–788, paras 16–24).

[99] On this account, Judge Donoghue in her separate opinion criticised the utility of the distinction between procedural and substantive obligations made by the Court (ibidem p. 765, para 9).

[100] See supra note 87.

[101] *Certain Activities/Construction of a Road*, p. 712, para 119. In the same vein, the Court excluded the violation of substantive obligations by Costa Rica on the account that "Nicaragua has not established that the fact that sediment concentrations in the river increased as the result of the construction of a road in and of itself caused significant transboundary harm" (ibidem, p. 731, para 196).

[102] Ibidem, p. 743, para 207.

[103] Ibidem, p. 736, para 213.

[104] See Maljean-Dubois (2018), pp. 155–156 ("la Cour recherche si le Costa Rica a causé un dommage, et non s'il a mis en œuvre toutes les mesures pour éviter un dommage... le raisonnement de la Cour laisse à penser qu'un dommage est requis pour constater la violations des secondes [obligations substantielles]").

[105] See supra notes 39–41.

characterization of the principle of prevention as a rule of general international law having a due diligence nature is endorsed, with different degrees of clarity, in the subsequent decisions of different specialised courts and tribunals. At the same time, this subsequent case law also reveals the returning character of some of the unresolved theoretical issues already encountered by the ICJ. This warrants a cursory overview of the relevant opinions and awards bearing on environmental matters, issued respectively by the International Tribunal for the Law of the Sea (ITLOS) (Sect. 3.2.1), by *ad hoc* arbitral tribunals (Sect. 3.2.2) and by the Inter-American Court of Human Rights (Sect. 3.2.3).

3.2.1 The International Tribunal for the Law of the Sea

The advisory opinion issued on 1st February 2011 by the Seabed Chamber of the ITLOS (hereinafter "the Chamber"), concerning the responsibilities and obligations of States sponsoring persons or entities with respect to activities in the Area, is noteworthy especially for the general description of the obligations of conduct and of due diligence.

Called on to interpret the scope of States' "obligation to ensure" that activities by sponsored contractors in the Area are carried out in conformity with Part XI of the UN Convention on the Law of the Sea (UNCLOS),[106] the Chamber held that

> [t]he sponsoring State's obligation to 'ensure' is not an obligation to achieve, in each and every case, the result that the sponsored contractor complies with the aforementioned obligations. Rather, it is an obligation to deploy adequate means, to exercise best possible efforts, to do the utmost, to obtain this result. *To utilize the terminology current in international law*, this obligation may be characterised *as an obligation 'of conduct' and not of 'result'*, and as an obligation of 'due diligence'.[107]

The effect of the above statement is to settle one of the thorniest issues which has hindered past efforts by the ILC on the subject, namely the opposed meanings attributed to the notion of obligations of conduct and result. In fact, the Chamber upheld the "civil law" or "French" sense of the concept, underscoring that obligations of conduct are to be intended as "best efforts" engagements and not as stringent and absolute obligations to do something.[108] Having so clarified the point, the Chamber stressed that "the notion of obligations 'of due diligence' and obligation 'of conduct' are connected" and to illustrate this connection drew heavily on the

[106] See Article 139, para 1, United Nations Convention on the Law of the Sea.

[107] See *Responsibilities of States in the Area*, p. 41, para 110 (emphasis added). This analysis of the scope and meaning of obligations of conduct and due diligence obligations was to be reasserted some years later by the ITLOS in the case *Request for an Advisory Opinion Submitted by the Sub-regional Fisheries Commission (SFRC) (Request for Advisory Opinion Submitted to the Tribunal)*, Advisory Opinion of 2 April 2015, in ITLOS Reports, 2015, p. 4, at 40, para 39.

[108] See supra text accompanying note 46.

description of due diligence provided by the ICJ in *Pulp Mills*.[109] The Chamber then added its original contribution to the subject, specifying that the content of due diligence obligations "may not easily be described in precise terms" and that due diligence "is a variable concept", which may change over time and depend on factual circumstances, scientific or technological knowledge, as well as the degree of the risk involved in certain activities.[110]

Beyond these general assertions, the reasoning of the Chamber is especially intriguing in relation to the content of the due diligence obligations at stake. The Chamber points out that, beyond the obligation to adopt within their legal systems the laws, regulations and administrative measures necessary to ensure certain behaviours by the sponsored contractors,[111] the sponsoring States are bound by other "direct obligations" under UNCLOS and related instruments. Among these direct obligations there is the duty to conduct environmental impact assessments.[112] At the outset of its analysis of these direct obligations, the Chamber takes pains to point out

> that compliance with these obligations can also be seen as a relevant factor in meeting the 'due diligence obligation to ensure' and that the said obligations are in most cases *couched as obligations to ensure compliance with a specific rule*.[113]

The emphasised part of the latter statement makes sense when read in conjunction with the subsequent analysis of the obligation to conduct an environmental impact assessment. On the matter, the Chamber recalled the remarks made by the ICJ in *Pulp Mills* concerning the EIA as a general requirement under general international law.[114] However, contrary to the conclusion of the ICJ that general international law does not specify the scope and the content of EIA, the Chamber asserted that the Regulations and Recommendations issued by the International Seabed Authority "add precision and specificity to the obligation as it applies in the context of activities in the Area".[115]

---

[109] See *Responsibilities of States in the Area*, p. 41, para 111 and p. 42, para 115, quoting respectively paras 187 and 197 of *Pulp Mills*.

[110] *Responsibilities of States in the Area*, p. 43, para 117.

[111] Ibidem, pp. 43–44, paras 118–120. The Chamber refers to the obligation of the sponsoring State to adopt "laws and regulations... and administrative measures which are, within the framework of its legal system, reasonably appropriate for securing compliance by persons under its jurisdiction", provided for by Article 153, para 4 and Annex III, Article 4, para 4, UNCLOS. The content of the measures required for sponsoring States is further explored in the appropriate part of the advisory opinion (ibidem, pp. 68–69, paras 218–221 and pp. 70–73, paras 227–241). Interestingly, although the Chamber repeatedly underscores that "the scope and the extent of the laws and regulations and administrative measures required depend upon the legal system of the sponsoring State", it also points out "the existence of such laws, regulations and administrative measures... is a necessary requirement for compliance with the obligation of due diligence of the sponsoring State" (ibidem, p. 68, paras 218–219).

[112] Ibidem, p. 44, paras 121–122.

[113] Ibidem, p. 44, para 123 (emphasis added).

[114] Ibidem, pp. 50–51, paras 145–148.

[115] Ibidem, p. 51, para 149.

Unquestionably, the idea that States are bound to accomplish some precise actions in carrying out an EIA helps specify the criteria for determining the diligent conduct concerning sponsored activities in the Area.[116] In this sense, the reasoning of the Chamber seems to reflect a trend towards the progressive "objectivization" of due diligence obligations in the field of international environmental law. Yet, it is obvious that this reconstruction of due diligence obligations tends to fade out, if not to obscure altogether, the dividing line between obligations of conduct and obligations of result. When a State is bound to a very precise form of conduct in order to comply with its (due diligence) obligation to prevent harm, can the latter still be described as an obligation of "best effort" or of "conduct" in the sense enlightened by the Chamber in the relevant part of its opinion? In this respect, the inquiry developed by the Chamber seems to echo some of the perplexities on the categorization of due diligence obligations expressed by Ago during the ILC early discussions on the breach of preventive obligations in international law.[117]

3.2.2 Arbitral Tribunals

During the last two decades, different arbitral tribunals have occasionally considered questions bearing on the topic under consideration. For example, in 2003 the Tribunal established in the dispute between Ireland and the United Kingdom over the access to information under Article 9 of the OSPAR Convention held that this provision imposed an obligation of result, i.e. one which cannot be fulfilled by States merely by putting in place a domestic legal regime directed at the disclosure of information.[118] In 2005, the arbitral tribunal constituted in the dispute between Belgium and the Netherlands over the use of the Iron Rhine railway made some statements on the general principle of international law imposing on States a duty to prevent or mitigate significant harm to the environment.[119] In the same vein, the 2013 Indus Waters Kishenganga arbitration between India and Pakistan referred to the *dictum* of the ICJ in *Pulp Mills* concerning the requirement under general

---

[116] See Plakokefalos (2012), p. 34 (who speaks in this respect of "the first clear statement by an international tribunal on the content of a due diligence obligation to ensure that no environmental harm will occur from a certain type of activity").

[117] See supra notes 36–37 and accompanying text, for Ago's suggestion that due diligence obligations cannot be considered as obligations to prevent a given event, insofar as they impose on States, the adoption of a particular form of conduct.

[118] See *Dispute Concerning Access to Information Under Article 9 of the OSPAR Convention (Ireland v. United Kingdom)*, Final Award of 2 July 2003, reprinted in (2004) *Reports of International Arbitral Awards* 23:159, paras 132–137.

[119] See *Arbitration Regarding the Iron Rhine ("Ijzeren Rijn") Railway (The Kingdom of Belgium v. The Kingdom of the Netherlands)*, Award of 24 May 2005, reprinted in (2007) *Reports of International Arbitral Awards* 35:27, paras 59 and 222.

international law to undertake an EIA and its role as a component of the due diligence obligation to prevent environmental damage.[120]

A more elaborate consideration of the principle of prevention is found in the 2016 South China Sea arbitration, between the Philippines and China. Albeit the case involved several contentious issues, a specific section of the award was devoted to the alleged failure to protect and preserve the marine environment, arising from harmful fishing practices and harmful construction activities carried out by China in the South China Sea.[121] In this part, the Tribunal provided a sophisticated reading of Article 192 UNCLOS—setting forth the general obligation of States "to protect and preserve the marine environment"—the content of which was considered as being informed "by other applicable rules of international law", in particular by "the corpus of international law relating to the environment".[122] Above all, this reading was meant to incorporate into the scope of the provision the general duty to prevent significant harm to the environment,[123] especially as interpreted in the previous decisions of the ICJ and ITLOS, enlightening its character as an obligation of conduct requiring due diligence.[124] Hence, the Tribunal further expanded the scope of Article 192 UNCLOS to include both "a due diligence obligation to prevent the harvesting of species that are recognised internationally as being at risk of extinction" under instruments such as the CITES;[125] and "a due diligence obligation to take measures 'necessary to protect and preserve rare and fragile ecosystems as well as the habitat of depleted, threatened or endangered species and other forms of marine life".[126] This extensive reading of the obligations under Article 192 UNCLOS proved to be very challenging for China, especially because most activities carried out directly or indirectly by that State in the South China Sea impacted upon the very fragile ecosystem or affected species enjoying special protection under the CITES. On this score, the Tribunal "ha[d] no hesitation" in finding that China breached its obligation to protect and preserve the marine environment due to the failure to prevent, or due to the toleration and protection of, the harvesting of endangered

[120] *Indus Water Kishenganga Arbitration (The Islamic Republic of Pakistan v. The Republic of India)*, Partial Award of 18 February 2013, reprinted in (2018) *Reports of International Arbitral Awards* 31:55, paras 447–452.

[121] See for the factual background of this part of the dispute *South China Sea*, paras 815–890.

[122] Ibidem, para 941.

[123] Ibidem:

> Thus States have a positive 'duty to prevent, or at least mitigate significant harm to the environment when pursuing large-scale construction activities'. The Tribunal considers this duty informs the scope of the general obligation in Article 192 [UNCLOS].

The Tribunal cited in this respect an excerpt from the Indus Waters Kishenganga Arbitration (see supra note 120).

[124] Ibidem, para 944.

[125] Ibidem, para 956.

[126] Ibidem, para 959. The Tribunal referred here to the specific wording of Article 194, para 5, UNCLOS.

species by Chinese fishing vessels.[127] The Tribunal reached the same conclusion regarding the construction activities carried out by China in the South China Sea.[128]

It has been argued that, through recourse to systemic treaty interpretation, the Tribunal was able to inject a very high standard of due diligence, or a very precise engagement to prevent a certain event (i.e., the harvesting of endangered species) into the open-ended obligation outlined in Article 192 UNCLOS.[129] It can hardly be denied that the reasoning of the Tribunal in the South China Sea arbitration adds some fuel to the above-referred trend towards the "objectivization" of due diligence standards in international environmental law. However, it remains to be seen whether recourse to systemic interpretation to expand the scope of an obligation of prevention would necessarily clarify the conditions governing the breach of such an obligation and solve all the related uncertainties considered so far.

3.2.3 The Inter-American Court of Human Rights

The advisory opinion OC-23/17 on "The Environment and Human Rights", issued in 2017 by the Inter-American Court of Human Rights,[130] is noteworthy primarily for the significant part devoted to environmental obligations that States must fulfil to respect and ensure human rights under the American Convention.[131] Interestingly, after having referred to the general contours of due diligence and having observed that "most environmental obligations are based on th[e] duty of due diligence",[132] the Inter-American Court carried out a detailed analysis based on a clear differentiation of States' obligations concerning transboundary damage.[133]

Concerning the "obligation of prevention", the Inter-American Court endorsed the usual approach, holding that such an obligation must be fulfilled "in keeping with the standard of due diligence" and that it "is an obligation of means and not of results".[134] This being said, from a general point of view, the Inter-American Court deployed considerable effort in trying to define the specific measures that States must

[127] Ibidem, paras 964–966.

[128] Ibidem, para 983.

[129] See Mbengue (2016), p. 286; d'Argent and de Vaucleroy (2018), p. 273; Kerbrat (2018b), pp. 33–34.

[130] On opinion OC-23/17 see the contribution by Elena Carpanelli in this book.

[131] *Environment and human rights*, paras 123–241.

[132] Ibidem, paras 123–124.

[133] In particular, the Inter-American has considered the following general environmental obligations: the obligation of prevention (which encompasses a specific duty to require and approve environmental impact assessments); the precautionary principle; the obligation of cooperation (which encompasses both the duty to notify and the duty to consult and negotiate); and procedural obligations (which include subjects such as access to information, public participation and access to justice in environmental matters). It is interesting to compare this approach with the categorization of substantive and procedural obligations adopted by the ICJ in *Pulp Mills*.

[134] *Environment and human rights*, paras 142–143.

take to fulfil their general obligation to prevent transboundary damage. These specific measures would include the obligations to (i) regulate, (ii) supervise and monitor, (iii) require and approve environmental impact assessments, (iv) establish contingency plans, and (v) mitigate environmental damage when it has occurred.[135] Noteworthily, the first of these sub-duties, i.e. the "duty to regulate", is deemed to encompass not only domestic laws and regulations to prevent, reduce or control pollution,[136] but also regulations aimed at assessing the risk connected to activities likely to cause transboundary damage.[137] On this point, the Inter-American Court is prominent in stating that

> with regard to environmental impact assessments... this regulation *must be clear*, at least as regards: (i) the proposed activities and the impact that must be assessed (areas and aspects to be covered); (ii) the process for making an environmental impact assessment (requirements and procedures); (iii) the responsibilities and duties of project proponents, competent authorities and decision-making bodies (responsibilities and duties); (iv) how the environmental impact assessment process will be used in approval of the proposed actions (relationship to decision-making), and (v) the steps and measures that are to be taken in the event that due procedure is not followed in carrying out the environmental impact assessment or implementing the terms and conditions of approval (compliance and implementation).[138]

Needless to say, to expect that States ensure the conformity of their domestic regulations on environmental assessments to the detailed list of requirements referred to above amounts to setting a very demanding standard of conduct in the prevention of transboundary damages. Unfortunately however, the impact of this ambitious "wish list" elaborated by the Inter-American Court has proved to be modest. After a more detailed analysis of the content of the "duty to require and approve environmental impact assessment",[139] the Inter-American Court had to take note of the ICJ's findings in *Pulp Mills* to the effect that it is for each State to determine in its laws the content of the environmental impact assessment required in each case. On this account, the Inter-American Court concluded that

> States *should* determine and define, by law or by the project authorization process, the specific content required of an environmental impact assessment, taking into account the nature and size of the project and its potential impact on the environment.[140]

What is noticeable in the described approach is that, unlike the case law of the ICJ, the Inter-American Court straightforwardly considered the obligation to undertake an EIA as integral to the (substantive) obligation to prevent transboundary environmental damage. Whether this approach has been successful in clarifying the content

[135] Ibidem, paras 144–145.

[136] Ibidem, para 147.

[137] Ibidem, para 149 ("this Court considers that States, taking into account the existing level of risk, must regulate activities that could cause significant environmental damage in a way that reduce any threat to the rights to life and to personal integrity").

[138] Ibidem, para 150.

[139] Ibidem, paras 156–169.

[140] Ibidem, para 170.

of the due diligence obligation of prevention, as well as the conditions governing its breach, is, however, quite another matter.

4 Concluding Remarks

The review carried out in the previous section provides some room for countering one of the arguments which led to the ILC dismissing the notion of obligations of conduct, result, and prevention from the ARSIWA: namely, that the use of such distinction in judicial practice was scant and not consistent.[141] The case law considered above, although not exhaustive and confined to the field of international environmental law,[142] is significant and, at least as far as certain aspects are concerned, it allows some general indications on the category of obligations to prevent to be drawn.

A question that appears to have been definitively clarified is the terminological conundrum accompanying the distinction between obligations of conduct and obligations of result. With a remarkable grade of clarity, all the decisions considered above converge in upholding the "civil" or "French" law meaning of the distinction. Under this meaning, obligations of conduct are conceived as flexible obligations, calling upon States to exercise best efforts but allowing them room for manoeuvre in the performance of their duties; conversely, obligations of results are meant to identify the most stringent obligations, committing States to the realization of a definite outcome.[143] With the same clarity, in the relevant case law the obligation of States to prevent transboundary environmental harm, with the underlying principle of prevention, are altogether filed within the category of obligations of conduct. Furthermore, prevention is consistently associated with the notion of due diligence, which is eminently used in this context as a conceptual tool for injecting flexibility into the scope of the international obligation.[144]

Yet, the crux of the matter is whether, beyond the terminological and conceptual clarifications, this case law has been successful in solving the critical issue at the core

---

[141] See supra text accompanying notes 47 and 51.

[142] This of course raises the problem of the significance that an inquiry limited to a particular field of international relations may have from the point of view of the general secondary rules on State responsibility. With all due caution, we can simply note that—as suggested for example by the advisory opinion OC-23/17 of the Inter-American Court of Human in respect to due diligence obligations (see *Environment and Human Rights*, paras 123–124)—some of the general findings formulated by judges concerning the nature and the character of the obligation of States to prevent transboundary harm may be also transferred to other fields of international law where preventive obligations are at work.

[143] See especially the ITLOS advisory opinion *Responsibilities of States in the Area*, supra note 107 and accompanying text.

[144] See *Genocide*, supra notes 62–63; *Pulp Mills*, supra note 75; *Certain Activities/Construction of a Road*, supra note 88; *Responsibilities of States in the Area*, supra notes 109–110; *South China Sea*, supra note 124; *Environment and Human Rights*, supra note 134.

of the early ILC efforts on the topic, namely the conditions under which a breach of an obligation to prevent may occur. In this respect, a classic problem re-emerges. Having stated that the obligation at stake is one of conduct and due diligence, the question is open as to whether demonstrating that a State has failed to deploy its best efforts in preventing damage suffices for a breach to accrue, or whether some other element (i.e. the occurrence of the harmful event to be prevented) is also necessary. To cope with the issue, one can usefully refer to a statement made by Roberto Ago when introducing his proposal on the (then) Draft Article 23 to the ILC: the former ILC Special Rapporteur maintained that

> to our knowledge, decisions of international tribunals have never affirmed, even indirectly or incidentally, that failure to adopt measures to prevent the occurrence of a possible event sufficed in itself – i.e., without the actual occurrence of such event – to constitute a breach of the obligation incumbent of the State.[145]

A look at the recent judicial practice in environmental matters does not seem to justify a departure from the above statement. On one hand, there is no case among those reviewed in the previous section in which a judge has clearly affirmed that, absent the evidence of a current damage or of a causal link between the detrimental effects caused by an activity and the negligent conduct of a State, the *substantive* obligation to prevent significant harm has been breached. On the other hand, with different nuances and a variable degree of clarity, courts and tribunals have insisted on the *procedural* dimension of the obligation to prevent transboundary harm and, in that context, they have struggled to "objectivize" the standards of the diligent conduct required of States.[146]

In this regard, it has been poignantly suggested that the emphasis put on the procedural dimension of prevention would be functional to the idea that certain due diligence obligations in the environmental field (i.e., those pertaining to procedure) can be violated even without the occurrence of a specific harmful event; and that through the category of procedural obligations, material obligations to prevent are transformed into full obligations of result.[147] Beyond the delicate methodological questions raised by this approach,[148] the different assessments provided by international courts on issues such as the nature and the content of EIAs demonstrate that the distinction between procedure and substance is far from clear-cut in the area under consideration.[149] What is more, the distinction risks further obfuscating, rather

[145] Ago, Seventh Report, supra note 32, p. 34, para 11.

[146] See for example supra text accompanying notes 95, 116–117.

[147] See especially Besson (2020), pp. 256–257, 263–264 and 325–326.

[148] As already pointed out, these methodological questions mainly consist of splitting the unitary principle of prevention into a bundle of separate and unconnected procedural and substantive obligations: see references supra notes 72–74.

[149] See again in this respect the outcomes of the *Pulps Mills* and *Certain activities/Construction of a road* cases and compare the different assessment of obligations of procedure and substance respectively made by the ICJ and the Inter-American Court of Human Rights, supra sections 3.1.2, 3.1.3 and 3.2.3.

than clarifying, the problem of determining when the obligation to prevent significant harm has been breached.

Yet, this brings us back to the central question of this essay, that is to wonder what clues can be expected on the above issues from the secondary rules on State responsibility. After a rather long journey, we are ultimately faced with the disappointing conclusion that the utility of the distinction between obligations of conduct, result, and prevention must not be overestimated and that, after all, the ILC decision to omit this distinction from the Articles of 2001 was not so misplaced. As maintained by one author,

> [i]n most instances, the wording of the obligation concerned and its degree of precision – rather than its qualification as an obligation of result or of conduct – will be the controlling factor in assessing whether it has been breached.[150]

While the latter statement may contain some elements of truth, it does not detract from the assumption that the task of the ILC Articles would be "to make a series of general statements which are designed to guide an interpreter especially in the application of the law of State responsibility",[151] and this would also apply to the conditions governing the breach of international obligations. In this respect, we cannot but consider that the current answer offered by the ARSIWA is partial and unsatisfactory, being limited to a single provision, i.e. Article 14(3), which is moreover premised on the "blending of the traits of an obligation of conduct with those of an obligation of result".[152] The embarrassment felt by the ICJ in applying the above provision beyond the *Genocide* precedent is telling of the current state of affairs.[153]

If, therefore, the issue of the breach of the obligation to prevent under the ILC Articles on State Responsibility needs to be revisited, in order both to better reflect latest developments of international case law and to provide guidance on unsolved issues, the critical question of how to carry out such a revision stands open. In this regard, it can be asked whether the choice to leave the Articles in the current non-binding format and to expect substantial clarifications from judicial practice is wise, or whether some kind of more authoritative revision would be advisable. This question, which involves the impending decision to convene or not a diplomatic conference of States to negotiate a convention on State responsibility, is of course one which cannot be addressed in the present context.

Acknowledgment The author wishes to thank Dr. Alice Ollino for her invaluable comments on an earlier version of the text. All errors remain the author's sole responsibility.

---

150 Gautier (2012), p. 862. There could be some irony in finding that the logic behind this quotation is not so far from the perspective adopted by Roberto Ago when, in outlining the distinction between obligations of conduct and of result, he suggested using the "determinacy" of the primary obligation at stake as a guiding factor for classification (supra notes 29–37).

151 Gaja (2014), p. 990.

152 Brunnée (2020), p. 155. See also supra text accompanying notes 55–57.

153 See supra section 3.1.1.

References

Ago R (1939) Le délit international. In: Recueil des cours de l'Académie de droit international 68. Brill, Leiden-Boston, pp 417–554

Ago R (1991) Conclusions du colloque Responsabilité des Etats pour les dommages à l'environnement. In: Francioni F, Scovazzi T (eds) International Responsibility for Environmental Harm. Graham & Trotman, London/Dordrecht/Boston, pp 493–499

Anzilotti D (1906) La responsabilité internationale des Etats à raison des dommages soufferts par des étrangers. Revue Générale de Droit International Public 13:5–29 and 285–309

Aust HP, Feihle P (2020) Due diligence in the history of the codification of the law of state responsibility. In: Krieger H, Peters A (eds) Due diligence in international law. Oxford University Press, Oxford, pp 42–58

Bendel J, Harrison J (2017) Determining the legal nature and content of EIAs in international environmental law: what does the ICJ decision in the joined cases Costa Rica v. Nicaragua/ Nicaragua v. Costa Rica cases tell us? QIL-Quest Int Law 42:13–21

Besson S (2020) La due diligence en droit international. In: Recueil des cours de l'Académie de droit international 409. Brill, Leiden-Boston, pp 157–398

Brunnée J (2020) Procedure and substance in international environmental law. In: Recueil des cours de l'Académie de droit international 405. Brill, Leiden-Boston, pp 79–240

Combacau J (1981) Obligations de résultat et obligations de comportement. Quelques questions et pas de réponse. In: Mélanges Offerts à Paul Reuter. Le droit international, unité et diversité. Pedone, Paris, pp 181–204

Crawford J (2013) State responsibility. The general part. Cambridge University Press, Cambridge

D'Argent P, De Vaucleroy A (2018) Le contenu de l'omission illicite: la non utilisations de moyens raisonnables. In: Société Française de Droit International, Le standard de due diligence et la responsabilité internationale. Pedone, Paris, pp 255–278

Dupuy P-M (1999) Reviewing the difficulties of codification: on Ago's classification of obligations of means and obligations of result in relation to state responsibility. Eur J Int Law 10:371–385

Economides CP (2010) Content of the obligation: obligations of means and obligations of result. In: Crawford J et al (eds) The law of international responsibility. Oxford University Press, Oxford, pp 371–381

Gaja G (2014) Primary and secondary rules in the international law on state responsibility. Rivista di Diritto Internazionale 97:981–991

Gattini A (2014) Breach of international obligations. In: Nollkaemper A, Plakokefalos I (eds) Principles of shared responsibility in international law. An appraisal of the state of the art. Cambridge University Press, Cambridge, pp 25–59

Gautier P (2012) On the classification of obligations in international law. In: Hestermeyer H, König D, Matz-Lück N, Röben V, Seibert-Fohr A, Stoll P-T, Vöneky S (eds) Coexistence, cooperation and solidarity. Liber Amicorum Rüdiger Wolfrum. Brill, Leiden, pp 853–879

Kerbrat Y (2018a) Obligations procédurales et obligations de fond en droit international des dommages transfrontières. In: Prezas I (dir.), Substance et procédure en droit international public: dialectique et influences croisées. Pedone, Paris, pp 7–17

Kerbrat Y (2018b) Le standard de due diligence, catalyseur d'obligations conventionnelles et coutumières pour les Etats. In: Société Française de Droit International, Le standard de due diligence et la responsabilité internationale. Pedone, Paris, pp 27–38

Koskenniemi M (2020) Foreword. In: Creutz K (ed) State responsibility in the international legal order. Cambridge University Press, Cambridge, pp ix–xiii

Maljean-Dubois S (2018) Les obligations de diligence dans la pratique: la protection de l'environnement. In: Société Française de Droit International, Le standard de due diligence et la responsabilité internationale. Pedone, Paris, pp 145–162

Marchesi A (2004) The distinction between obligations of conduct and obligations of result following its deletion from the draft articles on state responsibility. In: Studi di diritto internazionale in onore di Gaetano Arangio-Ruiz, vol II. Editoriale Scientifica, Napoli, pp 827–852

Mbengue MM (2016) The South China arbitration: innovations in marine environmental-fact finding and due diligence obligations. AJIL Unbound 110:285–289
Milanović M (2007) State responsibility for genocide: a follow-up. Eur J Int Law 18:669–694
Nègre C (2010) Responsibility and international environmental harm. In: Crawford J, Pellet A, Olleson S, Parlett K (eds) The law of international responsibility. Oxford University Press, Oxford, pp 803–813
Paddeu FI (2018) To convene or not to convene? The future status of the articles on state responsibility: recent developments. Max Planck Yearb United Nations Law 21:83–123
Pisillo Mazzeschi R (1992) The due diligence rule and the nature of the international responsibility of states. German Yearb Int Law 35:9–51
Plakokefalos I (2012) Prevention obligations in international environmental law. Yearb Int Environ Law 23:3–43
Scovazzi T (2001) State responsibility for environmental harm. Yearb Int Environ Law 12:43–67
Wolfrum R (2010) Obligation of result and obligation of conduct: some thoughts about the implementation of international obligations. In: Arsanjani MH, Cogan J, Sloane R, Wiessner S (eds) Looking to the future. Essays on international law in Honour of W. Michael Reisman. Brill, Leiden, pp 363–383

Legal Personality for Nature: From National to International Law

Maria Clara Maffei

Abstract More and more frequently national Constitutions and legislative acts or decisions of national courts recognize specific natural/cultural entities, ecosystems, nature itself and certain animals as having rights. Such recognitions are intended to improve the protection of these "items" from both an environmental and a cultural, sometimes spiritual and religious, point of view. Notwithstanding the interconnections between the recognition of rights and the recognition of legal personality, the present chapter will focus mainly on questions concerning the granting of international legal personhood. The aim is to investigate whether the national model of legal personhood granted to natural/cultural entities and animals is exportable in international law, whether it may be useful and which problems would accompany such eventual recognition. The chapter, in particular, analyses the analogies with the case of individuals whose international legal personality is still controversial. As for individuals, the recognition of natural/cultural entities and animals as international subjects strictly depends on the will of States. The latter seem rather reluctant to undertake legal obligations at the international level concerning such recognition. And above all the possibility for entities and animals to put in motion procedures at the international level in order to obtain the protection of their rights is far from reality. Difficulties may also arise about the legal representation of entities and animals, their heterogeneous nature and the fact that in exercizing their rights the will of entities and animals would be, always and inevitably, filtered through the will of individuals. In the light of these and other peculiar problems and of States' practice, the conclusions concerning the international legal personality of nature can only be pessimistic, at least at present. However, something is progressively changing in the way nature's protection is conceived and attempts to reshaping the relationship between human beings and nature have also been made internationally.

M. C. Maffei (✉)
University of Parma, Parma, Italy
e-mail: mariaclara.maffei@unipr.it

M. Arcari et al. (eds.), *Trends and Challenges in International Law*,
https://doi.org/10.1007/978-3-030-94387-5_8

1 Introduction

More and more frequently national Constitutions and legislative acts or decisions of national courts have been willing to recognize[1] specific natural/cultural entities,[2] ecosystems, nature itself and certain animals as having rights.[3] The reason for such recognitions is the need to improve the protection of these "items" from both an environmental and a cultural, sometimes spiritual and religious, point of view.

The recognition of rights and the recognition of legal personality are often interconnected. Notwithstanding these interconnections,[4] the focus of the present chapter will be mainly on the questions concerning the granting of international legal personhood.[5] The study of national cases concerning the personhood of entities and animals is also beyond the scope of the present chapter, which will be limited to some issues of international law. In particular, following a legal and pragmatic approach instead of a moral, ethical or philosophical one,[6] the aim is to investigate whether the national model is exportable in international law. That is to say, is it useful? Is it a factual option? What problems are foreseeable and what are the possible solutions?

The first part of this chapter will focus on the problem of the (eventual) international legal personhood of natural/cultural entities; the second part is devoted to some reflections concerning the (eventual) international legal personhood of animals. The last part of the chapter contains some tentative conclusions on the practice of States in these matters in the light of some recent developments.

---

[1] Despite the semantic difference of the words, in this chapter, the terms "conferment/to confer", "recognition/to recognize", and "to grant" will be used indifferently.

[2] For practical reasons in this chapter, we refer to these "entities" as "natural/cultural entities" or "entities" *tout court*.

[3] It is impossible to ignore in this regard the well-known pioneering article by Stone (1972); see also Grear (2012). A list of the most recent "Key legislation adopted" concerning the rights of nature is contained in UN Doc A/75/266, Harmony with Nature, Report of the Secretary-General of 28 July 2020, paras 54–64 and in previous Reports of the Secretary General on the same issue (see *i.e.* UN Doc A/72/175 of 19 July 2017, para 28 ff.; UN Doc A/73/221 of 23 July 2018, para 23 ff.; UN Doc A/74/236 of 26 July 2019, para 23 ff.). An up-to-date list of national legislation and case-law on the rights of nature and recognition of legal personality is contained in www.harmonywithnatureun.org.

[4] It is worth noting that the literature on the rights of nature is already immense.

[5] Referring to the *granting* of international legal personhood, we share the opinion of those who consider that States can recognize other entities as international persons; this theory is one that Portmann (2010), p. 80, calls the "recognition conception". Of course, as in the case of international organizations, the simple recognition of legal personality "on paper" is not enough if it is not accompanied by a certain degree of effectiveness; see *infra* note 31 and note 48.

[6] For a more comprehensive approach see, for instance, Vallejo Galárraga (2019); see also Korsgaard (2013); Gordon (2018).

2 Preliminary Remarks

Te Urewera is an area of mostly forested land, in the North Island of New Zealand. Through the Te Urewera Act of 27 July 2014 this area became a "legal entity" with all the rights, powers, duties, and liabilities of a legal person. This implies that Te Urewera is freehold land. Before the 2014 Act, the Crown managed Te Urewera as a National Park. Te Urewera is now managed by the Te Urewera Board, which acts on behalf and in the name of Te Urewera.[7]

The Whanganui river is New Zealand's longest navigable river. According to the Te Awa Tupua (Whanganui River Claims Settlement) Act 2017, "Te Awa Tupua is a legal person and has all the rights, powers, duties, and liabilities of a legal person".[8] The Act recognises the need to protect the ecosystem and the spiritual and cultural values of indigenous people as regards the relationship of land and people. The Act also establishes the office of Te Pou Tupua, which is "the human face of Te Awa Tupua and act[s] in the name of Te Awa Tupua. [. . .] Te Pou Tupua has full capacity and all the powers reasonably necessary to achieve its purpose and perform and exercise its functions, powers, and duties in accordance with" the Act.[9] These functions are analogous to those of a trustee.[10]

The Yamuna is the second-largest tributary river of the Ganga. It is closely connected to religious beliefs and is one of the most polluted rivers in India and in the world. On 20 March 2017, the High Court of Uttarakhand at Nainital declared the Rivers Ganga and Yamuna and all their tributaries as juristic/legal persons/living entities having the status of a legal person with all corresponding rights, duties and liabilities of a living person in order to preserve and conserve them. Ten days later, the same Court declared "the Glaciers, including Gangotri & Yamunotri, rivers, streams, rivulets, lakes, air, meadows, dales, jungles, forests, wetlands, grasslands, springs and waterfalls" in the State of Uttarakhand legal persons.[11] On 7 July 2017, the Supreme Court of India stayed the operation of the first order of the High Court based on a petition reporting some legal and administrative issues among which is the fact that a single State cannot be responsible for a river flowing beyond its

---

[7] See the *Māori Law Review* (2014). See also Colwell and Carr-Wilson (2017), pp. 12–14; Athens (2018), pp. 213–215; Lillo (2018), pp. 174 ff.; Bieluk (2020), pp. 16–17.

[8] Section 14(1) of the Te Awa Tupua (Whanganui River Claims Settlement) Act 2017.

[9] Section 18(2) and (3) of the Te Awa Tupua (Whanganui River Claims Settlement) Act 2017.

[10] On the 2017 Act see Rodgers (2017); see also Shelton (2015), para 31 ff.; Tanasescu (2015), pp. 120–124; Colwell and Carr-Wilson (2017), pp. 6–12; Athens (2018), pp. 211–212; Clark et al. (2018), pp. 800–805; Collins and Esterling (2019); Bieluk (2020), pp. 14–16; Sheber (2020), pp. 152 ff.

[11] The High Court ruled in two cases: *Mohd Salim v. State of Uttarakhand and others*, and *Lalit Miglani v. State of Uttarakhand and others*; see Brara (2017); Colwell and Carr-Wilson (2017), pp. 15–19; Athens (2018), pp. 215–217; Clark et al. (2018), pp. 811–818; Lillo (2018), pp. 177 ff.; Alley (2020); Bieluk (2020), pp. 18–19; Sheber (2020), pp. 154–155.

borders.[12] In November 2017, the Supreme Court of India also stayed the ruling in the Miglani case.

Tamaqua is a borough in eastern Schuylkill County, Pennsylvania (US). In 2006, the municipal ordinance No. 612 recognized nature's right to the borough. The ordinance prohibited the discharge of sewage sludge without a rigorous system of testing. It recognized Tamaqua as a legal person:

> The Borough of Tamaqua, along with any resident of the Borough, shall have standing to seek declaratory, injunctive, and compensatory relief for damages caused to natural communities and ecosystems within the Borough, regardless of the relation of those natural communities and ecosystems to Borough residents or the Borough itself. Borough residents, natural communities, and ecosystems shall be considered to be 'persons' for purposes of the enforcement of the civil rights of those residents, natural communities, and ecosystems.[13]

The Atrato River is a river in northwestern Colombia. In November 2016, the Constitutional Court of Colombia ruled that the Atrato River basin possesses rights to protection, conservation, maintenance, and restoration. For the effective implementation of the declaration of the Court,

> la Corte dispondrá que el Estado colombiano ejerza la tutoría y representación legal de los derechos del río en conjunto con las comunidades étnicas que habitan en la cuenca del río Atrato en Chocó; de esta forma, el río Atrato y su cuenca – en adelante – estarán representados por un miembro de las comunidades accionantes y un delegado del Estado colombiano [. . .]. Adicionalmente y con el propósito de asegurar la protección, recuperación y debida conservación del río, ambas partes deberán diseñar y conformar una comisión de guardianes del río Atrato cuya integración y miembros se desarrollará en el acápite de órdenes a proferir en la presente sentencia.[14]

The Turag River is the upper tributary of the Buriganga, a major river in Bangladesh. On 30 January 2019, the High Court of Bangladesh recognized the Turag River as a living entity with legal rights and held that the same would apply to all rivers in Bangladesh. The Court identified the National River Conservation Commission of

---

[12] *State of Uttarakhand & Ors. v. Mohd. Salim & Ors.*

[13] Section 7.6 of ordinance No. 612. On this ordinance and other similar ones in the USA, see Tanasescu (2015), pp. 107–117.

[14] See República de Colombia, Corte Constitucional—Sala Sexta de Revisión, T-622 de 2016, Referencia: Expediente T-5.016.242, 10 November 2016, para 9.32 On 5 April 2018, the Colombian Supreme Court *(Corte Suprema de Justicia de Colombia)* recognized the Colombian Amazon rainforest and as an autonomous rights-bearing entity: "*en aras de proteger ese ecosistema vital para el devenir global, tal como la Corte Constitucional declaró al río Atrato, se reconoce a la Amazonia Colombiana como entitad, "sujeto de derechos", titular de la protección, de la conservación, mantenimiento y restauración a cargo del Estado y las entitades territoriales que la integran*" (STC4360-2018, Radicación n.° 11001-22-03-000-2018-00319-01). On these Judgments see Villavicencio Calzadilla (2019) who expresses some doubts: "It is also not clear what the real implications of recognising the Atrato River and the Amazon rainforest as being rights-bearing subjects will be. For example, if such recognition will be limited to a symbolic effect, or whether it will generate real practical changes in the governance, management and control of these (and others) ecosystems in Colombia or in the current national development model based on the exploitation of natural resources" (p. 10). See also Colwell and Carr-Wilson (2017), pp. 22–24; Clark et al. (2018), pp. 805–811; Bieluk (2020), pp. 19–20.

Bangladesh as a legal guardian for all rivers.[15] On 17 February 2020, the Appellate Division of the Supreme Court of Bangladesh upheld the decision of the High Court.

As may be inferred from the above short list and descriptions, all these areas (mostly rivers)[16] enjoy rights under the national law of the territory where they are located. The list could go on. Sometimes, ecosystems and nature itself are recognized as having rights.[17] This unusual recognition is becoming more frequent. In the aforementioned cases the granting of rights and legal personality was made through legislative acts (for instance, this is the case with Te Awa Tupua and Te Urewera) or through the decisions of national courts (as in the case of Ganga and Yamuna). To assess the relevance and the consequences of these legislative or jurisprudential acts of recognition they should be framed in the corresponding domestic legal contexts. This is not the appropriate place to examine these questions in depth and to dwell on the technicalities which characterize the different national legal systems. However, we shall draw some cues from these cases as far as might be useful for the topic of this chapter.

Animals are not entities in the meaning referred above and they have different characteristics: for instance, they move and can cross boundaries while forests, rivers, mountains etc. are static even if they potentially extend across two or more countries. Animals are living beings while natural/cultural entities usually constitute an ensemble of living components.[18] However, as regard the recognition of legal personality, some similarities between animals and entities may be stressed at least in the light of certain national decisions. First, the recognition of personhood for entities implies that they are incapable of being owned;[19] similarly, the recognition of animals as sentient beings—at least according to some scholars and animal rights activists—implies the same consequence and changes their nature of "things" to be possessed.[20] Second, for both categories, there are problems as regards the legal

[15] Serious concern may be expressed as regards the competence and the effectiveness of this Commission; see on this point Sajal (2019).

[16] On the legal personhood of rivers see, in general, Berros (2017), Cano Pecharroman (2018), Clark et al. (2018), Lillo (2018), O'Donnell and Talbot-Jones (2018), Eckstein et al. (2019) and Bieluk (2020).

[17] See, for instance, the Constitution of Ecuador quoted below at note 29.

[18] Natural/cultural entities may even be lifeless from a biological point of view but can be considered living entities according to a spiritual and religious meaning.

[19] For instance, "the conferment of legal personality on the river Whanganui was explicitly intended to reflect the iwi view that the river is a living entity in its own right and is incapable of being 'owned' in an absolute sense"; Rodgers (2017), p. 272 (in the Māori language, iwi means people or nation). "Granting legal personality to a non-human entity implies that the law shall treat it as a subject rather than an object. [. . .] When a society recognizes nature as a subject of law, its status shifts from being considered as a private good, common resource or a resource in the public trust to a specific person under the law, with all the consequences that entails"; Lillo (2018), p. 166.

[20] According to the Secretary-General of the United Nations, "[a] first step to recognizing the rights of Nature is the recognition that non-human animals are sentient beings, not mere property, and must be afforded respect and legal recognition"; UN Doc A/75/266, para 42. On these problems see Schaffner (2011), esp. Chapter 6, pp. 171 ff.

capacity to sue, to be sued and to be represented. Third, even if the protection of animals is often a consequence of their (sometimes) recognized nature of sentient beings, as discussed below, they can be protected also as part of the national cultural heritage. The same cultural value, as noted above, is often awarded to natural entities.[21]

The similarity of the legal problems posed by the recognition of personhood of entities and animals suggests some reflections which may fit both categories.

3 Rights, Intrinsic Value, Legal Personhood

The recognition of rights to nature or to natural/cultural entities must not be confused with the recognition of their legal personhood. Nonetheless the recognition of rights can be considered as a first step towards the recognition of personhood.

Up to now, international law seems merely to have acknowledged the national developments concerning the recognition of rights to natural/cultural entities. These recognitions are encouraged as far as they represent an improvement in the protection of the environment and of cultural rights. For instance, the United Nations have launched some initiatives concerning the re-thinking of the human-nature relationship which includes the possibility of granting rights to nature.[22] In his most recent report on Harmony with Nature,[23] focused on the COVID-19 pandemic, the Secretary-General of the United Nations noted that the pandemic

> obliges humankind to either continue its existence permanently conditioned to an endless state of crisis management with regard to its relationship with the natural world as a result of the objectification of Nature and all the uncertainty that such a worldview entails, or to choose to guide its existence through a steady and harmonious relationship with the natural world, with the subjectification of Nature at its source.

It is however doubtful whether the reference to subjectification necessarily implies the recognition of legal personhood, much less at the international level.

The problem of the legal personality of natural/cultural entities (or of nature as a whole) and the recognition of their rights should also not be confused with the recognition of the intrinsic value of nature and its elements.[24] In a sense, the

---

[21] On animal rights, see Peters (2020a), esp. Chapter VII.

[22] The most important of these initiatives is the United Nations Harmony with Nature programme launched in 2009; see www.harmonywithnatureun.org/. Every year, since 2009, the General Assembly of the United Nations adopts a resolution on Harmony with Nature (Resolutions 64/196 of 21 December 2009; 65/164 of 20 December 2010; 66/204 of 22 December 2011; 67/214 of 21 December 2012; 68/216 of 20 December 2013; 69/224 of 19 December 2014; 70/208 of 22 December 2015; 71/232 of 21 December 2016; 72/223 of 20 December 2017; 73/235 of 20 December 2018; 74/224 of 19 December 2019). Up to now, the Secretary General of the United Nations has presented ten Reports on Harmony with Nature.

[23] UN Doc A/75/266.

[24] On this point see Warnock (2012), pp. 59 ff. and the response of Stone (2012), pp. 107–112.

recognition of the intrinsic value of nature may be considered as an assumption for granting rights to nature itself.[25] The intrinsic value of nature (or of species, wildlife etc.) has long been recognized at the international level, not only in soft law instruments.[26] However, human beings continue to be the arbiters in assessing this intrinsic value. For example, they may decide, on the basis of, if not utilitarian, at least anthropocentric considerations, that an elephant or a lion do not have the same value as a grasshopper or that an Edelweiss deserves more protection than weed.[27]

In a recent Advisory opinion, the Inter-American Court of Human Rights[28] seemed to regard these two different issues as closely interrelated. In particular, the Court indicated that it

> considers it important to stress that, as an autonomous right, the right to a healthy environment, unlike other rights, protects the components of the environment, such as forests, rivers and seas, as legal interests in themselves, even in the absence of the certainty or evidence of a risk to individuals. This means that it protects nature and the environment, not only because of the benefits they provide to humanity or the effects that their degradation may have on other human rights, such as health, life or personal integrity, but because of their importance to the other living organisms with which we share the planet that also merit protection in their own right.[. . .] In this regard, the Court notes a tendency, not only in court judgments, [. . .] but also in Constitutions [. . .], to recognize legal personality and, consequently, rights to nature.[29]

[25] See in this sense UN Doc A/72/175, para 40.

[26] See, *e.g.*, the preamble of the Convention on the Conservation of European Wildlife and Natural Habitats (Bern, 19 September 1979, entered into force on 1 June 1982, 1284 UNTS 209) ("[. . .] Recognising that wild flora and fauna constitute a natural heritage of aesthetic, scientific, cultural, recreational, economic and *intrinsic value* that needs to be preserved and handed on to future generations [. . .]"), or the preamble of the Convention on Biological Diversity (Nairobi, 22 May 1992, entered into force on 29 December 1993, 1760 UNTS 79) ("[. . .] Conscious of the *intrinsic value* of biological diversity and of the ecological, genetic, social, economic, scientific, educational, cultural, recreational and aesthetic values of biological diversity and its components [. . .]"); emphasis added. The World Charter for Nature is one of the first non-legally binding international instruments that indirectly recognizes the intrinsic value of every form of life, refusing an anthropocentric approach to conservation. According to its preamble, "Every form of life is unique, warranting respect *regardless of its worth to man*" (UN General Assembly, 28 Oct 1982, UN Doc A/RES/37/7, emphasis added).

[27] See the pessimistic considerations of Naffine (2012), pp. 68–83 and the response of Stone (2012), pp. 113–117. Even the Secretary-General of the United Nations in Report A/75/266, para 42, admits a certain speciesism (and a very anthropocentric assessment) where he affirms that the recognition that non-human animals are sentient being "is growing around the world, in particular with regard to those animals best known and most easily appreciated by humans".

[28] Inter-American Court of Human Rights, Advisory Opinion Oc-23/17, 15 November 2017, requested by the Republic of Colombia, The Environment And Human Rights; on the Advisory opinion see the introductory note of Scovazzi (2019) to the Spanish version; see also Feria-Tinta, Milnes (2019) pp. 57–58; Lima (2020). In this volume see Carpanelli, esp. Sect. 4.

[29] Inter-American Court of Human Rights, Advisory Opinion Oc-23/17 *supra* note 28, para 62. To support its statement the Court quotes *inter alia* the International Union for Conservation of Nature (IUCN), the World Declaration on the Environmental Rule of Law of the International Union for Conservation of Nature adopted at the IUCN World Environmental Law Congress, held in Rio de Janeiro from April 26–29, 2016, Principles 1 and 2. As regards the national jurisprudence, the Court

The fact that, as far as the legal personality is concerned, the Court quoted only national judgments and Constitutions[30] may be read *a contrario* to confirm that the question of international legal personhood is not at stake.

4 International Legal Personhood of Natural/Cultural Entities: Not Yet; Perhaps Never?

4.1 The Subjects of International Law: Some Preliminary Remarks

States are the traditional and primary subjects of international law.[31] If certain conditions are met, international organizations may also be considered subjects of international law, but, as they are established by States, they are considered to be secondary subjects. A variety of other "entities" are also granted "selected" rights.

mentions, in particular, the following decisions: "Constitutional Court of Colombia, Judgment T-622-16 of November 10, 2016, paras. 9.27 to 9.31; Constitutional Court of Ecuador, Judgment No. 218-15-SEP-CC of July 9, 2015, pp. 9 and 10, and High Court of Uttarakhand At Naintal of India, Decision of March 30, 2017. Petition (PIL) No. 140 of 2015, pp. 61 to 63". As regards the national Constitutions, the Court quotes the preamble and Article 33 of the Constitution of Bolivia and Article 71 of the Constitution of Ecuador according to which "La naturaleza o Pacha Mama, donde se reproduce y realiza la vida, tiene derecho a que se respete integralmente su existencia y el mantenimiento y regeneración de sus ciclos vitales, estructura, funciones y procesos evolutivos. Toda persona, comunidad, pueblo o nacionalidad podrá exigir a la autoridad pública el cumplimiento de los derechos de la naturaleza. Para aplicar e interpretar estos derechos se observaran los principios establecidos en la Constitución, en lo que proceda. El Estado incentivará a las personas naturales y jurídicas, y a los colectivos, para que protejan la naturaleza, y promoverá el respeto a todos los elementos que forman un ecosistema".

[30] According to Tanasescu (2015), p. 124, the case of the Constitution of Ecuador "is the first one with international aspirations". This does not mean, of course, that it had an influence on the attitude of international law towards international legal personhood of nature but that Ecuador tried to apply the principle of extraterritoriality to the rights of nature recognized in its Constitution. On 30 March 2011, the Corte Provincial de Justicia de Loja—Sala Penal (Juicio No. 11121-2011-0010) applied Article 71 of the Constitution of Ecuador to the Vilcabamba River; see Berros (2017); Colwell and Carr-Wilson (2017), pp. 20–22; Clark et al. (2018), pp. 795–800; Sheber (2020), pp. 155 ff.

[31] "As a working definition, subjects of international law may be defined as entities which are capable of possessing international rights and duties"; Walter (2007), para 1.1. According to the International Court of Justice (which refers to international organizations), to be an international person means to be a subject of international law "capable of possessing international rights and duties" and having "capacity to maintain its rights by bringing international claims" (*Reparation for injuries suffered in the service of the United Nations*, Advisory Opinion, 11 April 1949, I.C.J. Reports 1949, p. 174 at p. 179). According to Portmann (2010), p. 10, and to many other scholars quoted by him, the definition of the Court "is not very illuminating for it neither addresses which entities actually are international persons nor does it state comprehensive criteria according to which personality is attributed. The latter aspect is further obscured by the somewhat tautological nature of the definition".

For instance, international law recognizes that *minorities* have rights (such as the right not to be discriminated against) and that *peoples* also have rights (such as the right to self-determination).[32] International law recognizes that even entities which do not in fact exist, such as *future generations*, may have rights; according to international law, *humankind* "enjoys" cultural and natural heritage, while some treaties seem to recognize (albeit limited) rights for *animals*, for instance the right not to be unnecessarily mistreated. Does such a recognition of rights confer international personality on these entities? Reasonably, it does not.[33]

Doubts even exist in terms of international legal personhood when it comes to the category of individuals.[34] The international legal personhood of individuals remains controversial.[35] That is even though more than 70 years has passed since the adoption of the Universal Declaration on Human Rights[36] and despite the fact that there are now many treaties recognizing human rights, more specifically recognizing the right to lodge individual complaints before international bodies, and indeed despite the existence of a number of international instruments affirming the criminal responsibility of individual for committing international crimes. Even if we accept that individuals are subjects of international law, their international personality seems to be limited to certain domains, that is: human rights law, international criminal law and humanitarian law.[37] For some distinguished scholars,[38] individuals are still simple beneficiaries of rights or bound by obligations, which States can decide respectively to either recognize, or to impose on them.

In the face of such reluctance, it can be doubted whether the time is now ripe for States to increase the number of international subjects and to recognize the full (or even partial) international legal personhood of natural/cultural entities or nature.

---

[32] The problem, in this case, may be to know the very notion of who the people are that enjoy such a right.

[33] According to Gorski (2013), para 10, "currently, the predominant view is that a subject of international law is whoever has rights and duties under public international law". See also the selected bibliography *ibidem*. For a more comprehensive approach to the issue of international legal personality see Portmann (2010).

[34] By using this term, in this context, we refer to human beings; in other contexts the term is used to refer also to groups of individuals or legal corporations.

[35] According to Shaw (2014), p. 188, "modern practice does demonstrate that individuals have become increasingly recognized as participants and subjects of international law". According to Daillier et al. (2009), p. 719, it is not possible to give "une description univoque du bilan actuel de leur [= personnes privées] personnalité juridique internationale". Similarly, according to McCorquodale (2014), p. 280, individuals are participants in the international legal system and are not solely objects that are subject to States' consent, though their degree of participation varies.

[36] Proclaimed by the General Assembly, A/RES/3/217 A, 10 December 1948.

[37] Some scholars refer to individuals as partial subjects. Peters (2016a) extends considerably the number of the above-mentioned domains; she considers that the individual is an original (and not only a derivative) subject of international law and the owner of international individual rights.

[38] See, among the others, Crawford (2019), p. 111; according to Treves (2019), p. 110, there is not "a descriptive advantage in including individuals in the list of subjects of international law".

However, in a well-known Advisory opinion, the International Court of Justice, referring to international organizations, affirmed that

> the subjects of law in any legal system are not necessarily identical in their nature or in the extent of their rights, and their nature depends upon the needs of the community. Throughout its history, the development of international law has been influenced by the requirements of international life [...]. [T]o achieve these ends [= purposes and principles of the UN] the attribution of international personality is indispensable.[39]

Reading this statement by the ICJ in the context of the protection of environment and cultural values, is the attribution of international legal personality to the aforementioned natural/cultural entities or animals indispensable? As we will see, the practice of States does not support a move in this direction.

In the literature on this topic, in order to discuss the legal personality of nature or natural/cultural entities, scholars have taken into account different reference models, depending on what aspects are sought to be emphasized. For example, the comparison with the status of slaves serves because the latter have gone from being the object of rights of property, to subjects of law, as would also happen for natural/cultural entities, following the above-mentioned practice. The comparison with women or black people serves instead to justify that the unthinkable can become a reality: until a few decades ago in many States these subjects enjoyed no rights or an extremely limited number of rights.[40] The comparison with children or mentally disabled individuals serves to demonstrate that a reduced capacity or even a total lack of capacity is not an obstacle to being granted legal personhood. Finally, the comparison with corporations serves as in both cases the legal personhood is a legal fiction and the "subjects" are not human. From the point of view of international legal personhood, we would argue that the most useful reference model is that of the controversial legal personality of individuals.

4.2 Any Hints of a Trend in International Law?

All the above-mentioned natural/cultural entities are subject to national jurisdiction. Their protection, from both the environmental and cultural point of view is a competence of the territorial State. This does not exclude that the State could be obliged by international law to protect those entities.

As regards the protection of the environment, and of wildlife in particular, usually international law, and treaties more precisely, do not specify the means by which the

---

[39] *Reparation for injuries suffered in the service of the United Nations*, *supra* note 31, p. 178.

[40] This comparison has often been used for discussions concerning the possibility of recognizing the "rights" of animals. It is sometimes considered as politically incorrect and inappropriate. Athens (2018) examines in parallel the evolution of the rights of women and of the rights of nature; she considers that the extension of rights to women is no more, and no different, than extending rights to nature (p. 193). See also Peters (2016b), p. 31 ss.

State must comply with its obligations. This is particularly true as regards treaties protecting wildlife "generically", imposing obligations to adopt appropriate and necessary legislative and administrative measures to ensure conservation.[41] In these cases, the Parties remain free to assess the appropriateness and necessity of such measures, including, of course, the designation of protected areas.[42] Even when the treaty provides explicitly that the Parties must designate particular areas to protect and to be included in "international" lists, the requirements for inclusion and the protection measures are indicated in terms which leave a certain discretion to the Parties. This is the case of the 1971 Ramsar Convention on Wetlands[43] and of the 1972 Convention concerning the Protection of the World Cultural and Natural Heritage.[44] According to the 1972 UNESCO Convention, the Parties have the duty to ensure the identification, protection, conservation, presentation and transmission to future generations of the cultural and natural heritage covered by the Convention and situated on their territory. None of the provisions of the Convention mentions the attribution of legal personhood to the items included in the Lists.[45] Needless to say that if a State Party considers that the most appropriate way to ensure protection of a site of cultural or natural value, whether or not it is included in the Lists, is the recognition of its *national* legal personhood, it may recognize such personhood. In other words, such recognition constitutes an implementation of the provisions of the Convention. It is equally clear that the recognition of *national* legal personhood does not affect the eventual recognition of *international* legal personhood.[46] A different case would be that of a treaty, which provided for certain entities to be given *international* legal personhood to allow them to exercise the rights granted to them. This treaty obligation (however unlikely) could not go beyond the scope of application of the treaty itself. In other words, the treaty could not

[41] See for instance the 1979 Convention on the Conservation of European Wildlife and Natural Habitats (*supra* note 26).

[42] For instance, the Convention on Biological Diversity (*supra*, note 26) provides at Article 8.a (In-situ conservation) that "Each Contracting Party shall, as far as possible and as appropriate: (a) Establish a system of protected areas or areas where special measures need to be taken to conserve biological diversity".

[43] Convention on Wetlands of International Importance especially as Waterfowl Habitat (Ramsar, 2 February 1971, entered into force on 21 December 1975, 996 UNTS 245), amended by the Protocol of 1982 and the Amendment of 1987. The Convention provides for a List of Wetlands of International Importance; to become Parties to the Convention, States shall designate at least one wetland to be included in the List. To be such wetland it must meet certain specific requirements.

[44] Adopted by the General Conference of UNESCO, Paris, 23 November 1972 (hereinafter: 1972 UNESCO Convention), entered into force on 17 December 1975, 1037 UNTS 151.

[45] The Convention provides for two lists: the World Heritage List and the List of World Heritage in Danger.

[46] Similarly, the Parties may decide that granting *national* legal subjectivity to entities holding a cultural value for a certain community is an appropriate measure to take in order to implement certain provisions of a treaty, which provides for the protection of the cultural rights of such a community. In these cases, international legal personhood is not at stake.

recognize the international legal personality *erga omnes* but, if ever, only between the Parties[47] and therefore it would have very limited effects.[48]

In the light of the above, it is interesting to note that the conferment of legal personhood to Te Urewera is considered a belated implementation of the Treaty of Waitangi originally signed on 6 February 1840 by Great Britain and 44 Maori chiefs (and many more following the initial signatures) from the North Island of New Zealand.[49] However, nothing in the Treaty of Waitangi imposes on the Parties an obligation to recognize either the national or the international legal personhood of Te Urewera. And, by the way, the measures that the Te Urewera Board has to adopt to protect the area do not differ substantially from the "traditional" measures to be taken to protect, for instance, a national park. In this specific case, the most important difference is the attention the Te Urewera Act devotes to the cultural and spiritual values of Maori people. The conferment of national legal personhood to Te Awa Tupua represents a measure for the implementation of the Treaty of Waitangi[50] as well.

The judgment of the Colombian Constitutional Court concerning Atrato River also recalls *inter alia* international law

> [...] dimensionando *el ámbito de protección de los tratados internacionales suscritos por Colombia en materia de protección del medio ambiente*, la Constitución Ecológica y los derechos bioculturales [...] que predican la protección conjunta e interdependiente del ser humano con la naturaleza y sus recursos, es que la Corte declarará que el río Atrato es sujeto de derechos que implican su protección, conservación, mantenimiento y en el caso concreto, restauración.[51]

No one denies that the protection of cultural rights, together with the protection of the environment, is becoming increasingly important in international law and the same is true for the protection of the rights of indigenous people.[52] However, once

---

[47] This reasoning would correspond with the theory according to which there is a difference between "objective" (*erga omnes*) international legal subjects (States and, sometimes, international organizations) and merely "particular" international legal subjects (e.g. individuals); on this point see Peters (2016a), p. 43. See also Portmann (2010), pp. 82 ff.

[48] *Mutatis mutandis*, for the same reason, it is not enough for a treaty establishing an international organization to state that such an organization has an international legal personality in order to make it a subject of international law.

[49] On this Treaty (in particular on its interpretation), see Scovazzi (1994), pp. 725–736 and the bibliography quoted at note 1. The Te Urewera Act 2014 expressly mentions the Treaty of Waitangi. See also Colwell and Carr-Wilson (2017), pp. 6 ff.

[50] The Te Awa Tupua (Whanganui River Claims Settlement) Act 2017 (see *supra* Sect. 2) which confers legal personality on the river system, "resolves historical claims to restitution for alleged breaches by the Crown of the principles enshrined in the Treaty of Waitangi" (Rodgers (2017), pp. 267 and 271).

[51] Corte Constitucional—Sala Sexta de Revisión, T-622 de 2016, Referencia: Expediente T-5.016.242 *supra* note 14, para 9.32 (emphasis added).

[52] The two issues are strictly interconnected, at least in some contexts; as quoted above, the Judgment of the Colombian Constitutional Court refers to "biocultural rights", which are "los derechos que tienen las comunidades étnicas a administrar y a ejercer tutela de manera autónoma

again, the recognition of the national legal personhood of significant sites may constitute a way to protect such rights but it does not interfere with the recognition of their international legal personhood.

Thus, up to now, there are no treaties providing for the recognition of the international legal personhood of natural/cultural entities. Even more pessimistic are the conclusions as regards the possible existence of a customary rule recognizing such personhood. In fact, the practice of States in this respect is still too limited and fragmentary to make it possible to identify the *diuturnitas* and the *opinio juris ac necessitatis* which are the indispensable elements of the customary rules. Nor is it possible to hold that a corresponding "general principle of law recognized by civilized nations"[53] does exist. As a matter of fact, including in this case, it is true that the States' national practice evidences a trend but this practice is not widespread enough and homogeneous[54] to rise to the rank of a general principle.

4.3 Hypothetical Questions Raised by Hypothetical Recognition of International Legal Personhood

Let us now consider what possible consequences could derive from a hypothetical recognition of the international legal personhood of natural/cultural entities. As noted above, the discussions that usually characterize the question of the international subjectivity of individuals will serve as a model for the following reasoning.

The main characteristics of international subjects is the fact that they possess rights and duties conferred by international law and that they have the capacity to act at the international level using the legal instruments typical of international law. It is reasonable to conclude that if natural/cultural entities were subjects under international law they would have the rights and duties of international law. Who would confer or recognize such rights and duties? If the comparison with individuals holds, States, mainly through treaties, would have the power to confer and recognize rights (and obligations) on entities. But of course, as has happened for individuals, entities should be able to put in motion procedures at the international level in order to seek the protection of their rights and to make the recognition effective. This is actually the crucial element of enjoying rights and the element that distinguishes those

sobre sus territorios – de acuerdo con sus propias leyes, costumbres – y los recursos naturales que conforman su hábitat, en donde se desarrolla su cultura, sus tradiciones y su forma de vida con base en la especial relación que tienen con el medio ambiente y la biodiversidad"; see note 314 of the Judgment of the Colombian Constitutional Court *supra* note 14. In UN Doc A/75/266, para 46, the Secretary General of the United Nations notes that "[t]here has [. . .] been growing awareness that recognition of the rights of Nature is embedded in customary laws [of indigenous peoples] in contrast to modern environmental laws which remain grounded on an anthropocentric paradigm".

[53] See Article 38.1.c of the Statute of the International Court of Justice.

[54] "[I]l principio [. . .] deve essere presente nella maggior parte dei sistemi giuridici nazionali"; see Scovazzi (2015), p. 168.

protected by international law from those enjoying rights under international law. In other words, recognizing rights without instituting procedures to exercise those rights and to bring claims before international bodies in case of violations may be emotionally suggestive but is substantially useful only for academic disquisitions.[55]

Nevertheless, suppose that States establish at the international level a procedure which may be triggered to protect the rights enjoyed by entities and allegedly violated. Against which international subjects should the international procedure be activated? Probably against States, first of all, the State where the entity is located but also other States, if that is the case. And who could act to represent the entity? Once again, the treaty-based procedures used by individuals to safeguard their rights help as a model. For instance, Article 34 of the European Convention on Human Rights and Fundamental Freedoms[56] provides that the Court may receive applications from non-governmental organizations (NGO) namely legal persons.[57] Thus, the non-human nature of an NGO is not in principle an obstacle to going to the European Court,[58] even if, in relation to NGOs, their status as a victim of a violation of the Convention may be sometimes difficult to ascertain. However, the possibility for NGOs to bring cases before the supervisory bodies provided for in human rights treaties is not particularly widespread. For example, according to Article 2 of the Optional Protocol to the International Covenant on Civil and Political Rights,[59] only individuals may submit a written communication to the Human Rights Committee for consideration. The Committee itself excluded the possibility that associations can submit a communication.

The fact that, according to some treaties, NGOs can put in motion procedures seeking the protection of their rights does not grant them international legal personhood. A similar reasoning can be replicated for natural/cultural entities if they could, based on a treaty, refer the matter to an international mechanism of quasi-judicial or judicial nature for the protection of their rights. In particular, one may think that the natural/cultural entities, which enjoy rights granted by a treaty, might appeal to international courts or similar organs, as the treaty provides for, through the body, which, at the national level, represents and manages the entity and acts on its

[55] *Contra*, referring to animals, see Peters (2016b), pp. 47–48: "as a matter of legal theory and practice, the question of possessing a right (as part of substantive law) and the question of how and in which forums to enforce it (procedural law) are two separate issues. The usefulness of a right can lie elsewhere than in its judicial enforceability".

[56] Rome, 4 November 1950, entered into force on 3 September 1953, ETS No. 005.

[57] In the same way, Article 44 of the American Convention on Human Rights (San José, Costa Rica, 22 November 1969, entered into force on 18 July 1978, 1144 UNTS 23) provides that "any nongovernmental entity legally recognized in one or more member states of the Organization [of the American States], may lodge petitions with the [Inter-American] Commission [on Human Rights] containing denunciations or complaints of violation of this Convention by a State Party".

[58] The notion of NGO is "broad and flexible and is not subject to any formalities of registration" and "[t]he Convention does not expressly refer to corporate bodies; these are subsumed under the rubric of 'non-governmental organisations'"(Schabas 2015, p. 736).

[59] New York, 16 December 1966, entered into force on 23 March 1976, 999 UNTS 171.

behalf.[60] In this regard, some similarities with the representation of corporations may be envisaged. This is not the place to dwell on the issue of legal personhood of corporations, which surely deserves a more in-depth analysis.[61] The comparison between natural/cultural entities and corporations, as regards legal personhood, cannot be pushed too hard. In fact, in very rough terms, a corporation is "animated" by individuals who represent it. These individuals have, more or less, an interest in its activity and may express their will through different mechanisms. Instead, a natural/cultural entity would be "animated" by individuals who represent it, but who have no personal interests in exercising the rights of the natural/cultural entity. But, for sure and inevitably, the will of the entity is filtered through the will of the individuals who exercise those rights. This could also happen for those bodies that have been instituted to represent the natural/cultural entities with national legal personhood through a sort of trust or stewardship.[62]

Further problems may arise when the possibility of taking legal action to protect the rights of natural/cultural entity is not reserved for a specific representative body but is a faculty granted to any person, community, people or nationality. This is the case of the rights of nature recognized in the Ecuadorean Constitution;[63] according to Article 71, any person, community, people or nationality may require the public authority to comply with the rights of nature. When the possibility of recourse to a national court is so wide-ranging, at the international level there would be a risk of overwhelming the international bodies with too many claims.[64] To avoid this, the right to appeal these bodies should be restricted appropriately. The condition of the exhaustion of all domestic remedies, as usually required by the human rights treaties, might not be sufficient for the purpose.

Even before all these problems, which might be solved through treaties, a preliminary question should be addressed: which natural/cultural entities could be enabled to defend their rights before an international mechanism? As noted above, at the national level rights are sometimes granted to nature in general; even when rights are granted to specific entities, there are no common criteria to recognize the rights and to specify the rights themselves. National authorities have a great discretion in deciding which entities deserve to have their rights recognized. Should a treaty be concluded to grant procedural rights to natural/cultural entities, it would specify which entities could enjoy such rights, for instance through *ad hoc* lists or the

---

[60] These problems were already dealt with by Stone (1972), pp. 464 ff. who suggested, *inter alia*, a guardianship approach. This approach, however, is not without some drawbacks (as underlined at p. 471).

[61] On this point see e.g. the very articulate analysis of Gordon (2018), pp. 62 ff.

[62] On this point see also *infra* Sect. 6.

[63] See *supra* note 29.

[64] According to Sheber (2020) (who refers to national cases and quotes Stone (1996), p. 17), "[t]rends, at least in the U.S., have leaned toward liberalized standing where people have increasingly had the opportunity to bring cases into court for environmental harm. But, a guardianship approach would give the environment an effective voice in more situations, and would help prevent the potential flood of cases pouring into courts due to relaxed standards for standing" (p. 150).

identification of specific requirements. Here the comparison with human rights is of little help. After the elimination of the discrimination of the past, it was not difficult to identify the subjects (women, people of all colours, children, disabled individuals . . .) to whom to extend the rights previously enjoyed by white men only, as the new subjects were part of a homogeneous group, that of humankind. Instead, the characteristics of natural/cultural entities considered legal subjects under different national laws are heterogeneous. For instance, sometimes the conferment of national legal personhood to natural entities is based on cultural and spiritual values, which are strongly linked to certain territories. This makes it impossible, or at least very difficult, to identify a unique reference model for the granting of the international legal personhood. Once again, States, through the above-mentioned hypothetical treaty, should decide which entities deserve the status of legal subjects.

In any case, as regards legal personhood, it is quite unlikely that a treaty, which would also guarantee procedural rights to natural/cultural entities, would explicitly affirm their international legal personality. Legal standing does not necessarily mean legal personhood. Such recognition, in any event, could only relate to the Contracting Parties. What is more, the latter remain free to terminate the treaty and thus deprive entities of their personhood. As the case of human rights shows, the road to the formation of a rule of customary international law in this field would still be long and tortuous.

4.4 *New Solutions for Old Problems?*

Now let us go back to the initial question: is the attribution of international legal personality to the abovementioned natural/cultural entities indispensable *to improve the protection of the environment or the cultural/spiritual rights of peoples?* Is there a difference between protecting a river or a forest as a "thing" and protecting the same river as an international legal person? Is there a difference between protecting the cultural/spiritual rights of a people through the traditional measures and protecting the same rights through the recognition of the international legal personhood to the entities having a cultural value for that people? Indeed, measures adopted to protect the environment may be similar in the case of a traditional, anthropocentric approach and in the case of an Earth-centered approach through the attribution of legal personhood to environmental features; the basic assumption, however, is different. In the latter case the interests of natural/cultural entities *should* be protected in a way that do not necessarily correspond to the interests of human beings, such as natural resource exploitation, harvesting, recreational use of natural beauty etc. In other words, through legal personhood these entities "are given a robust and expansive legal footing that is independent of directly connected human interests".[65] However, our use of the verb form "*should* be protected" is not random. As noted

[65] Gordon (2018), pp. 61–62.

above, even when the natural/cultural entities have legal personhood, "their" interests are necessarily assessed by human beings. There cannot be actions "objectively" in the interest of natural/cultural entities because even the criteria for assessing the objectivity of such actions are established by human beings, although designated—once again by human beings—to represent and defend the interests of the natural/cultural entity. The best one can hope is that the assessment is reasonable and well-balanced in respect of all the other interests at stake.[66]

The traditional approach to the protection of the environment is a property-based approach. The greatest consequence from recognising the rights of nature is that it places limits on human property rights. In a national contest and, in particular, in English law, the conferring of legal status could ensure effective access to legal redress to protect the natural/cultural entity without the necessity of establishing a "sufficient interest" in an environmental dispute for standing in legal proceedings.[67] The widening of the possibility to stand in legal proceedings deriving from the recognition of legal personality at the domestic level might be useful also at the international level. As noted above, this is, however, subject to the fact that special procedures are established at the international level—inevitably through treaties—for the protection of one's rights. As in the simpler case of mechanisms for the protection of human rights, it is unnecessary to confer international personhood upon the applicants. From a substantive point of view, abandoning the property-based approach could substantially increase the scope of the protection as, at least in some cases, it should be due to the ecosystem as a whole and not to its single components. Once again, however, this improved protection does not imply that an international legal personhood is necessary. To achieve this result, broader protective measures provided for in the protection agreements may be sufficient (if implemented correctly, of course).

5 Animals as Sentient Beings: New Subjects of International Law?

As said above, it is becoming more and more frequent for international treaties and other international instruments to contain provisions which prohibit States from unnecessarily mistreating animals. This is the case, for instance, of the numerous treaties concluded in the framework of the Council of Europe which deal with the

[66] Unfortunately, as regards animals in particular, "[b]alancing the animals' interests against human interests typically ends up prioritising the human interests, even trivial ones. Arguably, this type of balancing is structurally biased against the animals"; Peters (2020a), p. 111; see also Peters (2016b), p. 49.

[67] On this point see for instance Rodgers (2017), pp. 273 ff. as regards Te Awa Tupua. As regards the right of rivers to stand in court and to be represented see Cano Pecharroman (2018).

treatment of some categories of animals.[68] Also some provisions of the CITES[69] provide that the risk of cruel treatment of living specimens is to be minimized. Article 13 of the Treaty on the Functioning of the European Union (TFEU, Lisbon, 2007) recognizes that animals are sentient beings and the Union and its Members have to pay full regard to their welfare requirements.[70]

None of these binding instruments mentions the "right" of these animals, which may be considered as simple beneficiaries of the obligations undertaken by States and only passive subjects of the protection. It is therefore not surprising that such instruments do not recognize the international legal personhood of animals. Instead, the rights of animals are proclaimed in the 1978 Universal Declaration of Animal Rights[71] and in other declarations, which are still at the draft stage. These declarations not only do not have a legal binding character but also do not provide for any obligation of States towards animals.

Notwithstanding such an unequivocal situation, the legal personhood of animals has been recurrently invoked before national judges and even before international

[68] See European Convention for the Protection of Animals during International Transport (Paris, 13 December 1968, entered into force on 20 February 1971, ETS No. 065), its Additional Protocol (Strasbourg, 10 May 1979, entered into force on 7 November 1989, ETS No. 103) and its revised version (Chişinau, 6 November 2003, entered into force on 14 March 2006, ETS No. 193); European Convention for the Protection of Animals Kept for Farming Purposes (Strasbourg, 10 March 1976, entered into force on 10 September 1978, ETS No. 087) and its Protocol of Amendment (Strasbourg, 6 February 1992, not in force, ETS No. 145); European Convention for the Protection of Animals for Slaughter (Strasbourg, 10 May 1979, entered into force on 11 June 1982, ETS No. 102); European Convention for the Protection of Vertebrate Animals used for Experimental and Other Scientific Purposes (Strasbourg, 18 March 1986, entered into force on 1 January 1991, ETS No. 123) and its Protocol of Amendment (Strasbourg, 22 June 1998, entered into force on 2 December 2005, ETS No. 170); European Convention for the Protection of Pet Animals (Strasbourg, 13 November 1987, entered into force on 1 May 1992, ETS No. 125).

[69] Convention on International Trade in Endangered Species of Wild Fauna and Flora (Washington, 3 March 1973, entered into force on 1 July 1975, 993 UNTS 243), Articles III, IV, V, VII and VIII.

[70] Article 13 TFEU: "In formulating and implementing the Union's agriculture, fisheries, transport, internal market, research and technological development and space policies, the Union and the Member States shall, since animals are sentient beings, pay full regard to the welfare requirements of animals, while respecting the legislative or administrative provisions and customs of the Member States relating in particular to religious rites, cultural traditions and regional heritage". On Article 13 of TFEU see Scovazzi (2014), pp. 177 ff.

[71] The Universal Declaration of Animal Rights is often referred to as a "UNESCO Declaration". Although it was in actual fact solemnly proclaimed in Paris on 15 October 1978 at the UNESCO headquarters (Paris, 15 October 1978), it seems that the Organization only served as host for the proclamation. The intent was that the text would be submitted to a vote of the General Assembly of the United Nations but this did not happen. The text, revised by the international League of Animal Rights in 1989, was submitted to the UNESCO Director General in 1990 and made public the same year. It is worth noting that Article 9.1 of the revised Universal Declaration provides that "The specific legal status of animals and their rights must be recognized by law". The same provision, in the French version, has a different meaning as it refers also to the legal personhood of the animal ("*La personnalité juridique de l'animal et ses droits doivent être reconnus par la loi*"). On the Universal Declaration see Neumann (2012); on the need for international animal rights see Peters (2020b), pp. 112–113.

bodies, albeit less successfully before the latter, as we will see below.[72] In fact some animals seem to enjoy special privileges before the law. The idea that certain animals are "better" than others and as such deserve more protection is not a new one even at the international level. We do not refer here to specimen of endangered species but to animals that for their similarity to man would even enjoy a right to life. This is the case, for instance of whales[73] or primates. Thus, similarity to human beings is the yardstick by which to recognize rights, special treatment or even legal personhood to some animals. This says a lot about the speciesism that characterizes this kind of assessments. This approach is just another way to make animal rights dependent on the value attributed by human beings and not a consequence of the intrinsic value of animals themselves. This makes it even more difficult to establish the discriminatory criteria according to which rights and possibly legal personality could be conferred on animals.

That said, it may be interesting to mention the case of the chimpanzee Cecilia which was decided by an Argentinian judge in 2016.[74] The case addresses some crucial aspects considered above as questions strictly connected with the attribution of legal personhood. Indeed, the Argentinian decision deals with the legal personhood of animals (primates, in particular), the persons or bodies legitimated to legally represent them[75] and the reasons for their protection. It is characterized by a widespread speciesism (though for good).

Generally speaking, the legal personhood of animals could be useful to guaranteeing them special protection as far as they are sentient beings or as part of the cultural heritage of a certain community. These two aspects are particularly evident in the case of Cecilia, a 30-year-old chimpanzee held in the zoo of Ciudad de Mendoza (Argentina). Through a *habeas corpus* action the President of A.F.A.D.A.[76] requested freedom for Cecilia. He insisted on her right to freedom of movement and to a decent life. The arguments of the President of A.F.A.D.A. are particularly specist.[77] According to him, Cecilia—and with her the other hominids like gorillas,

[72]On this issue see for instance Schaffner (2011) (esp. chapter 6); Tanasescu (2015), esp. chapter 3.

[73]D'Amato and Chopra (1991).

[74]Tercer Juzgado de Garantías, Poder Judicial Mendoza, Expte. Nro. P-72.254/15 presentación efectuada por A.F.A.D.A. respecto del chimpancé "Cecilia". "Sujeto no humano", Mendoza 3 de noviembre de 2016 (available online; a translation by Ana María Hernández Marti is also available online).

[75]On the representation of the interests of animals see, in general, Peters (2020b), esp. p. 509 ss.; on the problem of legal standing of animals (especially as regards the Canadian case of elephant Lucy) see Totten (2015) esp. pp. 7 ff.

[76]*Asociación de Funcionarios y Abogados por los Derechos de los Animales.*

[77]"[...] un chimpancé no es una mascota y tampoco puede ser usado como mero objeto de diversión, cobayo de experimentación o mera exhibición. Ellos piensan, sienten, se afeccionan, odian, sufren, aprende e inclusive trasmiten lo aprendido" (Tercer Juzgado de Garantías, Poder Judicial Mendoza, Expte. Nro. P-72.254/15 *supra* note 74, at p. 4). This means *a contrario* that some less lucky animals may be used as mere entertainment objects, used for experiments or for mere exhibition. According to Staker (2017), pp. 505–506, notwithstanding criticism, "it may be necessary for strategic purposes initially to pursue legal personhood for a limited number of species

orangutans and bonobos—must enjoy some protection. In particular, as hominids they enjoy some of the rights of human beings, among which is the right to obtain a *habeas corpus*. This means, *a contrario*, that animals that are not hominids could not enjoy the same rights. In other words, this could lead to weakened protection for other less "privileged" animals.

In granting a writ of right—the *habeas corpus*—conceived for humans, the judge stressed the cultural value of Cecilia for the Argentinian community. According to the judge, the case of Cecilia involves the protection of a collective good or value (*bien o valor colectivo*). Since 1994 the Constitution of Argentina recognizes a new category of rights that is "rights of collective impact" (*derechos de incidencia colectiva*), referring *inter alia* to the right to the environment (Article 41 of the Constitution). The broad notion incorporated in Article 41 includes not only natural heritage[78] but also the cultural values and the quality of social life. Cecilia is part of the Argentinian wild fauna the protection and conservation of which is a matter of public interest. Thus, Cecilia is a part of the natural heritage but, according to the Argentinian judge, she is also a part of the cultural heritage of the human community because of her relationship with that community. Her wellbeing concerns the protection of a collective patrimony. Notwithstanding the link with the Argentinian community, the judge did not find that the decision to transfer Cecilia outside Argentina[79] was in contrast with the protection of the natural and cultural heritage and the quality of life of such community.

The judge's arguments suggest a short digression about her "innovative" position. In a different legal situation, dealing with the return of cultural property, Scovazzi refers to the "principle of preservation of the integrity of cultural context, which is deeply rooted in the nature of cultural property".[80] The same Author, referring to non-living items, observes that

> objects removed from their context [. . .] can provide little information about the history and culture of the often unknown places where they have been taken from and the civilizations to which they belonged. Since art and history are always associated with a geographical context, cultural evidence should be preserved *in situ*.[81]

Would these considerations have been different if they referred to a living being like Cecilia? Would they have been different if the survival of the living being were at stake? Whatever the answer could be, the Argentinian judge took a clear position on this point: aware of the fact that the Argentinian community could not provide Cecilia the due wellbeing, the judge recognized that her transfer beyond the national

---

only. [. . .] a more ambitious project would be unrealistic and may risk alienating the animal advocacy movement. [. . .] An incremental approach, initially focused on securing personhood for certain species, may be more viable, both legally and politically".

[78] In the judgment concerning Cecilia the term "patrimonio" is used, translated in this chapter as "heritage".

[79] In particular, Cecilia had to be relocated in the Chimpanzee Sanctuary of Sorocaba in Brazil.

[80] Scovazzi (2011), pp. 389–390. See also Scovazzi (2009).

[81] Scovazzi (2011), p. 390.

borders was the appropriate means to guarantee Cecilia—part of the Argentinian heritage—the best life conditions. The judge stated that

> [e]l lazo espiritual que vincula a una comunidad con los elementos de su patrimonio no depende de la proximidad fisica sino de la intensidad con la que la relación sea vivida y fortalecida a lo largo del tiempo, con independencia de la condición dominial del elemento o de la jurisdicción a la que él quede sometido.

The community will be satisfied knowing that "*actuando colectivamente como societad*" has granted Cecilia the life she deserves. Not only that. The community must thank Cecilia for giving it the opportunity to grow as a collective and to feel a little more human.

The Argentinian judge seems to overcome, in the name of the survival of the natural and cultural heritage—a living one, in this case—the arguments sometimes used by States in order to avoid returning elements of the cultural heritage of other States. According to these arguments, the element of the cultural heritage should be left where it is safeguarded more appropriately and not returned to the community to which it culturally belongs, especially when such a community cannot afford the costs of its preservation. In the case of Cecilia, the reasoning of the judge is quite simple: Cecilia, a non-human subject of law (*sujeto de derecho no humano*), is part of the natural and cultural heritage of Argentina; she cannot stand in process and needs to be represented; her best protection may be found outside the country without impoverishing the community.[82] It should be noted that Cecilia does not become common heritage (shared with another country or with humankind as a whole) only as a consequence of crossing the national borders.

The Argentinian judge deserves a mention also for the evolutionary interpretation of the law, which takes into account the change in the attitude of society and its moral evolution toward the awareness of animal rights, and the role of zoos in particular.

Notwithstanding these courageous statements, as noted above, the decision of the Argentinian judge is "affected" by a serious and dangerous speciesism. The specist arguments, which had supported the action of the President of A.F.A.D.A., recur in the decision as well: "no se intenta [. . .] elevar a la categoria de personas a todos los animales o flora y fauna existente,[83] sino reconocer que los primates son personas en tanto sujetos de derechos no humanos y que ellos poseen un catálogo de derechos fundamentales [. . .]".[84]

---

[82] One may argue that the decision of the Argentinian judge was "easier" because chimpanzees are numerous while the cultural objects are sometimes unique. However, the question here is whether the living or non-living items which constitute part of the cultural heritage of a certain State can be adequately protected in that State. Could their "export" be justified in order to ensure their survival?

[83] Emphasis added.

[84] The speciesism is partly mitigated in the operative part of the decision, where the judge requested a remedy to be found for the situation of keeping in inappropriate captivity conditions all exotic species which do not belong to the geographical and climate area of the Province of Mendoza. A similar speciesism seems to characterize another national statement: on 17 May 2013, the India's Ministry of environment and forests declared cetaceans (dolphins in particular) "non-human

The judge mentioned in particular, *inter alia*, the fundamental right to be born, to live, grow and die in the environment proper for each species. In the judge's opinion, the great apes are owners of the inherent right of sentient beings and have non-human rights; they are legal persons, with legal capacity but incompetent to act. According to the judge, animals could be represented by NGOs or State organisms or by any person who claims collective or diffuse interest.

Thus, in the Argentinian decision the questions concerning the preservation of the environment, the protection of cultural heritage, the moral and ethical aspects and even human dignity are dealt with together and partially overlap, supporting each other for the wellbeing of the great apes.[85]

Cultural values and protection of animals are instead in competition—and unfortunately, the former prevail upon the latter—in Article 13 of TFEU.[86] In this provision, the status of animals as sentient beings, often mentioned in the decision concerning Cecilia, finds a relevant confirmation at the legal level. As noted above, the main consequence of this recognition is that animals can no longer be considered as things to be owned. The possibility of being owned is considered to be one of the greatest obstacles to the development of animal rights.[87] From this point of view, Article 13 may be considered as progress from the same perspective of the recognition of (national) legal personhood of natural/cultural entities. It must be noted, however, that Article 13 does not even mention animal rights and the recognition of their status as sentient beings, so warmly welcomed by animal activists, is so much impaired by other (human) prevailing interests that it risks having a very limited impact on the wellbeing of animals.[88] In conclusion, Article 13 is irrelevant for the granting of the international legal personhood.

As noted above, the Argentinian judge in the case of Cecilia did not surrender to the shortcomings of the law. Lacking a legal procedure for protecting animals, she

---

persons"; as such, they "should have their own specific rights and [it] is morally unacceptable to keep them captive for entertainment purpose". This status, however, is granted to them because of their high intelligence as compared to other animals; see Ministry of Environment & Forests, Central Zoo Authority, Policy on establishment of dolphinarium – Regarding, Circular F. NO. 20-1/2010-CZA(M)/2840. According to Gordon (2018), p. 57, note 37, it is not "clear "what specific changes to legal status this declaration gave these species".

[85] According to the judge, "*[l]a desidia humana en la omisión del estudio y profundización sobre la calidad (o no) de sujeto de derecho no humano de los grandes simios conforma un comportamiento contrario al concepto de dignitad humana, dado que el hombre debe atender a su preservación en la posteridad, la que depende primordialmente del ecosistema que la rodea. Y en el él, claramente, están los grandes simios* [. . .]".

[86] See on this point Peters (2016b), p. 38 ss.

[87] See *e.g.* Morrish (2014), pp. 1149 and 1151–1152: "Animal rights will not be taken seriously or grow if animals are incorrectly labeled as property by the law". "The property status of animals severely hinders their rights through creating confusion, inconsistencies, inadequate enforcement, and obstacles in gaining standing to sue. Because animals are considered property and standing in animal protection cases is so difficult to obtain, animal rights are going unenforced and animals are needlessly suffering".

[88] Scovazzi (2014), p. 179, refers to Article 13 as a self-defeating norm (*norma autolesionista*).

interpreted and adjusted a procedure which was conceived for human beings—the *habeas corpus* procedure, in this case—to guarantee the right of Cecilia to live in an environment and conditions appropriate for her species. In the past, the European Court of Human Rights has not demonstrated the same "flexibility" of the Argentinian judge in extending to animals—chimpanzees again—the human rights provided for in the European Convention on Human Rights. In 2008, Martin Balluch, President of the *Verein Gegen Tierfabriken* (Association against animals in factories) submitted an application to the European Court on behalf of a chimpanzee. The application was rejected by a committee of the First Chamber for incompatibility *ratione materiae;*[89] an analogous application submitted by the British animal activist, Paula Stibbe, against Austria had the same outcome.[90] The scope of such applications was mainly to obtain a statement on the status of "persons" of the chimpanzees.[91]

Beyond the provocative intent of these two attempts, it is clear that the competence of the European Court is limited by treaty to the protection of *human* rights. Despite the courage shown by the Court on some occasions in interpreting extensively the European Convention on Human Rights and in extending its scope, the extension of the competence of the Court to protect animal rights does seem too much.[92] So much so, that it goes beyond thinking the unthinkable! What the Court can do, and actually did, is to consider the needs of animals only indirectly, by protecting the ethical principles individuals may hold or the affectionate relationship that they may have with the animals they own or possess.[93]

The above few examples show that as regards the *effective* recognition of animal rights international law is still stuttering.[94]

---

[89] Balluch v. Austria, application no. 26180/08 of 4 May 2008. Staker (2017), p. 504, quoting Bevilaqua (2013) p. 79, observes that although the Court refused to hear the claim, "it nevertheless acknowledged the application, thereby indirectly lending it legitimacy". See also Sparks (2020), p. 166.

[90] Stibbe v. Austria, application no. 26188/08 of 6 May 2008.

[91] The possibility to sue "on behalf of" or "to protect the right of" animals has been analysed by US scholars in particular; see *e.g.* Sunstein (2000), esp. 1359, who suggests, *inter alia*, that "animal welfare statutes should be amended to grant a private cause of action against those who violate them, so as to allow private claimants, either human beings or animals, to supplement currently weak agency enforcement efforts" (p. 1336). See also Staker (2017) for some cases in the United States and Europe.

[92] On the inappropriateness and impossibility of extending the human rights protection system including the non-human rights see Ash (2005).

[93] This happened, for instance, in some cases concerning hunting, farming and slaughter; on the jurisprudence on hunting see Scovazzi (2013). On the protection of animals through human rights see, in general, Sparks (2020).

[94] See Robin (2016). According to Staker (2017), p. 502, despite the failures, "cases that seek to establish legal personhood for animals should continue to be pursued [...]. Even when unsuccessful, these cases help to reshape societal views regarding animal rights and welfare, paving the way for future cases and strengthening the animal advocacy movement more generally".

6 Conclusions

In the light of the above, the conclusions concerning the international legal personality of nature can only be pessimistic. At the international level, many initiatives seem to have been shipwrecked on the rocks of the binding obligations that States are reluctant to assume. Let us mention just a couple of examples. In 2017, the NGO Nature's Rights launched a European Citizens' Initiative (ECI) to propose that the rights of nature be entered onto the EU legislative agenda. The members of the NGO had prepared a draft directive,[95] which has also been reviewed by the UN Harmony with Nature experts and experts from the IUCN.[96] Article 4.1 of the draft directive provided that

> Nature shall have legal personality, be recognised as having fundamental rights that arise from its inherent dignity as the source of life and those rights shall be respected, applied and protected by the law of the Union and the laws of the Member States.[97]

Even assuming that the recognition of legal personhood was not limited to national law but extended to the wider area of the European Union, nothing in the draft directive suggests that nature can be regarded as a subject of international law. In any case, the lack of success of the initiative[98] leads to the conclusion that many States—and in particular, the EU Members—are not yet ready to recognize the legal personality of nature even at the level of national law. A shipwreck?

In May 2019, on the occasion of the European Parliamentary elections, the Liste Europe Écologie presented the text of a "traité environnemental de l'Union européenne" to be adopted by "les peuples de l'Europe".[99] The draft Treaty sets out a number of rights of nature (Article 5) and, in particular, provided that "Tout écosystème et tous les êtres vivants ont droit à être défendus en justice à travers des représentantes légaux et des mécanismes permettant aux résidentes de l'Union de saisir les tribunaux" (Article 5.3).

Notwithstanding its "visionary" character, the draft Treaty does not explicitly mention the legal personhood of nature. It goes without saying that no treaty has yet been concluded or adopted in the framework of the European Union. Another shipwreck?

It has been claimed that it is necessary to dare to turn the unthinkable into reality. As noted above, the model for thinking the unthinkable—that is the legal personhood of nature—may be what happened in the case of the extension of rights to

---

[95] The text of the draft is available at http://natures-rights.org/ECI-DraftDirective-Draft.pdf.

[96] See Mumta Ito (2017).

[97] Article 5 of the draft provided for procedural rights of nature; in particular, according to Article 5.1 "Nature possesses a fundamental right to the defence, protection, and enforcement of its rights under this Directive by any physical person acting individually or collectively, government, or non-governmental organisation of the European Union".

[98] In fact, the draft seems not to have had a following.

[99] The text of the Treaty is available at http://files.harmonywithnatureun.org/uploads/upload856.pdf.

slaves, women, black people, children, disabled individuals, etc.[100] As we have tried to illustrate, in the case of nature and animals the unthinkable is even more unthinkable.[101] The question is not simple; we have tried to point out some difficulties, first of all the fact that the aforementioned subjects belong to the same category (that is human beings) while natural/cultural entities and animals are heterogeneous. The rights and interests of individuals belonging to humankind find their limit in the rights and interests of other individuals on an equal footing. The rights and interests of nature, natural/cultural entities and animals are often competing with the rights and interests of human beings: an unfair competition indeed. As in the case of juridical persons, the conferment of legal personality to nature, natural/cultural entities and animals, if any, is "artificial", based on different factors assessed by the society (of human beings) in a certain moment.[102] Moreover, international law continues to be State-centric; every recognition of rights, duties, and legal personhood must "pass" through the will and consent of States. The fact that a certain entity is shared by two or more States, far from facilitating the recognition of rights and legal personhood to that entity and thus strengthening its protection, without an agreement between the States involved, can even lead to the nullification of measures taken at the national level. As mentioned above, this happened, for instance, for the Ganga river which extends through India into Bangladesh. A few months after the High Court decision identifying the Ganga and Yamuna as living entities, the Supreme Court of India stayed the operation of that decision. In its appeal, the State government of Uttarakhand, from which these two rivers originate, raised concerns *inter alia* about the fact that the High Court did not consider other States where the river flows, and hence it was outside the limits of the State court's jurisdiction.

No one denies that something is progressively changing in the way nature's protection is conceived. From an exclusively anthropocentric and utilitarian approach, there is a growing number of cases in which, in the context of national rights, nature is granted rights and legal personality, according to an Earth-centred approach. Attempts to reshape the relationship between human beings and nature have also been made internationally through a dual path: protecting the environment and respecting the cultural and spiritual rights of peoples. Pressures to grant rights to

---

[100] "[T]hroughout legal history, each successive extension of rights to some new entity has been, therefore, a bit unthinkable"; Stone (1972), p. 453. See also Athens (2018).

[101] Even at the national level, thinking the unthinkable sometimes works sometimes it does not. In September 2017 the *Colorado River Ecosystem/Deep Green Resistance et al. v. State of Colorado* case was filed in the Federal District Court for the recognition of personhood of the Colorado River. As the Colorado Attorney General's Office threatened serious sanctions, the plaintiff withdrew the case. The Attorney General's Office considered "the "rights of nature" case unlawful and frivolous; see on this point Walker (2017); Clark et al. (2018), pp. 818–823.

[102] As regards animals, Shelton (2015), para 23, mentions for instance "biological life, genetic humanness, brain development, ability to feel pain, consciousness/sentience, ability to communicate, ability to form relationships, higher reasoning ability, and rationality". As shown above, some of these factors underly the decision of the judge in the case of Cecilia. The factors are subjective and imply value judgments that change over time and space.

nature are strongest where the cultural link with the earth and the native spiritual traditions are most felt.[103]

If one were to construe the international legal personhood of natural entities, nature and animals on the basis of arguments similar to those that led to the considerations behind individuals becoming (perhaps) subjects of international law, the conclusion would be that certainly entities, nature, animals are not subjects. At present, no international treaty allows natural entities, nature or animals to file a complaint with international bodies, through suitable representatives.[104] And the answer to the initial question ("is the attribution of international legal personality to nature, natural/cultural entities or animals indispensable?") is: no, it is not.

However, the 1948 Universal Declaration on Human Rights demonstrates that the rights recognized in a soft law instrument may become treaty law and even customary law.[105] In the case of nature and animals the "universal" declarations are more

[103] The UN Secretary General underlined a generalized trend: "[c]ountries around the world, despite their cultural and historical differences, are converging towards a holistic relationship with Nature, specifically granting rights to Nature" UN Doc A/72/175, para 91. On the other side, some doubts concerning the correspondence between the conferral of legal personality and the way in which indigenous peoples (in Canada) conceive the relationship with the environment and its protection are expressed by Curran in Eckstein et al. (2019), pp. 12–15; moreover, as Eckstein observes (in Eckstein et al. 2019, p. 21), "whether rights of personhood recognized in rivers will lead to cleaner and more bountiful water for people and the nature is still unknown". Also Collins and Esterling (2019), pp. 213 ff., raise some doubts on the impact of the recognition of legal personality of Te Urewera and Te Awa Tupua as regards the protection of the rights of indigenous people: "the [2017 Te Awa Tupua] *Act* fails to go beyond the current ethos of human rights in its recent embrace of the Indigenous cosmovision and claims rooted in culture and identity. It does not meet the real demands of Indigenous peoples, in this case for ownership of water – a demand that might not fit succinctly into this worldview. The *Act's* focus on cultural aspects comes at the expense of claims to property and so fails to provide the real material gains that human rights law purports to offer Indigenous peoples. Consequently, the *Act* reflects the gloss but not the substance of human rights; its bark without its bite" (p. 217).

[104] It would be even more difficult to find provisions of international law which provide for criminal responsibility of natural/cultural entities. At the national level, in some cases, the law provides for possible liabilities for the entity (see *supra* Sect. 2 for the Te Urewera and the Yamuna). Indeed, the fact that an entity (or animal) has legal personhood should imply that it also has duties and liability. The problem was raised as regards the possible liability of the Ganga and Yamuna in case of flood and victims; see Alley (2020), esp. p. 30.

[105] According to Peters (2016b), pp. 51–52 "the question needs to be addressed whether animal rights would need to be endorsed at the global level, in parallel with international human rights, or should solely be enshrined in domestic law. I submit that the principled arguments which have led to the codification of human rights in international catalogues are equally relevant for potential animal rights. Firstly, from the perspective of fairness and justice, such rights (once accepted as a matter of principle) are incumbent on animals independently of their place of birth and abode. Secondly, international rights would serve as a benchmark for domestic law. International instruments would potentially allow for some monitoring of, or at least facilitate the formulation of criticism against domestic practices which do not satisfy the international standard. Thirdly, the endorsement of animal rights in only one state would probably lead to the outsourcing of the relevant industries. This risk is already present when one state has higher protective standards than others, and it could be exacerbated when one but not all states embrace a rights-based approach to

than one. Unfortunately, while the Universal Declaration on Human Rights was adopted by the General Assembly of the United Nations, made up by States, the universal declarations on nature and animals do not imply any commitment by States, not even a soft one. This is the case, for instance, of the Universal Declaration of Animal Rights[106] and of the Universal Declaration of the Rights of Mother Earth.[107] It is true that national law and jurisprudence may also contribute to the formation of international customary law but only time will tell whether and to what extent the national practice will affect international law.[108]

Finally, if States really wanted to overcome their reluctance to attributing rights and legal personality to nature, natural/cultural entities and animals, then one might even think about recognizing rights to inanimate objects. We refer, in particular, to those items which have a cultural or religious value for a certain community. This is not meant to be provocative. As regards rights and their exercise, nature, animals and inanimate objects share certain features. Even when a law, a statement, a declaration or a judgment affirm that nature, entities or animals have an intrinsic value or enjoy inherent rights, it is human beings that assess which value is intrinsic and which rights are inherent. Human beings decide the limits of these rights and their content. Human beings may decide that whales have a right to live, while cows, pigs or even dogs may be slaughtered. Nature and animals have no voice. Their representatives—as trustees or stewards or whatever they may be—are human beings that exercise the rights of nature and animals on the basis of human laws and before human judges.[109] The same could happen for cultural objects whose value would correspond to the

---

animal protection. In order to prevent a competitive disadvantage for industries subject to higher domestic standards, and in order to forestall a race to the bottom, harmonized universal standards and a level playing field must be sought. [. . .] Such harmonization is also desirable to accommodate consumers' concerns about the importation of animal products from low-standard countries, and would obviate import prohibitions based on such public morality concerns".

[106] On the proclamation of this Declaration see *supra* note 71.

[107] The Declaration was proclaimed at the World People's Conference on Climate Change and the Rights of Mother Earth held in Cochabamba, Bolivia on 22 April 2010. The Conference was convened by President of Bolivia, Evo Morales Aymaa. The draft of the declaration was submitted to the Secretary General of the United Nations by a letter dated 7 May 2010 from the Permanent Representative of Bolivia to the United Nations; see UN Doc A/64/777 of 7 May 2010. The Declaration was proclaimed by the "peoples of the Earth", not by States. Tanasescu (2015), p. 125, considers this Declaration as an example of "internationalism of the rights of nature, and their connection to human rights".

[108] It is worth noting that some scholars have raised doubts about the effective relevance of certain recognitions. For instance, according to Gordon (2018), p. 85 "Arguably, personhood for natural features in New Zealand was an easy change that changes little"; as regards the provisions of the Constitutions of Ecuador and Bolivia, she observes that "perhaps, [. . .] these revolutionary-sounding rights for nature regimes are just for show". On the problems concerning the implementation of the relevant provisions of the Bolivian Constitution see also Villavicencio Calzadilla and Kotzé (2018). See also Shelton (2015), para 25 ff.

[109] Staker (2017), p. 500, quoting Naffine (2009), pp. 9 and 11, observes that "the law 'plays critical and creative role' in making legal persons and will expand the category of personhood only to the extent that this reflects societal understandings of 'who is of value and why'".

cultural assessment of a certain community and to the need to better protect the cultural rights of such community. It is just a problem of thinking the unthinkable.

References

Alley KD (2020) River goddesses, personhood and rights of nature: implications for spiritual ecology. In: Sponsel Leslie E (ed) Religious environmental activism in Asia, case studies in spiritual ecology. MDPI, Basel, pp 19–35

Ash K (2005) International animal rights: speciesism and exclusionary human dignity. Anim Law Rev 11:195–213

Athens AK (2018) An indivisible and living whole: do we value nature enough to grant it personhood? Ecol Law Q 45:187–226

Berros MV (2017) Defending rivers: Vilcabamba in the South of Ecuador. In: Hillebrecht T, Leah A, Berros MV (eds) Can nature have rights? Legal and political insights. RCC Perspectives Transformations in Environment and Society 6, pp 37–44

Bevilaqua B (2013) Chimpanzee in court: what difference does it make? In: Otomo Y, Mussawir E (eds) Law and the question of animal: a critical jurisprudence. Routledge, London, p 79

Bieluk J (2020) River as a legal person. Studia Iuridica Lublinensia 29:11–23

Brara R (2017) Courting nature: advances in Indian jurisprudence. In: Hillebrecht T, Leah A, Berros MV (eds) Can nature have rights? Legal and political insights. RCC Perspectives Transformations in Environment and Society 6, pp 31–36

Cano Pecharroman L (2018) Rights of nature: rivers that can stand in court. Resources 7:13

Clark C et al (2018) Can you hear the rivers sing: legal personhood, ontology, and the nitty-gritty of governance. Ecol Law Q 45:787–844

Collins T, Esterling S (2019) Fluid personality: indigenous rights and the Te Awa Tupua (Whanganui River Claims Settlement) Act 2017 in Aotearoa New Zealand. Melbourne J Int Law 20:197–220

Colwell R, Carr-Wilson S (supervised by Calvin Sandborn, Calvin) (2017) Legal Personality of Natural Features: Recent International Developments and Applicability in Canada. Environmental Law Clinic University of Victoria. http://www.elc.uvic.ca/wordpress/wp-content/uploads/2018/05/2017-02-03-LegalPersonalityNatural-Features_web-version.pdf

Crawford J (2019) Brownlie's principles of public international law. Oxford University Press, Oxford

D'Amato A, Chopra SK (1991) Whales: their emerging right to life. Am J Int Law 85:21–62

Daillier P, Forteau M, Pellet A (2009) Droit international public. L.G.D.J, Paris

Eckstein G et al (2019) Conferring legal personality on the world's rivers: a brief intellectual assessment. Water International 1. https://scholarship.law.tamu.edu/facscholar/1321

Feria-Tinta M, Milnes SC (2019) International environmental law for the 21st century: the constitutionalization of the right to a healthy environment in the Inter-American Court of Human Rights Advisory Opinion 23. Anuario Colombiano de Derecho Internacional (Colombian Yearbook of Int L Law) 12:43–84

Gordon GJ (2018) Environmental personhood. Columbia J Environ Law 43:49–91

Gorski S (2013) Individuals in international law. Max Planck Encyclopedia of Public International Law

Grear A (ed) (2012) Should trees have standing? 40 Years on. Edward Elgar, Cheltenham

Korsgaard C (2013) Personhood, animals, and the law. Think 12:25–32. https://doi.org/10.1017/S1477175613000018

Lillo A (2018) Is water simply a flow: exploring an alternative mindset for recognizing water as a legal person. Vermont J Environ Law 19:164–190

Lima LC (2020) The protection of the environment before the Inter-American Court of Human Rights: recent developments. Rivista Giuridica dell'Ambiente 35:495–522

Māori Law Review. October 2014 – Whiringa-ā-nuku 2014. Special issue - The Tūhoe-Crown Settlement. https://www.ngaituhoe.iwi.nz/vdb/document/77

McCorquodale R (2014) The individual and the International Legal System. In: Evans MD (ed) International law, 4th edn. Oxford University Press, Oxford, pp 280-305

Morrish LM (2014) The elephant in the room: detrimental effects of animals' property status on standing in animal protection cases. Santa Clara Law Rev 53:1127–1154

Mumta Ito (2017) Nature's rights: a new paradigm for environmental protection. Ecologist. https://theecologist.org/2017/may/09/natures-rights-new-paradigm-environmental-protection

Naffine N (2009) Law's meaning of life: philosophy, religion, Darwin and the legal person. Hart, pp 9 and 11

Naffine N (2012) Legal personality and the natural world: on the persistence of the human measure of value. In: Anna G (ed) Should trees have standing? 40 Years on. Edward Elgar, Cheltenham, pp 68–83

Neumann J-M (2012) The universal declaration of animal rights or the creation of a new equilibrium between species. Anim Law 19:91–104

O'Donnell E, Talbot-Jones J (2018) Creating legal rights for rivers: lessons from Australia, New Zealand, and India. Ecol Soc 23:7. https://doi.org/10.5751/ES-09854-230107

Peters A (2016a) Beyond human rights. Cambridge University Press, Cambridge

Peters A (2016b) Liberté, Égalité, Animalité: human-animal comparisons in law. Transnatl Environ Law 5:25–54

Peters A (2020a) Animals in international law. Recueil des cours de l'Académie de droit international 410:95–544

Peters A (2020b) Toward international animal rights. In: Peters A (ed) Studies in global animal law. Springer, Heidelberg, pp 109–120

Portmann R (2010) Legal personality in international law. Cambridge University Press, Cambridge

Robin D-S (2016) Statut et bien-être des animaux: quelques remarques sur les balbutiements d'un droit international animalier. Revue du droit international 143:455–485

Rodgers C (2017) A new approach to protecting ecosystems: The Te Awa Tupua (Whanganui River Claims Settlement) Act 2017. Environ Law Rev 19:266–279

Sajal IA (2019) A strengthening the National River Conservation Commission of Bangladesh. The Daily Star

Schabas WA (2015) The European Convention on Human Rights - a commentary. Oxford University Press, New York

Schaffner JE (2011) An introduction to animals and the law. Palgrave Macmillan, Basingstoke

Scovazzi T (1994) T Kawanatanga e Rangatiratanga: a proposito del Trattato di Waitangi. Rivista di Diritto Internazionale 78:725–736

Scovazzi T (2009) La restituzione dell'obelisco di Axum e della Venere di Cirene. n Rivista di Diritto Internazionale Privato e Processuale 45:555–566

Scovazzi T (2011) Diviser c'est Détruire: Ethical principles and legal rules in the field of return of cultural property. Rivista di Diritto Internazionale 94:341–395

Scovazzi T (2013) Un'altra sentenza della Corte Europea dei Diritti Umani in tema di caccia su terreni altrui. Rivista Giuridica dell'Ambiente 28:117–124

Scovazzi T (2014) Art. 13. In: Pocar F, Baruffi MC (a cura di) Commentario breve ai Trattati dell'Unione Europea. Cedam, Padova pp 177–181

Scovazzi T (a cura di) (2015) Corso di diritto internazionale. Parte II. Giuffrè, Milano

Scovazzi T (2019) La Corte interamericana dei diritti umani svolge una trattazione sistematica del diritto umano a un ambiente sano. Rivista Giuridica dell'Ambiente 34:713–706

Shaw MN (2014) International law. Cambridge University Press, Cambridge

Sheber K (2020) Legal rights for nature: how the idea of recognizing nature as a legal entity can spread and make a difference globally. Hastings Environ Law J 26:147–168

Shelton D (2015) Nature as a legal person. VertigO – la revue électronique en sciences de l'environnement http://journals.openedition.org/vertigo/16188. https://doi.org/10.4000/vertigo.16188
Sparks T (2020) Protection of animals through human rights: the case-law of the European Court of Human Rights. In: Peters A (ed) Studies in global animal law. Springer, Heidelberg, pp 153–171
Staker A (2017) Should chimpanzee have standing? The case for pursuing legal personhood for non-human animals. Transnatl Environ Law 6:485–508
Stone CD (1972) Should trees have standing? – Toward legal rights for natural objects. South Calif Law Rev 45:450–501
Stone CD (1996) Should trees have standing? And other essays on law, morals and the environment. Dobbs Ferry, Oceana Publications, New York
Stone CD (2012) Response to commentators. In: Grear A (ed) Should trees have standing? 40 Years on. Edward Elgar, Cheltenham, pp 100–120
Sunstein CR (2000) Standing for animals (with notes on animal rights). UCLA Law Rev 47:1333–1368
Tanasescu M (2015) Environment, political representation, and the challenge of rights. Palgrave Macmillan, London
Totten T (2015) Should elephants have standing? West J Leg Stud 6:1–16
Treves T (2019) The expansion of international law. Recueil des cours de l'Académie de droit international 398:9–398
Vallejo Galárraga S (2019) The international legal personhood of nature and other ecosystems: a legal approach based on ecocentric ethics. Dissertation, University of Szeged. http://www.juris.u-szeged.hu/download.php?docID=90638
Villavicencio Calzadilla P (2019) A paradigm shift in courts' view on nature: the Atrato River and Amazon Basin cases in Colombia. Law Environ Dev J (LEAD J) 15:1–11
Villavicencio Calzadilla P, Kotzé LJ (2018) Living in harmony with nature? A critical appraisal of the rights of Mother Earth in Bolivia. Transnatl Environ Law 7:397–424
Walker C (2017) Attorney to withdraw Colorado River Lawsuit under threat of sanctions. Westword. https://www.westword.com/news/colorado-river-lawsuit-to-be-withdrawn-due-to-potential-sanctions-9746311
Walter C (2007) Subjects of international law. Max Planck Encyclopedia of Public International Law
Warnock M (2012) Should trees have standing? In: Grear A (ed) Should trees have standing? 40 Years on. Edward Elgar, Cheltenham, pp 56–67

Climate Change and Intercommunal Conflicts in West Africa: A New Challenge for the UN System of Collective Security or Much Ado About Nothing?

Laura Pineschi

Abstract Several UN documents have identified climate trends as a security concern in recent years. A remarkable development can be seen in the incorporation by the UN of the climate change issue within its security dimension, through the unanimous adoption of recent UNSC resolutions. But what is the extent of the UNSC commitment to address intercommunal conflicts exacerbated by climate related effects in the Sahel region? What are the legal and practical implications of the UNSC recommendations for the UN and its subsidiary bodies in areas characterized by generalized State weaknesses and weak enforcement of the rule of law? Has the UNSC really succeeded in ensuring an adequate integrated approach to multidimensional threats in the Sahel? The present contribution tries to answer these questions by analyzing selected provisions of UNSC Resolution 2423 (2018), concerning the situation in Mali, and their implementation. In a tentative conclusion, a few reflections will be developed on the possible impact of the UNSC approach to climate security threats in the Sahel on the evolution of the UN system of collective security: new wine in old bottles or a first step towards a change in the overall security architecture of the Organization?

1 Introduction

In recent years, intercommunal conflicts characterised by unprecedented violence have grown at an alarming rate in various parts of West Africa and the Sahel.[1] Although the frequency and severity of conflicts differ within various States in the

[1]For an accurate survey on the situation in Burkina Faso, Guinea, Mali, Mauritania, Niger and Nigeria, see the report of the United Nations Office for West Africa and the Sahel (UNOWAS) on *Pastoralism and Security in West Africa and the Sahel: Towards Peaceful Coexistence. UNOWAS Study*, 2018 (hereinafter: *UNOWAS Study*). On violent clashes between Arab (herders) and

L. Pineschi (✉)
Department of Law, Politics and International Studies, Center for Studies in European and International Affairs (CSEIA), University of Parma, Parma, Italy
e-mail: laura.pineschi@unipr.it

M. Arcari et al. (eds.), *Trends and Challenges in International Law*,
https://doi.org/10.1007/978-3-030-94387-5_9

region, violent clashes usually break out in areas affected by structural instability, as for instance in Mali, where the implementation of the Peace Agreement of 2015[2] is progressing very slowly.[3]

In Central Mali—and, in particular, in the Mopti region—43 attacks were documented in 2018 between Fulani herders (the largest pastoralist group spread across West Africa and the Sahel) and farmers of the Dogon community.[4] A peace agreement was concluded by more than 30 leaders of the two communities in August 2018;[5] nevertheless, large scale massacres and retaliatory attacks occurred in the months following. In 2019, the deadliest assault took place in Ogossagou, a village of the Mopti region where at least 145 civilians of the Fulani community were killed and 95 per cent of the houses were burned down.[6] According to a preliminary investigation by the *United Nations Multidimensional Integrated Stabilization Mission in Mali* (MINUSMA), the attack was planned, organised and coordinated and could amount to a crime against humanity.[7] Dogon villages in the same region were assaulted by Fulani "self-defence" groups in June 2019[8] and violence against Dogon communities also continued in Burkina Faso, Mali and Niger in 2020.[9]

non-Arab (farmers) communities in the eastern Chad in 2019, see International Crisis Group, *Avoiding Resurgence of Intercommunal Violence in Eastern Chad*, Report No. 284, December 2019. More generally, see Day and Caus (2020).

[2] *Accord pour la paix et la réconciliation au Mali issu du processus d'Alger*, https://peacemaker.un.org.

[3] See e.g.: *Final Report of the Panel of Experts established pursuant to Security Council resolution 2374 (2017) on Mali and renewed pursuant to resolution 2484 (2019)*, UN Doc. S/2020/785, 13 August 2020. See also infra, Sect. 5.1.

[4] See e.g. UN Doc.S/2018/273, 29 March 2018, para 41.

[5] Text available in French at: https://www.hdcentre.org/wp-content/uploads/2018/08/Accord-de-paix-entre-les-communautés-Dogon-et-Peulh-du-cercle-de-Koro-28-août-2018.pdf.

[6] UN Doc. S/2019/782, 1 October 2019, para 35. A second attack against Ogossogou was launched on 14 February 2020: 35 civilians of the Fulani community, including women and children were killed and horribly mutilated, while over 19 other civilians remain unaccounted for. UN Doc. S/2020/785, p. 8. For further details see Human Rights Watch, *Mali: Army, UN Fail to Stop Massacre. Second Militia Attack on Ogossagou Village Killed at least 35*, 18 March 2020, available at https://www.hrw.org/news/2020/03/18/mali-army-un-fail-stop-massacre.

[7] UN Doc. S/2019/782, para 35. In March 2019, the Prosecutor of the International Criminal Court (ICC), Fatou Bensouda, declared that her Office "will take all necessary steps to ensure the investigation and prosecution of those who participated in or otherwise contributed to what appears to be egregious crimes which may fall under the jurisdiction of the (...) ICC", available at https://www.icc-cpi.int/Pages/item.aspx?name=190325-otp-stat-mali. See also the joint Statement on attacks against civilians in Central Mali by the UN Special Adviser on the Prevention of Genocide, the UN Special Adviser on Responsibility to Protect and the Special Representative of the Secretary-General for Children and Armed Conflict, Press release, 12 June 2019, https://peacekeeping.un.org/en/joint-statement-attacks-against-civilians-central-mali-united-nations-special-advisers-prevention-of.

[8] UN Doc. S/2019/782, para 68.

[9] UN Doc. S/2020/785, pp. 8–9. It may be useful to recall that "(...) members of Fulani communities are stigmatized as members of extremist groups and lumped together with them, and (...) members of the Dogon community are cast as traditional hunters in the pay of the State", *Report of*

Violent clashes among nomadic pastoralists and sedentary farmers across the Sahel region are driven and exacerbated by various economic, political and social issues, including poverty, a strong overpopulation[10] and the widespread presence, in the whole region, of violent extremists, who find in local conflicts fertile ground for their expansion strategies.[11] In addition, in the absence of a State authority and with the proliferation of small arms and light weapons, self-defence groups grow stronger and contribute to fuelling the situation of insecurity.

Other serious factors, however, may be regarded as part of the root causes of local tensions between herders and farmers. In particular, increased competition for land, water and other natural resources is exacerbated by climate-related effects (*i.e.* drought, desertification, land degradation and food insecurity), as various United Nations (UN) documents,[12] including Presidential Statements of the UN Security Council (UNSC), explicitly recognise.

In this context, the incorporation of climate change as a security issue in some UNSC resolutions unanimously adopted deserves special consideration. Although the Council has been debating the climate change issue since 2007,[13] its legitimacy and role in addressing this topic remains contentious for some States.[14] In addition, various regional organizations, including the African Union (AU),[15] European Union (EU)[16] and NATO,[17] have shown increasing attention to the security

---

the Independent Expert on the situation of human rights in Mali to the Human Rights Council, UN Doc. A/HRC/40/77, 21 January 2019, para 42.

[10] "In the Sahel, where the average age of marriage can be as low as 14 and women [have on] average six or seven children, the population is growing more rapidly than the food supply or the economy. The population of the Sahel could jump from just over 100 million today to between 250 and 300 million by 2050", People and the Planet, *World Must Wake up to the Coming Crisis in the Sahel*, 2020. http://unohrlls.org/news/world-must-wake-up-to-the-coming-crisis-in-the-sahel/.

[11] See e.g. UN Doc. A/HRC/40/77, 21 January 2019, para 42: "The formation of a new armed, self-styled self-defence group for the Fulani community, l'Alliance pour le Salut au Sahel (. . .), has been announced on social networks, and the activities of the brotherhoods of traditional hunters, or dozos, have gradually shifted to the defence of the Dogon community or to attacks that are increasingly targeting members of the Fulani community". See also UN Doc. S/2019/983, 30 December 2019, para 51, and UN Doc. S/2020/476, 2 June 2020, para 100.

[12] See e.g. *Activities of the United Nations Office for West Africa and the Sahel. Report of the Secretary-General*, UN Doc. S/2019/1005, 30 December 2019, para 95. According to the UN Secretary-General report on the situation in Mali of December 2020, the combined effect of the COVID-19 pandemic, the inter-community violence and climate change, the number of internally displaced persons increased from 287,496 in July to 311,193 in October 2020. Some 143,300 Malian refugees remained in neighbouring countries, UN Doc. S/2020/1281, 28 December 2020, para 80.

[13] See infra, Sect. 3.

[14] See infra, Sect. 3.

[15] See Aminga (2000); Aminga and Krampe (2000).

[16] See Far and Youngs (2018); Fetzek and van Schaik (2018); Bremberg (2019); Bremberg et al. (2019).

[17] See Lippert (2019).

dimension of climate change in recent years. The same issue has also been included in their strategies or has been the subject of *ad hoc* measures. The implications are however quite different, due to the primary responsibility in maintaining international peace and security that the UN Charter has conferred to the UNSC under Article 24.

Against this background, it may be useful to explore whether, and to what extent, climate change in its security dimension has been addressed by the Council with regard to the Sahel region. In particular, starting from the assumption that "Security in Mali has an impact on the entire Sahel, which in turn affects global stability",[18] the attention will be focused on some selected provisions of UNSC Resolution 2423 (2018) of 28 June 2018, providing for the consideration of the security implications of climate change and other ecological changes when activities, programmes and strategies in Mali are planned and implemented.

To this end, a few preliminary remarks will be made on climate change and its security implications in West Africa and the UNSC's approach to tensions and instability exacerbated by climate-related effects in the Sahel region. The legal and practical implications of relevant provisions of Resolution 2423 (2018) will be then examined with regard to the Malian government and the UN. An overall assessment will ultimately be made of the UNSC's approach to the challenge of climate securitization in the Sahel and its possible impact on the evolution of the UN system of collective security: new wine in old bottles or a first step towards a change in the security architecture of the Organization?

2 Changes in Climate Trends and Security Implications in West Africa and the Sahel

The existence of a mutual interconnection between security and environmental degradation was clearly highlighted in the 1987 Report of the World Commission on Environment and Development (hereinafter: *Brundtland Report*) on *Our Common Future*: "Environmental stress is both a cause and an effect of political tension and military conflict".[19] The document also underscored that, although "[e]

[18] UN Doc. S/2019/454, 31 May 2019, para 92. See also the Statement by the President of the Security Council on *Peace Consolidation in West Africa* of 7 August 2019, UN Doc. S/PRST/2019/7, para 7.

[19] UN Doc. A/42/427, 4 August 1987, Annex, Chapter 11, para 2, 286. See also the Rio Declaration on Environment and Development, UN Doc. A/CONF.151/26 (Vol. I), 12 August 1992 (hereinafter: Rio Declaration), Principle 25 ("Peace, development and environmental protection are interdependent and indivisible"). On the consideration of "environmental security" within the outcome of the UN Conference on Environment and Development (Rio de Janeiro, 3–14 June, 1992), the World Summit on Sustainable Development (Johannesburg, 26 August–4 September 2002), and the UN Conference on Sustainable Development (Rio+20) (Rio de Janeiro, 20–22 June 2012), see Ebbesson (2014), p. 74 ff.

nvironmental stress is seldom the only cause of major conflicts within or among nations (...)", it "can be (...) an important part of the web of causality associated with any conflict and can in some cases be catalytic".[20]

What is more difficult to prove is the existence of a direct causal link between climate change and conflicts. On the one hand, there is still a lack of consensus among scholars about the origins of some climatic variables and their effects. On the other hand, it is very arduous to predict conflict occurrences as the causes of conflict are so numerous so as to make the use of any econometric model ineffective.[21]

There is, however, a growing consensus on a basic assumption. As the UN Secretary-General emphasised in his report on *Climate change and its possible security implications* in 2009:

> (...) the fact that quantitative studies fail to confirm statistically significant links between environmental factors and conflict does not mean they do not exist. Rather, environmental factors may exacerbate conflict dynamics and risk through multiple and indirect pathways, interacting in complex ways with social, political, and economic factors, which tend to be more direct and proximate drivers of armed conflict.[22]

Accordingly, climate change was identified as a "threat multiplier", *i.e.* "as a factor that can work through several channels (...) to exacerbate existing sources of conflict and insecurity".[23] The security dimension of climate-related effects will therefore be considered from this perspective with specific reference to the Sahel.

Indeed, the five countries in the West African Sahel (Burkina Faso, Chad, Mali, Mauritania, Niger and Nigeria) make only a modest contribution to global warming.[24] By contrast, they are among the most vulnerable to climate change,[25] because of the overall status of food, water, environment, health, and infrastructure in their territories.[26] More generally, during the last decades, the Sahel region has been affected by a consistent increase in temperature (between 1.5 °C and 2 °C in far eastern Chad and the northern regions of Mali and Mauritania)[27] and by extreme

---

[20] "Brundtland Report", para 5, 287.

[21] See e.g. "Climate change and its possible security implications. Report of the Secretary-General", UN Doc. A/64/350, 11 September 2009, para 64 and Gray (2012), p. 221. More generally, on the need to avoid dangerous automatisms between conflicts and climate change, see Venturi and Barana (2021).

[22] Ibidem, para 67. See also UNEP, From Conflict to Peacebuilding: The Role of Natural Resources and Environment, February 2009 (hereinafter: 'UNEP Report 2009'), 5.

[23] 'Climate change', ibidem, para 13.

[24] See e.g. Ministry of Foreign Affairs of the Netherlands, 'Climate Change Profile. West African Sahel', April 2018.

[25] "[A]ll but one of the Sahel countries (Nigeria) rank among the 20% most vulnerable to climate change, and three (Burkina Faso, Chad, Mali) are among the most vulnerable 10%", ibid, p. 4.

[26] Ibidem, p. 4.

[27] See e.g. UNEP, 'Livelihood Security, Climate Change, Migration and Conflict in the Sahel', 2011 (hereinafter: 'UNEP Report 2011'), pp. 30–34.

events, including a substantial variability in precipitation, with a persistence of drought,[28] on the one hand, and torrential rains and frequent flooding on the other.[29] Flooding and draught can lead to major crop losses, serious food crisis[30] and massive displacement.[31] A lack of available grassland can also force nomadic herders to move earlier than usual, with consequent "(. . .) increased competition for resources and the destruction of crops before they have been harvested in the receiving areas"[32] that may lead to conflicts with local farmers.[33]

Clashes among nomadic pastoralists and sedentary farmers across West African Sahel have occasionally occurred for centuries; however, increased competition over natural resources is triggering a growing number of conflicts:

> Although pastoralists have traditionally migrated southwards along established livestock pathways, agriculturalists often spread their cultivation onto these pathways, preventing the safe passage of herds. Some studies have found that such planting can be considered a deliberate act of 'claiming' the space and diverting pastoralists. Often with the same deliberation, pastoralists will 'ignore' their animals, allowing them to graze within the claimed farmland.[34]

What is more, in recent years, intercommunal violence has been characterised by unprecedented levels of magnitude and brutality.[35]

Local tensions in relation to access to available natural resources are also fuelled and exacerbated by factors that are not determined by climate change including, for instance, strong overpopulation. The widespread presence, in the whole region, of violent extremists and armed groups who find in local conflicts fertile ground for their expansion strategies[36] is equally remarkable. In this context, the recruitment of

[28] As highlighted by the 'UNEP Report 2011' (ibidem, p. 38), large areas of Chad, Mali, Mauritania and Niger faced between six and ten drought seasons between 1982 and 2009.

[29] The entirety of Burkina Faso, a large part of Southern Niger and southern Chad experienced between seven and eight floods from 1985 to 2009. Over the same period, large parts of Mali, Niger and Chad were affected by five to six floods; for further details see: *UNEP Report 2011*, 39. In Mali, in 2020, seasonal floods affected 80,760 persons, killed 18 and injured 25, damaged 6478 houses, destroyed 7030 tons of food and washed away 274 hectares of crops, UN Doc. S/2020/1281, para 83.

[30] For a detailed account see: UN Doc. S/2018/541, 6 June 2018, para 45.

[31] See e.g. 'UNEP Report 2011', p. 46.

[32] Ibidem, p. 56. See also *Report of the Secretary-General in the Sahel region*, UN Doc. S/2013/354, 14 June 2013, paras. 13–14.

[33] This situation may have devastating implications on the area of the inland delta of the Niger River—*i.e.* the largest wetland in Western Africa, mostly covered by the population of the Mopti region—whose seasonal flooding supports fisheries, pasture, and rice farming. See e.g.: USGS (United States Geological Survey), *Inland Delta of the Niger River, Mali*, https://eros.usgs.gov/image-gallery/earthshot/inland-delta-of-the-niger-river-mali.

[34] 'UNEP Report 2011', p. 60.

[35] 'Report of the Independent Expert on the situation of human rights in Mali', UN Doc. A/HRC/43/76, 15 January 2020, para 45.

[36] On the deterioration of the situation in Central Mali for the continued expansion of terrorist groups, see e.g. UN Doc. S/2020/223, 20 March 2020, para 38.

Fulani herders by terrorist groups,[37] on the one hand, and the forced enrolment of Dogon villagers by Dan Nan Ambassagou (the Dogon self-defence militia) into its ranks,[38] on the other, are a significant example of the exploitation of divisions within communities.

In conclusion, the inextricable link between climate-related effects and other manifold threats requires an integrated and comprehensive approach, which goes well beyond the capacity and resources of a weak national regime. But if that is indeed the case, what is the strategy that the UNSC has adopted to deal with a problem of this complexity? And above all, what powers may be used by the Council to address these new challenges according to an integrated and comprehensive approach?

3 The Security Council Approach to Climate Change and Security Challenges in the Sahel Region

During the last two decades, the issue of the possible implications of climate change for international peace and security has been addressed by the UNSC in various "open debates",[39] "briefings"[40] and "Arria-Formula meetings".[41] The first meeting was held in 2007, when the United Kingdom invited the other members of the

[37] 'Activities of the United Nations Office for West Africa and the Sahel. Report of the Secretary-General', UN Doc. S/2019/1005, 30 December 2019, paras. 36 and 89.

[38] UN Doc. S/2020/952, 29 September 2020, para 33.

[39] On the first open debate, see infra note 42. The subsequent open debates were organized by Germany (UN Doc. S/PV.6587, 20 July 2011), Sweden (*Maintenance of international peace and security. Understanding and addressing climate-related security risks*, UN Doc. S/PV.8307, 11 July 2018), and the Dominican Republic (*Addressing the impacts of climate-related disasters on international peace and security*, UN Doc. S/PV.8451, 25 January 2019).

[40] See e.g. the briefing with Dan Smith, Director of SIPRI, organized in February 2020 by the Belgian Presidency of the UNSC, on the particular obstacles that climate change is creating to the UN Mission in Somalia (UNSOM), https://www.sipri.org/media/press-release/2020/sipri-briefs-un-security-council-climate-related-security-risks-somalia.

[41] *Security dimensions of climate change* (15 February 2013); *Climate change as a threat multiplier for global security* (30 June 2015); *Security implications of climate change: sea level rise* (10 April 2017); *Climate change: preparing for security implications of rising temperatures* (14 December 2017); *Climate and security risks: the latest data* (22 April 2020). The "Arria-Formula meetings" consist of very informal meetings of the UNSC members with various stakeholders (e.g. member States not represented in the Council; representatives of intergovernmental and non governmental organizations; high level UN officials). For further information see: *UN Security Council Working Methods. Arria-Formula Meetings*, in *Security Council Report*, 16 July 2020.

Council to hold an open debate to "explor[e] the relationship between energy, security and climate",[42] with no formal outcome.[43]

Various open debates on climate change and security have been held at the UNSC in the subsequent years. In particular, remarkable progress was made in 2011, when, through a statement of its President, the Council expressed concern "(. . .) that possible adverse effects of climate change may, in the long run, aggravate certain existing threats to international peace and security".[44] The UNSC also noted that:

> (. . .) in matters relating to the maintenance of international peace and security under its consideration, conflict analysis and contextual information on, *inter alia*, possible security implications of climate change is important, when such issues are drivers of conflict, represent a challenge to the implementation of Council mandates or endanger the process of consolidation of peace.[45]

It cannot be overlooked, however, that the legitimacy of the UNSC to address climate change has been contested by some States. In particular, China considers that this issue should be tackled within the intergovernmental framework of the UN Climate Change Convention (UNFCC),[46] in accordance with the principle of common but differentiated responsibilities.[47] In the opinion of the Russian Federation, "(. . .) the Council has neither the specialized expertise nor the tools to put together viable solutions for effectively combating climate change".[48] Accordingly, the UNSC should avoid any conflict with other competent organs, in strict compliance with the general principle of the "division of labour" among the UN bodies.[49]

With respect to the Sahel, climate-related effects on the security of the region have been raised during the most recent UNSC open debates.[50] In particular, various Presidential statements, expressing concern over "the security and political challenges to the stability and development of the Sahel region", have highlighted the Council's "(. . .) continued commitment to address all these challenges, which are

---

[42] UN Doc. S/2007/186, 5 April 2007, Annex, 2. The open debate was held on 17 April 2007; for the verbatim records see UN Doc. S/PV.5663, 17 April 2007.

[43] UN Doc. S/2007/186, 1. On the evolution of the debate on the climate issue by the UNSC, see in particular: Scott and Ku (2018), p. 11 ff.; Koivurova (2014), p. 171 ff.; and Conca (2019).

[44] Statement by the President of the Security Council, UN Doc. S/SPRST/2011/2015, 20 July 2011, 1.

[45] UN Doc. S/SPRST/2011/2015, 2.

[46] United Nations Framework Convention on Climate Change (New York, 9 May 1992). Text available at https://unfccc.int/files/essential_background/background_publications_htmlpdf/application/pdf/conveng.pdf.

[47] Rio Declaration, Principle 7.

[48] UN Doc. S/PV.8307, p. 16.

[49] Ibidem. On the UNSC competence to address (and engage in) climate change as a security issue, see: Szasz (1992); Tinker (1992); Malone (1996); Reilly (1996); Elliott (2005); Gray (2012); Koivurova (2014); Scott (2015); Davies and Riddell (2017); Binder and Heupel (2018); Kravik (2018). On various approaches by countries or groups of countries to the topic, see: Sindico (2007); Scott (2018).

[50] See e.g. UN Doc. S/PV.8307, pp. 6–7.

interrelated with humanitarian and development issues as well as the *adverse effects of climate and ecological changes*".[51] In August 2018, after the publication of a study on *Pastoralism and Security in West Africa and the Sahel* by UNOWAS,[52] a Presidential statement for the first time mentioned intercommunal conflicts and linked these tensions, *inter alia*, to the climate issue.[53]

The subsequent year, the Secretary-General was invited to present recommendations to the Council

> on potential areas of improvement or new or refocused priorities, including (...) *effects of climate change on security, intercommunal violence* as part of a broad prevention and sustaining peace agenda.[54]

The most significant development, however, is represented by the inclusion of the consideration of climate-related effects, as a security concern, within some UNSC resolutions. The first to be adopted was Resolution 2349 (2017) on Lake Chad Basin, where the Council recognised "(...) the adverse effects of *climate change and ecological changes* among other factors on the stability of the Region, including through water scarcity, drought, desertification, land degradation, and food insecurity". It also emphasised the need for "adequate risk assessments and risk management strategies by governments and the United Nations relating to these factors".[55]

From 2018 onward, similar language was used by some UNSC resolutions extending the mandate of certain peacekeeping operations.[56] In particular, in the preamble of Resolution 2423 (2018), relating to the situation in Mali and the renewal of the mandate of MINUSMA, the Council expressly recognized: "(...) the adverse effects of climate change, ecological changes and natural disasters, among other factors, on the stability of Mali, including through drought, desertification, land degradation and food insecurity".[57] What is more, in the operative para. 68 of the resolution, under the general heading "Environmental issues", the Council recommended that the Government of Mali and the United Nations "(...) take into

---

[51] Statement by the President of the Security Council, UN Doc. S/SPRST/2015/24, 8 December 2015, para 1 (emphasis added).

[52] See *supra*, note 1.

[53] "The Security Council expresses its concern for *increased tensions between pastoralists and farmers* in the region driven by competition for natural resources, rapid population growth, weak governance, pressures related to *climate and ecological factors*, and the circulation of small arms and light weapons", UN Doc. S/PRST/2018/6, 10 August 2018, p. 3 (emphasis added).

[54] Statement by the President of the Security Council, UN Doc. S/PRST/2019/7, p. 1 (emphasis added).

[55] UN Doc. S/RES/2349 (2017), 31 March 2017, para 26 (emphasis added).

[56] See e.g. UNSC Resolution 2408 (2018), 27 March 2018, concerning UNSOM and Resolution 2431 (2018), 30 July 2018, concerning AMISOM (*African Union Mission in Somalia*), preamble, 3. Both resolutions were unanimously adopted. On UNSC Resolution 2349 (2017) and 2408 (2018), see: Kravik (2018).

[57] UN Doc. S/RES/2423 (2018), 28 June 2018, preamble, 4. The same wording characterized the preamble of Resolution 2429 (2018), 13 July 2018, concerning UNAMID (*United Nations-African Union Hybrid Operation in Darfur*).

consideration, as appropriate, the security implications of the adverse effects of climate change and other ecological changes and natural disasters, among other factors, in their activities, programs and strategies in Mali".[58]

Apparently, the wording of UNSC Resolution 2423 (2018), para. 68, is plain and clear. It may be useful, however, to better explore its exact implications at the legal and practical level. To this end, some thoughts will be developed on: (1) the object and purpose of this provision; (2) its legal nature; and (3) its addressees.

4 Legal Implications of Resolution 2423 (2018)

4.1 Object and Purpose

The prevention of climate change falls under the scope of various multilateral environmental agreements (MEAs), primarily, the UNFCC,[59] its Kyoto Protocol[60] and the Paris Agreement of 2015.[61] The UNSC and its member States have consistently stressed that the UNFCC legal system remains the multilateral frame of reference for the fight against climate change.[62] Therefore, all States parties to the Paris Agreement, including Mali,[63] are under the duty to reduce greenhouse gas emissions. Developed countries are also required to assist developing countries (for instance, Mali) with regard to the implementation of their mitigation and adaptation duties (Article 9) and to strengthen their co-operative efforts on technology development and transfer to improve resilience to climate change and to reduce greenhouse gas emissions (Article 10).

More controversial is, first, whether the UNSC has the legal authority to characterise climate change and its security consequences as threats to international peace and security[64] and, second, whether the Council can adopt enforcement measures to address these challenges.[65]

---

[58] Resolution 2423 (2018), para 68.

[59] See supra n. 46.

[60] Kyoto Protocol to the UN Framework Convention on Climate Change (Kyoto, 11 December 1997), entered into force on 16 February 2005; text available at https://unfccc.int/sites/default/files/resource/docs/cop3/l07a01.pdf.

[61] The Paris Agreement of 12 December 2015 entered into force on 4 November 2016; text available at: https://unfccc.int/files/essential_background/convention/application/pdf/english_paris_agreement.pdf.

[62] See e.g. the statement by the President of the Security Council, UN Doc. S/PRST/2011/15, para 3.

[63] Mali ratified the Paris Agreement on 26 September 2016. However, as with other countries of the Sahel region (see *supra*, Sect. 2), Mali is more a victim than a producer of greenhouse gases.

[64] On this issue, see e.g. Penny (2018), p. 39.

[65] In particular, see: Boyle et al. (2019).

A wide-ranging debate has been sparked in relation to these issues over the last few decades.[66] Suffice it here to stress—to avoid any misunderstanding—that the purpose of Resolution 2423 (2018), para. 68, is not to prevent climate change and other natural disasters either in the Sahel region or at the global level, but to address conflicts associated with the consequences of climate change at their roots. The UNSC resolution was adopted on the finding that the situation in Mali (*not climate change*) "continues to constitute a threat to international peace and security".[67] Therefore, the attention of the Council was focused on security challenges causing instability in Mali, including *inter alia* those associated with climate related effects. As a result, the purpose of the UNSC was not to combat climate change, characterised as a threat to peace a security, but to prevent or contain conflicts, *i.e.* a situation which traditionally falls within the primary responsibility of the UNSC to maintain international peace and security (Article 24 of the UN Charter).

Nonetheless, it is worth noting that the provision at hand was not accepted without controversy. Resolution 2423 (2018) was unanimously approved; however, the representative of the Russian Federation, who chaired the meeting, stressed that the resolution was supported by Russia for "(. . .) the importance of maintaining consensus in the Security Council and on the understanding that in helping the Malian authorities to rectify the situation in the country, MINUSMA is carrying out a very important task".[68] Yet, the inclusion of a provision on climate and other environmental issues was criticised as a *coup* made by the so-called penholders, e.g. the UNSC members who produced the draft resolution:[69]

> (. . .) We would like to draw the Council's attention to the resolution's provisions on climate and ecological issues. We believe that this issue, as it has always been, comes under the purview of the relevant bodies of the General Assembly and the Economic and Social Council. (. . .) the Council has neither the mandate nor the necessary expertise to deal with such issues. Its main aim, as established in the Charter of the United Nations, is to examine issues that directly relate to peace and security. Unfortunately, our reasoning on this, which other delegations also talked about during the negotiations on the resolution, was not taken into consideration. This is therefore another de facto case of penholders abusing their rights.[70]

In the subsequent year, when the mandate of MINUSMA was further extended, the recommendation to the Malian government and the UN relating to climate change was not renewed. Only a general reference to the issue, "among other factors", was placed in the preamble of Resolution 2480 (2019), where the UNSC emphasised

> (. . .) the need for adequate risk assessment and risk management strategies, by the government of Mali and the United Nations, of ecological changes, natural disasters, drought,

[66] For an in-depth study of the topic, see contributions mentioned above, note 43.

[67] Resolution 2423 (2018), preamble.

[68] UN Doc. S/PV.8298, 28 June 2018, p. 5.

[69] On this practice see e.g: 'The Penholder System, Security Council Report' (2018) No. 3, 21 December 2018 and Loiselle (2020).

[70] UN Doc. S/PV.8298, p. 5.

> desertification, land degradation, food insecurity, energy access, *climate change*, among other factors, on the security and stability of Mali.[71]

This time it was France who firmly reacted, recalling that

> (. . .) in the Sahel more than anywhere else it is important that the actions of the United Nations and local Governments fully take into account the impact of climate change and other environmental factors on security. Resolution 2480 (2019) recalls that, but we would like to continue to work with our partners with a view to going even further to develop the climate and security agenda within the Council.[72]

Disappointment was also expressed by other European Western countries. In particular, Germany declared:

> (. . .) we were very clear throughout negotiations that the adverse effects of climate change on the stability and security of Mali needed to be explicitly referenced in the resolution. Those are key challenges that the international community needs to address collectively and urgently.[73]

These tensions cannot be disregarded, as they clearly show that climate change remains a controversial issue within the UNSC not only when the competence of the Council to prevent climate change is under discussion, but also when climate-related effects are directly or indirectly interrelated with other (traditional) security threats.

4.2 Legal Nature

As already recalled, Resolution 2423 (2018) was adopted pursuant to Chapter VII of the Charter. It is widely known, however, that: "[t]he language of a resolution of the Security Council should be carefully analysed before a conclusion can be made as to its binding effect".[74]

Paragraph 68 of Resolution 2423 (2018) is not couched in mandatory language. The Security Council does not "decide"; it only "[*n*]*otes the importance* (. . .) to take into consideration, *as appropriate*".[75]

It might also be recalled that the issue at stake is part of a conflict prevention strategy.[76] Therefore, it should be framed within the context of the functions that the

---

[71] UN Doc. S/RES/2480, p. 2 (emphasis added). The same approach was adopted under UNSC Resolution 2531, 29 June 2020.

[72] UN Doc. S/PV.8568, 28 June 2019, 3.

[73] UN Doc. S/PV.8568, 5. See also the statement by Belgium, *ibid.*, 6.

[74] ICJ, *Legal Consequences for States of the Continued Presence of South Africa in Namibia (South-West Africa) Notwithstanding Security Council Resolution 276 (1970)*, Advisory Opinion, 21 June 1971, *ICJ Reports*, 1971, para 114.

[75] UNSC Resolution 2429 (2018), concerning the situation in Darfur, contained a similar recommendation (para 47) with slightly different language ("The Council (. . .) *requests* the United Nations and the Government of Sudan to consider (. . .)" (emphasis added).

[76] See infra, Sect. 6.2.

UNSC exercises under Chapter VI of the UN Charter in order to draw the attention of Member States to issues that can potentially affect the maintenance of international peace and security.[77]

Finally, the mere recommendatory effect of this provision is implicitly confirmed by the discussions that preceded the adoption of the resolution,[78] which can be used as a supplementary means of interpretation.[79] Due to the strong criticism expressed by Russia on this paragraph,[80] there are serious grounds to believe that a legally binding provision on this topic could never have been accepted.

If, against this background, it may be concluded that the provision at hand has no legally binding effect, it is equally important to recall that all UN member States, individually and jointly, are under the duty to co-operate in good faith with the Organization.[81] Accordingly, it may be argued that the addressees of the UNSC recommendation are expected to make reasonable efforts to integrate climate related effects within their planned activities in Mali.

5 Addressees of Resolution 2423 (2018)

The Malian government and the United Nations are the formal recipients of the UNSC recommendation under Resolution 2423 (2018), para. 68. It may therefore be useful to explore the possible implications of the UNSC's exhortation for both national authorities and the world Organization itself.

5.1 *Mali*

Any assessment of the Malian contribution to the implementation of the UNSC recommendation at issue cannot be separated from the objective difficulties faced by national institutions in the path of the effective restoration of State authority and the rule of law throughout their territory.[82] The situation became even more complex in

---

[77] In particular, see Articles 34 and 36 (1) and (2) of the UN Charter.

[78] Again, according to the ICJ, the binding effect of a UNSC resolution should be determined on a case by case basis, "(...) having regard to the terms of the resolution to be interpreted, the discussions leading to it, the Charter provisions invoked and, in general, all circumstances that might assist in determining the legal consequences of the resolution of the Security Council", ICJ, *Legal Consequence,* supra note 78, para 114.

[79] See Wood (2016), p. 94. Statements made in the Council after the adoption of a resolution are included by the Author in this category.

[80] See supra, Sect. 4.1.

[81] See UN Charter, Article 2 (5). For broader considerations see: Schreuer (1977); Giegerich (2012), pp. 1143–1145; Conforti and Focarelli (2017), pp. 468–469.

[82] In this sense see UNSC Resolution 2423 (2018), para 38 (i).

2020. The political tensions caused by widespread protests, arising from disputes around legislative elections held in Spring 2020 within a difficult context, due to the COVID-19 restrictions and other serious incidents,[83] culminated in a *coup d'état* on 18 August.

The political crisis contributed to further diverting the attention away from the implementation of the 2015 Peace Agreement. A transitional government was formed in October 2020[84] and the Transition Charter includes the implementation of the agreement among its objectives.[85] However, the advancement of key reforms remains critical.

An action plan for the re-organization of the national security system[86] was adopted in September 2019,[87] but the restructuring process was delayed due to disagreement between the parties at the local and national level.[88] As regards the promotion of justice and human rights protection, the Parties to the 2015 Peace Agreement pledged themselves to promote cultural diversity, inclusiveness, and respect for human rights. Mali is also party to the International Covenant on Civil and Political Rights (ICCPR) since 1974; accordingly, pursuant to Article 2 of the ICCPR, the Malian government is expected to adopt adequate preventive and repressive measures to ensure that there is respect for the rights recognised under the Covenant for all individuals within its territory and subject to its jurisdiction, without any distinction. However, the human rights situation continues to deteriorate, especially in central Mali, where most violations—including grave violations—and abuses are perpetrated by armed groups, judicial authorities, and national forces.[89]

Finally, the *Macina Liberation Front* (MLF)—one of the leading terrorist groups in the Sahel region which largely draws its membership from the Fulani herders—is not a party to the Peace agreement, as it was excluded from negotiations. Therefore, the MLF is released from any formal commitment.[90]

Against this backdrop, it can be argued that the Malian government is unable, on its own, to comply with all the undertakings that require adequate control of the

[83] Incidents included the kidnapping of the opposition leader and electoral officials; see UN Doc. S/2020/476, para 2.

[84] Presidential and legislative elections should be held in 2022; UN Doc. S/2020/1281, para 3.

[85] Décret N° 2020-0072/PT-RM du 1er Octobre portant promulgation de la Charte de la transition, *Journal Officiel de la Republique du Mali*, Special No. 17, 1er Octobre 2020, https://constitutionnet.org/sites/default/files/2020-10/mali-jo-2020-17-sp.pdf.

[86] 2015 Peace Agreement, Sections II and III.

[87] More details in *Activities of the United Nations Office for West Africa and the Sahel. Report of the Secretary-General*, UN Doc. S/2019/1005 of 30 December 2019, para 65.

[88] UN Doc. A/HRC/WG.6/29/MLI/1*, 6 November 2017, para 67.

[89] See e.g. the last Malian Government periodic report to the Human Rights Council, UN Doc. A/HRC/WG.6/29/MLI/1*, 6 November 2017, para 67 and the most recent reports by the UN Secretary-General on the situation in Mali: UN Docs. S/2020/476, para 76 ff.; S/2020/952, para 66 ff.; S/2020/1281, paras. 66–69.

[90] For further considerations see Drange (2018), p. 9.

territory and effective human rights protection. As a result, in a generalised context of State weakness, governmental action highly depends on the collaboration of the international community. Indeed, as we shall see below, the support of the UN, and in particular of MINUSMA, has been essential for the implementation of the UNSC Resolution 2423 (2018), para. 68, by the Malian authorities.

5.2 United Nations

The United Nations is the second addressee of the UNSC Resolution 2423 (2018), para. 68. Absent any further specification, "United Nations" is to be interpreted very broadly, *i.e.* as the whole UN system. Accordingly, all the primary and subsidiary bodies of the Organization (including, for instance, peacekeeping operations) specialised agencies, funds and programmes fall within the scope of the UNSC recommendation.

In the following pages the attention will only be focused on UNOWAS and MINUSMA. The former, as it plays an important role "in contributing to continuous strategic and integrated analysis of the opportunities, risks and challenges in support of efforts by national and local actors to sustain peace".[91] The latter, for MINUSMA is a peace operation, *i.e.* a UN subsidiary body, which has been operating on the ground, since 2013, in the areas most threatened by the interconnection of various factors of instability.

5.2.1 UNOWAS

UNOWAS is a UN political mission, which was established by the UN Secretary-General in 2016, pursuant to a specific request by the President of the UN Security Council.[92] According to its mandate, it is required to:

> (...) monitor political developments in West Africa and the Sahel and carry out good offices and special assignments on behalf of the Secretary-General to support conflict prevention, peacebuilding, sustaining peace and mediation efforts in the subregion.[93]

In particular, UNOWAS promotes partnerships with regional and subregional organizations in various areas, including

> (...) the development of networks of practitioners and subregional frameworks and mechanisms to address challenges related to security sector reform, transnational organized crime,

---

[91] Statement by the President of the Security Council, UN Doc. S/PRST/2018/16, 10 August 2018, 1.

[92] UN Doc. S/2016/89, 28 January 2016. In particular, UNOWAS is a unified structure resulting from the merger between two pre-existing offices: the Office for the Special Envoy for the Sahel (OSES) and the United Nations Office for West Africa (UNOWA).

[93] UNOWAS renewed mandate (2020–2023), UN Doc. S/2020/85, 31 January 2020, Objective 1.

> illicit trafficking, *conflicts between farmers and herders*, terrorism and violent extremism as and when conducive to terrorism.[94]

UNOWAS is also responsible for the implementation of the United Nations Integrated Strategy for the Sahel (UNISS), which the UNSC endorsed in 2013 to tackle security, political, and developmental challenges in the Sahel region according to a comprehensive approach.[95] In the report of the Secretary-General illustrating the objectives of this strategy,[96] UNISS was characterized as a new instrument for conflict prevention, with the aim "to support the Governments and people of the region in their efforts to address the causes of instability within a sustainable and long-term perspective".[97]

Starting from the assumption that global warming is one of the major causes of vulnerability in the region, the adoption of programmes specifically oriented to tackle this challenge was included among the indicative actions that UNISS promotes under its "third pillar" (long-term resilience).[98] One of its strategic goals consists of pursuing "environmental sustainability through national and regional natural resource management mechanisms and climate change adaptation and mitigation programmes, with a special focus on water".[99]

In 2018 UNISS was strengthened through the adoption of a Support Plan for the Sahel,[100] an instrument covering the period 2018–2030, to foster greater coherence, coordination and efficiency of the UN Strategy. The Support Plan aims, *inter alia*, to ensure an approach consistent with the goals of the 2030 Agenda for Sustainable Development[101] and the Paris Agreement in the Sahel Region.

---

[94] UN Doc. S/2020/85, Function 2.2, 3 (*emphasis added*).

[95] UNISS was established by the UN Secretary-General following UNSC Resolution 2056 (2012), 5 July 2012, para 28.

[96] UN Doc. S/2013/354. In this document, the Sahel was intended as the broad Sahelo-Saharan region, encompassing West, Central and North African countries, but placing a particular emphasis on five core Sahel countries: Burkina Faso, Chad, Mali, Mauritania and Niger.

[97] *Ibid.*, para 23.

[98] *Ibid.*, Annex, 22.

[99] Objective 3.5, UN Doc. S/2013/354, 24.

[100] See *UN Support Plan for the Sahel. Working together for a prosperous and Peaceful Sahel*, May 2018, available at https://www.un.org/africarenewal/sites/www.un.org.africarenewal/files/English%20Summary%20Report_0.pdf.

[101] Transforming our world: The 2030 Agenda for sustainable development, UN Doc. A/RES/70/1, 21 October 2015.

5.2.2 MINUSMA

MINUSMA was established by the UNSC in 2013,[102] after the Malian army, with the support of French and African forces, restored control over Timbuktu and Gao.[103]

MINUSMA is a "robust" peacekeeping operation, which has been authorized by the UNSC "to use all necessary means to carry out its mandate".[104] In particular, according to Resolution 2423 (2018), the mission is required "to continue to carry out its mandate with a proactive and robust posture" (para. 33) and to

> anticipate and deter threats and to take robust and active steps to counter asymmetric attacks against civilians or United Nations personnel, to ensure prompt and effective responses to threats of violence against civilians and to prevent a return of armed elements to those areas (para. 34).[105]

The very broad mandate held by MINUSMA was strengthened in 2019 by the addition of the security situation in Central Mali as a second strategic priority of the UN mission.[106]

Under UNSC Resolution 2423 (2018), the topic of climate change was addressed under the general heading "Environmental issues", which included two paragraphs. One was the already mentioned para. 68. The other paragraph required MINUSMA to consider the environmental impact of its activities and to manage them according to the relevant UN rules and regulations (para. 67). The latter recommendation was reiterated by the UNSC following the establishment of MINUSMA[107] and the Secretary-General has regularly reported on its implementation.[108]

---

[102] UN Doc. S/RES/2100, 25 April 2013, para 7. As at December 2020, the deployed number of personnel in MINUSMA amounted to 15,775 units, including military (12,877), police (1718) and civilian personnel (1180), which had been contributed by 60 countries; data available at https://minusma.unmissions.org/en/personnel.

[103] African-led International Support Mission in Mali (AFISMA) was established by ECOWAS in 2013, with prior UNSC authorization, Resolution 2085 (2012), 20 December 2012, para 9.

[104] See UNSC Resolution 2164 (2014), 25 June 2014, para 12. See also: Resolution 2423 (2018), para 32; Resolution 2480 (2019), para 19; and Resolution 2531 (2020), para 18.

[105] See also para 38 d) (ii) second hyphen.

[106] Resolution 2480 (2019), para 20. The primary strategic priority of MINUSMA remains to support the implementation of the 2015 Peace Agreement.

[107] See UN Doc. S/RES/2100, para 32. MINUSMA was the first UN peacekeeping operation to receive a direct mandate to address environmental concern for its ecological footprint. On the reduction of the environmental impact of UN peacekeeping operations see: UNEP, *Greening the Blue Helmets. Environment, Natural Resources and UN Peacekeeping Operations*, 2012; Maertens (2016); Maertens and Shoshan (2018); Diehl (2018), p. 131 ff. See also *Report of the High-level Independent Panel on Peace Operations on uniting our strengths for peace: politics, partnership and people*, UN Doc. A/70/95, S/2015/446, 17 June 2015 (hereinafter: *HIPPO Report*), para 292.

[108] See e.g. UN Doc. S/2018/541, para 52; UN Doc. S/2019/983, para 52; UN Doc. S/2020/223, para 92.

The environmental impact of military operations has been considered with growing attention paid to the issue at the international level in recent years.[109] Special provisions have also been incorporated within the Draft principles on protection of the environment in relation to armed conflicts, which the International Law Commission provisionally adopted on first reading on 8 July 2019.[110] Accordingly, a reduction of the so-called peacekeeping environmental footprint is a positive undertaking which fits into (and strengthens) the above-mentioned general trend.

It cannot be overlooked, however, that the contribution of UN peace operations to the global greenhouse gas emissions is very low if compared with the carbon emissions produced by leading industrial States.[111] Therefore, the reduction of their environmental footprint may only have a minor impact on global warming.

A major role can be played by MINUSMA in preventing and suppressing certain security implications of climate change through its actions and strategies. The mandate conferred on the mission is in fact flexible and broad enough to ensure an indirect, but meaningful, contribution to the implementation of the UNSC recommendation addressed to the UN in many respects. In particular, MINUSMA may co-operate in preventing and removing certain security implications arising from climate change in central Mali on three levels.

First, the military component of MINUSMA provides a deterrent presence in the Mopti region, *i.e.* the area where the most dramatic intercommunal clashes have occurred in recent years. It should be noted, however, that the priority tasks of the military component of MINUSMA are the protection of civilians and stabilization of areas where civilians are at risk,[112] not the settlement of intercommunal conflicts through the use of military force.[113] In addition, stabilization is a necessary precondition to prevent other causes of clashes between local communities, such as the exploitation of intercommunal violence by terrorists and ethnically-based self defence groups.

Second, MINUSMA is required to support the Malian authorities in reducing intercommunal tensions through mediation, good offices and reconciliation. In particular, according to UNSC Resolution 2480 (2019), the Mission's mandate

---

[109] See e.g. NATO, *supra* Sect. 1.

[110] UN Doc. A/CN.4/L.937, 6 June 2019, Draft principles 6 [7] and 7 [8], 2.

[111] With regard to MINUSMA, suffice here to mention the undertaking of a pilot project for the storage of solar energy in liquid form aimed at reducing greenhouse gas emissions, UN Doc. 2020/952, para 112.

[112] See e.g. UNSC Resolution 2423 (2018), para 38 *d*). Since March 2019, MINUSMA has increased the protection of civilians through the deployment of *ad hoc* patrols (*Operation Oryx*); see UN Doc. S/2019/454, para 33. MINUSMA is also supporting a Government programme, aimed at facilitating the reinsertion of young people associated with self-defence and militia groups in the Mopti Region into civilian life, UN Doc. S/2020/476, para 28.

[113] On the action to be adopted by UN peace operations to respond to different environments and threats, see United Nations Department on Peacekeeping Operations, *The Protection of Civilians in United Nations Peacekeeping Handbook*, 2020, 143 ff. and, in particular, 147–148 (threats of intercommunal violence).

includes "(...) interaction with civilians, community outreach, reconciliation, mediation, support to the resolution of local and intercommunal conflicts and public information", as well as the exercise of good offices to support efforts to reduce intercommunal tensions".[114]

Third, MINUSMA supports government efforts to combat impunity—which is one of the interconnected and aggravating factors of violence in Mali—through a strategy aimed at increasing criminal accountability.[115] As we shall see below, MINUSMA has achieved interesting results in supporting reconciliation and social cohesion efforts. Instead, the fight against human rights abuses and impunity continues to be hindered by serious challenges.[116]

6 Major Strengths and Open Challenges

From the previous survey it can be argued that various actions undertaken so far by UNOWAS and MINUSMA are consistent with the most urgent measures that have been highlighted during the UNSC debates on climate change and the situation in the Sahel, *i.e.*: the adoption of a comprehensive and integrated approach and conflict prevention. It may be useful, however, to assess whether and to what extent the objectives pursued by the UNSC recommendation at hand can be fully achieved.

6.1 Comprehensive and Integrated Approach

As noted above, the need for a holistic approach has been repeatedly highlighted during the UNSC open debates on climate change[117] and in various Presidential statements.[118] It should also be stressed that, in the opinion of some scholars, actions aimed at promoting human security[119] would be better framed if they were based on an interdependent and dynamic approach, similar to that characterizing sustainable development. Accordingly: "(...) the field of security should be broadened to a more comprehensive notion of '*sustainable security*'(...)", *i.e.* a more expanded field that

---

[114]Para 28 *c)* and *d)* (*ii*).

[115]See UN Doc. S/2019/454, para 34.

[116]Investigations relating to the attacks against the Fulani community in the Mopti region were conducted by the Specialized Investigation Brigade of MINUSMA in 2019 and 2020. Any progress in investigations and execution of arrest warrants is however affected by various challenges, including increasing insecurity and restrictions on movement due to the COVID-19 pandemic; see UN Docs S/2019/782, para 35; S/2020/476, para 78; S/2020/952, para 43.

[117]See e.g. UN Doc. S/PV.8307, *passim*.

[118]See e.g. UN Doc. S/PRST/2018/6, p. 3 and UN Doc. S/PRST/2019/7, para 26.

[119]On this notion see, in particular: Nasu (2013, 2016); Chinkin and Kaldor (2017).

"(. . .) facilitates critical integrations of state, human and environmental security".[120]

In addition, a cross-pillar approach (environment, development, human rights, peace and security)[121] is consistent with a basic principle of international environmental law, the principle of integration, according to which: "In order to achieve sustainable development, environmental protection shall constitute an integral part of the development process and cannot be considered in isolation from it".[122]

It would be reductive, however, to limit the scope of the principle of integration to the reconciliation between the three components of sustainable development, namely, i.e.: economic growth, social development and environmental protection. As the International Law Association (ILA) Committee on the International Law on Sustainable Development highlighted in 2006,[123] institutional integration (global, regional, national, sub-national and local) "(. . .) is both the most obvious form of integration and the one that most fully reflects what Principle 4 [of the Rio Declaration] was quite clearly referring to".[124]

Obviously, integration requires not only a better coordination between different subjects and initiatives to avoid duplicative or conflicting approaches,[125] but also a systemic inter-institutional integration, which leads to "a coherent and coordinated policy- and decision-making across institutions both *horizontally* and *vertically*".[126]

Are the United Nations prepared to lead this process?

6.1.1 The UN Legal Framework

If we look at the UN legal order, a broad legal framework for inter-institutional integration may be found in the UN Charter and in some general principles of law.

First, the UN Member States are under the duty to co-operate in good faith with the United Nations and its bodies (Article 2 (2) of the UN Charter) and all UN bodies, programmes, strategies and specialized agencies are expected to comply with

---

[120] Khagram et al. (2003), p. 290 (emphasis added).

[121] UN Doc. S/PRST/2019/7, para 26.

[122] Rio Declaration, Principle 4. See also Article 3 of the Global Pact for the Environment, that was drafted by an international network of one hundred experts from all over the world in 2017; text available at https://globalpactenvironment.org/uploads/EN.pdf. On the principle of integration, see in particular: Hernández (2012), p. 153 ff.; Voigt (2013); Barral and Dupuy (2015).

[123] ILA (2006) Report of the Seventy-Second Conference (Toronto 4–8 June 2006), London (hereinafter: ILA Report).

[124] 'ILA Report', p. 476.

[125] As the representative of the EU stressed during the UNSC briefing on the Sahel in 2016: "Coordination (. . .) is at the centre of our debate. If we count all the various initiatives and strategies on the Sahel, I believe that there may now be 16 or even more. It is clear that there is a real need for coordination. Such coordination does exist (. . .). But we must work very hard within that coordination; otherwise, we will find ourselves working against ourselves. It goes without saying that we must work together", UNSC briefing on Sahel 2016, p. 31.

[126] 'ILA Report', p. 478.

the general principle of loyal collaboration between organs and institutions. It is equally clear that UN Member States are bound to the duty of co-operation in good faith with the Organization both directly, in their individual actions, and indirectly, *i.e.* in the actions undertaken within the international organizations that they are members of (Article 48 (2) and Article 56 UN Charter).

Second, Chapter VIII of the UN Charter provides the legal basis for the co-operation between the United Nations and regional organizations in the maintenance of international peace and security. Notably, pursuant to Article 52 (3): "The Security Council shall encourage the development of pacific settlement of local disputes through such regional arrangements or by such regional agencies either on the initiative of the states concerned or by reference from the Security Council", while under Article 54: "The Security Council shall at all times be kept fully informed of activities undertaken or in contemplation under regional arrangements or by regional agencies for the maintenance of international peace and security".

It cannot be overlooked, however, that Articles 52 and 54 contain only programmatic, not prescriptive provisions. What is more, no general rules have ever been established to regulate forms and methods of operational coordination between the UN and regional organizations. Some generic exhortations have been made by the UNSC,[127] the UN General Assembly[128] and the Heads of States and Governments in the World Summit Outcome of 2005.[129] Nevertheless, both the United Nations and regional organizations seem reluctant to abandon the current flexibility, which allows them to take action, at the operational level, on a case by case basis.[130]

As a result, the legal framework provided for under Chapter VIII of the UN Charter has been replaced by a principle of co-operation "désormais omniprésent", but with a "faible consistence juridique", leading to a soft, flexible and pragmatic partnership between the UN and regional organizations.[131] Finally, a major problem arises from the highly complex and challenging context of the current political scenario, characterized by a plurality of actors and multiple, interconnected threats.[132]

---

[127] See e.g. UN Doc. S/RES/2457 (2019), 27 February 2019, in particular paras. 8–11.

[128] See e.g. the UN General Assembly *Declaration on the Enhancement of Cooperation between the United Nations and Regional Arrangements or Agencies in the Maintenance of International Peace and Security*, UN Doc. A/RES/49/57, 9 December 1994, Annex, para 9.

[129] See UN Doc. A/RES/60/1, 24 October 2005, para 170 a).

[130] For a thorough analysis of the evolution of co-operation and coordination between the United Nations and regional organizations and the reluctance of regional organizations to be bound by rules and standards that risk jeopardizing their operational freedom of choice, see Tanzi (2004), p. 24 ff.; Boisson de Chazournes (2016).

[131] Balmond (2008), pp. 67–79.

[132] For broader considerations, see: *Report of the Secretary-General on the United Nations and conflict prevention: a collective recommitment*, UN Doc. S/2015/730, 25 September 2015, para 43.

6.1.2 The Situation on the Ground

With respect to the Sahel, a recent UNSC Presidential statement, reiterating and broadening previous exhortations on the topic,[133] stressed the need for a *holistic approach* to address root causes of terrorism, intercommunal violence and all other major challenges in the region, including the promotion of sustainable development. It also encouraged "(. . .) *cross-pillar efforts to foster greater coherence and coordination* within the UN System as well as with partners in the region".[134]

As regards Resolution 2423 (2018), para. 68, it may be regarded as a concrete application of the principle of integration, since the security implications of the adverse effects of climate change are to be taken into account by the Government of Mali and the UN within all their decision-making processes ("activities, programs and strategies in Mali"). It should also be noted that other operative paragraphs of the UNSC resolution are characterized by the adoption of an integrated approach.[135] Accordingly, taking into account that para. 68 is to be read in conjunction with all the provisions of Resolution 2423 (2018) aimed at preventing conflicts or promoting integration, all measures under para. 68 are necessarily interrelated with (and strengthened by) other actions in accordance with that resolution.

With regard to the situation on the ground, UNOWAS has promoted initiatives to encourage collaboration with its main partner, ECOWAS,[136] and between ECOWAS and various UN agencies. Some positive results in the co-operation with other sub-regional entities have also been reported.[137] However, due to the variety of drivers of local conflicts, on the one hand, and the great number of different entities that fall within the broad reference to "the UN System"[138] and "partners in the region",[139] on the other, the adoption of a comprehensive and integrated approach remains a daunting undertaking.

In particular, a clearer legal framework would be required to clarify delicate issues, like the direction and the coordination of common undertakings, respective competencies and potential responsibilities. An effective mechanism for institutional integration should also be put in place between the UN system and regional organizations to move from the complementarity of actors working alongside one another to joint actions.

---

[133] See e.g. UN Doc. S/PRST/2015/24, 8 December 2015, para 2 and UN Doc. S/PRST/2016/11, 28 July 2016, 4.

[134] UN Doc. S/PRST/2020/2, 11 February 2020, pp. 2 and 3 (emphasis added).

[135] See e.g. paras. 17, 28, pp. 29, and 31.

[136] With respect to security and climate-related effects, see e.g. UN Doc. S/2019/1005, 30 December 2019, para 59.

[137] See e.g. UN Doc. S/2019/890, 19 November 2019, para 48.

[138] See e.g.: the Peace Building Commission; the UNDP; the FAO.

[139] Suffice here to mention: the African Union, EU, ECOWAS, the Group of Five for the Sahel, the Mano River Union, and the Lake Chad Basin Commission.

Some final considerations should be reserved to MINUSMA, an integrated mission with military, police and civilian components, which performs a wide range of activities on the ground.

For years, the effective implementation of this mission's mandate has been undermined by a gap in the integration and complementarity of its personnel at the organizational and operational level.[140] Recently, in compliance with UNSC Resolution 2423 (2018), para. 28,[141] MINUSMA adopted a strategic plan to enhance the complementarity of skills and to take a coordinated approach across its various units, with a view to better reflecting its strategic priorities.[142] An important development also consisted of the adoption of a three-year UN Integrated Strategic Framework (ISG) in 2019,[143] setting joint priorities and internal division of labour between the UN Country team, MINUSMA, UNDP and other UN agencies to strengthen stabilization efforts in Central Mali.[144]

A crucial issue for peacekeeping and peace-building operations is however represented by the difficult integration between short-term and long-term objectives. Various projects have been promoted by MINUSMA in recent years to contain or avoid conflicts between herders and farmers in the short term.[145] Nevertheless, broader actions in the area of climate change mitigation and adaptation may require long-term perspectives. Unfortunately, as the UN practice shows, those projects risk not being undertaken if they collide (or are perceived to collide) with the urgent needs of local and national actors and their expectations for quick results.[146]

6.2 *Conflict Prevention*

As noted above, the main purpose of Resolution 2423 (2018) is to address climate change-related conflicts at their roots. A similar approach may be found in the UNSC Presidential statements characterizing conflicts between herders and farmers in the Sahel region as a consequence of "competition for natural resources, rapid

---

[140] For further details see Rjetens and Ruffa (2019), p. 383 ff.

[141] In particular, the UNSC requested that MINUSMA "(…) strengthen its efforts to improve coordination between its civil, military and police components, including through an integrated approach to operational planning and intelligence as well as through the establishment of intra-mission dedicated coordination mechanisms"; UN Doc. 2423 (2018), para 28.

[142] See Spink (2019).

[143] See UN Doc. S/2019/207, 5 March 2019, paras. 15–18.

[144] This action was promoted by the UNSC under Resolution 2423 (2018), para 29, and Resolution 2480 (2019), para 25.

[145] See infra, Sect. 6.2.

[146] On the possible tension between the short-term objective of settling two million returnees in Rwanda in 1994 and the long-term goal of safeguarding endangered forest areas, see e.g. Matthew (2014), p. 83 ff.

population growth, weak governance, pressures related to climate and ecological factors, and the circulation of small arms and light weapons".[147]

More generally, during the last two decades, the UNSC has repeatedly stressed "(. . .) its determination to pursue the objective of prevention of armed conflict as an integral part of its primary responsibility for the maintenance of international peace and security".[148] It also committed itself "(. . .) to consider and use the tools of the UN system to ensure that early warning of potential conflicts translates into early, concrete preventive action".[149] The following year, although recognizing that "[i]t is a difficult time to write about conflict prevention", the UN Secretary-General emphasized that conflict prevention is not only "the core function of the United Nations", but also the most convenient solution at the practical level.[150]

Against this background, it can be argued that actions under Resolution 2423 (2018), para. 68, should be undertaken pursuant to a conflict prevention approach. Both UNOWAS and MINUSMA mandates include support to conflict prevention efforts—in the Sahel region and Mali, respectively—through preventive diplomacy and mediation.[151] Therefore, it may be useful to briefly recall some concrete steps that the two UN missions have taken in this direction.

6.2.1 UNOWAS

Conflict prevention and the adoption of an integrated approach are strictly interrelated in the mandate and the subsequent practice of UNOWAS. As the UN Secretary-General stressed, the UN mission chairs the working group on the prevention and resolution of farmer-herder conflicts "(. . .) with the aim of strengthening United Nations system cooperation, contributing to unified messaging and building bridges between local, national and regional responses".[152] Meanwhile, the Head of UNOWAS continues his efforts,

---

[147] See e.g. UN Doc. S/PRST/2019/7, para 26 and UN Doc. S/PRST/2020/2, pp. 2 and 3.

[148] See e.g. UN Doc. S/RES/1366, 30 August 2001, para 1 and UN Doc. S/RES/2171 (2014), 21 August 2014, para 1.

[149] UN Doc. S/RES/2171 (2014), para 20. See also UNSC, 'Declaration on strengthening the effectiveness of the Security Council's role in conflict prevention, particularly in Africa', where the Council emphasized the close interrelation between conflict prevention and sustainable development (UN Doc. S/RES/1625, 14 September 2005, Preamble, recital 6). For a systematic survey on the topic, see: International Peace Institute, The UN Security Council and Conflict Prevention, October 2011, available at https://www.jstor.org/stable/pdf/resrep09518.pdf?refreqid=excelsior%3Ad747d18331f9787ce1c6472f58437c11.

[150] 'Report of the Secretary-General on the United Nations and conflict prevention: a collective recommitment' UN Doc. S/2015/730, paras. 1, 13 and 14.

[151] See supra Sect. 5.2.

[152] Activities of the United Nations Office for West Africa and the Sahel. Report of the Secretary-General, UN Doc. S/2019/1005, 30 December 2019, para 67.

> in close collaboration with United Nations resident coordinators, relevant United Nations system entities, ECOWAS, civil society organizations and think tanks, to strengthen regional and cross-border initiatives to address conflicts between herders and farmers.[153]

In this respect, it is worth remembering that the establishment of regional political offices like UNOWAS is generally regarded as one of the most appreciated innovations in the UN practice with regard to preventive diplomacy and mediation of recent years.[154] The experience of the current Head of UNOWAS, Mohamed Ibn Chambas, in conflict settling in the region is an additional element to be taken into account in evaluating the role that the UN political mission can also play in relation to climate-related security risks in the Sahel.[155]

6.2.2 MINUSMA

MINUSMA's mandate includes supporting the national authorities to reduce intercommunal tensions and facilitate reconciliation and social cohesion through mediation and good offices.[156] If "good offices" is intended in its broad meaning,[157] MINUSMA plays an active role on the ground. Moreover, its civilian component (which usually, in a peace operation "is at the forefront of the mission's engagement with local communities")[158] has recently been strengthened in the Mopti region, *i.e.* the area of Central Mali where violent clashes between herders and farmers are more numerous and frequent.[159]

In the UN practice, there are only a few precedents (with a limited scope)[160] of a direct engagement of Civil Affairs officers in promoting social cohesion in areas affected by intercommunal tensions.[161] More generally, every UN mission is a *sui generis* case, due to its mandate, composition, strength and the context in which it operates. Some useful lessons can however be drawn from previous experience.

[153] Ibidem.

[154] See e.g. HIPPO Report, para 69 and Day (2019), p. 79.

[155] See Day (2019), p. 79.

[156] See supra Sect. 5.2.

[157] On the meaning of "good offices" and their role in UN peace operations, see: Day (2019), p. 69 ff.

[158] UNEP, Greening the Blue Helmets, supra note 107, p. 71.

[159] "A total of 19 additional civilian personnel, including a planning officer, have been redeployed to Mopti", UN Doc. S/2020/223, para 76.

[160] See Da Costa and Karlsrud (2010) and Karlsrud (2015), p. 796.

[161] For instance, MINURCAT (*United Nations Mission in the Central African Republic and Chad*) facilitated dialogue and reconciliation between farmers and herders in eastern Chad, while UNOCI (*United Nations Operation in Côte d'Ivoire*) promoted justice and reconciliation in northern areas of Côte d'Ivoire.

First, adequate skills, experience[162] and collaboration with various stakeholders are obvious, but necessary, requirements.[163]

Inclusivity is another basic requirement. Notably, public participation should be enhanced, but with care taken not "to further exacerbate conflicts between ethnic groups and [to] unwittingly endorse one particular clan over another".[164] This implies, primarily, that all those who make efforts under a strategy of preventive diplomacy behave in good faith.[165] From this perspective, impartiality—one of the basic principles of UN peacekeeping operations—may also play a crucial role in a positive outcome for these undertakings and the credibility of the peace operation as a whole.

Finally, a successful preventive approach cannot be separated from: the capacity to collect (and exchange) adequate and reliable information in a constant and timely manner; the availability of early warning systems and adequate analytical capability.[166] The latter is also instrumental in providing the Security Council with sufficient analysis on potential peace and security risks posed by environmental challenges, as explicitly called for under the *HIPPO Report*[167] and, in a more nuanced way, under the Preamble of UNSC Resolution 2423 (2018).[168]

Taking into account all these elements on the one hand, and the competences and resources they imply on the other, it may be wondered whether MINUSMA is prepared to tackle a similar challenge.

The Civil Affairs Division of MINUSMA works closely with local authorities and communities to provide reconciliation and mediation services in an effort to resolve local conflicts.[169] In Ogossagou, the area most affected by violence, local peace agreements were signed in 2020, allowing for the return of 500 internally displaced persons to Djenné.[170] MINUSMA has also promoted joint intercommunity activities to reduce the risk of new conflicts between the Dogon and the Fulani communities.[171] Finally, quick impact projects have been

[162] See e.g. HIPPO Report, para 75, and Da Costa and Karlsrud (2010).

[163] See Day (2019), p. 78.

[164] Da Costa and Karlsrud (2010).

[165] "The Council further encourages concerned parties to act in good faith when engaging with prevention and mediation efforts, including those undertaken by the United Nations", UN Doc. S/PRST/2011/18, 22 September 2011, 2.

[166] See e.g. Day (2019), p. 80.

[167] *HIPPO Report*, para 292.

[168] Preamble, recital 28.

[169] For more details see the periodic reports by the UN Secretary-General on the situation in Mali in 2019 and 2020. See also the Budget for MINUSMA for the period 1 July 2019–30 June 2020, UN Doc. A/73/760, 22 February 2019.

[170] UN Doc. S/2020/952, para 36.

[171] See UN Docs. S/2020/223, para 25; S/2020/476, para 12; S/2020/1281, para 36.

implemented to support the local population in relation to agricultural activities, water supply and the organization of income-generating projects.[172]

It cannot be overlooked, however, that structural problems may affect the positive outcome of the entire process. A positive impact will also depend on a number of variables, such as the scarcity of reliable data, operational constraints,[173] or the lack of commitment from local actors.

What is more, MINUSMA is a large multidimensional operation, with the mandate to pursue a variety of complex objectives in a highly unstable and dangerous context. The UNSC has been consistently called upon to adopt a different strategy in planning peace operations, avoiding, on the one hand, over-ambitious mandates (the so called "Christmas-tree mandates")[174] and a disparity between their mandate and their resources on the other. It can hardly be said, however, that Christmas is really over.[175] In addition, despite the extension of the MINUSMA mandate from the North to the centre of Mali in 2019, budgetary pressures continue.[176] What is more, since its establishment, MINUSMA has been operating in a dangerous and asymmetrical environment. The situation on the ground is characterized by a constant expansion of terrorist groups,[177] violent attacks on UN personnel by armed extremists,[178] and the absence of any (or scant) co-operation by self-defence Dogon and Fulani militias.[179]

7 Concluding Remarks

An overall assessment of the measures taken within the UN after the adoption of Resolution 2423 (2018) highlights some strengths, but also weaknesses.

---

[172] UN Doc. S/2020/1281, para 87. See also QIPs Overview—Mali at https://minusma.unmissions.org/sites/default/files/2013-2020_qips_overview_en_0.pdf.

[173] Suffice here to recall that the reduction of patrols and interaction with communities—due to COVID-19 prevention measures—have negatively affected information collection and performance in 2020; see UN Doc. S/2020/952, para 105.

[174] The Security Council Report and UN Peace Operations: Reform and Deliver, Security Council Report, 5 May 2016, p. 9.

[175] See UNSC, 'Is Christmas Really Over? Improving the Mandating of Peace Operations', Security Council Report, 22 February 2019.

[176] For further details see Spink, *Strengthened* cit., at 9.

[177] UN Doc. S/2020/223, para 38.

[178] As of December 2020, fatalities within MINUSMA included 135 lives lost, as a result of malicious acts, and 358 seriously injured; data available at https://minusma.unmissions.org/en/personnel.

[179] See UN Doc. S/2019/983, para 51. More generally, on the need for better coordination between the many actors in the Sahel through a broad and inclusive agreement on peacekeeping and peacebuilding in the area, see Baudas et al. (2001), p. 32.

The UNSC recommendation may be regarded as a first attempt of the Council to move from discussion[180] to action with regard to climate change and security issues. Some permanent members continue to resist any role for the Council in addressing climate change, including the adoption of uncontroversial measures under Chapter VI of the UN Charter. Nevertheless, Resolution 2423 (2018) and similar resolutions concerning the situation in other Sahel countries mark a precedent in the UN practice which could prove impossible to ignore in the future.

A considerable advance on previous UNSC practice is also represented by the adoption of a preventive and integrated approach to the root causes of crisis and tensions, including climate change. This might be taken for granted, due to the multidimensional challenge posed by climate securitization in the Sahel region. Nevertheless, as repeatedly warned by various groups of independent experts over the last two decades, for too long conflict prevention has remained "the poor relative" of huge operations deployed during and after armed conflicts,[181] with consequent flaws in the functioning of an effective system of collective security.[182] Similarly, the adoption of a comprehensive and integrated approach to sustainable development and human security has been constantly advocated in a number of UN documents in recent years. Yet, theoretical assertions have rarely been translated into concrete actions.

It cannot be ignored, however, that the fulfilment of the objectives pursued by the UNSC recommendation risks being hampered by various structural problems. In particular, the groundbreaking approach adopted by the Council is not supported by innovative tools. As a result, multidimensional threats and complex security issues are tackled by the UNSC within a legal framework that has remained substantially unchanged since 1945 and with the support of operational means (in particular, peace operations) whose reform has been repeatedly called for by various groups of independent experts, but in reality has not seen any substantial reform being undertaken.

Suffice here to mention, on the one hand, that the lack of a clear legal framework outlining the nature and extent of co-operation between the UN and regional or sub-regional organizations means may result in multiple actions, taken by multiple actors, according to a fragmented approach. On the other hand, it is striking to note that large peace operations, already burdened with a heavy mandate, continue to be

---

[180] "(. . .) for the time being (. . .) the role of the Security Council cannot be much more than to organise debates on climate change and international security" Koivurova (2014), p. 186; "At the moment, it seems that the best possible role for the UNSC in relation to climate change is to discuss the issue rather than act upon it", ibidem, p. 187.

[181] 'Hippo Report' para 63. See also paras. 72 and 73.

[182] "The biggest source of inefficiency in our collective security institutions has simply been an unwillingness to get serious about preventing deadly violence. The failure to invest time and resources early in order to prevent the outbreak and escalation of conflicts leads to much larger and deadlier conflagrations that are much costlier to handle later", *A More Secure World: Our Shared Responsibility. Report of the High-Level Panel on Threats, Challenges and Change*, UN Doc. A/59/565, 2 December 2004, para 39.

considered as a useful instrument to deal with whatever problem arises, including overly ambitious security tasks, with scant consideration for their own structural flaws and the extreme complexity of situations on the ground.

Against this background, it can be argued that the securitization of climate change may be regarded not only as a clear example of the complexity of new security threats, but also as a paradigm of the major limits of the (traditional) collective security system in addressing multidimensional challenges.[183] Should we therefore conclude that the Security Council is not the appropriate body to deal with climate change issues and their detrimental effects as some States claim?

In the opinion of the present writer, the problem is not an alleged lack of competence by the UNSC, but a shortage of adequate tools, specifically tailored to address the complexity of the new challenges. In other words, it is not sufficient that the UNSC members agree to address climate change as a security threat through a combination of various actors and skills. Multidimensional threats require a multidimensional strategy, both at the legal and the institutional level, in accordance with an integrated approach, with the support of highly competent subjects in various areas (including agro-ecology[184] and human rights[185]) from different national and international bodies and institutions, who work synergically, within a clear legal framework.

In addition, due to the inherent characterization of climate change as a global threat, a genuine integrated approach requires that measures adopted in the Sahel region are complemented by appropriate UNSC actions at the global level. In principle, the Council could make a direct contribution to the reduction of global warming by exercising its "legislative powers". For instance, it might strengthen obligations or extend duties already enshrined in existing multilateral treaties to all UN Member States.[186] The UNSC could also exercise its enforcement powers against States failing to comply with their climate change treaty obligations.[187] It is unlikely, however, that the above measures will be put into practice in the short term.[188] More generally, it cannot be ignored that three permanent members of the Council (China, United States and Russia) are among the world's major contributors

[183] See e.g. Arcari (2012), p. 37: "(...) la problematique institutionnelle ne saurait facilement être dissociée de celle relative à la recherche des moyens opérationnels aptes à assurer une gouvernance efficace des problèmes sécuritaires. Finalement, l'inadéquation institutionnelle du Conseil de sécurité à la gouvernance des problématiques posées par les nouvelles menaces à la paix est aussi liée, pour une bonne part, à l'inadaptation des instruments opérationnels à la disposition de l'organe".

[184] See e.g. Ide et al. (2021); Kalilou (2021).

[185] See supra Sect. 5.1 and Committee on Economic, Social and Cultural Rights, Concluding observations on the initial report of Mali, UN Doc. E/C.12/MLI/CO/1 of 6 November 2018, in particular, paras. 4–5, 38–40 and 53–54.

[186] Outstanding precedents may be found in the fight against terrorism and the use of weapons of mass destruction. For further considerations, see Boyle et al. (2019), p. 107 ff.

[187] In this sense, ibidem, pp. 117–118.

[188] See Boyle et al. (2019), p. 115 ff.

to greenhouse gas emissions and that only recently has the United States re-joined the Paris Agreement.[189] The evolution of the negotiations which preceded the Paris Agreement and the agreement itself[190] also show a clear reluctance by the majority of States to accept any stringent obligations on the prevention of climate change at the global level.

Returning to our initial question (new wine in old bottles or a first step towards a change in the security architecture of the Organization?), it can be argued that some new wine (but perhaps not so new) has been added to the old bottles of the UN legal and institutional framework. However, more structural changes have yet to be agreed upon to reshape and strengthen the capacity of the UN system to address climate change as a non-traditional security challenge in the Sahel region and in other areas of the world.

Obviously, this is primarily a political problem, which should be adequately addressed at the UN level. It is unlikely, however, that effective progress in this direction is possible as long as climate change in its security dimension is not perceived by UN member States first as a matter of urgency within their national boundaries. Unfortunately, however, too many States, including major powers, seem unprepared to tackle this challenge.

References

Aminga V, Krampe F (2000) Climate-related security risks and the African Union. Stockholm, SIPRI Policy Brief

Arcari M (2012) Gouvernance globale et sécurité collective. Quelques éléments de dissonance. In: Arcari M, Balmond L (sous la direction de), La gouvernance globale face aux defis de la sécurité collective, Editoriale Scientifica, Napoli

Balmond L (2008) La sécurité collective, du droit des Nations Unies au droit régional? In: Arcari M, Balmond L (sous la direction de), La sécurité collective entre légalité et défis à la légalité, Giuffrè, Milano

Barral V, Dupuy PM (2015) Sustainable development through integration. In: Viñuales JE (ed) The Rio Declaration on environment and development: a commentary. Oxford University Press, Oxford, pp 157–180

Baudas V et al (2001) Conflict mediation and peacebuilding in the Sahel: the role of the Maghreb countries in an African framework. SIPRI Policy Paper No. 58

[189] The decision of the United States to withdraw from the Paris Agreement on 4 November 2019 took effect on 4 November 2020. Following the deposit by the US Government of a new instrument of acceptance on 20 January 2021, the Agreement will enter into force for the United States on 19 February 2021.

[190] The Paris Agreement is in fact based on a system of (unilateral, voluntary and not quantified or quantifiable) "nationally determined contributions" to the global response to climate change (Article 3). Accordingly, the Agreement "(. . .) is a reflection of national politics more than a driver. The architecture will grow stronger when and if countries become comfortable and confident on the path toward decarbonization. Whether that happens depends on forces far larger than the UN", Roberts (2015).

Binder M, Heupel M (2018) Contested legitimacy: the UN Security Council and climate change. In: Scott VS, Ku C (eds) Climate change and the UN Security Council. Edward Elgar Publishing, Cheltenham, Northampton, pp 186–208

Boisson de Chazournes L (2016) Interactions between regional and universal organizations: a legal perspective. Brill, Nijhoff, Leiden, Boston

Boyle A et al (2019) The United Nations Security Council's legislative and enforcement powers and climate change. In: Scott VS, Ku C (eds) Climate change and the UN Security Council. Edward Elgar Publishing, Cheltenham, Northampton, pp 101–130

Bremberg N (2019) EU foreign and security policy on climate-related security risks. SIPRI Policy Brief: 1–7

Bremberg N et al (2019) The EU and climate related security risks: a community of practice in the making? J Eur Integrat 41:623–639

Chinkin C, Kaldor M (2017) International law and new wars. Cambridge University Press, Cambridge

Conca K (2019) Is there a role for the UN Security Council on climate change? Environ: Sci Policy Sustain Dev 61:4–15

Conforti B, Focarelli C (2017) Le Nazioni Unite, XI edn. Cedam, Naples

Da Costa F, Karlsrud J (2010) A role for civil affairs. Community conflict resolution? MINURCATs Intercommunity Dialogue Strategy in Eastern Chad. In Humanitarian Exchange Magazine 48

Davies K, Riddell T (2017) The warming war: how climate change is creating threats to international peace and security. Georgetown Environ Law Rev 30:47–74

Day A (2019) Politics in the driving seat: good offices, UN peace operations, and modern conflict. In: De Conig C, Peter M (eds) United Nations peace operations in a changing global order. Springer, Berlin, pp 67–89

Day A, Caus J (2020) Conflict prevention in an era of climate change. Adapting the UN to climate security risks. United Nations University, New York

Diehl PF (2018) Mainstreaming climate change adaptation into peace missions. In: Scott VS, Ku C (eds) Climate change and the UN Security Council. Edward Elgar Publishing, Cheltenham, Northampton, pp 131–146

Drange B (2018) The potential and limits of peace agreements. Colombia and Mali. Conflict Trends 4:12–20

Ebbesson J (2014) Social-ecological security and international law in the anthropocene. In: Ebbesson J et al (eds) International law and changing perception of security: Liber Amicorum Said Mahmoudi. Brill, Leiden, Boston, pp 71–92

Elliott L (2005) Expanding the mandate of the United Nations Security Council. In: Chambers WV, Green JF (eds) Reforming international environmental governance: from institutional limits to innovative reforms. United Nations University Press, Tokyo, New York, Paris, pp 204–226

Far S, Youngs R (2018) The EU's distinctive approach to climate security. In: Scott VS, Ku C (eds) Climate change and the UN Security Council. Edward Elgar Publishing, Cheltenham, Northampton, pp 147–161

Fetzek S, van Schaik L (2018) Europe's responsibility to prepare: managing climate security risks in a changing world. The Center for Climate and Security, Washington

Giegerich T (2012) Article 36. In: Simma B et al (eds) The Charter of the United Nations. A commentary, vol I. Oxford University Press, Oxford, pp 1119–1145

Gray C (2012) Climate change and the law on the use of force. In: Rayfuse R, Scott SV (eds) International law in the era of climate change. Edward Elgar Publishing, Cheltenham, Northampton, pp 219–241

Hernández AJR (2012) El principio de integración de los aspectos económicos, sociales y medioambientales del desarrollo sostenibile. Revista Española de Derecho Internacional LXIV:133–161

Ide T et al (2021) The past and future(s) of environmental peacebuilding. Int Aff 97:2–16

Kalilou O (2021) Climate change and conflict in the Sahel: the Acacia Gum Tree as a tool for environmental peacebuilding. Int Aff 97:201–218

Karlsrud J (2015) United Nations Mission in the Central African Republic and Chad I and II (MINURCAT I and II). In: Koops J et al (eds) The Oxford handbook of United Nations peacekeeping operations. Oxford University Press, Oxford, pp 791–802

Khagram S et al (2003) From the environment and human security to sustainable security and development. J Hum Dev 4:289–313

Koivurova T (2014) Climate change and international security. In: Ebbesson et al (eds) International law and changing perception of security: Liber Amicorum Said Mahmoudi. Brill, Leiden, Boston, pp 171–188

Kravik A (2018) The Security Council and climate change – Too hot to handle? In EJIL Talk!

Lippert TH (2019) NATO, climate change, and international security. A risk governance approach. Palgrave Macmillan, Chicago

Loiselle ME (2020) The penholder system and the rule of law in the Security Council decision-making: setback or improvement? Leiden J Int Law 33:139–156

Maertens L (2016) Quand les Casques bleus passent au vert: environnementalisation des activités de maintien de la paix de l'ONU. Études internationales 47:57–80

Maertens L, Shoshan M (2018) Greening peacekeeping: the environmental impact of UN peace operations. International Peace Institute, New York

Malone LA (1996) 'Green Helmets': a conceptual framework for Security Council authority in environmental emergencies. Mich J Int Law 17:515–536

Matthew R (2014) Integrating climate change into peacebuilding. Climatic Change 183:83–93

Nasu H (2013) The place of human security in collective security. J Confl Secur Law 18:95–129

Nasu H (2016) Human security and international law: the potential scope for legal development within the analytical framework of security. In: Footer ME et al (eds) Security and international law. Hart Publishing, Oxford, pp 25–42

Penny CK (2018) Climate change as a 'threat to international peace and security'. In: Scott VS, Ku C (eds) Climate change and the UN Security Council. Edward Elgar Publishing, Cheltenham, Northampton, pp 25–46

Reilly B (1996) 'Clear and present danger': a role for the United Nations Security Council in protecting the global environment. Melb Univ Law Rev 20:763–804

Rjetens S, Ruffa C (2019) Understanding coherence in UN peacekeeping: a conceptual framework. Int Peacekeep 26:383–407

Roberts D (2015) The conceptual breakthrough behind the Paris Climate Treaty, Vox, 15 December 2015. https://www.vox.com/2015/12/15/10172238/paris-climate-treaty-conceptual-breakthrough

Schreuer C (1977) Recommendations and the traditional sources of international law. German Yearb Int Law 20:103–118

Scott SW (2015) Implications of climate change for the UN Security Council: mapping the range of potential policy responses. Int Aff 91:1317–1333

Scott SW (2018) The attitude of the P5 towards a climate change role for the council. In: Scott VS, Ku C (eds) Climate change and the UN Security Council. Edward Elgar Publishing, Cheltenham, Northampton, pp 209–228

Scott SW, Ku C (2018) The UN Security Council and global action on climate change. In: Scott VS, Ku C (eds) Climate change and the UN Security Council. Edward Elgar Publishing, Cheltenham, Northampton, pp 1–24

Sindico F (2007) Climate change: a Security (Council) issue? Carbon Clim Law Rev 1:29–34

Spink L (2019) Strengthened planning in UN peacekeeping operations: how MINUSMA is reinforcing its strategic planning unit. Center for Civilians in Conflict

Szasz PC (1992) Restructuring the international organizational framework. In: Brown Weiss E (ed) Environmental change and international law: new challenges and dimensions. United Nations University Press, Tokyo, pp 340–384

Tanzi A (2004) Il ruolo delle organizzazioni regionali nel dibattito alle Nazioni Unite. In: Lattanzi F, Spinedi M (eds) Le organizzazioni regionali e il mantenimento della pace nella prassi di fine XX secolo. Editoriale Scientifica, Napoli, pp 1–31

Tinker C (1992) "Environmental security" in the United Nations: not a matter for the Security Council. Tenn Law Rev 59:787–801

Venturi B, Barana L (2021) Lake Chad: another protracted crisis or a regional exception?. IAI Papers 21: 10 March 2021

Voigt C (2013) The principle of sustainable development. Integration and ecological integrity. In: Voigt C (ed) Rule of law for nature. New dimensions and ideas in environmental law. Cambridge University Press, Cambridge, pp 146–157

Wood M (2016) The interpretation of Security Council resolutions, revisited. In Max Planck Yearbook of UN Law 20:3-35

Part IV
Law of the Sea

On the Nature of the Law of the Sea

Irini Papanicolopulu

Abstract The law of the sea is one of the oldest fields of international law and one that is still very much studied and applied. Yet there seem to be few definitions of what the law of the sea exactly is, what it includes and what falls outside its scope. This chapter tries to provide some elements to move towards a better understanding of the nature of the law of the sea, through a historical analysis, which examines definitions provided from the seventeenth century until today. It thus identifies some elements which characterise the current definitions of the law of the sea and which pertain to its relationship with maritime law, its subject and its substantive content.

1 "Intellectual Attraction and Intrinsic Elegance"

There is no description that captivates the fascination with the law of the sea so well as the brief title with which Professor Tullio Scovazzi opens his Hague course: "Intellectual Attraction and Intrinsic Elegance".[1] The law of the sea has fascinated international lawyers for centuries and has been one of the building blocks upon which modern international law has been developed. Past eminent scholars such as Grotius and Vattel have discussed issues pertaining to the freedom of the high seas and the sovereignty over coastal waters, but also of access to resources and the rights of states with respect to their vessels. Modern lawyers, be they scholars or practitioners, are also often engaged with the basic concepts of the law of the sea, as well as with their adaptation to the current needs of the international community. The law of the sea still forms part of many international law textbooks and is taught at universities worldwide, continuing to fascinate many young lawyers that choose to make it their preferred field of study, research and practice.

[1] Scovazzi (2001), p. 53; see also Scovazzi (2015).

I. Papanicolopulu (✉)
School of Law, University of Milano-Bicocca, Milan, Italy
e-mail: irini.papanicolopulu@unimib.it

M. Arcari et al. (eds.), *Trends and Challenges in International Law*,
https://doi.org/10.1007/978-3-030-94387-5_10

Yet, it would be hard to find any extensive and precise definition of what the "law of the sea" is. Most textbooks, not to mention the many volumes that deal with specific issues of this branch of law, do not provide much conceptual elaboration of what the law of the sea is, apart from some occasional definitions that tend to refer either to its addressees or to its substantive issues.[2] Indeed, the majority of us who work on the law of the sea do not ordinarily address the nature of this branch of international law. Somehow, we take it for granted that the law of the sea exists and that it has a certain content or "we know it when we see it".

Having had the good fortune of approaching the law of the sea under the guidance of Professor Tullio Scovazzi, the author of this chapter has since been entrapped by the "intellectual attraction and intrinsic elegance" of this field of law. It therefore came as an obvious choice, at a time when she wanted to pay a tribute to him, to address, among his many fields of work, this one. In his many writings, Professor Scovazzi has explored old and new problems and has contributed to the advancement of this discipline, questioning strongly held beliefs and advancing novel approaches with clear and rigorous analysis and persuasive language. Having had the chance to discuss with him whether specific issues were part of the law of the sea or not, and thus to wonder about what was actually included in this field of law, it seems a fitting tribute to try and offer some remarks on the nature of the law of the sea and its content. This chapter therefore begins from the obvious starting point, the United Nations Convention on the Law of the Sea (UNCLOS or Convention),[3] which is discussed in Sect. 2. It then goes back to the beginnings of the discipline and follows doctrinal definitions from the past centuries (Sects. 3 and 4) until the present day (Sect. 5), before offering some conclusive remarks (Sect. 6).

2 The UNCLOS as *the* Law of the Sea

Any effort to deal with the law of the sea needs to take into account the UNCLOS. After all, the UNCLOS has purported to "settle, in a spirit of mutual understanding and cooperation, all issues relating to the law of the sea".[4] This objective developed out of the need, particularly felt by developing States in the 1960s and 1970s, to revise the traditional rules of the law of the sea and to adapt them to the new political, economic and social framework generated by the process of decolonisation. As has been noted:

[2]For an overview of such definitions see Sects. 4 and 5 below. An exception is provided in Lucchini and Voelckel (1990), who devote particular attention to defining the law of the sea and distinguishing it from similar concepts.

[3]United Nations Convention on the Law of the Sea (adopted 10 December 1982, entered into force 16 November 1994) 1833 UNTS 397.

[4]UNCLOS Preamble.

> Pour la majorité des Etats, la Conférence était chargée de substituer au droit Classique de la mer un droit nouveau, ayant pour finalité explicite d'être radicalement plus favorable aux intérêts des pays en développement et dont les dispositions devaient concourir à la réalisation de cet objectif.[5]

This goal was reflected in the mandate of the Third United Nations Conference on the Law of the Sea, which would eventually produce the UNCLOS. In 1970, the United Nations (UN) General Assembly decided to convene "a conference on the law of the sea", the mandate of which would include:

> the establishment of an equitable international regime – including an international machinery – for the area and the resources of the sea-bed and the ocean floor, and the subsoil thereof, beyond the limits of national jurisdiction, a precise definition of the area, and a broad range of related issues including those concerning the regime of the high seas, the continental shelf, the territorial sea (including the question of its breadth and the question of international straights) and contiguous zone, fishing and conservation of the living resources of the high seas (including the question of the preferential rights of coastal States), the preservation of the marine environment (including, *inter alia*, the prevention of pollution) and scientific research.[6]

The UN General Assembly, therefore, did not provide a definition of the law of the sea but rather decided to list the issues that this field of international law included. These issues concern both maritime zoning, i.e. the maritime zones into which the ocean is divided and their legal regime, and functional issues that straddle across the boundaries of maritime zones, such as fishing and protection of the marine environment.

Comparing the mandate with the product of the Conference two facts become evident. First, that the law of the sea, at least as incorporated in the final text of the UNCLOS, consists very much of the issues already identified by the UN General Assembly in 1970. Second, that the UNCLOS, and therefore the law of the sea also deals with issues other than those expressly mentioned in the 1970 mandate. These additional issues are both substantive, such as the protection of archaeological objects[7] and the transfer of technology,[8] and procedural, such as the settlement of disputes.[9] The fact that the UNCLOS deals with all law of the sea issues identified by the UN General Assembly as being worthy of (re)statement, joined with the fact that the Convention itself goes beyond this list and also addresses other issues closely tied to human activities in the seas and oceans, raises the question: does the content of the UNCLOS coincide, totally, with the content of the law of the sea?

The UN General Assembly seems to give a positive answer to this question. In its annual Resolution on Oceans and the Law of the Sea the UN General Assembly, for decades now, has

[5] De Lacharrière (1983), p. 12.

[6] UNGA Res. 2750(XXV) of 17 December 1970.

[7] Art. 303 UNCLOS. Garabello and Scovazzi (2003); Scovazzi (2004).

[8] Part XIV UNCLOS.

[9] Part XV UNCLOS.

> [emphasised] the universal and unified character of the Convention, and [reaffirmed] that the Convention sets out *the legal framework within which all activities in the oceans and seas must be carried out* and is of strategic importance as the basis for national, regional and global action and cooperation in the marine sector, and that its integrity needs to be maintained.[10]

However, as Professor Scovazzi has brilliantly demonstrated, in some instances the UNCLOS may not be the legal framework for all activities at sea.[11] The UNCLOS may present some gaps, notably with respect to bioprospecting, but also with respect to other issues, that were either not known about at the time when this treaty was adopted, or that were avoided for a number of reasons. In fact, the UNCLOS itself cautions the attentive reader that there is more law of the sea out there than he or she may find in the Convention text. In the first place, the repeated reference to other treaties and legal instruments in many UNCLOS provisions points towards the fact that law of the sea rules may also be incorporated in other treaties, either preceding or following the Convention. Furthermore, the UNCLOS preamble ends by "affirming that matters not regulated by this Convention continue to be governed by the rules and principles of general international law". It seems plausible to consider that these other "matters" do not fall outwith the law of the sea, but are rather part of this legal field. Any other interpretation, that would refer to "matters" that do not fall within the law of the sea, would render the provision redundant, if not totally useless.

In conclusion, the UNCLOS certainly incorporates much of the rules and principles of the law of the sea. However, this treaty does not provide a definition of what the "law of the sea" is, nor does it contain an exhaustive list of all matters that fall within this field of international law.[12] Since the treaty does not provide an answer, one must turn to subsidiary sources, in particular legal doctrine, in search of some guidance.[13]

3 Law of the Sea in Early International Legal Doctrine

Early international law scholars do not generally seem to have conceived of the law of the sea as a discrete field. For example, Hugo Grotius, who is considered by many to be the father of the modern law of the sea, actually never wrote a real law of the sea treatise. Indeed, he addressed only some points relating to the law of the sea, both in his famous *Mare Liberum*[14] and in his all-encompassing treatise on international

[10] See, for the most recent text, UNGA Res. 75/239 of 31 December 2020 (emphasis added).

[11] Scovazzi (2010). See also Treves (1995), p. vii; Brown (1994), p. 1.

[12] This is not a limitation of the UNCLOS. The purpose of a treaty is to provide clear legal regulation, rather than abstract definitions, and certainly the UNCLOS goes as far as any other treaty in achieving this aim.

[13] Customary international law is out of the question, since this source of international law, even more than treaties, aims at regulating conduct and not providing abstract definitions.

[14] Grotius (1609).

law.[15] At the very moment when he forcefully argues in favour of the freedom of the seas, he does not use the phrase "law of the sea", much less provide any conceptual abstraction or definition. Grotius conceived of the rules that apply to marine space as part of international law, the "ius (commune) gentium" that regulated inter-state relationships. This was indeed a great development by itself, since international law was in its infancy when Grotius was writing[16] and the primary issue for Grotius was to consolidate the existence of the "ius gentium"—rather than, one might surmise, argue in favour of a subfield that would include the rules of the sea. The same conclusions may be drawn for other scholars writing on "law of the sea" issues and involved in the battle of books.[17]

There were exceptions, however. Welwod, one of the opponents of Grotius, did use the phrase "sea-lawes", which even formed the title of one of his books.[18] Interestingly, what he referred to were primarily the maritime rules that regulated mostly "private" aspects of maritime matters. All the same, in his treatise, Welwod did also address some "public" issues related to sea uses, in particular issues of "property" (sovereignty) over the sea as well as the regulation of fishing, in open contrast to the theories advanced by Grotius. The author thus seems to have a conception of "sea lawes" that includes both public and private elements—one that is surprisingly close to the modern conception.[19]

The reason for Welwod's composite notion of "sea lawes" is probably to be found in the fact that, by the beginning of the seventeenth century, there was a well-established body of rules concerning maritime matters, that was only partially affected by the new rules that were being developed concerning freedom and possession of the seas. This body of laws included, as the subtitle to the book illustrated, both uses developed within the seafaring communities and the acts of sovereigns.[20] The genesis of this body of law, as Welwod recorded, had originated in the Mediterranean Sea and dated back to the laws of the Rhodians, later picked up by the Romans and, following a break in the first part of the middle ages, by the

---

[15] Grotius (1625).

[16] Scovazzi (2018), p. 48 points to the fact that Grotius was the first to elaborate comprehensively what we call today "international law".

[17] As Gidel (1932), p. 105 noted,

> ni Grotius dans son *Mare Liberum*, ni Selden dans son *Mare Clausum*, ni Bynkershoek dans son *Dominio Maris*, ni les autres auteurs, moins célèbres, dont nous aurons à mentionner les noms lorsque nous étudierons le développement de l'idée de liberté de la mer ou de l'idée de mer territoriale, ne se sont proposé d'écrire un traité général de droit maritime.

[18] Welwod (1613). Curiously, Gidel (1932) does not mention Welwod in his overview over the law of the sea doctrine.

[19] Infra Sect. 5.1.

[20] The full title of the book was "An Abridgement of All Sea-Lawes; Gathered Forth from all Writings and Monuments, which are to be found among any people or Nation, upon the coasts of the great Ocean and Mediterranean Sea: And specially ordered and disposed for the use and benefit of all benevolent Sea-farers, within his Majesties Dominions of Great Britanne, Ireland, and the adjacent Isles thereof".

maritime communities of the Mediterranean.[21] While there is no terminological consistency in either old or new scholars, this body of rules will be referred to as "maritime law" for the purposes of this chapter.

The new rules on the freedom or the dominion of the seas, which were considered by Grotius and other contemporaries as rules of the "new" law of nations, could also be perceived, as Welwod did, as part of the "old" common maritime law. In fact, they were both. On the one hand, they were rules that concerned the relationship between States at sea, therefore they were certainly part of the law of nations. On the other hand, they also closely affected navigation and therefore issues related to the well-established maritime law, of which they could be seen as a part. It probably depended on the background and the objectives of each scholar whether they were posited within one or the other regime.

A concept similar to that advanced by Welwod emerged in nineteenth century legal doctrine, which considered the substantive rules embodied in the different, private and public, national and international formal sources as part of the 'common law of the sea'. In his 1884 treatise on the law of nations, the British scholar and practitioner Twiss described the rules that apply at sea in the following words:

> [the open sea] is the public highway of Nations, upon which the vessels of all Nations meet in terms of equality, each vessel carrying with it the laws of its own Nation for the government of those on board of it in their mutual relations with one another, but all subject to a Common Law of Nations in matters of mutual relation between the vessels themselves and their crews. The origin of this *Common Law of the Sea* is lost in the darkness of a very remote antiquity, but it sprang into existence with the earliest necessities of maritime commerce. We find the rudiments of such a law amongst the Athenians; and the Rhodian Law of the Sea, of which a very few fragments have been preserved in the Digest, are supposed to have been a collection of Maritime Customs observed amongst the Nations established on the shores of the Mediterranean, and which formed at such time their Common Law on maritime matters. Rules of Law which prevailed amongst those Nations are still recognized by the Maritime tribunals of existing European Nations, as rules for the decision of analogous questions.[22]

Putting aside the romantic tones characterising that era, the use of the term "law of the sea" by Twiss is very much alike that already used, two centuries before, by Welwod. And he is not alone: the narrative of a 'common law of the sea' that derives from old customs applied by the maritime communities, and which partakes of acts by both public and private actors, is generally recognised throughout the nineteenth century. The American Captain Colomb, writing to the ILA in 1883, notes that

> [i]n days gone by, before the rules regulating sea traffic were authoritatively formulated, nations recognised a general 'custom of the sea', on the main points of which it was understood that all mariners worthy of authority were agreed, and owing to such understood agreement, National Courts were able to administer a law which was accepted as fairly international.[23]

---

[21] Welwod (1613).

[22] Twiss (1884), p. 286 (emphasis added). Twiss had been Advocate-General to the Admiralty and Queen's Advocate-General.

[23] 11 Ass'n Reform & Codification L. Nations Rep. Conf. 133 (1883), 134.

Furthermore, the idea of a common core of principles applicable beyond state boundaries is common also to those who considered that national legislation had in fact taken over the common (international) law. Thus Reddie considered that

> [a]s there grows up, however, an internal common or customary law in each particular nation, [. . .] so a similar common law appears to have gradually formed and cultivated between or among the inhabitants of different countries engaged in maritime traffic, who [. . .] are brought into contact, and have frequent intercourse in their mercantile dealings, and thus become connected for the purposes of gain or profit, and interested in the adoption and observance of similar general and uniform modes or rules of proceeding. For the observance or establishment of such a jus maritimum universal, an express legislative act of the supreme powers of states does not appear to have been necessary.[24]

This common law of the sea went beyond what came to be understood as the 'law of the sea' in the second half of the twentieth century, i.e. rules that concerned only states.[25] It included rules originating from and binding also other actors, such as the master and the crew of a vessel, and the shipowner. It contained a mixture of 'public' norms, 'private' norms, and norms that were located in between the public and the private spheres. 'Public' norms included those relating to the status of maritime waters, freedom of navigation and State jurisdiction upon vessels, while 'private' norms addressed, among others, maritime contracts, ownership of vessels, and conflicts of laws. Rules in between concerned matters such as the safety of vessels and salvage. Using terms commonly utilised today, we can say that it included public international law, maritime law, admiralty law, private international law and commercial law.

The rules of the 'common law of the sea' applied beyond the territory of states and to actors coming from different states. This way, the law applicable to maritime activities, whether termed the common law of the sea or international maritime law, was truly international.[26] Apart from this general consideration, the 'common law of the sea' as a conceptual category seems not to have formed the object of much elaboration and it falls beyond the scope of this article to discuss the exact nature of the 'common law of the sea' and its relationship with maritime law and international law. Suffice it to say that for those writing in the nineteenth century, the common law of the sea was considered as part of international law and its rules were therefore rules of international law.

---

[24] Reddie (1841), pp. 24–25. He goes on however to argue that 'from the time [. . .] nations began to improve their own internal law by statutes and ordinances, and to commit it to writing in digests general or particular, this maritime universal consuetudinary law, however valuable as a model for imitation, however rich in materials for the construction of new codes, cannot be said to have existed as a general compulsory or coercive body of law' (ibid., p. 27).

[25] Section 4.

[26] See for example Lauterpacht (1970), p. 155, according to whom the '. . . origins of international law as grounded in natural law and as expressive, together with the law merchant and maritime law, of a universal law of mankind'.

4 The Twentieth Century

The narrative of a 'common law of the sea' was resilient as a notional category and was still used well into the twentieth century, at least by British scholars. Higgins and Colombos, writing in 1943, considered that

> from the earliest days of navigation, seafaring men have been subject to rules dealing with collisions and salvage which may be said to form a "common law of the sea, adopted by the common consent of States". This "common law" was binding, not because it was imposed by any superior Power, but because it had generally been accepted as a rule of conduct. Whatever may have been its origin, whether in the usages of navigation or in the ordinances of maritime States, or in both, it has become the law of the sea only by the concurrent sanction of those who may be said to constitute the shipping and commercial world. As regards changes in these rules, they have been accomplished by the concurrent assent, express or understood, of maritime nations.[27]

This concept could indeed be seen as separate from the main topic of their work, which, as defined in the beginning of the book includes "[i]nternational law, of which the principles which govern maritime intercourse, naval warfare and neutrality, form a substantial part, is a body of rules which States consider they are bound to observe in their mutual relations".[28]

While the "common law of the sea" could be seen as antithetical to the "international law governing maritime intercourse", the treatment of the former concept by Higgins and Colombos is rather ambiguous and appears to signal the transition from a public/private conception to a purely 'public' one. On the one hand, they consider that the 'common law of the sea' is adopted 'by the common consent of States' and that its modification happens with the assent of 'maritime nations'. The reference to "states" exclusively signals a "public international law" approach, according to which international law is made by states. On the other hand, however, they still consider that it has become such by the 'concurrent sanction of . . . the shipping and commercial world', a statement that seems to attribute a certain role in the creation and adoption of rules also to non State actors. This position could be considered as further strengthened by the reference, in discussing the source of the international law of the sea, to the "Rhodian Sea Law", the "Consolato del Mare" and other similar acts, adopted not by states, but rather by other actors.[29]

In fact, during the end of the nineteenth century and the beginning of the twentieth century, the terms "international maritime law" and "international law of the sea" were quite often used interchangeably,[30] and it was only due to the work of some authors that the two fields were eventually separated.

---

[27] Higgins and Colombos (1943), p. 223.

[28] Higgins and Colombos (1943), p. 7.

[29] Higgins and Colombos (1943), pp. 24–29.

[30] For example, Berlingieri (1918) adopts the title "Towards the Unification of the Law of the Sea" for a book that actually discusses mostly (private) maritime law. Similarly, in Higgins and Colombos (1943), p. iii, which deals with the (public) law of the sea, Colombos refers to Higgin's "idea of writing a book on maritime international law".

The tendency to distinguish the 'public' law of the sea from the 'private' law of the sea characterised, in particular, what can probably be considered as the first modern treatise on the law of the sea. In his 1932 book "The Public International Law of the Sea",[31] Gidel avowedly addressed "public international maritime law", which was defined in the following terms:

> Le droit maritime a pour objet l'ordre juridique qui régit le milieu marin et les diverses utilisations dont il est susceptible. [. . .] De cette définition du droit maritime, il résulte que c'est essentiellement le droit du milieu marin. Ce milieu présente, au point de vue du droit, un aspect différent de celui que présente le milieu Terrestre. [. . .] Les règles de l'ordre juridique régissant le milieu marin appartiennent, suivant la terminologie habituelle des juristes, au droit public ou au droit privé. Il ne faudrait pas cependant exagérer cette division : elle a surtout une valeur d'exposition. [. . .] Le droit maritime, étant le droit d'un milieu, ne saurait être, sans arbitraire, divisé en cloisons étanches, l'une comportant le droit public maritime e l'autre le droit privé maritime. [. . .] On peut toutefois distinguer dans le droit maritime trois grands groupes de questions correspondant à ce que l'on peut appeler le droit commercial maritime, le droit administratif maritime (dans lequel on peut faire entrer le droit pénal maritime), le droit international public maritime. C'est de ce dernier seulement que nous avons à nous occuper. [. . .] Le droit international public maritime est, d'après Calvo, « l'ensemble des lois, des règlements et des usages observés pour la navigation, le commerce par mer et dans les rapports, soit de paix soit d'hostilités, des puissances maritime entre elles ».[32]

Gidel's definition highlights some interesting elements of the law of the sea, that are still valid to this day. Rather than being the law that regulates a certain activity, the law of the sea is the law that applies in a certain environment ('milieu') and which, therefore, regulates everything that happens in that environment. As a consequence, it is necessary to consider the place where it applies, rather than the addressees or the activities concerned, in order to encompass a certain rule within the law of the sea. Furthermore, according to Gidel, the law of the sea presents both public and private aspects that are closely interconnected and which it is artificial, to a certain extent, to divide.

Gidel marked both a continuity with previous authors and a departure from older treatises. On the one hand, he considered that 'maritime law' was unique and that it included both public and private aspects, which could not easily be separated into 'watertight partitions'. In this respect, he seems to follow the same lines as those advanced by earlier scholars. On the other hand, there was a part of 'maritime law', namely 'public international maritime law' that had its own existence and which could form the object of a treatise such as the one that Gidel himself wrote. This 'public international maritime law' related to the relationships between states and is therefore to be assimilated into what we call today 'law of the sea'—as the title of his oeuvre shows. Gidel, therefore, signals the passage from a common law of the sea that involved actors other than States, to a 'modern' 'public international law of the

---

[31] Gidel (1932).

[32] Gidel (1932), pp. 4–6.

sea' which aimed at discussing the rules that applied solely in the relationship between States.[33]

This distinction, together with the preference of international lawyers to treat solely the 'public' part of the law of the sea, is evident in the other treatises in this legal field up to the end of the twentieth century, written by scholars that carry different conceptual approaches to international law. For example, according to McDougal and Burke:

> Within the more comprehensive earth-space process of authoritative decision, the international law of the sea is, however, a clearly distinguishable component process, characterised by its own relatively unique features. These distinctive features may be observed in varying phases of the process of interaction by which peoples exploit the oceans and their resources, of the process of claim by which authority is invoked for the regulation of interactions, and of the process of decision by which authority is allocated and exercised in such regulation.[34]

Setting aside the particular language used, which conforms to their conception of international law, the authors actually address the public part of the law of the sea, that is, maritime zones and the jurisdiction of states over vessels flying their flag.

Similarly, Lucchini and Voelckel, while to some extent deploring the scission between maritime law and the law of the sea, prefer to address the latter only,[35] which they define in the following words:

> Tout un système de règles a, en effet, été édicté : règles nationales, mais aussi internationales. Pour ces dernières, certaines s'appliquent aux rapports prives ; d'autres – qui nous intéressent principalement ici – ont pour fonction de repartir les espaces, d'en fixer le statut, de canaliser et régir les activités sociales qui s'exercent en milieu marin etc . . . L'expression « droit de la mer » est utilisée pour designer ce dernier corps de règles.[36]

At the turn of the century, Churchill and Lowe still defined the law of the sea as "the rules and principles that bind States in their international relations concerning maritime matters".[37] As the two authors go on to specify, these are rules of public international law and therefore distinct from both private (international) maritime law and from municipal law.[38] They deal with mainly two sets of issues, maritime zones, on the one hand, and particular uses of the sea, on the other.

[33] It should be remembered that at the time when Gidel was writing, legal positivism was in its heyday, as were efforts by international lawyers to break clear from older conceptions of international law that went beyond the State as the subject of international law, such as natural law.

[34] McDougal and Burke (1962), p. vii.

[35] Lucchini and Voelckel (1990), p. 9.

[36] Lucchini and Voelckel (1990), p. v.

[37] Churchill and Lowe (1999), p. 1.

[38] Ibid., according to which the law of the sea does not include "rules of private maritime law" or "municipal law".

5 Modern Understandings of the "Law of the Sea"

The current understanding of the "law of the sea" does not depart much from the conception that was advanced during the twentieth century, although it is certainly influenced by current debates, relating both to the law of the sea itself and to public international law more generally. Three trends are particularly visible: first, the enduring close relationship between the law of the sea and maritime law; second, the tendency to broaden the subjects (or actors) of the law of the sea; third the extension of its reach, which today includes many more issues than were originally considered.

5.1 Law of the Sea and Maritime Law

Starting with the first trend, it is necessary to keep in mind, as already discussed above, that the law of the sea appears to have become a discrete field of (public) international law, and thus opposed to (private) maritime law, only in the twentieth century. Yet the close relationship between these two branches of law did not die and is now and again rekindled in different sorts of works. On one hand, some authors still use the phrase "maritime law" to identify the rules of public international law that apply to maritime spaces,[39] whilst others question the necessity to separate into watertight compartments the two disciplines.[40] On the other hand, there are works which try to bridge what is perceived as an artificial divide and bring the different rules that apply at sea all together. For example, the first volume of a leading manual on "international maritime law" is entitled "the law of the sea".[41] In its introduction, it is argued that

> [w]hile there is a trend in certain legal literature to treat the law of the sea and shipping law (or admiralty law) separately, it is submitted that these public and private branches of international maritime law have today become intimately interdependent [. . .] some argue that they are now fused together into a single body of law.[42]

Most law of the sea textbooks and treatises, nonetheless, tend still to focus on the public international law of the sea, albeit they do include references to rules and instruments that *stricto sensu* would belong to international maritime law.[43]

---

[39] Conforti (2013).

[40] Lucchini and Voelckel (1990), p. 7.

[41] Attard et al. (2014).

[42] Attard (2014), p. vii.

[43] For example, Forteau and Thouvenin (2017), p. 31 openly acknowledge that they feel justified "losque le besoin s'en fera sentir, de procéder dans cet ouvrage à quelques incursions ponctuelles dans le droit interne de la mer ou le droit (international) privé maritime".

5.2 The Subjects of the Law of the Sea

At the close of the nineteenth century, positivism prevailed over natural law, shaping the "traditional" understanding of international law, as it is conceived today. This development consolidated, among others, the belief that only States are subjects of international law.[44] The establishment, in the course of the twentieth century, of international organisations composed of States, altered this conclusion only in the measure in which international legal subjectivity was recognised to these organisations.[45] This subjectivity, however, was derivative, and depended to a significant extent upon the will of States.[46]

In recent times, however, this assumption has been challenged. Scholars have increasingly argued in favour of an international subjectivity of other actors, which include natural and legal persons. The development of international human rights[47] has paved the way for a recognition of an—at least limited—legal personality for individuals. Furthermore, it is possible to consider that individuals also enjoy "other" rights, beyond human rights.[48] Corporate entities have also been recognised as having a certain legal personality, at least in the field of international investment law.[49] More recently, the legal subjectivity of other entities, and even of elements such as nature, is being discussed.[50]

These developments have been visible also with respect to the law of the sea, an area of international law which has, in certain respects, rather led the move towards the recognition of international personality for actors other than States. Two

[44] Anzilotti (1956), p. 211, according to whom "La dottrina prevalente considera il Diritto internazionale come un complesso di norme giuridiche aventi valore soltanto per gli stati e fra gli stati".

[45] ICJ, *Reparation for Injuries Suffered in the Service of the United Nations*, Advisory Opinion of 11 April 1949, 8

> Throughout its history, the development of international law has been influenced by the requirements of international life, and the progressive increase in the collective activities of States has already given rise to instances of action upon the international plane by certain entities which are not States.

[46] Ibid., 9 "It must be acknowledged that its Members, by entrusting certain functions to it, with the attendant duties and responsibilities, have clothed it with the competence required to enable those functions to be effectively discharged".

[47] Universal Declaration of Human Rights, UNGA Res. 217 A of 10 December 1948. The Declaration was followed by numerous treaties, including the International Covenant on Civil and Political Rights (adopted 16 December 1966, entered into force 23 May 1976) 999 UNTS 171, and the International Covenant on Economic, Social and Cultural Rights (adopted 16 December 1966, entered into force 3 January 1976) 993 UNTS 3.

[48] Peters (2016).

[49] ICSID, *Urbaser S.A. and Consorcio de Aguas Bilbao Bizkaia, Bilbao Biskaia Ur Partzuergoa v The Argentine Republic*, ICSID Case No. ARB/07/26, Award of 8 December 2016, para. 1195. See also *Guiding Principles on Business and Human Rights*, Human Rights Council Res. 17/4 of 16 June 2011.

[50] On the legal subjectivity of nature, see the contribution by Maria Clara Maffei in this volume.

examples seem useful to illustrate this tendency. In the first place, the UNCLOS has explicitly recognised the rights and obligations of natural and legal persons in connection with activities in the International Seabed Area. Part XI of the UNCLOS includes provisions that not only attribute to these persons substantive rights and duties,[51] but also allows them to bring actions against States and other entities before the Seabed Disputes Chamber of the International Tribunal for the Law of the Sea.[52] In the second place, the law of the sea, as codified in international treaties that include the International Convention on the Safety of Life at Sea (SOLAS) and the International Convention on Salvage, attribute a duty directly on masters of vessels to rescue people in distress at sea.[53]

The growing relevance of actors other than States has led scholars to provide definitions of the law of the sea that take into account this diversity. Thus, today the law of the sea has been considered to include "[t]he body of rules that bind States and other subjects of international law in their maritime affairs".[54] This definition, while similar to that provided at the close of the twentieth century, departs from the latter in its inclusion of subjects other than states.

5.3 The Substantive Enlargement of the Law of the Sea

The greatest departure from traditional understanding of the law of the sea is perhaps to be noted with respect to the substantive content of this field. Early scholars who wrote about the law of the sea, such as Grotius, focused almost exclusively upon the tension between the principle of freedom (of the high seas) and state sovereignty (upon the territorial sea). Even today, it is commonplace to consider that "[a]ny discussion of the law of the sea takes as its starting point the fundamental principle of the freedoms of the seas".[55]

On the other hand, modern exponents of the doctrine tend to focus on many different aspects of the law of the sea. In this respect, it has been noted that

> Whilst the law had its initial origins in determining the status and control of ocean space, the contemporary international law of the sea goes well beyond focussing on the extent of coastal State sovereignty and jurisdiction to encompass the ongoing interests of the international community in the deep seabed, high seas, and fish stocks, whilst also regulating marine scientific research, military uses of the oceans, and marine environmental protection.[56]

---

[51] Including Art. 137(3) UNCLOS, Art. 151(6) UNCLOS, and Art. 153(2)(b) UNCLOS.

[52] Art. 187(c) and (d) UNCLOS.

[53] Reg. V/33.1 International Convention for the Safety of Life at Sea (adopted 1 November 1974, entered into force 25 May 1980) 1184 UNTS 278, as amended, and Art. 10 International Convention on Salvage (adopted 28 April 1989, entered into force 14 July 1996).

[54] Tanaka (2018), p. 3.

[55] Kelin (2011).

[56] Rothwell and Stephens (2010), p. 1.

Similarly, changing language but not content, it has been noted that

> le droit international de la mer, longtemps réduit à quelques principes, répond de nos jours à des préoccupations fort diverses de la communauté internationale, que tente de satisfaire un réseau normative de plus en plus dense.[57]

This development is probably due, to a certain extent, to the development of international law itself, which has notoriously moved from a law on the coexistence of States to a law on the cooperation of states. Already in 1950, it was noted, with respect to the broadening of the law of the sea:

> cette société – qui, après avoir occupé la terre, tende à présent à occuper une partie de la haute mer – évolue vers l'interdépendance de ses membres et vers un nouveau droit de la mer, en concordance avec le nouveau droit des gens; ce droit aura à règlementer juridiquement la tendance de chaque Etat à s'approprier les richesses naturelles et minérales d'une parties de la haute mer avec l'intérêt général de co-existence et d'interdépendance sociale, économique, politique, culturelle et même démographique internationale.[58]

Today, international law includes not only the law of diplomatic relations and the laws of war, which formed the initial subjects of interest to jurists, but also a wealth of other fields, ranging from environmental law, to investment law, to human rights law, to space law.[59] Some of these fields are discrete in that they apply to a particular space, such as the polar regions (polar law) or the outer space (space law). Most subfields of international law, however, are characterised by their addressing a particular substantive issue, such as investments, human rights, or the environment. As long as these issues pertain also to the seas and oceans, it follows as a natural consequence that rules concerning these aspects will become part of the law of the sea.

Some of these issues were indeed already incorporated into the UNCLOS, following the mandate given to the Third United Nations Conference on the Law of the Sea by the UN General Assembly, as well as following the negotiations in the context of the Conference.[60] Alongside "traditional" law of the sea issues, including maritime zones and the delimitation of maritime boundaries, the UNCLOS does also contain rules concerning, among others, access to fisheries[61] and exploitation of other resources,[62] safety of life,[63] protection of the environment,[64] marine scientific

---

[57] Forteau and Thouvenin (2017), p. 23.

[58] Mateesco (1950), p. 152.

[59] So much so, that Tullio Treves has titled his general course to the Hague Academy "The Expansion of International Law"; Treves (2018).

[60] Supra, Sect. 2.

[61] Eg Art 87(1)(e) UNCLOS.

[62] Eg Art 77 UNCLOS.

[63] Art 98 and Art 146 UNCLOS.

[64] Eg Art 192 UNCLOS and the entire Part XII UNCLOS.

research,[65] transfer of technology,[66] labour conditions,[67] protection of archaeological and historical objects,[68] creation of new bodies[69] and settlement of disputes.[70] A similar trend may be seen in other treaties that are generally considered as (also being) part of the law of the sea,[71] such as the 2000 Smuggling Protocol[72] and the 2001 UNESCO Convention on the Protection of the Underwater Cultural Heritage.[73] Furthermore, the progressive expansion of the topics covered under the law of the sea is well documented in the textbooks, which today include sections dealing with "conservation of marine biological diversity",[74] "maintenance of international peace and security at sea",[75] "oceans governance",[76] or "les personnes privées".[77]

A theoretical issue that is raised by this multiplication and diversification of issues dealt under the umbrella of the law of the sea pertains to their taxonomy. Should they be considered as truly part and parcel of the law of the sea, or are they just rules of other legal regimes which are lent to the law of the sea in order to serve a particular policy aim? In this respect, it has been argued that the UNCLOS "and the law of the sea in general also include some provisions belonging to other distinctive parts of international law".[78] At the same time, one could also argue that rules such as the duty to protect the marine environment, prescribed by Art. 192 UNCLOS, the prohibition of slavery, enshrined in Art. 99 UNCLOS, or the duty to save life at sea, as incorporated in Art. 98 UNCLOS, are an integral part of the law of the sea. The choice between the two approaches, far from being a mere theoretical decision, carries some important practical implications, in particular with respect to issues of interpretation and systemic integration. The UNCLOS itself contains norms dedicated to the interaction between its provisions and other rules of law of the sea and international law, notably Art. 293 UNCLOS and Art. 311 UNCLOS. Its drafters

[65] Part XIII UNCLOS.

[66] Part XIV UNCLOS.

[67] Art 94(3)(b) UNCLOS.

[68] Art. 303 UNCLOS.

[69] Such as the International Seabed Authority, the International Tribunal for the Law of the Sea (ITLOS) and the Commission on the Limits of the Continental Shelf.

[70] Part XV UNCLOS.

[71] An issue which will not be addressed in this chapter concerns the question of whether these issues belong to only one, or rather to two or more, regimes of international law.

[72] Protocol against the Smuggling of Migrants by Land, Sea and Air Supplementing the United Nations Convention against Transnational Organized Crime (adopted 15 November 2000, entered into force 28 January 2004) 2241 UNTS 480.

[73] Convention on the Protection of the Underwater Cultural Heritage (adopted 2 November 2001, entered into force 2 January 2009).

[74] Tanaka (2018), p. 404.

[75] Tanaka (2018), p. 451.

[76] Rothwell and Stephens (2010), p. 461.

[77] Forteau and Thouvenin (2017), p. 305.

[78] Vukas (2004), p. 5. The author continues, remarking that "for example, there are in the [UNCLOS] some well-known rules on human rights".

conceived of it as an open treaty, as evidenced by the last preambular paragraph, according to which "matters not regulated by this Convention continue to be governed by the rules and principles of general international law".

A further conceptual issue generated by this expansion and diversity concerns the boundaries of the discipline. The introduction of so many "new" issues may indeed beg the question whether there are *any* issues that do not belong to the law of the sea. Put in other words, are there any topics which cannot be considered as part of this regime and cannot be analysed under the framework of the law of the sea? The inclusion of Part XII on the protection of the marine environment in the UNCLOS would seem to solve the question, as to whether the protection of the marine environment falls within the law of the sea, rather than within international environmental law.

Other topics, however, still raise some issues.

Until a few years ago, for example, few would consider that the protection of people who are at sea was indeed a part of the law of the sea.[79] Following the upsurge of piracy off the coasts of Somalia and the exponential increase in irregular migration in the Mediterranean Sea, however, this issue has come to the forefront and has been examined in an number of international fora,[80] in addition to scholarly writings,[81] which are specifically dedicated to the law of the sea. Maritime migration, a topic which is closely linked to the protection of people at sea, is also on the upsurge and demands to be considered within law of the sea textbooks and dedicated volumes.[82]

Another topic for which some doubts have been raised relates to gender issues. It has indeed been questioned whether there are "any notable gender implications in international law of the sea".[83] Any conclusion depends, once again, on the personal understanding that one has of the law of the sea. If one considers that the law of the sea is only about maritime zones, boundary lines and the freedom of navigation, then the nexus between this field of international law and gender issues might be harder to

[79]Early articles on human rights and the law of the sea include Sohn (1988); Oxman (1997); Cacciaguidi-Fahy (2007); Treves (2010).

[80]Including both law of the sea courts and tribunals (e.g. ITLOS, *The M/V "SAIGA" (No. 2) Case (Saint Vincent and the Grenadines v. Guinea)*, Judgment of 1 July 1999; *The Arctic Sunrise Arbitration (Netherlands v. Russia)*, Award of 10 July 2017) and human rights courts (e.g. ECtHR, *Women on Waves and Others v Portugal*, App no 31276/05, Judgment of 3 February 2009; *Medvedyev and Others v France*, App no 3394/03, Judgment (GC) of 29 March 2010; *Hirsi Jamaa and Others v Italy*, App no 27765/09, Judgment (GC) of 23 February 2012; *Drieman and Others v Norway*, App no 33678/96 (Decision of 4 May 2000); *Bakanova v Lithuania*, App no 11167/12, Judgment of 31 May 2016); HRC, *A.S., D.I., O.I. and G.D. v. Italy*, Communication No. 3042/2017, Views of 27 January 2021.

[81]Papanicolopulu (2018); Petrig (2014); Attard (2020).

[82]Moreno Law & Papastavridis (2017).

[83]Scovazzi (2019).

establish.[84] However, as already illustrated, there is more to the law of the sea than just lines in the sea; therefore, it may be argued that the law of the sea relates also to gender issues, insofar as they pertain to maritime matters.[85]

6 Concluding Thoughts

Like the sea itself, the law that governs it is varied and ever changing. Nonetheless, as this brief overview has tried to show, there are some common threads that have characterised our understanding of what the law of the sea is since at least the development of the modern conception of international law.

In the first place, the law of the sea is a law that pertains to a certain space—"a certain milieu", as Gidel put it—rather than to any specific activity.[86] As such, it encompasses all human activities that may happen in this space and evolves as these activities develop and multiply. The content of the law of the sea thus changes to reflect new uses, but also new concerns of the international community, such as the need to protect the environment, the commitment to protect human rights and the advancement of gender considerations.

In the second place, the law of the sea—a law of States, in its strictest understanding—is profoundly intertwined with the rules developed by the seagoing communities, which have been identified in this chapter as "maritime law". As such, it has always had a dual nature. On the one hand, there are the rules that allocate power among States, so as to ensure a certain order for the oceans. On the other, there are the rules that concern directly the conduct of other actors at sea, first and foremost the master of a vessel, but also the crew, the fishers, and even the natural or legal persons that engage in the exploitation of the riches of the sea. The latter rules are more substantive in nature and tend to regulate the conduct of these actors, imposing on them duties or attributing them rights. While many efforts have been made in the twentieth century to distinguish the two and to address the (public) law of the sea only, it has proven rather impossible to entirely do with some of the fundamental rules dating back to the times that preceded Grotius, such as the duty to save life at sea.

[84] Yet, even the most fundamental and apparently gender-neutral principles of the law of the sea may unexpectedly present a gender lining; for a discussion of the gender implications of fundamental law of the sea rules such as the freedom of navigation Hodson (2019); Heathcote (2019).

[85] In cases in which there are women directly involved in the activity considered, taking into consideration the gender dimension seems obvious. In addition, the absence (or near absence) of women in specific activities and sectors, such as shipping or marine scientific research, requires an examination to be carried out from a gender perspective in order to identify whether there are any legal or factual obstacles to their entry into this field. For a further discussion Papanicolopulu (2019).

[86] See also Lucchini and Voelckel (1990), pp. 10–16.

Apart from these basic concepts, the law of the sea has changed and is still changing. This change is visible, in the first place, in its content, as that has been shaped by the adoption, first of the four Geneva Conventions of 1958 and then by the UNCLOS, but also by numerous other treaties that are today included in a general understanding of the law of the sea. This change is also visible in the approach of scholars to the law of the sea. In fact, one could say that while the rules of the law of the sea are made by States, the definitions of the law of the sea are made by scholars—or, in other words, that the law of the sea is what States and scholars make of it. In this light, the lawyer must show a sensibility towards not only legal thinking, but also the wider concerns of the community. As Professor Scovazzi concludes "[t]he present challenges of international law of the sea are to be found in the practical capacity of States to adapt and change old principles to conform with new needs".

References

Anzilotti D (1956) Scritti di diritto internazionale pubblico, vol I. Cedam, Padova
Attard DJ (2014) Preface. In: Attard DJ, Fitzmaurice M, Martinez Gutierrez NA (eds) The IMLI manual on international maritime law. Volume I: the law of the sea. Oxford University Press, Oxford, p vii
Attard FG (2020) The duty of the shipmaster to render assistance at sea under international law. Brill/Nijhoff, Leiden/Boston
Attard DJ, Fitzmaurice M, Martinez Gutierrez NA (eds) (2014) The IMLI manual on international maritime law. Volume I: the law of the sea. Oxford University Press, Oxford
Berlingieri F (1918) Verso l'Unificazione del Diritto del Mare. Athenaeum, Roma
Brown (1994) The international law of the sea, vol I. Dartmouth, Aldershot
Cacciaguidi-Fahy S (2007) The law of the sea and human rights. Sri Lanka J Int Law 19:85
Churchill RR, Lowe AV (1999) The law of the sea. Manchester University Press, Manchester
Conforti B (2013) Diritto internazionale, 3rd edn. Editoriale Scientifica, Napoli
De Lacharrière G (1983) La réforme du droit de la mer et le role de la Conference des Nations Unies. In: Bardonnet D, Virally M (eds) Le nouveau droit international de la mer. Pedone, Paris, p 1
Forteau M, Thouvenin JM (2017) Traité de Droit International de la Mer. Pedone, Paris
Garabello R, Scovazzi T (2003) The protection of the underwater cultural heritage: before and after the 2001 UNESCO Convention. Martinus Nijhoff, Leiden/Boston
Gidel G (1932) Le droit international public de la mer. Etablissements Mellottée, Chateauroux
Grotius H (1609) Mare Liberum sive de Jure, quod Batavis Competit ad Indicana Commercia, Dissertatio. Lugduni Batavorum
Grotius H (1625) De Jure Belli ac Pacis Libri Tres
Heathcote GV (2019) Feminism and the law of the sea: a preliminary Inquiry. In: Papanicolopulu (ed) Gender and the law of the sea. Brill/Nijhoff, Leiden/Boston, p 83
Higgins AP, Colombos CJ (1943) The international law of the sea. Longmans - Green, London
Hodson L (2019) Mermaids and Utopias: the high seas as feminist space? In: Papanicolopulu (ed) Gender and the law of the sea. Brill/Nijhoff, Leiden/Boston, p 122
Kelin N (2011) Maritime security and the law of the sea. Oxford University Press, Oxford
Lauterpacht H (1970) International law: being the collected papers of Hersch Lauterpacht, vol 1. Cambridge University Press, Cambridge
Lucchini L, Voelckel M (1990) Droit de la mer, vol I. Pedone, Paris

Mateesco N (1950) Vers un nouveau droit international de la mer. Pedone, Paris
McDougal MS, Burke WT (1962) The public order of the oceans – a contemporary international law of the sea. Yale University Press, New Haven/London
Moreno Law & Papastavridis (2017) 'Boat Refugees' and migrants at sea: a comprehensive approach. Brill/Nijhoff, Leiden/Boston
Oxman BH (1997) Human rights and the United Nations Convention on the law of the sea. In: Charney JI, Anton DK (eds) Politics, values and functions: international law in the 21st century. Essays in Honor of Professor Louis Henkin. Martinus Nijhoff, Leiden
Papanicolopulu (2018) International law and the protection of people at sea. Oxford University Press, Oxford
Papanicolopulu (2019) Gender and the law of the sea. Brill/Nijhoff, Leiden/Boston
Peters A (2016) Beyond human rights. The legal status of the individual in international law. Cambridge University Press, Cambridge
Petrig A (2014) Human rights and law enforcement at sea. Brill/Nijhoff, Leiden/Boston
Reddie J (1841) An historical view of the law of maritime commerce. William Blackwood and Sons, Edinburgh and London
Rothwell DR, Stephens T (2010) The international law of the sea. Hart, Oxford and Portland
Scovazzi T (2001) The evolution of international law of the sea: new issues, new challenges. Recueil des Cours 286:39–243
Scovazzi T (2004) La protezione del patrimonio culturale sottomarino nel mare Mediterraneo. Giuffré, Milano
Scovazzi T (2010) Is the UN Convention on the law of the sea the legal framework for all activities in the sea? The case of bioprospecting. In: Vidas D (ed) Law, technology and science for oceans in globalisation. Martinus Nijhoff, Leiden/Boston, p 309
Scovazzi T (2015) The origin of the theory of sovereignty of the sea. In: del Castillo L (ed) Law of the sea, from Grotius to the international tribunal for the law of the sea. Liber Amicorum Judge Hugo Caminos, Leiden, Brill, pp 48–63
Scovazzi T (2018) Corso di diritto internazionale - Parte I. Giuffrè, Milano
Scovazzi T (2019) Some doubts on the gender implications of the law of the sea. In: Papanicolopulu (ed) Gender and the law of the sea. Brill/Nijhoff, Leiden/Boston, p 144
Sohn LB (1988) International law of the sea and human rights issues. In: Clingan TA (ed) The law of the sea: what lies ahead? The Law of the Sea Institute, Honolulu, p 51
Tanaka Y (2018) The international law of the sea, 3rd edn. Cambridge University Press, Cambridge
Treves T (1995) Il diritto del mare e l'Italia. Giuffrè, Milano
Treves T (2010) Human rights and the law of the sea. Berkeley J Int Law 28:1
Treves T (2018) The expansion of international law: general course on public international law. Recueil des Cours 398
Twiss T (1884) The law of nations considered as independent political communities. Clarendon Press, Oxford
Vukas B (2004) The law of the sea – selected writings. Martinus Nijhoff, Leiden/Boston
Welwod W (1613) An abridgment of all sea-lawes

The Last Frontier: Trends and Challenges Related to the Delineation of the Outer Limits of the Continental Shelf Beyond 200 Nautical Miles

Luigi Santosuosso

Abstract The legal certainty sought through the adoption of convention norms is at odds with the constant evolution of science and technology. This chapter addresses the delineation of the outer limits of the continental shelf as a case study into the interplay between international law, on the one hand, and science and technology, on the other hand. The 1958 Convention on the Continental Shelf and the 1982 United Nations Convention on the Law of the Sea (UNCLOS) offer opposite methods to address these difficulties. The 1958 Convention contained an open-ended reference to technology that translated into a real-time evolution of the outer limits of the continental shelf at the expense of the stability that all jurisdictional limits should guarantee. UNCLOS incorporated complex scientific and technical concepts, but neutralized their evolutionary nature by freezing them into the definition contained in its Article 76; the difficulty of implementing its criteria for the delineation of the outer limits of the continental shelf beyond 200 nautical miles has increased as the theoretical model on which Article 76 rests has aged due to the progress in our understanding of the seafloors. This chapter provides an overview of the evolution of the continental shelf doctrine as well as an analysis of recent trends and challenges in the delineation of the outer limits of the continental shelf beyond 200 nautical miles as by-products of the obsolescence of the theoretical model contained in Article 76.

1 Introduction

The provisions of a treaty establish rights and obligations for the States that have consented to be bound by that treaty. They also provide fascinating insights about the place and time in which those provisions took form.

The views expressed herein are those of the author and do not necessarily reflect the views of the United Nations.

L. Santosuosso (✉)
Division for Ocean Affairs and the Law of the Sea, Office of Legal Affairs, United Nations, New York, NY, USA

M. Arcari et al. (eds.), *Trends and Challenges in International Law*,
https://doi.org/10.1007/978-3-030-94387-5_11

In between the paragraphs of a treaty, the inquisitive reader never fails to discover a not-so-hidden trap-door to sneak into the conference rooms and the corridors in which nouns, verbs and verb forms, adverbs, articles and conjunctions were carefully proposed, traded, replaced, reinstated, and finally adopted because delegations found them acceptable, or at least not unacceptable. In between those same paragraphs, the adventurous reader can also find a portal to get to the world-views, legal doctrines, mind-sets and underlying political inclinations prevailing at the time of the negotiations. When treaties incorporate scientific notions, or address technical issues, their provisions also lay bare the "state of the art" which shaped their drafting.

Just like a chapter in a novel, or the lyrics of a song, the text of a treaty is where the evolving perspectives of generations of readers meet the crystallized aspirations of the drafters. Whereas in literature the widening of the gap between these two vantage points often adds a veneer of glamour and mystery to the reading act, in treaty-law it may lead to a chasm that can only be filled through evolutionary interpretations or, if necessary and possible, through amendments, revisions or treaty supersessions. For treaty provisions rooted in science and technology, the passage of time adds a further, internal, line of evolutionary tension. Whereas treaties are concluded to establish the permanency necessary to ensure legal certainty and stable international relations, science and technology are in constant evolution. The very moment a scientific or technical concept is incorporated in a treaty provision, it instantaneously "carbon dates" it. Looking at the scientific and technical models incorporated in that provision, future generations of jurists will be able to determine its age, and how much the law has fallen behind science and technology. As soon as such a treaty provision enters into force, it starts to both bind the parties to the treaty and to decay from a scientific and technical point of view.

Article 76 of the United Nations Convention on the Law of the Sea[1] (hereinafter "the Convention"), may represent a good case-study. The provisions of this article are so scientifically and technically dense that its drafters provided for a body of experts, the Commission on the Limits of the Continental Shelf (hereinafter "the Commission" or "CLCS"), to be established in order to assist States to accurately implement it and furthermore to provide reassurance to the international community as to the extent of States' adherence to Article 76. If delegations that took part in the Third United Nations Conference on the Law of the Sea (hereinafter "UNCLOS III") had known what we know today as a result of the intervening dramatic advances that geo-sciences have undergone, the first seven paragraphs of Article 76 would have looked very different. In view of the wealth of data and information that is now available to coastal States which wish to establish the outer limits of their continental shelves beyond 200 nautical miles from the baselines from which the breadth of the territorial sea is measured, the procedural and institutional arrangements that were constructed on the vintage scientific and technical foundations of article 76, paragraphs 1–7, could not but become challenging and laborious, and ultimately inefficient, to implement.

[1] UNTS 1833, p. 3.

Together with internal waters, territorial sea, archipelagic waters, contiguous zone, and exclusive economic zone, the continental shelf is one of the maritime zones under national jurisdiction envisaged by Convention. Article 76, paragraphs 1 and 3, of the Convention defines it as follows:

> The continental shelf of a coastal State comprises the seabed and subsoil of the submarine areas that extend beyond its territorial sea throughout the natural prolongation of its land territory to the outer edge of the continental margin, or to a distance of 200 nautical miles from the baselines from which the breadth of the territorial sea is measured where the outer edge of the continental margin does not extend up to that distance. [...]
>
> The continental margin comprises the submerged prolongation of the land mass of the coastal State, and consists of the seabed and subsoil of the shelf, the slope and the rise.[2] It does not include the deep ocean floor with its oceanic ridges or the subsoil thereof.

How did we get here?

2 The Evolution of the Continental Shelf Doctrine

2.1 How Deep Is the Ocean?

On the morning of 13 September 1893, the five-year-old Israel Baline and his family disembarked from the Belgian-flagged *SS Rhynland* before going through the immigration procedures at Ellis Island. They had taken the 11-day journey across the Atlantic Ocean after the Cossacks had burnt their family home to the ground. They were relocating from Talachyn, Belarus, to New York's Lower East Side. By the mid-'20s, Israel, who in the meantime had adopted the professional name of Irving Berlin, had become an established composer and songwriter whose compositions were destined to enter into the canon of American popular music and jazz. Following the sudden death of his three-week old son, and the troubles that affected his finances after the 1929 stock market crash, he had slumped into what seemed like an inextricable circle of self-doubt during which inspiration eluded him. In 1932, while the rest of the United States had sunk into the depths of the Great Depression, Irving Berlin managed to get over this compositional drought. Thanks to the

[2] "The continental shelf extends from the shore to the top of the continental slope. The continental slope is the section of the seabed bordering the continental shelf. It is rather steep and brings the water depth from a few hundred metres, at the edge of the shelf, down to anywhere between 3,500 and 5,500 metres at the foot of the continental slope. In general, the continental slope is formed near the edge of the continental mass where the continental crust thins considerably and merges with the oceanic crust. [...] The continental rise, a feature of many coastal States, is an area of very gentle dip between the foot of the continental slope and the deep ocean floor. The typical continental rise is a wedge-shaped layer of sediments derived from the shelf areas and accumulated next to the base of the slope – in many places prograding partly onto the oceanic crust." United Nations (2006), Module I, p. 11.

increasing success of the radio, a medium that he had long distrusted, a number of his new songs became major hits.

One of them, "How Deep Is the Ocean?", vividly described the pangs of unrequited love through a metaphor perhaps rooted in the curiosity mixed with anxiety that young Israel Baline must have experienced during that early transatlantic voyage. How deep is the Ocean?

We live at a time when the answer to that question is just one quick online search away: on average, the ocean is 2.3 miles deep.[3] Not quite the metaphor for infinite love, today. But back in 1932 the deep Ocean must have appeared at once mysterious and immeasurable; and its floor inaccessible. It certainly did to the lover in Irving Berlin's song. And it most likely did to diplomats of that generation.

2.2 *Out of Sight, Out of Mind*

For this reason, when delegates convened in The Hague for the 1930 League of Nations Codification Conference, the question of jurisdiction and sovereign rights over marine resources on the seabed and subsoil located beyond the relatively shallow territorial waters was not pressing enough to be discussed.[4]

It is not that the ocean floor and its depths were completely unknown to people of their generation. Depth-sounding[5] was a technique used by vessels approaching the port of Alexandria as early as 450 B.C., according to Herodotus.[6] By the second half of the eighteenth century navigators relying on lead-lines to probe the bottom of the ocean had established that at approximately 200 m of depth the seafloor dramatically dropped, a circumstance that was seen as marking the end of continents and the beginning of "really high" seas.[7] The techniques available were more art than science and remained rudimentary until a series of concurrent factors like the increased reliance on transatlantic submarine cables, the sinking of the Titanic in 1912, and the unfolding of World War I's submarine warfare, led to a push towards increased investment and research aimed at documenting the bottom of the ocean. A scientific breakthrough took place following the Titanic disaster with the introduction of echo-sounding as a result of experiments conducted by the German physicist Alexander Dehm.[8] However, even though the first continuous profile of the ocean floor along the course of a ship had been drawn in 1922 between Rhode Island and

---

[3]3 Last searched on 30 January 2022, at https://www.google.com/search?q=how+deep+is+the+ocean.

[4]Churchill and Lowe (1991), p. 122.

[5]For an account of early depth measurement techniques, see Shipman and Laughton (2000).

[6]Vaughan (1940), p. 1.

[7]Ibidem, p. 2. See also Shipman and Laughton (2000), p. 124.

[8]Vaughan (1940), p. 8.

Gibraltar,[9] at the time of the Hague Conference the veil of the deep ocean floor had been barely scraped, certainly not pierced.

It is not that States had remained completely indifferent to the submarine areas adjacent to their coasts either. Sovereignty over the territorial sea already extended to its seabed and subsoil.[10] To the degree that some coastal States could effectively occupy the seabed and subsoil under the high seas they also claimed title over the resources of those submarine areas; sometimes even over the areas themselves, eliciting objections from States that considered them *res communis*.[11]

Coral and amber mining,[12] as well as sponge, pearl, oysters and chank fisheries were traditional in various parts of the world.[13] Underwater coal, iron, and tin mining activities through tunnels originating on land were not uncommon either.[14] Oil drilling from a platform built on shallow waters had already become viable in the late 1800s.[15]

At a time in which the territorial sea was much narrower than today, however, these activities were taking place at relatively low depths and short distances from the shore. Beyond the territorial sea, the sea floor was virtually out of scientists' sight and definitely out of diplomats' minds. The scant activities that had taken place on the sea floor below the high seas were tolerated as long as they did not interfere with the traditional freedoms of the high seas.[16] The technological advances in offshore drilling techniques, however, pointed to an inevitable growth in coastal States' interest in the seabed and subsoil at progressively increasing distances from the shore, and depths. They also portended a future need to reconcile the traditional freedom of navigation on the high seas with some degree of interference from exploration and exploitation activities.

After the continental shelf had entered into diplomats' "field of vision", the limited scientific understanding of seafloors available to them would affect the quality of their "sight" and, ultimately, the destiny of the continental shelf regime.

2.3 *Descriptions, Pudding Dishes and Press Releases*

The part of the sea floor located between the shore and that edge which had already been sensed by navigators of the late eighteenth century was first described as a "continental shelf" in the late nineteenth century. In "The Realm of Nature", a

---

[9]Edvalson and Miscoski (1969), p. 2.

[10]Churchill and Lowe (1991), p. 121.

[11]ILC (1950), p. 73.

[12]Hurst (1923–1924), pp. 42–43.

[13]Churchill and Lowe (1991), p 121.

[14]Hurst (1923–1924), pp. 34–35; ILC (1950), p. 51.

[15]Hardwicke (1949), p. 22.

[16]ILC (1950), p. 75.

treatise destined to revolutionize the teachings of geography, Scottish geographer Hugh Robert Mill wrote of a "shore flat, or [. . .] continental shelf" which he described as being located where the "world ridges forming the walls of the ocean-basins are flattened at the top like the rim of a pudding-dish".[17]

It would take more than half a century for international law to follow geography's lead and whole-heartedly embrace the continental shelf concept. Rare elaborations of the legal aspects of a continental shelf could be found in some academic circles between the two World Wars.[18] In State practice and international law, the concept of the continental shelf timidly emerged in relation to fisheries first, with a view to securing access to significant fish-stocks that found ideal living conditions in the waters above the continental shelf.[19]

Foreshadowed by a 1944 Argentinean decree concerning mineral reserves which introduced the concept of entitlement over an "epicontinental sea",[20] the 1945 Truman Proclamation[21] is commonly seen as the first instance of State practice in which the term "continental shelf" was utilized. It famously declared that

> the Government of the United States regards the natural resources of the subsoil and seabed of the continental shelf beneath the high seas but contiguous to the coasts of the United States as appertaining to the United States, subject to its jurisdiction and control.

The Proclamation laid the foundation for the further evolution of the continental shelf doctrine. Since the prospects of foreign countries conducting exploration and exploitation activities on the continental shelf of the United States were far from imminent, the Proclamation did not define with precision what the continental shelf was. It simply aimed at staking a claim and establishing a new policy. It was also intended to alert other States that the United States did not regard the "natural resources of the subsoil and seabed of the continental shelf beneath the high seas but contiguous to the coasts of the United States" as *res nullius*.

---

[17] Mill (1892), p. 194.

[18] E.g. Miguel Ruelas (1930).

[19] "[C]ertain states have participated in the continental shelf race principally to extend their claims over high seas fisheries"—Morris (1958), p. 38. Cosford (1958), p. 246, traces back the introduction of the concept of the continental shelf to a 1910 decree enacted by Portugal to prohibit trawl fishing practices which were destroying the environment of the continental shelf and affecting the fish stocks which relied on it. For the decree's purposes the continental shelf was defined by reference to the 100 fathom isobath. The Portuguese Decree Regulating Fishing by Steam Vessels of 9 November 1910 is reproduced in United Nations, High Seas Laws, pp. 19–21. See also ILC (1950), p. 48, p. 54, and especially pp. 56–57 citing additional examples dating back to 1916.

[20] Argentina's decree No. 1386 concerning mineral reserves, 24 January 1944 (Boletin Oficial de la Republica Argentina, Vol. 52, No. 14,583, 17 March 1944). ILC (1950), p. 60; Mouton (1952), p. 250.

[21] Proclamation 2667 of September 28, 1945 - Policy of the United States with Respect to the Natural Resources of the Subsoil and Sea Bed of the Continental Shelf. 10 Fed. Reg. 12,305 (1945). Reproduced in United Nations Legislative Series, Laws and Regulations on the Regime of the High Seas (ST/LEG/SER.B/1), at 38 (UN Sales No. 1951.V.2 (1951).

The Proclamation *per se*, however, did not enable anyone to identify the precise shape and size of the continental shelf of the United States on a nautical chart. A continental shelf description, still based on the 200 m criterion, was relegated in the press release which accompanied the issuance of the Proclamation. According to the press release "submerged land which is contiguous to the continent and which is covered by no more than 100 fathoms (600 feet) of water is considered as the continental shelf", which the reader could infer to be located beyond territorial waters.[22] What the press release did not explain was at what distance from the shore a depth of 100 fathoms, equivalent to approximately 200 m, could be found. According to estimates available at the time, this could be as far as two hundred and fifty miles.[23]

The Proclamation was seminal in articulating a number of aspects that were destined to shape future developments of the continental shelf doctrine. It framed the new policy in terms of the "land dominates the sea" principle, by invoking continuity[24] and contiguity.[25] It described the prerogative of the coastal States as "jurisdiction and control" rather than full sovereignty, vague as that distinction may be in practice.[26] It linked such jurisdiction and control to the natural resources of the continental shelf and the security interests of the coastal State.[27] The Proclamation also reassured that the new policy did not alter the nature of the superjacent waters as high-seas.[28]

---

[22] United Nations Legislative Series, Laws and Regulations on the Regime of the High Seas (ST/LEG/SER.B/1), p. 39 (UN Sales No. 1951.V.2 (1951).

[23] Colombos (1967), p. 71.

[24] "[...] since the continental shelf may be regarded as an extension of the land-mass of the coastal nation and thus naturally appurtenant to it [...]"; "[...] since [its natural] resources frequently form a seaward extension of a pool or deposit lying with the territory [...]". An interesting example of State practice in which the concept of continuity of the continental shelf was relied on prior to the Truman Proclamation, but for different purposes, is that of a 1916 declaration made by the Imperial Russian Government claiming a number of uninhabited islands because "they formed the northern continuation of the Siberian continental shelf"—ILC (1950), p. 56.

[25] "[...] the continental shelf beneath the high seas but contiguous to the coasts of the United States [...]". The proclamation also established a conceptual link between contiguousness and effectiveness as follows:

> [...] the exercise of jurisdiction over the natural resources of the subsoil and sea bed of the continental shelf by the contiguous nation is reasonable and just, since the effectiveness of measures to utilize or conserve these resources would be contingent upon cooperation and protection from the shore [...].

[26] Hurst (1948), p. 161.

[27] "[...] self-protection compels the coastal nation to keep close watch over activities off its shores which are of the nature necessary for utilization of these resources [...]".

[28] "The character as high seas of the waters above the continental shelf and the right to their free and unimpeded navigation are in no way [...] affected." The press release which accompanied the issuance of the Proclamation further clarified that the new policy did not purport to "extend the present limits of the territorial waters of the United States".

What may be most relevant for the purposes of the present analysis of the relationship between law/policy and science/technology is the fact that the Truman Proclamation is almost exclusively law/policy. Its tacit reliance on the 200 m criterion derived from the prevailing use of that depth mark as an accepted locator of the continental shelf. Its suitability resulted from the fact that extraction activities were not projected to reach greater depths in the foreseeable future. The Proclamation articulated a need, access to underwater resources, and selected a straightforward criterion that enabled the fulfillment of that need. Over time, criteria selected to address the need to access underwater resources would become increasingly complicated.

2.4 From Washington D.C. to the Rest of the World

The Truman Proclamation paved the way for State practice so significant, focused and unchallenged that it gave rise to a customary entitlement to the continental shelf. This custom may not have been as "instantaneous" in its emergence as in the case of space law, which—significantly—is another branch of public international law devoted to areas considered hitherto *res nullius*—but it was expeditious enough that just two years after the Truman Proclamation a number of States were framing their own continental shelf proclamations as being a matter of customary law.[29]

Less than five years after the Truman Proclamation, a review of the existing State practice could yield almost thirty declarations, proclamations, and various forms of domestic legislation concerning the continental shelf.[30] Even more significant was the fact that these acts, despite being rather ambitious in nature, did not elicit objections insofar as they aimed at asserting claims over the seabed and subsoil of the continental shelf, leaving the high seas unaffected.[31]

These developments consistently pointed to the fact that coastal States had some form of entitlement over their continental shelf. The exact nature (sovereignty or jurisdiction and control), the object (seabed, subsoil and their natural resources or just natural resources), the scope (seabed, subsoil and superjacent waters or just seabed and subsoil) and the outer limits (200 miles of distance from the shore or 200 m of depth)[32] of such entitlement were much less clear.

---

[29]E.g. Chile's Presidential Declaration Concerning the Continental Shelf enacted on 23 July 1947, reproduced in *Maritime Dispute (Peru v. Chile), Memorial of the Government of Peru, Volume 1, p. 108.* Peru's Supreme Decree No. 781 of 1 August 1947, - reproduced in *Maritime Dispute (Peru v. Chile), Judgment I.C.J. Report 2014,* p. 3, at para 38.

[30]For a review of early State practice concerning the continental shelf see Lauterpacht (1950), especially at pp. 380–382; Mouton (1952), Chapter IV, Section 1; and ILC (1950), especially at pp. 59–63. Later examples are also described in Colombos (1967), p. 75.

[31]Lauterpacht (1950), p. 393. Also ILC (1950), p. 60.

[32]For references to the 200 nautical miles criterion see e.g. the Proclamations by Chile (Decree of 23 June 1947); Peru (Decreto Supremo of 1 August 1947, No. 781 - Revista Peruana de derecho

The fragmentation of this practice was so pronounced that in 1952, when Lord Asquith of Bishopstone rendered his award in the *Abu Dhabi Arbitration,*[33] he observed that

> Neither the practice of nations nor the pronouncements of learned jurists give any certain or consistent answer to many, perhaps most, of these questions. I am of the opinion that there are in this field so many ragged ends and unfilled blanks, so much that is merely tentative and exploratory, that in no form can the doctrine be claimed, as yet, to have assumed hitherto the hard lineaments or the definitive status of an established rule of international law.

The growing interest in the promised riches of the continental shelf, coupled with the need to create some order in this matter, were among the key drivers that led to the convening of the First United Nations Conference on the Law of the Sea (hereinafter "UNCLOS I") and, ultimately, to the adoption of the 1958 Convention on the Continental Shelf[34] (hereinafter "Continental Shelf Convention").[35]

Up to this point, nothing had changed in the law/policy vs. science/technology balance since the Truman Proclamation; it had all been about law/policy.

2.5 *Depth or Exploitability?*

At its first session in 1949, the International Law Commission (hereinafter "ILC") included the regime of the high seas among its priority topics, deeming it "suitable for rapid codification".[36] A year later, in reporting to the General Assembly about the progress of its work, the ILC listed the continental shelf among the topics falling within the general scope of the regime of the high seas.

In the course of its consideration of this matter, shaped by the intention to curtail excessive claims and informed by the thorough work of the special rapporteur J.P.A. Francois, whose codification experience dated back to his work as rapporteur on the topic of the territorial sea at the 1930 Hague Conference, the ILC oscillated

---

internacional, Vol. 7, p. 301) and Costa Rica (Decree of 27 July 1943, No. 116, Gaceta, Costa Rica, 29 July 1948; Decree of 2 November 1949, No. 803, ibid., 5 November 1949). For references to the 200 m depth, see e.g. the above-mentioned press-release issued in connection with the Truman Proclamation or Mexico's Decree of 25 February 1949 (Diario Oficial, 11 March 1949).

[33] *Matter of an Arbitration between the Petroleum Development (Trucial Coast) Limited and His Excellency Sheikh Shakhbut Bin Sultan Bin Za'id, Ruler of Abu Dhabi and its Dependencies* - 1 ICLQ 247. On the continental shelf aspects of this arbitration see Cosford (1953).

[34] UNTS vol. 499, p. 311.

[35] For a general account of the negotiations concerning the Continental Shelf Convention, see Gutteridge (1959); Whiteman (1958).

[36] Yearbook of the International Law Commission 1949, p. 43, at para 62. For a brief overview of the work of the ILC in the field of the law of the Sea, see United Nations (2017), pp. 130–138. In general, all documents of the ILC are available on the website maintained by the Codification Division of the Office of Legal Affairs of the United Nations at https://legal.un.org/ilc/documentation/.

between two approaches on the delineation[37] of the outer limits of the continental shelf, exploitability and 200 m depth, ultimately combining them in the final version of its draft articles.

The exploitability approach may have had the advantage of allowing the nascent continental shelf ambitions to grow at the same pace of deep sea technology but had the disadvantage of lacking clarity and certainty as to where at any given time in history the outer limits of the continental shelf theoretically rested, and for how long they would stay the same. The 200 m depth criterion, remedied this by pragmatically referring to the age old depth criterion, which the ILC deemed "sufficient for all practical purposes at present and probably for a long time to come", striking a Solomonic pose that acknowledged the need for legal certainty over a significant period of time while leaving open the possibility of a future revision at a time when progress would dictate it. The fact that the 200 m isobath, i.e. the line consisting of points having the same 200 m depth, was traditionally marked on the nautical charts of the time, added a dimension of expediency to the legal certainty inherent in this criterion.[38] Conversely, this criterion could be a reaction against some coastal States' aspirations to broader areas under national jurisdiction, which were growing as a result of the geopolitical shifts and the increasing resistance against rules that were perceived as defending the interests of the traditional commercial and military powers.[39]

At UNCLOS I,[40] given the fact that neither method of delineation would encounter majority support, combining them in a single provision proved to be successful in ensuring the acceptance of this definition. Nevertheless, the dual delineation criterion had many detractors and could not be approved by unanimity or consensus. It required a vote.[41] Ultimately, its acceptance resulted from the inability to find sufficient support for an alternative approach, among the many that were proposed during UNCLOS I.[42] Identifying a single criterion to define the outer limits of the continental shelf evidently would have required a higher degree of progressive

[37] Given the inconsistent and interchangeable use of the terms "delineation" and "delimitation" that can be found in both literature and official documents, it is noted that for the purposes of this article the term "delineation" is utilized in relation to the outer limits of a maritime zone, whereas "delimitation" is used with regard to maritime boundaries.

[38] Colombos (1967), p. 77.

[39] The fact that in 1956 a number of Latin American Governments emphatically supported the exploitability criterion, at a time when it appeared to have been set aside by the ILC in favour of the 200 m criterion, could be interpreted in that light. See Final Act - Inter-American Specialized Conference on Conservation of Natural Resources of the Continental Shelf and Marine Waters, Ciudad Trujillo, 15–28 March 1956. Pan American Union, 1956, 13.

[40] In general, all documents of UNCLOS I are available on the website maintained by the Codification Division of the Office of Legal Affairs of the United Nations at https://legal.un.org/diplomaticconferences/1958_los/.

[41] 51 votes in favour, nine against, and ten abstentions - A/CONF.13/C.4/SR.19, pp. 4–5.

[42] A wide range of proposals can be found in A/CONF.13/C.4/L.1; UNCLOS I, Official Records, Vol. VI, pp. 2–3; A/CONF.13/C.4/L.11; A/CONF.13/C.4/L.7; A/CONF.13/C.4/L.8; A/CONF.13/C.4/L.29/Rev. 1; A/CONF.13/2, especially pp. 40–41; A/CONF.13/C.4/L.12; A/CONF.13/C.4/

development than delegations at UNCLOS I were ready for. Article 1 of the Continental Shelf Convention, as a result, amounted to a codification of the existing confusion in using the term continental shelf as referring to

> the seabed and subsoil of the submarine areas adjacent to the coast but outside the area of the territorial sea, to a depth of 200 metres or, beyond that limit, to where the depth of the superjacent waters admits of the exploitation of the natural resources of the said areas.

State practice and case law strengthened the status of the definition of continental shelf contained in Article 1 of the Continental Shelf Convention, which by 1969 was considered by the International Court of Justice (hereinafter "ICJ") as reflecting customary international law.[43] It also revealed the challenges posed by the application of the exploitability criterion, as it was not clear whether such exploitability was supposed to be just technically possible or economically viable, and whether it was dependent on the technical capacity of the coastal State concerned or, rather, that of any State.[44] In addition, exploitability implied that at some point in the future, when technology would allow it, the entirety of the sea-floor, not just the physical continental shelf, could fall under national jurisdiction.[45]

The impact of UNCLOS I on the uneasy relationship between law/policy and science/technology was the introduction of a criterion, exploitability, that would allow a real-time evolution of the outer limits of the continental shelf. Article 1 of the Continental Shelf Convention was not self-contained. Exploitability was an empty box that needed to be filled every day with the technology *du jour* to determine the outer limits of the continental shelf. In order to cater to delegations that had not lost sight of their ambition to extend their prerogatives to 200 nautical miles, legal certainty had been traded for technological currentness.

The uncertainties introduced by the exploitability criterion, combined with the fact that UNCLOS I had failed to find agreement on the outer limits of the territorial sea, which also mark the inner limits of the continental shelf, meant that for a number of years the exact configuration of coastal States' continental shelves would have to be determined on a State by State basis.

At the end of 1969, the perceived shortcomings of Article 1 of the Continental Shelf Convention saw a formal elaboration by the General Assembly, which observed that the 1958 Convention did not define

L.30; A/CONF.13/C.4/SR. 19, pp. 2, 3; A/CONF.13/C.4/L.30; A/CONF. 13/C.4/SR.19, p. 3); 28 A/CONF.13/C.4/L.4.

[43]See the *obiter dictum* contained in the Judgment of 20 February 1969 in the North Sea Continental Shelf Cases (Federal Republic of Germany v. Denmark; Federal Republic of Germany v. Netherlands), para 63 - I.C.J. Reports 1969, p. 3, at p. 39.

[44]Churchill and Lowe (1991), p. 125.

[45]Consider the statement by the ILC in A/13/19.

with sufficient precision the limits of the area over which a coastal State exercises sovereign rights for the purpose of exploration and exploitation of the natural resources, and that customary international law on the subject is inconclusive.[46]

2.6 *Sediments, Ridges, Breadths and Biscuits*

The ensuing developments did not originate within the ILC. They started in the Seabed Committee,[47] whose deliberations provided a preview of both the challenges that delegations would face at the Third United Nations Conference on the Law of the Sea (UNCLOS III) and of the different approaches for the delineation of the outer limits of the continental shelf.[48]

When UNCLOS III[49] started, one of the principal concerns with regard to the continental shelf regime was—like in the pre-UNCLOS I days—the exact delineation of the outer limits of the continental shelf. This was consistent with the overall goal of the Conference to bring about clarity with respect to the breadth and configuration of all maritime zones, not only the continental shelf.

Propelled by the shortcomings of the open-ended reliance on technology contained in Article 1 of the Continental Shelf Convention, at UNCLOS III the pendulum swung to the opposite extreme. Whereas UNCLOS I made it possible for the evolution of technology to impact the delineation of the outer limits of the continental shelf "in real time", UNCLOS III froze in time concepts which were destined to evolve significantly in the scientific and technical domains. The following pages will try and outline how this came to be, leading to future implementation challenges for States parties. Since our purpose is not to analyse the merits of the scientific and technical notions tabled during UNCLOS III, these notions will be reproduced in the next paragraphs only to the degree necessary to illustrate how their introduction has shaped today's trends and challenges concerning the delineation of the outer limits of the continental shelf, which will be described in Sect. 3.

As far as maritime zones which included submerged regions were concerned, delegations' primary focus at UNCLOS III were the concepts of the exclusive economic zone (EEZ) and the international seabed area (Area), the two maritime zones which, unlike the continental shelf, had not yet been the object of any treaty

---

[46]Third preambular paragraph of resolution 2574A (XXIV) of 15 December 1969 https://undocs.org/en/A/RES/2574(XXIV).

[47]Committee on the Peaceful Uses of the Sea-Bed and the Ocean Floor Beyond the Limits of National Jurisdiction, established by General Assembly resolution 2467A (XXIII) of 21 December 1968 https://undocs.org/en/A/RES/2467(XXIII).

[48]Report of Sub-Committee II, A/AC.138/95, para 51, reproduced in I SBC Report 1973, Annex I, at 38. For an overview of the deliberations that took place within the Sea-bed Committee see Virginia Commentary, sections 76.3–76.4.

[49]For a practical yet comprehensive synopsis of UNCLOS III's Second Committee negotiations concerning the continental shelf regime, see Virginia Commentary, Part VI.

regime. Deliberations concerning the criteria for the delineation of the outer limits of the continental shelf gained steam as the regimes concerning EEZ and Area progressively emerged.

The negotiating stances[50] of delegations depended on the size of the continental shelf their Government laid claims on (States with broad continental margins approaching the negotiation from a perspective of national and territorial integrity and defence of "acquired rights"[51] vs. States with narrow continental margins which tried to limit those ambitions); how much they supported the concept of "common heritage of mankind"[52] applicable to the Area; and whether they deemed that the introduction of an EEZ, whose scope included the seabed and subsoil, rendered the continental shelf regime redundant.[53] A related subset of positions depended on whether, in the presence of a continental shelf extending beyond 200 nautical miles, there should be a mechanism for the sharing of revenues generated by resources located beyond that limit. As was the case for many other important topics at UNCLOS III, a significant amount of work was conducted informally.[54]

The basis for the switch from the "depth & exploitability" approach of 1958 to the "breadth & geomorphology" approach found today in Article 76 emerged in the early stages of UNCLOS III and, after the third session in 1975, was reflected in the Informal Single Negotiating Text (ISNT). It described the continental shelf of a coastal State by reference to the sea-bed and subsoil of the submarine areas beyond the territorial sea (i) "throughout the natural prolongation of its land territory to the outer edge of the continental margin", or "to a distance of 200 nautical miles from the baselines from which the breadth of the territorial sea is measured where the outer edge of the continental margin does not extend up to that distance".[55]

The so-called "Irish formula",[56] informally introduced during the fourth session, proposed two concrete criteria to delineate the outer limits of the continental margin defined in the ISNT. Both criteria were based on the concept of the "foot of the

---

[50]For an overview of the early positions of delegations with regard to the definition of the continental shelf see the so-called Main Trends Working Paper (official title: Statement of activities of the Conference during its first and second sessions - A/CONF.62/L. 8/Rev.1) p. 117.

[51]See e.g. A/CONF.62/ SR.46, para 46.

[52]Declaration of Principles Governing the Sea-Bed and Ocean Floor, and the Subsoil Thereof, beyond the Limits of National Jurisdiction - General Assembly resolution 2749 (XXV) of 17 December 1970. For the purposes of this article, the gender-biased formulation of "common heritage of mankind" is used insofar as it reflects the language of the Convention. The more appropriate way to refer to it would otherwise be the common heritage of "humankind" or "humanity".

[53]Virginia Commentary, part VI.8.

[54]Within the Second Committee an informal consultative group on the continental shelf was established during the third session, A/CONF.62/C.2/L.89/Rev. 1, para 5.

[55]Article 61 - A/CONF.62/WP.8/PART II, available at https://legal.un.org/diplomaticconferences/1973_los/vol4.shtml. A similar proposal had been made to the plenary of the second session by a group of nine States, see Article 19 in A/CONF.62/L.4, available at https://legal.un.org/diplomaticconferences/1973_los/vol3.shtml.

[56]A/CONF.62/C.2/L.98, footnote at p. 189.

continental slope", a point found at the base of the continental slope. The "base of the continental slope" was not defined, but the "foot of the continental slope" was to be identified as follows: "[i]n the absence of evidence to the contrary, the foot of the continental slope shall be determined as the point of maximum change in the gradient at its base". In other words, this definition described the foot of the continental slope as the point at which the steep incline of the slope gave way to the gentler incline of the rise.[57] According to this formula, the foot of the slope would then be used as a "continental shelf baseline",[58] i.e. a reference from which to construct two alternative lines aimed at establishing the outer edge of the continental margin: (i) a simple-to-construct line located at a distance of 60 M from the foot of the slope; or (ii) a much more complex line delineated by reference to "fixed points at each of which the thickness of sedimentary rocks is at least 1 per cent of the shortest distance from such point to the foot of the continental slope."[59] The rationale behind these formulae was that they enabled coastal States to include the vast majority of their continental rises, a segment of the sea-floor which, if present, was known to host significant natural resources.

It quickly became apparent that the technical nature of these criteria required an in-depth examination,[60] which took place during the fifth session, in the context of Negotiating Group No. 3.[61] A symptom of the difficulties inherent in taming the concrete realities described by geo-sciences into a general and abstract legal definition was the fact that, at the sixth session of the Conference, the Secretariat of the United Nations servicing the Conference was requested to prepare a study showing how the various formulae proposed to date would work in practice, i.e. the difference in area between the formulae for the definition of the continental shelf.[62]

The Secretariat presented its preliminary study at the seventh session.[63] In hindsight, this study comes across as a disregarded canary in the UNCLOS III coalmine. After months of expensive work by top experts in the field, the study contained observations like "[t]he data used as a basis for the lines illustrated are, it must be emphasized, extremely irregular in both quantity and quality between different areas". Equally, or perhaps even more, telling of the difficulties posed by

---

[57] For a description of the concepts of continental slope and rise see fn 2.

[58] A metaphor used in Carleton and Cook (2000), p. 271.

[59] A/CONF.62/C.2/L.98, footnote at p. 189.

[60] Para. 13 of the introductory note to the Revised Single Negotiating Text (RSNT), A/CONF.62/WP.8/Rev.1/PartII.

[61] A/CONF.62/L.17, paras. 33–39.

[62] A preliminary study and map were made available at the seventh session (A/CONF.62/C.2/L.98), whereas the final version of the study and map were issued at the eighth session (A/CONF.62/C.2/L.98/dd.1-3). This study and maps reflected the contribution of the Lamont-Doherty Geological Observatory of Columbia University, selected on the basis of its expertise and database, and were reviewed by Guiding Committee for the General Bathymetric Chart of the Oceans (GEBCO), a joint expert group of the Intergovernmental Oceanographic Commission (IOC) of UNESCO and the International Hydrographic Organization (IHO).

[63] See previous footnote.

the proposed sediment thickness criterion was the fact even the very delegation that advocated it had to acknowledge that a global assessment of its impact was made difficult by the fact that data and information was incomplete:

> [...] the concept of determining a limit by means of the thickness of sediments [...] was entirely practicable, techniques were available for that purpose and the data at present available had confirmed that such determination was possible. However, it was unlikely that countries would wish to undertake the work involved unless required to do so under the convention *and it was therefore virtually impossible to do so currently on a global scale.*[64]

Coming from a developed country, this statement must have rendered the implementation of the sediment thickness criterion daunting in the eyes of developed country delegates. In another study, the Secretariat warned about the practical implications of another concept included in the drafts under consideration, the foot of the continental slope: "[...] at least three years will be necessary to complete a delineation of the foot of the slope line to the accuracy appropriate to a scale of 1: 10,000,000 and [...] the cost could exceed one million dollars".[65] The study contained similar considerations concerning the delineation of a sediment thickness line.[66] These considerations, of course, were made in the context of a global study. For a single country the time and financial investment would be proportionally smaller, but still much higher than those necessary to delineate a line based on a breadth criterion. For comparative purposes, according to the same study a line calculated a breadth criterion like the 200 nautical miles line "would take between 6 and 16 months and would cost approximately $50,000". For an individual State the cost would be a fraction of that amount.

Legal norms are meant to be general and abstract. Geo-sciences, on the contrary, describe the infinite variations in the seafloors that exist around the world. Having undertaken the path of incorporating scientific and technical notions into the legal definitions of the continental shelf, it could be expected that delegations would soon have to address local features that could not be easily accommodated by the two abstract formulae described above. Negotiations therefore were further complicated by (i) the need to identify an overall limit, or constraint, beyond which the claims of coastal States could not extend, because in some parts of the world the formulae described above could extend to a distance from the baselines that was considered excessive by many States; (ii) the existence of certain sea-floor highs which could equally extend the coastal State claims farther than many delegations were ready to accept;[67] (iii) the fact that off the coast of Sri Lanka the combination of a foot of the slope which was very close to the shore and the presence of an extraordinarily large continental rise, which resulted from the massive sedimentary depositions generated

[64] A/CONF.62/C.2/SR.50 para 23 (emphasis added).

[65] Study of the implications of preparing large-scale maps for the Third United Nations Conference on the Law of the Sea (A/CONF.62/C.2/L.99), at para 24.

[66] Id. at para 29.

[67] For a review of the types of ridges and issues related to them see Symonds et al. (2000).

by the river Ganges over millions of years, rendered the application of the two proposed formulae inequitable.

Taken as a whole, the developments concerning constraints, ridges and the Sri Lanka circumstances illustrate (i) that reliance on the tenets of science and technology does not necessarily simplify the solution of legal issues, it just influences the nature and form of the arguments used to pursue national interests, and (ii) that when the scientific notions utilized are not easily applicable everywhere, they may prove inequitable to certain States. Exceptions to the general rules, or constraint criteria that would allow the coastal State to extend the continental shelf well beyond 200 nautical miles were a "slippery slope"—an idiom that seems quite well placed in a discussion concerning the continental shelf—that caused concern in several delegations that felt "occasional remorse about the extent of the limits already reached".[68] A straight-forward breadth criterion would have avoided these complications.

That the Conference was able to reconcile not only all the conflicting interests concerning the continental shelf regime, but also incorporate complex scientific and technical considerations in the deliberations, is one more reason why it should be considered a pinnacle of modern diplomacy. The definition of continental shelf that emerged from those efforts is contained in Article 76. Those who see its criteria as unnecessarily complex, should also remember that they were seen by broad margin States to be "a major compromise" on their part, because they "would prevent them from claiming the full extent of their adjacent continental margin",[69] as they had set up to do at the beginning of the Conference. Given the length and complexity of Article 76, it will suffice to summarize the following aspects of its provisions:

a. The definition of continental shelf is rooted in scientific concepts, but is legal in nature, a circumstance that generates a dichotomy between what a geo-scientist and a jurist mean when they use the term "continental shelf";
b. The dual 60 nautical miles/sediment thickness formula accommodated different coastal configurations where there may or may not be large amounts of sediment, but also added a significant layer of complexity where sediment thickness had to be measured;
c. Narrow-margin States would be recognized to have a default continental shelf extending from the outer limits of the territorial sea up to 200 nautical miles even if their continental margins did not naturally reach that distance from the shore, whereas broad-margin States would be able to lay claim over a continental shelf extending as a single entity from the outer limits of the territorial beyond 200 nautical miles.[70]

---

[68] Oxman (1980), at fn 75.

[69] A/CONF.62/C.2/SR.50, para 22.

[70] In this regard, see the Arbitration between Barbados and the Republic of Trinidad and Tobago, relating to the delimitation of the exclusive economic zone and the continental shelf between them, decision of 11 April 2006, para 213. Available at https://pca-cpa.org/en/cases/104/. 27 United Nations Reports of International Arbitral Awards (*RIAA*) 147, at 208–9.

d. To prevent excessive claims, beyond 200 nautical miles two constraints criteria were introduced. A constraint located at 350 nautical miles from the baselines and a constraint determined by reference to a distance of 100 nautical miles from the 2500-m isobath, if that was further seaward. Originally proposed as an alternative, the two constraints were combined in an approach that, according to UNCLOS lore, became known as the 'biscuit formula';[71]
e. Sea floor highs, and the special circumstances of Sri Lanka, required specific provisions, in paragraph 6 of Article 76, and in the Statement of Understanding annexed to the Final Act of the Conference,[72] respectively;
f. A Commission would be established to assist coastal States in implementing Article 76 through recommendations on matters related to the establishment of the outer limits of their continental shelf. Outer limits established on the basis of these recommendations would be final and binding.

It seems appropriate at this stage to address the Commission on the Limits of the Continental Shelf.

2.7 *It's a Watchdog ... It's an Adviser ... It's a Guarantor... It's the Commission on the Limits of the Continental Shelf!*

The establishment of the outer limits of any maritime zone is a unilateral act of the coastal State concerned. In order to perform this act with regard to the continental shelf, however, the coastal State may need to undertake the procedure envisaged in Article 76.8, namely submitting information on the limits of its continental shelf to the Commission. This procedure is only necessary to establish the outer limits of the continental shelf beyond 200 nautical miles from the baselines from which the breadth of the territorial sea is measured.

---

[71] "So stylized was the relationship between the opposing sides that for a considerable period, to symbolize its emergence from the center rather than from any delegations, and perhaps to suggest a customary affection for tea among the original chefs, the proposal was called the 'biscuit'". Oxman (1980), fn 66.

[72] The fact that provisions of the Statement of Understanding were not included in Article 76 but annexed to the Final Act of the Conference has to do with the fact that they were introduced at a late stage of the Conference, when delegations were weary of reopening deliberations on Article 76. Annex II to the Convention makes sure that the Commission applies the Statement of Understanding by describing its main function as follows:

> to consider the data and other material submitted by coastal States concerning the outer limits of the continental shelf in areas where those limits extend beyond 200 nautical miles, and to make recommendations in accordance with article 76 *and the Statement of Understanding* adopted on 29 August 1980 by the Third United Nations Conference on the Law of the Sea (Article 3, para 1(a) - emphasis added).

The genesis of the Commission during UNCLOS III sheds additional light on the complexities resulting from the reliance on concepts of scientific and technical origin to delineate the outer limits of the continental shelf.

The idea of an independent international commission that would review the outer limits of the continental shelf dates back to the Seabed Committee.[73] At UNCLOS III it resurfaced during informal consultations, like many other UNCLOS concepts. This took place as early as the second session,[74] when the definition of the outer limits of the continental shelf had not yet reached the level of complexity that it would reach in its final incarnation, a circumstance that points to the fact that the initial role of the Commission appeared to be one of "watchdog" aimed at ensuring that in establishing the outer limits of the continental shelf beyond 200 nautical miles, coastal States would not unduly chip-away areas of the sea-floor appertaining to the Area, as "common heritage of mankind". The Commission made its formal appearance in the revised Informal Composite Negotiating Text before the eighth session[75] but several delegations questioned the idea of a Commission or reserved their positions in the absence of more details about its role and functions.[76]

The concept of the Commission was, therefore, fleshed out informally[77] at the resumed eighth and ninth sessions, in terms of expertise (geology, geophysics, hydrography), membership (30 members to be appointed by a procedure established by the Intergovernmental Oceanographic Commission and the International Hydrographic Bureau), and functions (certification of conformity of the outer limits with the provisions of the Convention and technical advice, upon the request of the coastal State). The proposal also envisaged that such a Commission would examine each submission by a "special committee" of five members, who may not include members that have advised the submitting State. The special committee would issue a final and binding certification for the outer limits—referred to as a "boundary" at the time—if satisfied by the evidence supplied by the coastal State that the outer limit was correctly delineated under the Convention. If not satisfied, the special committee would give its reasons in writing to the submitting State who could submit revised outer limits within a reasonable time. Cognizant of the technical demands associated with the preparation of such a submission, coastal States were given ample time to prepare it, namely ten years from the entry into force of the Convention for the State in question. Finally, to underscore that the Commission was not a court of law, but a technical body solely seized with the delineation of the outer limits of the continental shelf, the proposal also emphasized that matters relating to the delimitation of boundaries between opposite or adjacent States did not fall within the purview of the Commission.

[73] A/AC.138/25 (1970), outlining the role of an International Seabed Boundary Review Commission.

[74] Stevenson and Oxman (1975), p. 782.

[75] A/CONF.62/WP. 10/Rev.1, Article 76, para 7.

[76] Suarez (2008), p. 77.

[77] Virginia Commentary, section A.II.6 and A.II.7.

These informal elements provided the basis for further negotiations, and, during the first part of the ninth session, they were enshrined, with modifications, in what would become Annex II to the Convention.[78] Certain elements that had been flagged during the earlier consultations did not make it to Annex II, including the possibility that the International Seabed Authority (ISA) could make a submission to the Commission, the possibility for "appeal procedures" by submitting States and the inclusion of legal experts in the Commission.[79]

The other major change introduced in the final text of Annex II was the fact that the concept of 'certification' was replaced by that of 'recommendation' which the Commission would issue to the submitting State, at the end of the examination of its submission. The limits would not be established by the Commission—something that would have been unacceptable to delegations—but by the coastal State, "on the basis of" the recommendations it received.[80] Pursuant to this regime, outer limits of the continental shelf beyond 200 nautical miles established in this manner "shall be final and binding".

The fact that limits so established could not be objected to responded to the need for the certainty necessary both for the ISA and for the coastal State, since an investment-intensive industry like that of mining demanded jurisdictional certainty as a pre-condition for engaging in the costly prospecting and exploration activities that precede the exploitation of mineral resources.[81] Evidently, the complex regime established in Article 76 was so steeped in technicalities that, without knowing how its criteria would be applied by a coastal State, other States would not be able to assess the conformity of those outer limits to the Convention. This emerges from the eloquent statement of one delegation according to which "[t]he commission is primarily an instrument which will provide the international community with reassurances that coastal States will establish their continental shelf limits in strict accordance with the provisions of Article 76."[82] Such a need for reassurances would not have arisen under a maximum breadth approach, the application of which could have been more easily verified by third States. Without a Commission, the risks of objections by third States stemming from Article 76 was so high that it would have defeated the aim of giving the Area certain limits. The role of the Commission that emerges from Article 76 and Annex II to the Convention is hybrid, that is to say advisor towards the coastal State in its implementation of Article 76, and guarantor towards the international community with regard to the conformity of the outer limits of the continental shelf to Article 76.

[78] A/CONF.62/WP.10/Rev.3, pp. 128–129.

[79] Virginia Commentary, p. 850.

[80] A late proposal to change "recommendations" into "decisions" was not successful (see Virginia Commentary, section 76.15).

[81] Oxman (1981), p. 230.

[82] A/CONF.62/WS/4, para 15.

3 Trends and Challenges Related to the Delineation of the Outer Limits of the Continental Shelf

One often reads that we know more about the surfaces of Mars, Mercury and the Moon than about the seafloor, since the vast majority of the ocean remains unmapped.[83] The scientific understanding of the continental margin, however, has progressed in leaps and bounds since the adoption of the Convention.

The legal definition of the continental shelf contained in Article 76 and the scientific knowledge that was used to shape it were once in harmonious touch. Their relationship now has changed, causing areas of friction like those that exist at a metaphorical convergent plate boundary, where the inert legal definition has been given primacy—for better or for worse—and sits on an overriding plate while the forward-moving developments of science and technology are being pushed underneath on a subducting plate. The phenomenon is not smooth, and it causes tremors that have made the implementation of Article 76 increasingly challenging, from both a substantive and a procedural point of view, and both for coastal States and the CLCS, as the following paragraphs will attempt to illustrate.

3.1 The Quantitative and Qualitative Impacts of the Evolution of Science and Technology on the Implementation of Article 76

3.1.1 Timelines

The amount of data and information available at the time of UNCLOS III was relatively small. A ten-year time-period for States to prepare their submissions to the CLCS from the date of the entry into force of the Convention for that State must have appeared reasonable—albeit suggestive of the fact that the drafters of the Convention understood that the task at hand would be time and resource intensive. Even such a substantial time-line, however, has proved challenging, especially for coastal States that were early-ratifiers of the Convention and for coastal States with limited resources and/or lengthy coastlines and proportionally larger needs for data and information.

In 2001, about three and a half years before the expiration of the ten-year time period for early-ratifiers, the Meeting of States Parties to the Convention (MSP), a treaty-body that, *inter alia,* elects the members of the CLCS every five years, annually receives information reported by its Chairperson, and traditionally steers

[83]E.g. National Oceanic and Atmospheric Administration, How Much of the Ocean Have We Explored? https://oceanservice.noaa.gov/facts/exploration.html; and Jon Copley, Just How Little Do We Know about the Ocean Floor? Scientific American https://www.scientificamerican.com/article/just-how-little-do-we-know-about-the-ocean-floor/.

clear of substantive determinations concerning the Convention, took a rare decision. At its eleventh meeting, it established an understanding according to which for a State Party for which the Convention entered into force before 13 May 1999, the ten-year time period “shall be taken to have commenced on 13 May 1999”.[84]

13 May 1999 was the date of the adoption of the “Scientific and Technical Guidelines of the Commission on the Limits of the Continental Shelf” (hereinafter “the Guidelines”).[85] The Guidelines have both an internal and an external relevance: they represent “the basis for the Commission to make its recommendations with respect to submissions prepared by States according to Article 76 and Annex II to the Convention in a manner that is consistent with the Convention and international law”,[86] and they provide “direction to coastal States which intend to submit data and other material concerning the outer limits of the continental shelf in areas where those limits extend beyond 200 nautical miles from the baselines from which the breadth of the territorial sea is measured”.[87] In preparing the Guidelines, the Commission was aware of the difficulties that coastal States would face in implementing Article 76 and of the ensuing need for clarity

> required in particular because the Convention makes use of scientific terms in a legal context which at times departs significantly from accepted scientific definitions and terminology. In other cases, clarification is required because various terms in the Convention might be left open to several possible and equally acceptable interpretations. It is also possible that it may not have been felt necessary at the time of the Third United Nations Conference on the Law of the Sea to determine the precise definition of various scientific and technical terms. In still other cases, the need for clarification arises as a result of the complexity of several provisions and the potential scientific and technical difficulties which might be encountered by States in making a single and unequivocal interpretation of each of them.[88]

Before having even commenced the examination of submissions, the CLCS was acknowledging receipt of the burden shifted onto it, and onto coastal States, by the drafters of the Convention.

The adoption of the Guidelines was a “game-changer” for all potential submitting States, whether they had started the preparation of a submission or not. By “resetting the clock” to 13 May 1999 the MSP not only levelled the playing field for all early-ratifiers, but also indirectly recognized the challenges placed on all submitting States by the complex scientific and technical activities and analysis required for the implementation of Article 76.

The MSP also decided that “[t]he general issue of the ability of States, particularly developing States, to fulfil the requirements of Article 4 of Annex II to the Convention be kept under review” recognizing that many early-ratifiers might not be able to

---

84 CLCS/72. All documents of the MSP are available at https://www.un.org/depts/los/meeting_states_parties/SPLOS_documents.htm.

85 CLCS/11, and /Corr.1, /Corr.2, /Add.1, /Add.1/Corr.1, /Add.1/Corr.2. All documents of the CLCS are available at https://www.un.org/Depts/los/clcs_new/commission_documents.htm.

86 Guidelines, para 1.1.

87 Guidelines, para 1.2.

88 Guidelines, para 1.3.

make a submission even by May 2009. Following a review of the matter in 2008, the MSP further articulated its understanding of the ten-year time period. At its eighteenth meeting, it decided that it would be understood that

> [. . .] the time period referred to in Article 4 of Annex II to the Convention and the decision contained in SPLOS/72, paragraph (a), may be satisfied by submitting to the Secretary-General preliminary information indicative of the outer limits of the continental shelf beyond 200 nautical miles and a description of the status of preparation and intended date of making a submission [. . .].[89]

After that decision, tens of coastal States have submitted such preliminary information.[90] The subsequent conduct of such coastal States has been quite diverse. Several coastal States have made submissions covering, in full or in part, the area they had included in the preliminary information. Others have transmitted updates to the original preliminary information postponing the intended date for the making of their submission. There have also been examples of preliminary information not including an intended date for the making of a submission, or cases of expiration of the intended date followed neither by a submission nor by a notification of its further postponement.

3.1.2 Queueing and Obsolescence

Despite the just-described elasticity to which the ten-year time period has been subjected, the compiling of data and information of sufficient quality to demonstrate an entitlement to a continental shelf beyond 200 nautical miles remains challenging for many coastal States. The progress of science and technology since the entry into force of the Convention, has been such that a coastal State wishing to make a submission to the CLCS has to plan for an expensive and time-consuming process involving a multi-disciplinary team of legal, scientific and technical experts. After an initial "desktop study" phase aimed at allowing the Coastal State to determine whether its continental shelf is indeed likely to extend beyond 200 nautical miles, a phase of acquisition of data and information and analysis precedes the preparation of the actual submission.[91] When a submission is finally made, it is placed in a queue which has become so long that the submitting State should consider developing a "maintenance plan" to prevent the obsolescence of the submission, in terms of compatibility with the evolving software and scientific and technical currentness, and in terms of team-continuity.[92] As the Chairperson of the CLCS has noted in his annual letter to the President of the MSP, almost 12 years will pass between the making of a submission and the establishment of a subcommission to consider it, a

[89] SPLOS/183, para. 1(a).

[90] https://www.un.org/depts/los/clcs_new/commission_preliminary.htm.

[91] For an insider overview of the process of the preparation of a submission see Roest (2017).

[92] E.g. SPLOS/310, para 27; or CLCS/95, para 111.

figure that is expected to increase further.[93] And this brings us to a discussion on how the challenges posed by this trend are, again, rooted in the scientific and technical models available during UNCLOS III.

3.1.3 Number of Submissions

Based on the information available at the time of UNCLOS III, delegations had estimated that approximately three-dozen coastal States might be able to extend their continental shelf beyond 200M.[94] Six years after the entry into force of the Convention the estimate had grown to 54 coastal States.[95] Five years later to 65.[96] Seven years after that to 85.[97] To date 74 States have already made a submission and an additional nine have transmitted preliminary information but not made any submission yet. Speculating on the number of potential submitting States, however, is partially misleading. A more accurate assessment of the workload of the Commission, and its repercussion on the wait-time for submitting States that are at the bottom of the queue, should be done by reference to the number of submissions received by the Commission. This number is determined by the number of submissions received to date, 97,[98] plus the number of potential future submissions, which can be calculated taking into account a number of factors and variables which are quite speculative. These include (i) the fact that a number of States that have transmitted preliminary information on their continental shelf are likely to make a submission (even though it cannot be predicted whether that will be a full submission or multiple partial submissions); (ii) the possibility that a number of submitting States which have already received recommendations may submit a new or revised submission, full or partial, as has already happened in a number of cases;[99] (iii) the possibility of submissions being made by recent States parties for which the ten-year time period has not expired yet; (iv) the fact that a number of coastal States have opted to make multiple partial submissions, covering various segments of their coastlines, rather than a single submission. It is impossible to determine whether States that are still in the process of implementing Article 76 will do so by way of a single submission or multiple partial submissions;[100] and (v) the possibility of submissions being made by

[93] SPLOS/31/6, para 16.

[94] The estimates were based on the study referred to in footnote 62. See also Taft (2007), p. 470.

[95] Carleton and Cook (2000), p. 268.

[96] Monahan (2005), p. 77.

[97] Schofield and van der Poll (2012), p. 72.

[98] As at 30 January 2022. The list of submission is available at https://www.un.org/Depts/los/clcs_new/commission_submissions.htm.

[99] The making of revised submissions alters the progress of the queue. At its twenty-sixth session the Commission decided that revised submissions would be considered on a priority basis notwithstanding the queue—CLCS/68, para 57.

[100] Partial submissions inevitably extend the workload of the Commission. A submission that, for argument's sake, includes only one third of a coastal State's potential continental shelf beyond

future parties to the Convention. As a result, surmising that UNCLOS III' projections concerning the number of submissions will ultimately quadruple, or worse, does not seem hyperbolic. It has already almost tripled.

3.1.4 Size of Submissions

Another trend that is impacting the workload of the CLCS is the constant increase in available data and information, a considerable portion of which is resulting from surveys conducted for the very purpose of preparing submissions to the CLCS. A submission prepared at the time of UNCLOS III would have been a relatively small document. Delegates at the Conference would have been astounded to learn that a few decades later a submission could amount to hard copy documents weighing as much as a ton and requiring Terabytes of hard-disk storage space, as is the case today. As noted at the second open meeting of the CLCS, which was held to mark the twentieth anniversary of its establishment, "[t]he amount of scientific and technical data contained in a single national submission surpasses the size of the full World data set used in 1978".[101]

3.1.5 Content of Submissions

In addition to impacting the number and size of the submissions made to the CLCS, the progress in science and technology has brought about a more substantive development, namely the difficulty of reconciling the conceptual model underpinning the definition of continental margin enshrined in Article 76 with the natural configuration of various areas of seafloor around the world. At the time of the Conference, the best studied sea-floors were those of the Atlantic Ocean, especially the North Atlantic. The sea-floors of this part of the world are relatively straightforward in terms of conformation. The continental shelf/slope/rise paradigm of Article 76 fits the shape of continents on the two sides of the Atlantic. The transition zones from one part of the continental margin to another are relatively easy to identify; so are the base of the slope and, within that base, the foot of the continental slope.

It has been observed that the fact that the prevailing documentation of the time had been produced by institutions that were located close to margins with this configuration, and the fact that these illustrations present a vertical exaggeration aimed at facilitating their interpretation, may have led many delegates to believe that "(i) all continental margins were of this type; (ii) the transitions from one zone to

200 nautical miles will in all likelihood require much more than one third of the time that a full submission for the entire area would have entailed.

[101] Carrera Hurtado (2017), p. 19.

another were clearly delineated; and (iii) therefore, it would be relatively simple to map any of the features shown. None of this is true".[102]

Whatever the reason may be, the two formulae utilized to identify the outer edge of the continental margin were proposed by scientists that belonged to two delegations on the opposite ends of the Atlantic Ocean. The 60 M formula was conceived by Hollis Dow Hedberg,[103] the geologist that advised the delegation of the United States, and the sediment thickness formula was the brainchild of Piers Gardiner, the geologist who was a member of the Irish Delegation. Both formulae relied on the same continental shelf/rise/slope/base of the slope/foot of the continental slope paradigm, despite the different methodologies they proposed, which had been shaped by the different configurations of the margins found off the coasts of the United States and Ireland.

That paradigm could not be as easily applied to areas of the world where the seafloor was less straightforward and more rugged, making the identification of the foot of the slope a baffling task. It is a matter of speculation whether delegations from those parts of the world did not push for a different paradigm because they lacked detailed information about their continental margins or because they sensed that the incongruence between Article 76 conceptual model and the configuration of their continental margin could later be used to their advantage.

In other parts of the world that conceptual model could theoretically be applied but it would lead to inequitable results. The delegation of Sri Lanka may have been late in the game in drawing attention to the model's adverse impact on its continental shelf entitlement,[104] but at least it did present its case in a manner that gathered enough support to be reflected in the Statement of Understanding[105]

Issues concerning the location of the foot of the continental slope, as well as the interpretation of data and information relating to sea-floor highs and how they impact the application of the constraint lines, take up the majority of the interactions between Commission/subcommissions and submitting States. Had the information outlined in this section been available to the delegates of UNCLOS III, they might have rethought the approach enshrined in Article 76. The 1958 Convention showed the shortcomings of an open-ended incorporation of technological criteria in terms of a lack of legal certainty. UNCLOS neutralized the evolutionary impact of these

[102] Carleton and Cook (2000), p. 271.

[103] For the background to this formula see Hedberg (1973).

[104] Statement of the delegate of Sri Lanka at the seventh session, 104th plenary meeting, in A/CONF.62/SR.104, paras. 27–29.

[105] Other coastal States have subsequently argued that the Statement of Understanding could also be applied in areas other than the Bay of Bengal, provided that the criteria outlined in the Statement of Understanding are met, a position that Sri Lanka has refuted on the basis of its interpretation of the legislative history of the Statement of Understanding. See e.g. the communications of Sri Lanka dated 2 March 2009 and 22 July 2009 concerning the submissions to the CLCS made, respectively by Myanmar and Kenya, respectively, available at https://www.un.org/Depts/los/clcs_new/submissions_files/submission_mmr.htm and https://www.un.org/Depts/los/clcs_new/submissions_files/submission_ken_35_2009.htm.

criteria by locking them into provisions leading to stable outer limits and legal certainty; the difficulty of their implementation, however, has grown at the same pace as the inexorable advances of science and technology. This becomes even clearer when looking into the institutional architecture of the CLCS and its interactions with coastal States.

3.2 The Institutional Architecture of the CLCS

Since during UNCLOS III delegations could not anticipate the developments described above, they assumed that the CLCS would not have a long-lasting and heavy workload and consequently did not need to have the same stature as the ISA and the International Tribunal of the Law of the Sea (ITLOS), and it certainly would not need the same level of infrastructure.

During the course of the Conference, the number of members of the Commission was brought down from 30[106] to 21. This adjustment, together with the fact that the membership of the subcommissions was brought up from five to seven[107] members, reducing the number of potential subcommissions which could operate in parallel from six to three, showed that the drafters expected the workload of the Commission to be moderate to low.

At a pretty advanced stage of the negotiations, the ninth session, a request was made to the Secretariat to "prepare a concise study showing how each State party would have to contribute to the administrative budgets of the International Sea-Bed Authority, the International Tribunal for the Law of the Sea and *other organs* to be established under the convention".[108] In response to that request, operating on the delegations' understanding that the CLCS would be tasked with the technical review of relatively small submissions from a limited number of coastal States, the study presented by the Secretariat at the tenth session outlined two revealing assumptions: (i) that "the secretariat of the Commission may be provided by the Secretary-General of the United Nations"[109] (as opposed to the dedicated secretariats that would be established for the ISA and the ITLOS), as Article 2(5) of Annex II to the Convention would later confirm; and (ii) that "the Commission and each subcommission *might* hold one session of three weeks duration each year."[110] One could almost picture how at that stage the members of the CLCS must have been envisioned as some sort of marine cadastral officers that would carry out the relatively menial work of verification of the outer limits of the continental shelf. Once again, the intervening developments have turned these assumptions into glaring under-estimations. At the

[106] See Virginia Commentary, p. 1004.

[107] Ibidem.

[108] A/CONF.62/L.65, para 1 (emphasis added).

[109] Ibidem, para 46.

[110] Ibidem, para 47 (emphasis added).

pace of three weeks a year, it would have taken the Commission up to nine years to approve some of its recent recommendations. Multiplying that amount of time by the above described total potential number of submissions, the CLCS work would have to be calculated in centuries, not years, if estimated at the pace envisaged by UNCLOS III. In order to avoid this scenario, the CLCS has progressively lengthened its sessions and, in response to a request from the MSP,[111] since 2012 it has increased its meeting time seven-fold compared to the UNCLOS III projections, working 21 weeks a year[112] (comprising four weeks of plenary meetings and 17 weeks involving up to ten subcommissions per session).

An often-overlooked procedural detail confirms the impression that the Commission may have been regarded as an expert body not requiring the same level of attention and safeguards as other institutions established under the Convention. Whereas the electoral mechanism set up for ITLOS provides for a staggered renewal of its membership, with only seven of the 21 seats becoming vacant every three years,[113] all 21 seats of the CLCS become vacant at the same time, every five years.[114] It is unlikely that none of the incumbent members are re-elected from one term of office to the next. The fact that the Conference did not model the election of the members of the CLCS after that of the members of the ITLOS, however, may be the result of a lack of understanding and appreciation of the level of complexity required in the examination of submissions, for which institutional memory is as important as that preserved in any other institution. One can only imagine the impact that an election replacing two thirds or more of the members would have on the efficiency of the Commission. The trends in the nominations of members of the Commission have prevented this pitfall from happening. However, if there is no improvement in the conditions of service of the members of the Commission[115]—a *vexata questio*, which has not been resolved yet by the MSP and falls beyond the scope of this analysis—that situation could change in the future, adding yet another challenge.

Further shortcomings of the CLCS setup concern its financing. As far as the secretariat of the CLCS is concerned, when States conducted the respective assessment of the financial implications associated with becoming parties to the Convention, they did not factor in the costs of a dedicated secretariat for the CLCS, which would have only made sense if the CLCS had been conceived as a permanent body, like the ISA and the ITLOS. Given the rigidities of internal budget approvals at the domestic level, especially if involving the introduction of new budget lines generated from a convention, the financial impact of which had already been assessed

[111] SPLOS/229, para 1.

[112] CLCS/76, para 11; CLCS/100, para 14.

[113] See Article 5, para 1, of Annex VI to the Convention.

[114] See Article 2, paras 1 and 4, of annex II to the Convention.

[115] Both the CLCS and the MSP, including through a working group established ad hoc, have included the review of the conditions of service of the members of the Commission, as reported in the statements of the Chairperson in regard to the CLCS sessions and the reports of the MSP.

prior to its ratification, one could consider any future attempt to remedy the lack of a dedicated Secretariat for the CLCS as doomed from the start, thus making the option of a CLCS working on a full-time basis moot.

In addition, the Conference determined that "[t]he State Party which submitted the nomination of a member of the Commission shall defray the expenses of that member while in performance of Commission duties."[116] The trend that has characterized the implementation of this provision illustrates that since the first election of members of the Commission, the only States parties that could secure a budget to nominate a member of the Commission were those that could justify that expense because they had a direct interest in the outer limits of the continental shelf. From an abstract point of view, it could be argued that all States parties, including land-locked ones, have a direct interest in ensuring that the outer limits of the Area, as "common heritage of mankind", are established in conformity with article 76. In practice, however, nominations have been received almost exclusively from States that had an interest in their own outer limits of the continental shelf beyond 200 nautical miles, or in those of neighbouring States.

In this respect, another recent trend can be better understood by analyzing the above circumstance in conjunction with the provision of Article 2.3 of Annex II to the Convention, according to which "[n]ot less than three members shall be elected from each geographical region." In one of the geographical regions, the total number of coastal States with the potential for a continental shelf beyond 200 nautical miles might be smaller than three. Not surprisingly, this has led to a long-lasting vacancy in the Commission resulting from a lack of sufficient nominations of members from that regional group, a situation that has further impacted the efficiency of the Commission and its subcommissions and that the MSP continues to monitor without having found a solution yet.[117]

4 Conclusions

UNCLOS was the first large multilateral treaty to introduce the concept of "efficiency", in addition to that of "equity",[118] with regard to the utilization of natural resources, when it recognized "the desirability of establishing [. . .] a legal order for

[116] Article 2.5, Annex II to the Convention. The same paragraph also clarified how the costs relate to the provision of scientific and technical advice to coastal States that requested it, establishing that "[t]he coastal State concerned shall defray the expenses incurred in respect of the advice referred to in Article 3, paragraph 1(b), of this Annex." The shortcomings of this approach were outlined by a number of delegations during the Conference—see e.g. A/CONF.62/SR.127, A/CONF.62/SR.128, A/CONF.62/SR.135, A/CONF.62/SR.136, and A/CONF.62/SR.138.

[117] As at 30 January 2022, the latest developments in this regard can be found at SPLOS/31/9, paras 60-63.

[118] See Oxman (1981), p. 255.

the seas and oceans which [...] will promote [...] the equitable *and efficient* utilization of their resources" in its preamble.[119]

As far as the utilization of the resources of the continental shelf beyond 200 nautical miles and of the Area is concerned, however, this efficiency is purely aspirational.

The wisdom of the international community develops—not unlike that of any individual—taking stock and learning from experience. Article 76 was shaped by a desire to remedy the shortcomings of Article 1 of the 1958 Continental Shelf Convention. In looking for alternatives to the "depth & exploitability" approach of 1958, delegations at UNCLOS IIII were searching for a way to justify the extension of the prerogatives of the coastal States to areas traditionally subject to a freedom regime. The concept of "natural prolongation" of the land territory lent itself to that end.[120] Having to identify the precise extent of this natural prolongation, it became necessary to enter into a balancing act of considerations aimed at identifying a continental shelf definition which could generate consensus despite the widely differing geological configurations of the States represented at UNCLOS III. This, in turn, gave rise to a complex definition steeped in scientific and technical notions. In this search for both clarity and consensus, diplomats looked for guidance from scientific and technical experts. The help from these experts, however, came packaged with another set of uncertainties. A jurist will find considerable comfort in discovering that interpretation is not a struggle exclusive to the legal profession. Consultations involving marine geologists or geophysicists provide ample evidence about the divergent conclusions that can be reached on the basis of different schools of geoscientific thought.

It did not have to go that way, but attempts at reducing the complexity of this approach were dismissed as they "ignore[d] the geological basis of the continental shelf doctrine, eliminat[ing] existing rights of the coastal State over the entire 'natural prolongation'".[121]

Even though rooted in science, however, the definition contained in Article 76 was legal in nature, codified in a provision the implementation of which—unlike that of Article 1 of the Continental Shelf Convention—was not meant to change over time. What we have tried to outline above are the unintended consequences of relying on this approach in the face of the natural evolution of science and technology. These consequences include temporal, financial, logistical and substantive challenges faced by States, especially developing ones, in preparing a submission to the CLCS; the unexpected number of submissions which have been, and will

[119]Emphasis added.

[120]Citing the first report by Francois, however, Mouton (1952) expressed doubt that the fact that the shelf could be considered as "an extension of the continent into the sea" would have any legal relevance; the fact that the continental shelf is covered by the sea, which has a different regime than the land, for instance, would appear to be more relevant—p. 33.

[121]Oxman (1979), p. 21.

continue to be, made; the consequent inadequacy of the institutional setup of the CLCS and the unlikelihood that States will be able to improve it in the future.

The resulting uneasy relationship between delineation of the outer limits of the continental shelf and delimitation of continental shelf boundaries, as evidenced in the practice of coastal States, the CLCS and recent judicial arbitral and judicial pronouncements, deserves an analysis of its own. It may suffice to note here that interesting developments have emerged from a number of rulings that have reversed the hitherto held view that the recommendations of the CLCS are a temporal and logical antecedent to the existence of overlapping claims beyond 200 nautical miles.[122] These developments, inaugurated by the 2012 judgment of ITLOS in the *Dispute concerning delimitation of the maritime boundary between Bangladesh and Myanmar in the Bay of Bengal (Bangladesh/Myanmar),*[123] might have been a way to avoid letting the above-described delays in the process of the delineation of the outer limits of the continental shelf beyond 200 nautical miles impact the judicial resolution of continental shelf delimitation disputes. Otherwise, they could be seen as the manifestation of a belief that if the mandate of the CLCS is without prejudice to the question of the delimitation of the continental shelf between States with opposite or adjacent coasts, then awards and judgements concerning overlapping claims over the continental shelf beyond 200 nautical miles must be without prejudice to the work of the Commission.[124] Alternatively, these judicial and arbitral developments could be seen as aimed at fracking open a reservoir of potential new cases as the continental

[122]Consider e.g. this dictum by the ICJ:

> [i]t should also be noted in this regard that in no case may the line be interpreted as extending more than 200 nautical miles from the baselines from which the breadth of the territorial sea is measured; any claim of continental shelf rights beyond 200 miles must be in accordance with Article 76 of the Convention and reviewed by the Commission on the Limits of the Continental Shelf established thereunder.

Territorial and Maritime Dispute between Nicaragua and Honduras in the Caribbean Sea (Nicaragua v. Honduras), Judgment, I.C.J. Reports 2007, p. 659, at para 319. Available at https://www.icj-cij.org/en/case/120.

[123]Available at https://www.itlos.org/index.php?id=108. See also the 2014 Award in the Matter of the Bay of Bengal Maritime Boundary Arbitration between The People's Republic of Bangladesh and The Republic of India, available at https://pca-cpa.org/en/cases/18/ and the 2017 Judgement in the Delimitation of the Maritime Boundary in the Atlantic Ocean (Ghana/Côte d'Ivoire) available at https://www.itlos.org/en/main/cases/list-of-cases/case-no-23/.

[124]E.g. para 394 of the Judgment of the International Tribunal for the Law of the Sea of 14 March 2012 in the *Dispute concerning delimitation of the maritime boundary between Bangladesh and Myanmar in the Bay of Bengal (Bangladesh/Myanmar)* - Available at https://www.itlos.org/index.php?id=108. After concluding that it had an obligation to adjudicate the dispute, the Tribunal observed that "[s]uch delimitation is without prejudice to the establishment of the outer limits of the continental shelf in accordance with Article 76, paragraph 8, of the Convention". The roots of this position could be found in the Arbitral Award in the *Matter of an Arbitration Between Barbados and the Republic of Trinidad and Tobago* of 2006. On that occasion, the Arbitral Tribunal rejected Barbados' contention that "delimitation of the outer continental shelf in the way proposed by Trinidad and Tobago would, in Barbados' view, interfere with the core function of the Commission on the Limits of the Continental Shelf" (paragraph 28 of the Award).

shelf beyond 200 M has come to be considered as holding lucrative areas of litigation worth pursuing, not just natural resources. Whatever the reason, this propensity seems to have flipped the "without prejudice" safeguard by opening a way for coastal States to possibly resort to a judicial or arbitral institution, to influence the delineation of the outer limits of their continental shelves beyond 200 nautical miles.

In conclusion, a lesson can be drawn from the tension between the stability sought by law, on the one hand, and the inevitable advances of science and technology, on the other hand. As outlined above, both the 1958 open-ended reference to real time technological evolutions and the 1982 crystallization of scientific concepts cause implementation difficulties. A theoretical happier medium could be the identification of stable principles in a "constitutional" normative instrument which is unlikely to change for a long period of time but is complemented by an operational annex that is subject to periodic reviews. This approach may work in many areas, for instance with regard to marine pollution, but is not suitable in relation to a coastal State's sovereign rights and jurisdiction which demand stable maritime zone outer limits.

A simpler "breadth approach" would have avoided such problems. For other maritime zones under national jurisdiction, delegations had identified the need those zones were to address, and the appropriate breadth of the maritime zone within which a regime would be established to address that need. The same could have been done also for the continental shelf. After all, the Conference was not after a scientifically accurate definition of continental shelf. It aimed at addressing the interests of a considerable amount of delegations, namely securing access to the riches of the continental shelf. If these riches had been located not on the continental shelf, but—for argument's sake—at the beginning of the deep ocean floor just beyond the continental margin, delegates would have resorted to different paradigms - perhaps the concepts of relative propinquity or optimal use of natural resources - to justify their inclusion under national jurisdiction and the consequent limitations to the traditional freedoms.

Since delegates were open to enter into a legal fiction—given that some coastal States had a continental shelf of 200 nautical miles recognized even in the absence of a continental margin that extended to that distance—then that legal fiction could have been adjusted to a more seaward, and simpler to establish, limit located at a distance acceptable to all delegations. In addition to greater efficiency, this approach would have also ensured greater equity, in so far as the coastal States' continental shelf would have been dictated by agreement rather than by the uneven generosity of nature. But at the time of UNCLOS III, with the EEZ's 200 nautical miles being an outer limit which was already considered generous by delegations which had traditionally defended the freedoms of the high seas, any possibility to extend coastal States' prerogatives beyond 200 nautical miles could only take place if limited and qualified. Article 76 provided the framework for that qualification.

The drafters of Article 76 may have found a definition that all delegations at UNCLOS III could live with, but they ended up shifting the burden of translating that abstract definition into a concrete delineation onto coastal States and the CLCS, without equipping the latter with the infrastructure to discharge its mandate efficiently. The interests of States had already been largely satisfied with the recognition of their prerogatives up to 200 nautical miles—where the vast majority of hydrocarbon resources of the world are located.[125] After that was achieved, the need for outer limits of the continental shelf beyond 200 nautical miles became relatively less urgent, especially considering that exploitation activities at those depths were known not to be economically viable for several decades and that approximately 87% of maritime hydrocarbon resources would be kept out of the Area.[126] This pursuit of national interests, though, quelled one of the ideals behind UNCLOS III by failing the "common heritage of mankind", for which the efficiency predicated in the preamble to the Convention will not be achieved.[127]

Unless States adopt significant measures to support the institutional setup of the Commission, it will take decades to complete the process of the delineation of the outer limits of the continental shelf. This, in turn, will affect the definition of the Area, as well as the exact identification of natural resources of the continental shelf that are subject to the redistribution regime of article 82 of the Convention. In this respect, it may be worth remembering that it was the promise of this redistribution that contributed to convincing delegations that opposed the extension of the continental shelf regime beyond 200 nautical miles to drop their objections.

It may be a stretch, but seen through this lens, the definition of the outer limits of the continental shelf by the drafters of Article 76 shelf can be considered as the harbinger of the debacle of Part XI of the Convention. The following observation from one of the most insightful commentators of UNCLOS III seems to confirm that, by the end of the Conference, the "common heritage of mankind" had lost a good deal of momentum:

> [i]t is assumed that [. . .] both the coastal state and the subcommission will do their best to ensure that the Commission will not approve even initial recommendations that are likely to be rejected by the coastal state. This was considered one of the advantages of using non contentious ex parte review by an international commission of experts independent of the Sea-Bed Authority.[128]

---

[125] United Nations, The United Nations Convention on the Law of the Sea (A Historical Perspective). http://www.un.org/Depts/los/convention_agreements/convention_historical_perspective.htm.

[126] Tuerk (2021), pp. 237–238.

[127] This circumstance is made even more concerning when considering that coastal States that have received recommendations do not seem to be in any hurry to establish their outer limits on the basis of those recommendations. As at 30 January 2022 only 10 outer limits of the continental shelf have been deposited with the Secretary-General of the United Nations out of 35 recommendations approved by the Commission. Compare the information available at https://www.un.org/Depts/los/clcs_new/commission_submissions.htm with that at https://www.un.org/Depts/los/LEGISLATIONANDTREATIES/regionslist.htm. On this matter see: Lodge (2017), pp. 1–2. It should be noted in this regard that the Convention does not specify a time-line for the establishment of these outer limits.

[128] Oxman (1981), p. 231.

There are significant silver linings in the regime established by the Convention, though. In addition to the fact that the delineation of the outer limits of the continental shelf is infinitely more fascinating than it would have been through a breadth approach—even though it is doubtful that entertainment is what the drafters of the Convention were after—there have been a number of positive developments resulting from the choice of drafting Article 76 by reference to scientific and technical criteria. The need to prepare a submission to the CLCS has spurred a considerable amount of scientific activities aimed at gathering data and information. As a result, the current understanding of the sea-floor has greatly improved, an unintended—but this time positive—consequence of Article 76. Within the limits of its institutional setup, and despite the non-ideal conditions of service of its members, the CLCS has been working professionally and has adopted 35 recommendations since its establishment. Technical cooperation among States has also benefited from the existing regime. A number of States have lent their expertise to assist other States in preparing submissions, a cooperation that is likely to pave the way for closer relationships and further technical cooperation among them. Other States have decided to forego the issues concerning pending overlapping claims by making joint submissions to the Commission, a positive and creative take on the "without prejudice" clause of Article 76.10. The confidence built, especially at the technical level, through joint surveys at sea, cooperative analysis of data and preparation of submission, sharing of costs, combined with the countless hours of preparations for meetings with the Commission and its subcommissions, might well be the best confidence-building measure required to ensure a smooth negotiation of a continental shelf boundary beyond 200 nautical miles.

References

Carleton C, Cook PJ (2000) Continental shelf limits - the scientific and legal interface. Oxford. https://www.google.com/books/edition/Continental_Shelf_Limits/ABVfvyi-8IAC?hl=en&gbpv=0

Carrera Hurtado G (2017) The implementation of the mandate of the Commission on the Limits of the Continental Shelf: 1997 to 2017. https://www.un.org/depts/los/clcs_new/clcsopen_2017.htm

Center for Oceans Law and Policy, University of Virginia, (2014) United Nations Convention on the Law of the Sea Commentary: Volumes I-VII ["Virginia Commentary"]

Churchill RR, Lowe AV (1991) The law of the sea. Manchester University Press, Manchester

Colombos CJ (1967) The International Law of the Sea - 6th revised edition. Longmans, London

Cosford EJ (1953) The continental shelf and the *Abu Dhabi* award. McGill Law J 1:109

Cosford EJ (1958) The continental shelf 1910-1945. McGill Law J 4(2):245

Edvalson FM, Miscoski VT (1969) Bathymetric charts. Their development and use. U.S. Naval Oceanographic Office, Washington D.C. https://www.google.com/books/edition/Bathymetric_Charts/sJETAAAAYAAJ?hl=en&gbpv=0

Gutteridge JJ (1959) The 1958 Geneva Convention on the Continental Shelf. Br Yearb Int Law 35: 102–123

Hardwicke RE (1949) The tidelands and oil. Atlantic 183(6):21–36

Hedberg HD (1973) The national-international jurisdictional boundary on the ocean floor. Ocean Manag 1:83–118
Hurst CJB (1923–1924) Whose is the bed of the sea? Sedentary fisheries outside the three-mile limit. Br Yearb Int Law 4:34–43
Hurst CJB (1948) The continental shelf. Transactions of the Grotius Society Vol. 34, Problems of Public and Private International Law, Transactions for the Year 1948 (1948) 153–169
International Law Commission (1950) Memorandum on the Regime of the High Seas - Prepared by the Secretariat (U.N. Doc A/CN.4/32)
Lauterpacht H (1950) Sovereignty over submarine areas. Br Yearb Int Law 27:376–433
Lodge M (2017) The relevance and importance of the work of the Commission to the International Seabed Authority, available at https://www.un.org/depts/los/clcs_new/clcsopen_2017.htm
Mill HR (1892) The realm of nature - an outline of physiography. Charles Scribner's Sons, New York (1899 edition). https://www.google.com/books/edition/The_Realm_of_Nature/ku08AAAAYAAJ?hl=en&gbpv=0
Monahan D (2005) Applying the test of appurtenance globally - a new inventory of wide margin states from public domain data. Int Hydrogr Rev 6 No. 1 (New Series):77–84
Morris HG (1958) The continental shelf-an international dilemma. Osgoode Hall Law J 1:137–146
Mouton MW (1952) The continental shelf. Martinus Nijhoff, The Hague. https://books.google.com/books?id=DSn2CAAAQBAJ&printsec=frontcover&source=gbs_ge_summary_r&cad=0#v=onepage&q&f=false
Oxman BH (1979) The Third United Nations Conference on the Law of the Sea: the seventh session (1978). Am J Int Law 73(1):1–41
Oxman BH (1980) The Third United Nations Conference on the Law of the Sea: the eighth session (1979). Am J Int Law 74(1):1–47
Oxman BH (1981) The third United Nations Conference on the Law of the Sea: the ninth session (1980). Am J Int Law 75(2):211–256
Roest WR (2017) An external and internal view of the work of the Commission. https://www.un.org/depts/los/clcs_new/clcsopen_2017.htm
Ruelas M (1930) La Cornisa Continental Territorial. Revista de Derecho Internacional, Organo del Instituto Americano de Derecho Internacional, Habana, Año. IX, Tomo XVII, Enero-Junio 1930
Schofield C, van der Poll R (2012) Exploring the Outer Continental Shelf in Implementation of Article 82 of the United Nations Convention on the Law of the Sea - ISA Technical Study: No. 12. https://isa.org.jm/files/files/documents/ts12-web.pdf
Shipman S, Laughton A (2000) Historical methods of depth measurement. In: Cook, Carleton (eds) Continental shelf limits - the scientific and legal interface. Oxford, 124-13
Stevenson JR, Oxman BH (1975) The third United Nations Conference on the Law of the Sea: the 1975 Geneva session. Am J Int Law 69(4):763–797
Suarez SV (2008) The outer limits of the continental shelf: legal aspects of their establishment. Springer
Symonds PA et al (2000) Ridge issues. In: Carleton C, Cook PJ (eds) Continental shelf limits – the scientific and legal interface, Oxford. https://www.google.com/books/edition/Continental_Shelf_Limits/ABVfvyi-8IAC?hl=en&gbpv=0
Taft G (2007) Applying the law of the sea convention and the role of the scientific community relating to establishing the outer limit of the continental shelf where it extends beyond the 200 mile limit. In: Nordquist MH et al (eds) L, Science & Ocean Management, Brill | Nijhoff
Tuerk H (2021) Questions relating to the continental shelf beyond 200 nautical miles: delimitation, delineation, and revenue sharing. Int Law Stud 97:232–257

United Nations (2006) Training manual for delineation of the outer limits of the continental shelf beyond 200 nautical miles and for preparation of submissions to the commission on the limits of the continental shelf. United Nations, New York

United Nations (2017) The work of the International Law Commission, 9th edn. United Nations, New York

Vaughan HB (ed) (1940) The history and development of sounding, with particular reference to precise super-sonic echo sounding methods as recently developed in the U.S. Engineer Department. The Engineer School, United States Army - Occasional paper No. 73, Washington, D.C. https://www.google.com/books/edition/The_History_and_Development_of_Sounding/bLv9jmsu6ZcC?hl=en&gbpv=0

Whiteman MM (1958) Conference on the law of the sea: convention on the continental shelf. Am J Int Law 52(4):629–659

Conclusions

Tullio Treves

It is difficult to draw "conclusions" from a book as this, that examines in ten essays a selected and small number of issues covering four apparently disparate chapters of international law, without being tempted to look for a "red thread" connecting these essays. I had no doubt that a red thread there would be once the editors, Professors Arcari, Papanicolopulu and Pineschi, approached me because their competence in international law and seriousness in organizing collective research endeavours were well known to me. As a matter of fact, the red thread was easy to find. It is the fact that the ten authors have one mentor whose main fields of interest correspond to the four sections in which the book is divided, namely, human rights law, cultural heritage law, environmental law and law of the sea. To this—as mentioned in the Introduction—was to be added that the retirement from his teaching position of their mentor was approaching and that they wished to honor him with a collection of essays. The complicating factor was that the Editors were aware of their mentor's aversion for the very notion of *Festschrift* in general and, especially, to the idea of a *Festschrift* in his honor.

They knew well their mentor, Professor Tullio Scovazzi, and thought that a book as different as possible from the monumental, sometimes pluri-volume Studies in Honor, whose vastness seems a projection of the ego of the honoured scholar or of his pupils, could be acceptable and hopefully welcome to him as a sign of affection of his direct pupils and as a testimony of how his teachings have been followed by them in the fields dear to him.

Of course, for reasons of age, I do not belong to the group of Tullio Scovazzi's pupils. But I was honoured and sentimentally touched by the request to be involved in this book writing the present few lines. Tullio Scovazzi and I, the "two Tullios" as we are sometimes referred to, go back many decades. In 1974 I supervised Tullio's dissertation on the then new subject of the exclusive economic zone. I remember

T. Treves (✉)
University of Milano, Milan, Italy

M. Arcari et al. (eds.), *Trends and Challenges in International Law*,
https://doi.org/10.1007/978-3-030-94387-5_12

bringing him from Caracas, where I had been involved in the Italian Delegation to the Third UN Conference on the Law of the Sea, the fresh documents on this subject—something quite extraordinary in a time in which documents on line did not exist. Since then, Tullio and I have been working together in many ways: as collaborators of our common mentor, the late Professor Mario Giuliano, as colleagues at the University of Torino, where Laura Pineschi, one of the editors of the present book, was our pupil, as co-authors of a new edition of Professor Giuliano's treatise on international law, as planners and coordinators of various collective research endeavours on law of the sea and environmental law and in many other circumstances, including when, in 1984, Tullio participated as my assistant in the work of the UN General Assembly's Sixth Committee.

Moreover, Tullio Scovazzi, together with my pupils Nerina Boschiero, Cesare Pitea and Chiara Ragni, was co-editor of a book published in 2012 on the occasion of my retirement form the University. In working at this book Tullio must have overcome his aversion to Studies in Honor, and I am grateful that he did it as a token of affection for me. I have thus a debt of gratitude to Tullio in matters concerning Studies in Honor. This encourages me to think that when the printed volume is given to him he will see in it more than an homage to academic custom a testimony of serious work on subjects that have occupied his professional life and of the affection of younger scholars that are grateful for the teaching and example they have received from him.

But what is the teaching of Tullio Scovazzi? He expounded his views in the Foreword to the second edition of Part I of his *Corso di diritto internazionale* (Giuffré, Milan, 2014). He describes his method as "descriptive and non-reconstructive" based on international practice without resort to "pre-determined and apparently consistent logical schemes", keeping in mind that, in a primitive and inconsistent system as the international law one, "dissonances are more interesting than assonances". This method, that Tullio follows rigorously, is clearly derived from that followed and taught to us through example by our mentor Mario Giuliano. What is new is the statement of an "emotional" profile in his approach. This "emotional" profile includes his "unrestrained anti-nationalism that by instinct brings [him] to search for, and to underline, cases in which Italy does not comply with the obligations derived from international law rules". It also includes his point of departure namely, "that the typical function of any system of law is to demonstrate . . .that it is not true that the strongest is always right".

This emotional, we could say "political", element is also present, as background, in the teaching and scholarly contributions of our mentor Mario Giuliano and is shared by the scholars, including the present writer, belonging to his "school", including the contributors to the present volume as clearly evidenced by their essays. However, different from the writings of Giuliano and other members of his "school", Tullio Scovazzi openly proclaims his "emotional" points of departure. This strengthens, not diminishes, the cogency of his reasoning and the impact of his conclusions.

GPSR Compliance
The European Union's (EU) General Product Safety Regulation (GPSR) is a set of rules that requires consumer products to be safe and our obligations to ensure this.

If you have any concerns about our products, you can contact us on

ProductSafety@springernature.com

In case Publisher is established outside the EU, the EU authorized representative is:

Springer Nature Customer Service Center GmbH
Europaplatz 3
69115 Heidelberg, Germany

www.ingramcontent.com/pod-product-compliance
Ingram Content Group UK Ltd.
Pitfield, Milton Keynes, MK11 3LW, UK
UKHW020238290926
15470UKWH00002B/597
* 9 7 8 3 0 3 0 9 4 3 8 6 8 *